REGULATING FOOD-BORNE ILLNESS

When faced with tackling food-borne illness, regulators have a number of competing goals. They must investigate in order to discover the source of the illness. Once the source is identified, they must take action to prevent further cases of illness occurring. Finally, once the illness is under control, they may wish to take enforcement action against those responsible. *Regulating Food-borne Illness* uses interviews and documentary analysis to examine the actions of regulators, and considers how they balance these three tasks. Central to the regulators' role is the collection of information. Without information about the source, control or enforcement action cannot be taken. Investigation must therefore take place to produce the necessary information. Utilising theoretical frameworks drawn from regulation and biosecurity, *Regulating Food-borne Illness* shows that control is prioritised, and that investigatory steps are chosen in order to ensure that the information necessary for control, rather than enforcement, is collected. This has the effect of reducing the possibility that enforcement action can be taken. The difficulty of evidence gathering and case building in food-borne illness cases is exposed, and the author considers the methods aimed at reducing the difficulty of bringing successful enforcement action.

Regulating Food-borne Illness

Investigation, Control and Enforcement

Richard Hyde

•HART•
PUBLISHING
OXFORD AND PORTLAND, OREGON
2017

Hart Publishing
An imprint of Bloomsbury Publishing Plc

Hart Publishing Ltd
Kemp House
Chawley Park
Cumnor Hill
Oxford OX2 9PH
UK

Bloomsbury Publishing Plc
50 Bedford Square
London
WC1B 3DP
UK

www.hartpub.co.uk
www.bloomsbury.com

Published in North America (US and Canada) by
Hart Publishing
c/o International Specialized Book Services
920 NE 58th Avenue, Suite 300
Portland, OR 97213-3786
USA

www.isbs.com

First published in hardback, 2015
Paperback edition, 2017

British Library Cataloguing-in-Publication Data
A catalogue record for this book is available from the British Library.

ISBN: PB: 978-1-50991-784-6
HB: 978-1-84946-673-8

Typeset by Compuscript Ltd, Shannon
Printed and bound in Great Britain by
Lightning Source UK Ltd

Acknowledgements

A number of people have assisted me greatly during this project, and thanks are due to them. Those Environmental Health Officers, lawyers, consultants, doctors and others who talked to me about this project, both on and off the record, have contributed to my understanding of food regulation, and food-borne illness in particular. Local authorities that were kind enough to allow me to study their practice deserve thanks.

This book is based on a PhD thesis conducted at the University of Nottingham and funded by an Economic and Social Research Council (ESRC) 1+3 Scholarship. Thanks are due to the ESRC for its financial support. My supervisors (and now my colleagues), Professor Peter Cartwright and Professor Paul Roberts, provided fantastic support, guidance and advice. My fellow PhD students at Nottingham between 2007 and 2011 provided an intellectually stimulating environment in which to conduct my research. My PhD examiners, Professor Maria Lee and Professor Paul Almond, provided really useful advice and guidance, and the anonymous reviewer of my book proposal should be thanked for helping me to make important changes, particularly to the first chapter.

Since the completion of my PhD, this book has taken a journey to Northumbria University and back to Nottingham. All of my colleagues, at both Nottingham and Northumbria Universities, should be thanked for their collegial assistance, which has really made it a pleasure to write. In particular, Dr Ashley Savage of Northumbria University has acted as a very useful sounding board for discussions regarding the book.

Thanks are also owed to my family, and particularly to my parents, Mick and Brenda Hyde. And most importantly, thank you to my wife, Catriona. You provided the necessary encouragement, love, sympathy, patience and stability that allowed this book to happen.

Lastly, all at Hart Publishing have once again been fantastic, and incredibly helpful when I have needed it.

I have attempted to state the law as at January 2015, but it must be borne in mind that the cases examined in this book were all dealt with under previous iterations of the legal framework that applies to food. It may therefore, at points, prove necessary to consider law that no longer applies, but it is hoped that this should be clear when this is so.

All errors and omissions, of course, remain my own.

Richard Hyde
Nottingham, 2015

Contents

Acknowledgements v
Explanation of Alpha-numeric Identifiers xiii
Table of Cases xv
Table of Legislation xix

1. The Response to Food-borne Illness 1
I. Introduction 1
II. Regulating Food 3
III. The Role of the Network 5
IV. Regulating Risk 7
V. The Issue of Illness 7
VI. Collection of Information 10
VII. The Control of Realised Risk 11
VIII. Enforcement and Sanctioning 11
IX. Examining the Response to Food-borne Illness: Methodological Considerations 12
X. Examining the Response to Food-borne Illness: A Structural Guide 14
XI. Summary 16

2. The Regulatory Network 17
I. Introduction 17
II. The EU and the UK Government 19
III. The Food Standards Agency 20
IV. Local Authorities 22
V. Medical Actors 26
VI. The Police 28
VII. Food Businesses and Their Employees 28
VIII. Consumers 29
IX. Conclusion 30

3. The Regulatory Landscape 31
I. The Governance of Food Production 31
A. Regulations Governing Food Products: Regulation 178/2002 32
i. Unsafe Per Se 33
ii. Injurious to Health 34
iii. Unfit for Human Consumption 35

B. Regulations Governing Food Premises: Food Hygiene Requirements 37
i. The General Obligation 38
ii. Temperature Control Requirements 39
iii. Microbiological Safety Requirements 39
iv. Hazard Analysis Critical Control Point 40
v. Condition 42
vi. Notification 42
II. The Control, Enforcement and Advisory Toolbox: Powers Available to Local Authorities 42
A. Four Species of Control Power Used During Incidents of Food-borne Illness 44
i. Powers that Control Products 45
ii. Powers that Control Premises and Processes 48
iii. Powers that Control People 50
iv. Powers that Control The Environment 52
B. Two Enforcement Powers Used Following Incidents of Food-borne Illness 53
i. Prosecution 53
ii. Caution 59
C. The Power to Advise 60
i. Improvement Notices 61
III. Conclusion: The Powers of the Network 62

4. The Investigation of Incidents of Food-borne Illness 64
I. Notification 64
II. Investigation of Incidents of Food-borne Illness 68
III. Epidemiological Investigations 69
A. Identifying Cases and Controls 70
i. Case Definition 70
ii. Snowballing from Consumers 73
iii. Utilising the Business 74
iv. Utilising the Event Organiser 75
v. Identification by Medical Professionals 76
B. Questioning Affected Persons 77
i. Information about the Case/Control 78
ii. Information about Symptoms 79
iii. Food History 81
iv. Information about Other Risk Factors 84
C. Analysing Epidemiological Information 86
i. Building a Hypothesis 87
ii. Testing a Hypothesis 88

IV. Microbiological Investigations ... 92
A. Human Samples ... 92
i. From Consumers ... 93
ii. From Employees ... 94
B. Food Samples ... 95
C. Environmental Samples ... 97
D. Testing and Analysis of Samples ... 98
V. Environmental Investigation ... 100
A. Contacting the Food Business ... 103
B. Physical Inspections of Premises ... 103
C. Examination of Documentation Retained at Premises ... 107
i. Food Safety Management System Documentation ... 108
ii. Temperature records ... 109
iii. Preparation Instructions ... 109
iv. Absence and Sickness Records ... 110
v. Other Documents ... 110
D. Questioning Businesses ... 111
i. Under Caution ... 111
ii. Not Under Caution ... 114
E. Questioning Employees of Food Businesses ... 117
F. Observation of Working Practices ... 118
VI. Supply Chain Investigations: Tracing ... 118
VII. Conclusion: Investigation of Incidents of Food-borne Illness ... 123

5. The Key Goal: Control of Food-borne Illness ... 124
I. Introduction ... 124
II. Biosecurity: The Theoretical Framework ... 126
III. Control in Action ... 127
IV. Two Techniques of Control ... 132
A. Control Through Spatial Separation ... 133
B. Control Through Market Management ... 136
V. Enforcing Biosecurity ... 139
VI. Control in a Regulatory Context ... 141
VII. Conclusion ... 145

6. Enforcement Following Incidents of Food-borne Illness ... 146
I. Introduction ... 146
II. Unavailability of Epidemiological Evidence and its Impact on Enforcement ... 148
A. Information Limited by Consumers' 'Source Fixation' ... 148

B. Information Limited by Consumers' Incomplete Memory 151
C. Information Limited by the Special Features of Buffets 153
D. The Effect of the Limitations on Enforcement Decisions 154
III. Unavailability of Food Sample Evidence and its Impact on Enforcement 156
IV. Unavailability of Faecal Sample Evidence and its Impact on Enforcement 159
V. 'Inadmissibility' Due to 'Medical Confidentiality' and its Impact on Enforcement 164
A. Two Case Studies 165
i. Cadbury *Salmonella* 165
ii. *R v South-West Water* (1997) 165
B. Three Legal and Ethical Reasons Offered for the Inadmissibility of Medical Information 166
i. 'Medical Privilege' 166
ii. Data Protection 167
iii. Ethical Obligations of Confidentiality 168
C. Policy Reasons for the 'Inadmissibility' of Medical Information 169
VI. Inadmissibility of Outbreak/Incident Control Team Reports and Its Impact on Enforcement 172
A. Case Study: *R v South-West Water* (1997)—The (In)Admissibility of OCT Reports on Hearsay Grounds 174
i. The Enforcement Decision 176
ii. The Prosecution 176
iii. The OCT Report 177
iv. After the Ruling 182
B. The Effect of Inadmissibility of OCT Reports on Enforcement Following Food-borne Illness 183
VII. Inadmissibility of Information Gained from Conversations with Businesses and Employees and Its Impact on Enforcement 186
A. Obtaining Information from Businesses 187
B. Obtaining Information from Employees 188
C. The Effect of Inadmissible Interview Information on Enforcement 189
VIII. Conclusion 191

7. Reacting to Incidents of Food-borne Illness: The (Im)Possibility of Investigation, Control and Enforcement 195
I. Key Themes in Investigation, Control and Enforcement 196
A. The Power of the Network 196
B. The Centrality of Information 197
C. Evidential Decision Making is not Discretionary 199
D. Strict Liability Cases are Epistemically Difficult 200
E. Prioritising Control over Enforcement 201
F. Difficulties Taking Enforcement Action—Four Additional Explanatory Factors 203
i. Delay in the Collection of Evidence 203
ii. Causation Matters 204
iii. Resourcing and Evidence Collection 205
iv. Inexperience of Environmental Health Officers 206
G. Environmental Health Officers as Risk-averse Actors 209
i. Desire for Success and Positive Results 209
ii. The Unwillingness to Rely upon Epidemiological Evidence 212
iii. Rejecting Risk Aversion 214
iv. Are Environmental Health Officers Risk-averse Actors? 216
H. Summary 217
II. Meeting the Epistemic Challenges of Incidents of Food-borne Illness 218
A. Improving the Collection of Evidence: Seven Suggestions for Increasing Expertise and Experience 219
i. The Need to Build an 'Evidential Culture' 219
ii. Greater Use of Guidelines, Check-lists and Aides-memoires 220
iii. A Two-team Solution—Dividing Control and Enforcement 221
iv. A National Body with Responsibility for Incidents of Food-borne Illness 222
v. Increased Investigative Cooperation on a Regional Basis 225

vi. Involvement of Specialist Lawyers in Case-building 226
vii. The Possibility of Civil Sanctions 227
B. Easier Prosecution Case-building: Adapting to or Altering the Legal Framework 229
C. Can the Epistemic Challenges be Met? 230

8. **Conclusions** 231
I. Summary of Findings and Conclusions 231
II. Limitations 234
III. Recommendations 235

Bibliography 237
Index 245

Explanation of Alpha-numeric Identifiers

This book draws on substantial empirical research into the response to food-borne illness. Qualitative data was gathered through interviews with actors involved in the response to food-borne illness and from documents created during and after the response to food-borne illness, both publically available and held by network actors. The analysis of this data provides the basis for many of the conclusions drawn. Data referred to in the text and footnotes is identified through a series of alpha-numeric designators which anonymise the source, whilst allowing the reader to ascertain the source of the data. Three types of designator appear, and are explained in turn below.

A designator in the form EHO-A1 identifies a person interviewed as part of the research. The code before the dash identifies the individual's role in the response to food-borne illness, in this case as an Environmental Health Officer; the first letter following the dash identifies the local authority that employs the individual. Where the individual is not employed by a local authority the identifier does not appear; the number is a unique identifier of the individual. Various job roles are identified by the initial code; 'EHO' identifies Environmental Health Officers; 'SOL' identifies solicitors; 'BAR identifies barristers; 'CCDC' identified Consultants in Communicable Disease Control; 'MIC' identifies Microbiologists; 'CON' identifies environmental consultants; and 'EXP' identifies expert witnesses.

A designator in the form A/I/1 identifies a file associated with an investigation into an incident of food-borne illness. The initial designator identifies the local authority who led the investigation; the second letter is either I or O, I designating an incident of food-borne illness not rising to the level of an outbreak, and O indicating that an outbreak was declared; the number is a unique identifier of the case.

Where an identifier in the form PEN/DD/MCC.00003 appears the document is found in the archive of the Pennington Inquiry into the outbreak of *E. Coli* in South Wales in 2005. The archive can be accessed through the Inquiry website at <http://wales.gov.uk/ecoliinquiry/?lang=en>. The PEN signifies that this is a Pennington document; the second set of letters identifies the witness; and the final set of letters and numbers corresponds to the inquiry's pagination as it appears in the documents.

Table of Cases

Allan Rich Seafoods v Lincoln Magistrates' Court [2009] EWHC 3391 (Admin) 49
Ashworth Security Hospital v MGN [2000] 1 WLR 515 168
Attorney-General v Great Eastern Railway Company (1879) 11 ChD 449 53
Attorney-General's Reference (No 1 of 1975) [1975] 3 WLR 11 183
Boddington v British Transport Police [1999] 2 AC 143 53
British Steel Corp v Granada Television Ltd [1981] AC 1096 167
BT Fleet Limited v McKenna [2005] EWHC 387 (Admin) 61
Chibnall's Bakeries v Cope Brown [1956] Crim LR 263 37
Cunningham v Birmingham City Council (1998) 30 HLR 158 35
David Greig Ltd v Goldfinch (1961) 59 LGR 304 36
DDP v Myers [1965] AC 1001 178
Duchess of Kingston's case (1776) 20 St Tr 355 166
Dudley MBC v Debenhams (1994) 159 JP 18 111
Fisher v Barnett & Pomeroy (Bakers) Ltd [1954] 1 WLR 351 37
Fitzpatrick v Kelly (1872–73) LR 8 QB 337 31
Focus (DIY) Ltd v Hillingdon LBC [2008] EWHC 1152 (Admin) 157
Greater Manchester City Council v Lockwood Foods Ltd [1979] Crim LR 593 37
Guild v Gateway Foodmarkets Ltd 1990 JC 277 35–36
Hazlewood Grocery Limited v Lion Foods Limited [2007] EWHC 1887 32
Hunter v Mann [1974] QB 767 167
J Miller Ltd v Battersea BC [1956] 1 QB 43 36
Kenn v Bell 1910 SC(J) 13 35
Kyle v Laird 1951 JC 65 35
Leatherland and Pritchard v Powys CC [2007] EWHC 148 (Admin) 157
McNamara v Television Licensing Region Centre [2002] EWHC 2798 (Admin) 113
Meah v Roberts [1977] 1 WLR 1187 37
Monks v East Northamptonshire DC [2002] EWHC 473 (Admin) 54
Oakley v Birmingham City Council [2001] AC 617 35
R(Allan Rich Seafoods Ltd) v West Lindsey DC [2010] EWHC 1232 (Admin) 49
R (Environment Agency) v Drake [2009] EWHC 1344 (Admin) 157
R (Errington) v Metropolitan Police Authority [2006] EWHC 1155 (Admin) 61
R (Food Standards Agency) v Brent Justices [2004] EWHC 459 (Admin) 46
R (Maud) v Castle Point Borough Council [2003] RTR 7 48
R (Wellington) v DPP [2007] EWHC 1061 (Admin) 182

R v Absolam (1989) 88 Cr App R 332 ... 190
R v Adaway [2004] EWCA Crim 2831 ... 59
R v Adomako [1995] 1 AC 171 ... 32
R v Asif (1986) 82 Cr App R 123 ... 38
R v Barrow BC and Beckingham (Preston Crown Court, 31 July 2006) ... 223
R v Bedi and Bedi (1992) 95 Cr App R 21 ... 182
R v Brighton BC, ex p Bunch [1989] COD 558 ... 48
R v Burnett (1815) 4 Maule and Selwyn 272 ... 140
R v Delaney (1988) 88 Cr App R 338 ... 190
R v Director of Public Prosecutions, ex p C [1995] 1 Cr App R 136 ... 54
R v Gayle [1994] Crim LR 679 ... 166
R v Gill [2004] 1 WLR 469 ... 111, 190
R v Greenfield (1973) 57 Cr App R 849 ... 38
R v Henson (1852) 1 Dears 24 ... 140
R v Hertfordshire CC, ex p Green Industries [2000] 2 AC 412 ... 187
R v Ismail [1990] Crim LR 109 ... 191
R v Jarrett and Steward [1997] Crim LR 517 ... 54
R v Keenan [1990] 2 QB 54 ... 190
R v Mason [1988] 1 WLR 139 ... 190
R v McGillivray (1993) 97 Cr App R 232 ... 179
R v McSweeney, Kaya and Mitchells and Butlers plc (Snaresbrook Crown Court, 8 January 2015) ... 32, 107
R v Moys (1986) 79 Cr App R 72 ... 61
R v Muriel Morris (Birmingham Magistrates Court, 8 December 2010) ... 157, 192
R v Nelson and Rose [1998] 2 Cr App R 399 ... 112
R v Newton (1983) 77 Cr App R 13 ... 210
R v Oakwood Deli (Wood Green Crown Court, 2000) ... 109
R v Quadir [2005] EWCA Crim 2800 ... 211
R v Rimmington [2006] 1 AC 459 ... 140
R v Rodger [2002] EWCA Crim 660 ... 112, 115
R v Samuel [1988] QB 615 ... 190
R v Secretary of State for Health, ex p Eastside Cheese [1999] 3 CMLR 123 ... 20, 48
R v Seelig [1992] 1 WLR 148 ... 111
R v Shillibier [2006] EWCA Crim 793 ... 115
R v Singleton [2002] EWCA Crim 459 ... 191
R v South-West Water (Bristol Crown Court, 16 September 1997) ... 19, 58, 165–66, 169, 171, 173–74, 179, 183–85, 194, 202, 223
R v Sparkes [1991] Crim LR 128 ... 190
R v Vantandillo (1815) 4 Maule and Selwyn 75 ... 140–41
Roberts v Edgerton (1873-74) LR 9 QB 494 ... 31
Schering Corp v Pfizer, Inc 189 F 3d 218, 225 (2d Cir 1999) ... 184
Shearer v Rowe (1996) 84 LGR 196 ... 37
Smedleys v Breed [1974] AC 839 ... 37, 56
Stoke on Trent City Council v B&Q (Retail) Ltd [1984] AC 754 ... 47

Teper v R [1952] AC 480 178
The Borough of Bexley v Gardner Merchant Plc (CA,17 March 1993) 61
Turner & Son Ltd v Owen [1956] 1 QB 49 36
Walkers Snack Foods Ltd v Coventry City Council [1998] 3 All ER 163 .... 24, 102
Warren v Attorney-General of Jersey [2011] UKPC 10 158
West Midlands Probation Board v French [2009] 1 WLR 1715 184

Tables of Legislation

Table of Statutes

Civil Contingencies Act 2004 .... 20, 50
Consumer Rights Act 2015 .... 24, 227
Criminal Justice Act 1967 .... 106, 173, 185
Criminal Justice Act 1988 .... 166, 178, 180
Criminal Justice Act 2003 .... 166, 173, 182–84
Criminal Procedure and Investigations Act 1996 171
Data Protection Act 1998 76
Employment Rights Act 1996 29
Enterprise Act 2002 227–28
Food and Drugs (Scotland) Act 1956 35
Food and Drugs Act 1955 36
Food Safety Act 1990 .... 20, 23, 25, 37, 45–48, 54, 56, 61, 96, 99, 102, 108, 117, 156, 168, 170
Food (Scotland) Act 2015 21
Food Standards Act 1999 21
Greater London Authority Act 1999 22
Health and Safety at Work, etc Act 1974 223
Local Government Act 1972 .... 22, 25, 53, 60
Police and Criminal Evidence Act 1984 .... 28, 111, 113
Prosecution of Offences Act 1985 55
Public Health (Control of Disease) Act 1984 .... 6, 24, 26, 44–45, 51, 76, 79, 139, 169, 187
Public Health Act 1936 125
Regulatory Enforcement and Sanctions Act 2008 .... 25, 48, 227–28
Water Industry Act 1991 176

Table of Statutory Instruments

Contaminants in Food (England) Regulations 2013, SI 2013/2196 36
Coordination of Regulatory Enforcement (Enforcement Action) Order 2009, SI 2009/665 .... 25, 48
Criminal Procedure Rules 2014 .... 38, 159
Enterprise Act 2002 (Part 8 Domestic Infringements) Regulations 2003, SI 2003/1593 228
Food Hygiene (England) Regulations 2006, SI 2006/14 165
Food Safety and Hygiene (England) Regulations 2013, SI 2013/2996 .... 23, 32, 37, 96, 139, 156
Food Hygiene (Wales) Regulations 2006, SI 2006/31 .... 24, 37
Food Hygiene (Scotland) Regulations 2006, SI 2006/3 .... 24, 37

Food Safety (General Food Hygiene) Regulations 1995, SI 1995/1763 ... 211
General Food Regulations 2004, SI 2004/3279 ... 24, 156, 165, 215
General Product Safety Regulations 2005, SI 2005/1803 ... 8, 31, 131
Health Protection (Local Authority Powers) Regulations 2010, SI 2010/657 ... 51
Health Protection (Notification) Regulations 2010, SI 2010/659 ... 26, 65
Health Protection (Part 2A Orders) Regulations 2010, SI 2010/658 ... 51
Official Feed and Food Controls (England) Regulations 2009, SI 2009/3255 ... 50
Public Health Wales National Health Service Trust (Establishment) Order 2009, SI 2009/2058 ... 27
Water Supply (Water Quality) Regulations 2000, SI 2000/3184 ... 183

Table of EU Legislation

Regulation (EC) No 178/2002 of the European Parliament and of the Council of 28 January 2002 laying down the general principles and requirements of food law, establishing the European Food Safety Authority and laying down procedures in matters of food safety [2002] OJ L31/1 ... 2, 19–20, 23–24, 32–33, 35–37, 39, 47, 119–21, 164
Regulation (EC) No 2073/2005 of 15 November 2005 on microbiological criteria for foodstuffs [2005] OJ L338/1 ... 24, 33, 39–40
Regulation (EC) No 852/2004 of the European Parliament and of the Council of 29 April 2004 on the hygiene of foodstuffs [2004] L139/1 ... 24, 38–42, 45, 104, 134, 183, 188
Regulation (EC) No 853/2004 of the European Parliament and of the Council of 29 April 2004 laying down specific hygiene rules for food of animal origin [2004] L139/55 ... 24, 38, 45, 49
Regulation (EC) No 854/2004 of the European Parliament and of the Council of 29 April 2004 laying down specific rules for the organisation of official controls on products of animal origin intended for human consumption [2004] L139/206 ... 24, 50
Regulation (EC) No 882/2004 of the European Parliament and of the Council of 29 April 2004 on official controls performed to ensure the verification of compliance with feed and food law, animal health and animal welfare rules [2004] L165/1 ... 50
Treaty on the Functioning of the European Union [2012] OJ C326/1 ... 143

1

The Response to Food-borne Illness

I. INTRODUCTION

INVESTIGATIONS INTO FOOD-BORNE illness are important and frequent, because food-borne illness is a persistent problem in modern society. Risks to human health caused by micro-organisms are frequently in the news.[1] Food-borne illness can lead to economic, social and political instability (on a large or small scale).[2] In the last 20 years two major public inquiries in the United Kingdom (UK) have investigated large-scale fatal outbreaks of *E. coli* O157.[3] In 2011, a major outbreak of *E. coli* O104:H4 was responsible for 49 deaths in the European Union. In the United States, a massive *salmonella* outbreak traced to the Peanut Corporation of America forced the company out of business.[4] *E. coli*, *salmonella*, *listeria* and *norovirus* are illnesses in the public consciousness. Whilst death is the most publicised form of harm, illness, resulting in days lost from work but with a relatively short recovery period, is the usual result.

The regulation of food is a long-standing preoccupation of the regulatory state.[5] Food regulation is partly aimed at preventing food-borne illness

1 See the stories that frequently appear at <http://www.food.gov.uk/news/> and those which are collated at <http://www.barfblog.com>.

2 House of Lords Select Committee on Science and Technology Fourth Report, *Fighting Infection*. The social, political and economic effects of food-borne illness are clearly observable in the bovine spongiform encephalopathy (BSE) crisis (Harriet Ritvo, 'Mad Cow Mysteries' in James L Watson and Melissa L Caldwell (eds), *The cultural politics of food and eating: a reader* (Blackwell 2005)), and are visible on a micro-level in many of the incidents examined in this book.

3 Pennington Group, *Report on the circumstances leading to the 1996 outbreak of infection with* E. coli *O157 in Central Scotland, the implications for food safety and the lessons to be learned* (Scottish Office 1997); Hugh Pennington, *The public inquiry into the September 2005 outbreak of* E. coli *O157 in South Wales* (Welsh Assembly Government 2009).

4 Rena I Steinzor, 'High Crimes, Not Misdemeanors: Deterring the Production of Unsafe Food' (2010) 19 *Health Matrix: Journal of Law-Medicine* 175.

5 Ingeborg Paulus, *The search for pure food: a sociology of legislation in Britain* (Martin Robertson 1974); Richard Hyde, 'Why Separate the Regulatory Regimes Applicable to Food Safety and Product Safety?' (2013) 33(4) *Legal Studies* 509.

from causing harm to consumers.[6] In particular, the rationale of food safety and hygiene regulation is identified as securing a high level of consumer protection.[7] If food-borne illnesses cause harm, the regulatory regime has, in one sense, not met that aim. The regime of inspections and advice may, to an extent, have failed. Of course, regulatory failure may not be the direct cause of an incident of food-borne illness.[8] But regulatory failure is not the theme of this book; its focus is on what comes afterwards.

Response to food-borne illness gives rise to *sui generis* interactions between regulators and businesses. It is a domain where the preventive, diagnostic and therapeutic medicine, regulation and criminal law interact. Medicine identifies and treats those unfortunate enough to be affected; regulation in the widest sense seeks to control the actions of things, be they humans, micro-organisms, businesses or technologies, and in the food context attempts to prevent the existence or propagation of illness; criminal law seeks to punish those responsible. It is necessary to explore the complex interrelationship between the regulatory control of illness (and those entities that may circulate the illness) and enforcement action taken against those who cause the spread of food-borne illness.[9]

Food-borne illness requires a networked response.[10] Local authority regulators must cooperate with medical professionals, national regulators, consumer and regulated businesses and their employees in order to investigate an incident of illness and bring it under control. A network is necessary because the regulatory capacity of individual actors is insufficient to enable a complete response to an incident. In particular, the information-gathering capacity of individual actors is not enough to enable a complete picture of the incident to be built up. Both control and enforcement require information, and the information must be detailed as possible so that the appropriate action can be taken. Information is obtained during the investigation into food-borne illness, but the type and content of information necessary

[6] The regulation of food has other roles, such as facilitating consumer choice and enabling the circulation of goods within the single market; see Regulation 178/2002, art 8(1) and preambular paras 4 and 5.

[7] Regulation (EC) 178/2002 of the European Parliament and of the Council of 28 January 2002 laying down the general principles and requirements of food law, establishing the European Food Safety Authority and laying down procedures in matters of food safety [2002] OJ L31/1, preambular para 2; and see Tony Prosser, *The regulatory enterprise: Government, regulation, and legitimacy* (Oxford University Press 2010) 45ff.

[8] Regulatory failure was a theme of the Pennington Inquiry convened following the South Wales *E. Coli* outbreak (Pennington, above n 3).

[9] Note that formal action taken to control a risk and formal action taken against those who cause a risk are often not separated in the literature (Richard B Macrory, *Regulatory Justice: Making Sanctions Effective* (Better Regulation Executive 2006); Julia Black, 'A review of enforcement techniques' in Law Commission (ed), *Criminal Liability in Regulatory Contexts—Consultation Paper 195* (Law Commission 2010)).

[10] Julia Black, 'The decentred regulatory state?' in Peter Vass (ed), *CRI Regulatory Review 2006/2007* (Centre for the Study of Regulated Industries, University of Bath 2007).

for control and enforcement are different. The competition between these goals influences the information gathered within the network and the range of actions that may be taken in response to food-borne illness.

An investigation into food-borne illness produces 'an ever growing and seemingly never-ending tsunami of data, facts, interpretations, contestations, disputations, demonstrations, inter-correlations, inferences, deductions, obfuscations, and a pervasive sense of confusion'.[11] The challenge of controlling this torrent of information is not confined to investigation into food-borne illness but exists for all investigators. Roberts observes that 'it is the job of the investigator to unearth, recover, procure, amass, sort, compile, test, evaluate and arrange' it.[12] This information must then be used. The data compiled may be translated into enforcement action, demonstrating a breach of the law by proving the elements of the offence through admissible evidence. The information may be used to prevent the occurrence of further infection. It may be used to preclude future incidents. Or it may be used to do all of these things. Therefore, the insights into information gathering and processing derived from this study may be applicable beyond the context of food-borne illness investigation, and in particular may mirror the experience of many regulatory networks that seek to control current and future behaviour as well as sanctioning the behaviour of the past.

It is necessary to consider the specifically regulatory nature of the response to food-borne illness. This is not akin to a law enforcement response; it is more concerned with the governance of risky food-borne illness, rather than the allocation of responsibility for incidents. First we need to examine why food is regulated, and why it is regulated more stringently than other products (section II.), before specifically considering two important governance issues illustrated by the response to food-borne illness: the importance of regulatory networks (section III.), and the regulation of risks (section IV.). The key concepts in the response to incidents of food-borne illness, investigation, control and enforcement, are then briefly explored (sections V.–VIII.), before the methodology of the empirical work underpinning this book is outlined (section IX.). The structure of the book is outlined in section X. of this chapter.

II. REGULATING FOOD

In many cases regulations are introduced to prevent market failure. The regulatory efforts are put in place either to correct this failure, or to ensure

[11] Paul Rabinow, 'Episodes or incidents: Seeking significance' in Andrew Lakoff and Stephen J Collier (eds), *Biosecurity Interventions: Global Health and Security Questions* (Columbia University Press 2008).

[12] Paul Roberts, 'Law and Criminal Investigation' in Tim Newburn, Tom Williamson and Alan Wright (eds), *Handbook of Criminal Investigation* (Willan 2007) 92, 96.

that consumers are not adversely affected by the lack of a perfect market in a particular area. Market failure arises where the consumer is not able to play the role of disciplining the market by exercising choice, which, if safer food is the rational choice of consumers, should result in food businesses that offer unsafe products exiting the market, as consumers will not support such businesses. Consumers are not able to make the choice between safe and unsafe products and safe and unsafe food business operators, because consumers are unable to judge whether a particular product poses a risk.

Consumers who purchase food are exposed to a classical information deficit, with the risk of food-borne illness being impossible for consumers to judge. Food-borne illness organisms are microscopic, and a consumer is unable to see whether a food contains such organisms or not. Of course, consumers are able to identify food that is more or less risky, by considering the style of preparation or examining the physical condition of the food, but this does not provide sufficient information for a consumer to decide whether to purchase food based on its safety attributes.

Similarly, the hygiene conditions of food businesses are difficult for consumers to judge, with food preparation taking place away from public view, even in businesses to which the public have access, such as restaurants. Consumers do not see how food is stored, they do not see the pest control measures that are taken and they do not see the measures taken to prevent cross-contamination. This important information, which would allow consumers to make rational decisions regarding whether to purchase food from a particular food business operator, is simply not available to them. Whilst some information about the conditions of a food business is accessible through the national food hygiene rating scheme, which provides a hygiene rating for every retail-level food business operator in the UK (which can be accessed online and in Wales has to be displayed on the premises; a similar requirement is to be introduced in Northern Ireland, but in Scotland and England display remains at the discretion of the business), this does not provide a sufficient safeguard for consumers, as the inspections are one-off events and hygiene conditions may change on a day-to-day basis, and the rating scheme does not include information about the safety of food produced in premises above the retail level.

As well as the presence of market failure resulting in the inability of consumers to make choices to avoid illness, food is different.[13] It is a product unlike any other, and it cannot be treated in the same manner as other products. It is necessary to regulate food to prevent illness for a number of reasons. First, food is an essential product that is consumed orally. Consumers have to eat, and they place food in their mouths, which provides a pathway to those parts of the consumers' bodies less well protected by the immune system, meaning that the consequences of an unsafe product are more likely

[13] Hyde, above n 5.

to be severe when compared with the harm that could be caused by a product consumed through other senses, such as by sight or touch. This is particularly the case where a consumer is young, old or immuno-deficient, each of whom has a greater risk of food-borne illness due to an underdeveloped immune system.

Further, food-borne illness is different from the damage caused by other unsafe products. Such products are limited in number, and can be traced and identified through physical existence and appearance, whereas illness is more elusive. It can spread far beyond the original product, from the original consumer to other people with whom he or she comes into contact. One piece of unsafe food has the potential to lead to an exponentially larger level of damage than a typical single unsafe product.

All of these factors lead to the need to regulate food. Broad-ranging regulatory controls have been introduced to ensure that the risk posed by food is controlled. Such controls have been in place for many years, and food was one of the first industrial sectors to be regulated by the state, initially in response to public pressure that followed outbreaks of illness caused by adulterated food.[14] Both food itself and the method of production are regulated (as will be seen in chapter three). This regime seeks to prevent food-borne illness occurring, both by preventing the conditions in which food may become infected and by preventing unsafe food from entering the market. This regime requires a governance mechanism, and it is therefore necessary to consider how the state operationalises its response to an incident of food-borne illness.

III. THE ROLE OF THE NETWORK

The state responds to an incident of food-borne illness through a network of bodies that work together to respond. A network is necessary because cooperative working between a number of bodies, with different competences, can lead to a more efficient response, with a broader range of powers to investigate, control and enforce following incidents of food-borne illness. The rise of governance networks is a hallmark of the rise of the regulatory state. From the 1980s onwards, the state has been hollowed out, with the core functions of government concentrated, and other functions that had been performed by central government have been delegated to non-state actors.[15] In the case of food-borne illness, a network has always been necessary, as the competences of a local authority (which had the primary responsibility for responding to food-borne illness) have always been too

[14] Paulus, above n 5.

[15] Karen Yeung, 'The Regulatory State' in Robert Baldwin, Martin Cave and Martin Lodge, *The Oxford Handbook of Regulation* (Oxford University Press 2010).

limited to allow a complete response without the cooperation of other bodies. However, the network has expanded as the complexity of incidents of food-borne illness and the expertise required to respond to them have grown. Multiple actors, with differing competences, are better situated to respond than a single, limited actor.

In her analysis of the financial services sector, Black identifies at least 13 categories of regulatory actors.[16] The actors who may play a role in the response to food-borne illness are no less numerous. From the supranational regulators who play a role in determining the regulatory standards that apply, to the consumer who purchases and ingests food, each part of the network can play an important role in the response to food-borne illness. National and local regulators, public health professionals and frontline medical staff, food businesses and their employees, all feature in the complex network that responds to incidents of food-borne illness, and which is explored in more detail in chapter two.

To play a part, regulatory actors must enrol into the network. Some regulatory actors have specific responsibility to act in particular circumstances, and are therefore enrolled into the regulatory network in response to incidents that touch on their area of responsibility. Public health professionals, and particularly the nominated Consultant in Communicable Disease Control in an area, have particular responsibilities when responding to incidents of certain types. The Food Standards Agency has responsibility for coordinating information sharing where an incident of food-borne illness is on an international scale. Other regulatory actors will enrol themselves voluntarily into a regulatory network, offering their regulatory capacity on an ad hoc basis. Medical professionals who report illness outside the framework provided by the Public Health (Control of Disease) Act 1984, consumers who report their illness and businesses that notify regulators of an incident connected to their premises are all voluntarily enrolling in a regulatory network. The regulatory actors with central responsibility for the response to food-borne illness, particularly local authorities, will take steps to encourage more actors to enrol voluntarily.

It is the need for information that drives the need to enrol actors into the network. Network actors can provide the data that identify people, places or products in need of control. This information cannot be harvested by a single, monolithic entity, subject to limited resources and facing a temporal challenge in gathering information, as it cannot be present in food establishments at all times, and much of the information that it needs when responding to incidents of food-borne illness relates to occurrences that pre-date the incident's coming to the attention of the regulators. A broader network, which takes advantage of the different competences of the regulatory actors

[16] Julia Black, 'Enrolling Actors in Regulatory Systems: Examples from UK Financial Services Regulation' [2003] *Public Law* 63, 70.

that are enrolled into the network, is better informed about the incident of food-borne illness. A consumer can provide information about what he or she has eaten; a business can provide information about the identity of its customers; employees can provide information about corners that have been cut in complying with regulatory requirements. Together, the network is able to identify those people, places and premises that pose risks, and therefore that require action to manage that risk.

IV. REGULATING RISK

Hutter conceptualises the governance mechanisms that apply to food as being aimed at the prevention of risk.[17] This book clearly shows that the regulatory network is concerned with risks posed by food, both general and specific, and takes steps to ensure that those risks do not eventuate and cause harm to consumers. At the highest level, the regulatory norms that govern the production of food, and which are outlined in chapter three, are intended to prevent the initial contamination of food by food-borne illness micro-organisms, and to prevent both primary and secondary spread of illness once food has become contaminated with such viral or bacterial micro-organisms.

Regulators are also concerned with more specific risks, which are identified by the investigation into an incident of food-borne illness, with risky foods, people or places forming the subject of regulatory action. This action is tailored to reduce the risk of these identified objects, ensuring that further individuals are not affected by food-borne illness identified in an investigation. Regulators may err on the side of preventing the future eventuation of risk, with their actions in response to these identified risks being taken on a precautionary basis.

Whilst it would be possible to consider measures that seek to prevent the occurrence of hazards, this book examines how regulatory networks respond to the second type of risk, considering the responses of the regulatory network when the hazard eventuates, and how networks seek to prevent spread and apportion responsibility.

V. THE ISSUE OF ILLNESS

The literature in this area has not engaged with the complexities of illness. The incidents of concern to criminal or regulatory scholars are generally

[17] Bridget M Hutter, *Managing food safety and hygiene: governance and regulation as risk management* (Edward Elgar 2011) 2. See also Bridget M Hutter and Tola Amodu, *Risk Regulation and Compliance: Food Safety in the UK* (LSE Enterprise 2009).

discrete activities, single actions that have ended by the time officers assemble information about the incident and take decisions about further steps. Whilst regulatory activities may be concerned with on-going risk to the public, as in product safety cases necessitating recall, these risks are fixed on discrete and identifiable products or classes of products.[18] Food-borne illness, on the other hand, is a dynamic biological risk, which spreads from place to place and from person to person, meaning that efforts to stop the spread of illness need to be both responsive to detected sites of illness and proactive to prevent new sites of infection arising. The fluid nature of the risk sets this enforcement context apart from most risks considered in the literature surrounding regulatory decision-making.

One strand of the emerging discipline of biosecurity focuses on the steps taken to prevent the spread of human and animal illnesses.[19] It examines the gathering of information about illness, and judgements taken about preventing illness spread. However, biosecurity literature tends to examine illness on a large, national or international scale. Foot and mouth, severe acute respiratory syndrome (SARS) and avian influenza have formed the basis for studies of the control of illness.[20] Each of these incidents played out on a massive scale, where illness (or precautions to prevent the spread of illness) affected a large number of widely dispersed people, products, places and environments. While food-borne illness may have an international reach, the events studied in this book are smaller in scope, with local rather than national populations, products, places and environments being the objects of inspection and control.[21]

Biosecurity examines the measures taken to prevent the mixing of infected (and/or infectious) people, products, places and environments with people,

[18] Eg, the General Product Safety Regulations 2005, SI 2005/1803, reg 15 provides that 'dangerous products' may be recalled. This is a binary designation: a product is either dangerous or not. With illness, people, products, places and environments can become dangerous, depending on their interactions with infected products.

[19] Biosecurity also looks at (i) steps taken to prevent 'foreign' species invading environments (eg Kezia Barker, 'Flexible boundaries in biosecurity: accommodating gorse in Aotearoa New Zealand' (2008) 40 *Environment and Planning A* 1598), and (ii) the prevention of the proliferation of bioweapons and the defence against such weapons (eg Kathleen M Vogel, 'Biodefence: Considering the Sociotechnological Dimension' in Andrew Lakoff and Stephen J Collier (eds), *Biosecurity Interventions: Global Health and Security in Question* (Columbia University Press 2008) 227). This book does not consider these dimensions of biosecurity, focusing instead on the question of 'making life safe' from illness, rather than from invasive species or bioweapons.

[20] See Steven Hinchliffe and Nick Bingham, 'Securing life: the emerging practices of biosecurity' (2008) 40 *Environment and Planning A* 1534; Andrew Donaldson, 'Biosecurity after the event: risk politics and animal disease' (2008) 40 *Environment and Planning A* 1552; Estair Van Wagner, 'The practice of biosecurity in Canada: public health legal preparedness and Toronto's SARS crisis' (2008) 40 *Environment and Planning A* 1647; Charles Mather and Amy Marshall, 'Biosecurity's unruly spaces' (2011) 177 *Geographical Journal* 300.

[21] Although smaller-scale control is beginning to be considered as part of the biosecurity literature, see Nick Bingham and Stephanie Lavau, 'The object of regulation: Tending the tensions of food safety' (2012) 44 *Environment and Planning A* 1589.

products, places and environments that are not (yet) infected. It can be seen as requiring separation, which is usually geographic but may be technological, between that which is diseased and that which is not. However, complete separation is unrealistic. Biosecurity should be seen as regulating the interactions between diseased and non-diseased, and managing the risk of spread of disease. The recent work of Hinchliffe *et al* has conceptualised biosecurity as regulating interfaces between 'clean' and 'unclean', and regulating areas of high risk.[22] In responses to cases of food-borne illness, it will become clear that this management of interactions is often closer to the reality than complete exclusion of the infected or complete elimination of risk.

Whilst biosecurity considers the measures put in place to control food-borne illness, it rarely examines the legal foundations of these powers. This book describes the detailed legal basis of Environmental Health Officers' (EHOs') powers, and considers factors that must be established in order to take lawful action.

Biosecurity literature does not consider the enforcement process following the control of food-borne illness. Whilst Van Wagner examines the legal challenges to measures put in place to control the spread of SARS,[23] biosecurity literature in general does not examine the process that attempts to fix responsibility for illness and to sanction those deemed responsible. This is often because the notion of responsibility for illness does not arise in large-scale events, where illness is understood as 'both integral to, and always part of, an entangled interplay of environments, hosts, pathogens and humans'.[24] Whilst the criminal law seeks to apportion responsibility, this is not seen as central to the goal of preventing the spread of illness. This tension looms large in the empirical findings presented below.

Perhaps the research most similar to that set out in this book is North's study of food-poisoning surveillance, which examined reported *salmonella* outbreaks between 1988 and 1992 and asked whether the response was high-quality or otherwise.[25] North found some of the challenges of turning information into useable evidence that are replicated in this study. Specifically, North reported that evidential difficulties arose from information created by the medical profession. He also found challenges, similar to those reported in this study, around obtaining food history evidence and information about food preparation. However, North's focus was on the techniques used to reach *scientific* conclusions. He did not consider the additional *legal* element of the response to food-borne illness, or the collection and use of

[22] Steven Hinchliffe *et al*, 'Biosecurity and the topologies of infected life: From borderlines to borderlands' (2013) 38(4) *Transactions of the Institute of British Geographers* 531.

[23] Van Wagner, above n 20.

[24] Hinchliffe *et al*, above n 22.

[25] Richard AE North, Jim PI Duguid and Michael A Sheard, 'The quality of public sector food-poisoning surveillance in England and Wales, with specific reference to salmonella food poisoning' (1996) 98 *British Food Journal* 1.

information to reach *legal* conclusions, which are the focus of this study. Further, the relationship between information obtained for the purposes of enforcement and information obtained for the purposes of control was not explored in his research.

Whilst illness has been a focus of some literature, it is necessary to consider the key concepts that underpin its regulation. Varying terms are used in the scholarly literature and in practice to classify the events of food-borne illness that give rise to regulatory intervention. 'Outbreak' is the only term afforded a formal definition, but those offered are diverse and varied.[26] Outbreaks, roughly speaking, are those events where there is a large increase in the number of people infected with a particular illness, which can be linked to a particular source, and which are dealt with formally by an Outbreak Control Team (OCT). By narrowing or widening the definition of the situations of interest, it would be possible to decrease or increase the number of cases in the study population. 'Outbreak' is too narrow and uncertain a term to be useful for methodological purposes. Local authorities also investigate sporadic natural occurrences of illness, and may take formal control action following such events to prevent further spread of illness. The response to such events has been included in this study. In order to capture outbreaks and sporadic events (and everything in between), the term 'incident' is used in this book. 'Incident' means all events of food-borne illness of which the regulatory network becomes aware. Once a network is aware of the food-borne illness, it will act to investigate and take the necessary action to control its spread. The first step it will take is to collect information about the incident, which is considered in detail in chapter four.

VI. COLLECTION OF INFORMATION

Information is central to the response to food-borne illness. It is the need for information that drives the need to enrol actors into the regulatory network. This information is necessary so that the regulators can form a clear picture of an incident of food-borne illness, its genesis, nature and extent. Drawing upon the literature examining the control of illness and case building, it is clear that obtaining, documenting and using information forms a central part of the activity of enforcement officers. Therefore, the research methods

[26] See Eileen A O'Neil and Elena N Naumova, 'Defining outbreak: Breaking out of confusion' (2007) 28 *Journal of Public Health Policy* 442; James M Wilson, 'Infectious Disease Events, Crises, and Disasters: An Operational Definition' (*Biosurveillance Blog*, 2010), available at <http://biosurveillance.typepad.com/biosurveillance/infectious-disease-events-crises-and-disasters-an-operational-definition.html>, accessed 12 October 2010; Food Standards Agency, *Management of outbreaks of foodborne illness in England and Wales* (Food Standards Agency 2008) 17; Directive 2003/99 on the monitoring of zoonoses and zoonotic agents, amending Council Decision 90/424/EEC and repealing Council Directive 92/117/EEC, art 2(2)(d).

adopted attempt to excavate information gathered during incidents of food-borne illness, and to explore the ways in which it was analysed, transmitted to third parties and used to take formal or informal action.

Within the institutional architecture of local authorities, EHOs are 'knowledge workers'.[27] An emphasis is placed on acquiring knowledge about risks posed by food-borne illness. The acquisition of this information is central to the role of EHOs in responding to such illness. They encounter huge amounts of information in their investigations.[28] The information is sifted, sorted and arranged to construct a narrative about the 'source' of an illness and about the 'risks' of transmission, which forms a basis for the intervention of network actors.

VII. THE CONTROL OF REALISED RISK

If information shows that something poses a risk to the public, action may be taken to control that risk. This is examined further in chapter five. Items that pose a risk to the public include food products, food premises, (possibly) infected individuals and (potentially) contaminated environments. Regulatory networks have powers that allow them to intervene to ensure that the risks are reduced. For example, products may be seized and destroyed, businesses may be closed and individuals prevented from working. The environment may be altered to reduce the risk of infection. However, such action depends on the regulatory network's having accurate information about the risks that require control.

VIII. ENFORCEMENT AND SANCTIONING

As well as control, the information gathered by the regulatory network may be used for the purposes of enforcement. Enforcement powers respond to and sanction regulatory breaches. This book adopts a purposive conception of enforcement powers. If a power is used after an illness has stopped spreading, to take action against a business suspected of being responsible for the incident, then this is treated as enforcement. In contrast to the approach taken in the Macrory Report,[29] only enforcement actions will be treated as sanctions, to differentiate them from formal powers used to *investigate* or *control* food borne-illness.

Enforcement can be both formal and informal. The classical enforcement power is the power of prosecution, but other formal enforcement powers

[27] Richard V Ericson and Kevin D Haggerty, *Policing the risk society* (Clarendon Press 1997) 19.
[28] Rabinow, above n 11.
[29] Macrory, above n 9.

are available, including cautions. Informally, businesses may be warned, either orally or in writing, regarding breaches that give rise to an incident of food-borne illness.

Enforcement forms the third prong of the response to food-borne illness, and tends to take place once an incident has been controlled. Particularly where prosecution is used, enforcement action tends to take place over a longer timescale than control, although, at least of the beginning of the enforcement process, it tends to take place concurrently with control.

As well as backward-looking powers that seek to apportion responsibility for an incident of food-borne illness, some actions taken by enforcement officers are advisory, looking to prevent the next incident, rather than controlling the current incident or sanctioning those responsible. Advice is not a central focus of officers responding to incidents of food-borne illness, and is instead a by-product of investigations aimed at securing control and facilitating enforcement.

IX. EXAMINING THE RESPONSE TO FOOD-BORNE ILLNESS: METHODOLOGICAL CONSIDERATIONS[30]

In order to examine the response to food-borne illness, it is necessary to consider the experiences of the network participants who work to investigate, control and enforce incidents. The response cannot be considered simply by looking at the law in the books; it is necessary to engage in empirical examination of the practice of enforcement professionals.[31] However, empirical research into regulation has been described as 'messy and uncertain', and as 'haphazard'.[32] It is therefore necessary briefly to outline the methods adopted in gathering and processing the data that form the core of this book.

As the enforcement activities of EHOs had not been subject to detailed examination by a socio-legal scholar since Hutter's study,[33] the work was somewhat exploratory. Therefore, an empirical, qualitative approach was chosen, with the goal of understanding 'the process by which agency outcomes are produced'.[34] The research drew on a wide range of available data

[30] A much more full consideration of the methodological considerations that shaped the research can be found in Richard Hyde, *Responding to Incidents of Food-borne Illness: An Empirical Study* (PhD Thesis, University of Nottingham 2013), ch 2.

[31] Paul Almond, 'An inspector's-eye view—The prospective enforcement of work-related fatality cases' (2006) 46 *British Journal of Criminology* 893.

[32] Paul Almond, 'Investigating health and safety regulation: Finding room for small-scale projects' (2008) 35 *Journal of Law and Society* 108, 117.

[33] Bridget M Hutter, *The reasonable arm of the law?: the law enforcement procedures of environmental health officers* (Clarendon 1988).

[34] Almond, above n 32, 110.

to shed light on an under-examined phenomenon.[35] This allowed exploration of the research questions from a variety of perspectives, giving a more holistic answer to the research questions posed.[36]

As noted above, the response to food-borne illness is led by local authorities.[37] The response involves a network of bodies and individuals working together, and produces large amounts of information. This is contained in contemporaneous files, which provide a reliable and in-depth source of information about EHOs' perceptions and priorities at the relevant time. A typical file contains details of the initial contact, including ways that the consumer-complainant, or other notifying individual, can be contacted; an activity log recording the time spent investigating the incident; *aides-mémoire* to assist with the investigation; questionnaires completed by 'cases' (symptomatic individuals) and 'controls'; a list detailing the samples taken and the analysis returns; notes of visits to premises and of interviews with businesses and staff; documentation taken from the businesses during the investigation; miscellaneous correspondence (with consumers, with businesses, with other local authority EHOs and with lawyers); documentation relating to formal or informal enforcement action; and a wrap-up setting out any lessons learnt during the investigation (including, where appropriate, an OCT report). Files from one local authority, Local Authority A, were examined in this research.

Alongside the contemporaneous files, 22 actors within the regulatory network, EHOs, lawyers and other professionals,[38] were interviewed, both generally about their response to incidents of food-borne illness and specifically about the responses referred to in the files.[39] These interviews lasted between 30 minutes and two hours, and were recorded and subsequently transcribed. Further information about incidents of food-borne illness was gathered from publicly available data (particularly from media stories, published official reports that considered the response to an incident, and the exceptionally large archive of data published by the *Pennington Inquiry*)[40] and from decided cases where businesses were accused of violating regulatory requirements

[35] Similar to Michael Levi, *The phantom capitalists: the organization and control of long-firm fraud* (rev edn, Aldershot 2008).

[36] Observation of the regulatory network responding to an incident of food-borne illness in person was not possible, for the simple reason that the network actors who granted access did not encounter an incident of food-borne illness during the period of access.

[37] Four local authorities were examined during this research: Local Authority A was an urban unitary authority, Local Authorities B and D were rural district authorities, and Local Authority C was an urban district authority.

[38] Including microbiologists, epidemiologists and medical professionals.

[39] These interviewees are denoted by alpha-numeric designators throughout the book. These designations identify for which of the four local authorities (if any) the interviewee worked, and the role that person held within that authority. So EHO-A1 worked for Local Authority A and was an EHO; SOL-A1 was a solicitor employed by Local Authority A; BAR-1 was a barrister, etc.

[40] Available at <http://wales.gov.uk/ecoliinquiry/?lang=en>, with documentary evidence and transcripts of hearings archived at <http://wales.gov.uk/ecoliinquiry/hearings/?lang=en>.

applicable to food. By relying on multiple data sources, information could be triangulated, affording enhanced validity.

The data gathered from these various sources were analysed by creating analytical categories and applying these to the data.[41] When data, whether interview transcripts, files or public documents, no longer offered novel insight into a particular area, it could be said with confidence that the repeated concept was a material finding, representing authentic responses to incidents of food-borne illness. This provides a rich account of institutional behaviours, and a solid evidence-based foundation to inform further academic work and policy-making in this area.

X. EXAMINING THE RESPONSE TO FOOD-BORNE ILLNESS: A STRUCTURAL GUIDE

Chapters two and three of this book consider the field in which enforcement decisions are made. By identifying the professional and institutional participants involved in responding to food-borne illness, and their formal powers of enforcement and control, the central position of EHOs in the response to such illness is demonstrated. Environmental Health Officers have a central role in investigation, control and enforcement of food-borne illness, working with other agencies to respond to it. By setting their role in context, it is possible to better understand their actions.

As noted above, the central themes of the book are the priority of control in responses to food-borne illness, and the way that the need to control food-borne illness influences the way in which information is collected, and how this impacts upon formal responses to an incident of illness. This book aims to tell the story of how information gathering, control of illness and the desire to take enforcement action interact with and influence each other.

The findings of the empirical research that form the heart of the study are set out in chapter four. The steps taken by enforcement officers to secure epidemiological, microbiological and environmental information about the illness are detailed, and the EHOs' reasons for taking these steps, are described and examined. In determining the actions to be taken by the EHO, the importance of preventing further cases of the illness is highlighted. The EHOs perceive the need for cooperation by businesses in order to achieve their goal of preventing further cases of food-borne illness, and may be disinclined to do anything that will damage this cooperation.

While chapter four highlights the influence on investigative steps of the need to control food-borne illness, chapter five explores further the concept of 'control'. Possible conceptions of control are examined and compared

[41] Using the grounded theory approach developed by Barney G Glaser and Anselm L Strauss, *The Discovery of Grounded Theory: Strategies for Qualitative Research* (Aldine 1967).

with EHOs' views of their role. Control rather than enforcement is seen as the main goal by those responding to an incident of food-borne illness. The imperative of control ensures that information is collected and used in a way that facilitates regulation of food-borne illness.

Chapter six explores the influence of investigative practices on the formal enforcement action that can be taken by EHOs. It argues that investigative practices aimed at ensuring control of food-borne illness are detrimental to formal enforcement action. This detriment arises in two ways: either information is gathered in a manner that (in the view of EHOs) renders it inadmissible to support enforcement action, or it is not gathered at all. This can be attributed to practical factors, such as the organic nature of food, but also to the working practices of EHOs, who seek information in ways that may fail to preserve its evidential value. As noted, in a 'real-crime' context, by Roberts, officers 'simply ignore legislation perceived as too complex to accommodate the operational imperatives of their daily working lives'.[42] With control as an operational imperative, legislation governing the collection of evidence is ignored, with inadmissibility the 'penalty' for non-compliance. This influences the extent to which formal enforcement action can be taken following incidents of food-borne illness.

Chapter six also shows that, in some cases, the admissibility of the information gathered during an investigation is assessed by EHOs rather than lawyers, and that EHOs use bright-line working rules to determine evidential admissibility. If they perceive the evidence to be inadmissible, they will not use such information for building a case.

Whilst control is the central goal of EHOs investigating food-borne illness, this does not mean that enforcement is impossible in all cases. Information is collected, and may appear to be both available and admissible. However, enforcement action is still typically not taken, despite the seriousness of the incident. Chapter seven examines key themes relevant to the muted, prosecution averse response to food-borne illness. It examines how EHOs process information that they gain during an investigation, highlighting the chief characteristics of EHOs' thinking and seeking to examine their decision making in response to incidents of food-borne illness. Considering EHOs' perceptions of the regulatory requirements and the evidential rules that apply to investigations, this chapter examines the institutional factors that influence non-enforcement strategies in relation to food-borne illness, even in circumstances where enforcement may be a realistic option, objectively speaking. Consideration is given to attitudinal and educational factors that may explain a risk-averse approach, which (echoing other regulatory literature)[43] seems to inform some decisions not to take enforcement action.

[42] Roberts, above n 12, 124.

[43] Ross Cranston, *Regulating Business: Law and Consumer Agencies* (The Macmillan Press 1979).

Turning to the scope for reform, the second half of chapter seven considers suggestions that have been put forward to tackle the evidential difficulties that prevent enforcement action. It concludes that none of the standard options is likely to lead to increased enforcement. Indeed, increased enforcement should not necessarily be a goal sought by local authorities, as the need to control the spread of food-borne illness properly takes precedence. Some suggestions are made, but these focus on soft changes to regulatory cultures, rather than on amendments to hard law instruments.

XI. SUMMARY

Scholarship on regulatory behaviour discloses an increasing interest on the ways in which regulatory networks respond to risk. This book, for the first time, seeks to explore this question in the context of the response to food-borne illness. When they become aware of an incident of food-borne illness, regulatory networks, centred on EHOs, attempt to gather information, take action to prevent further cases of the illness arising and bring enforcement action against those responsible. This book, through an empirical examination of the response, considers how these aspects of the response are put into practice. The interrelationship between investigation, control and enforcement is scrutinised, and the opportunities and challenges presented by the response to illness are explored. Drawing on both regulatory theory and literature that examines the control of illness, particularly the literature surrounding biosecurity, a narrative of information gathering, control action and the difficulty of enforcement is constructed, emphasising both the difference between food-borne illness and other regulated risks, and the similarities, in order that lessons may be drawn.

2

The Regulatory Network

I. INTRODUCTION

INVESTIGATION, CONTROL AND enforcement following incidents of food-borne illness are carried out by a network of actors. These actors have different regulatory competences, and by combining them the network should be better able to manage the risks arising from food-borne illness. As biological risks emerge from a relational entanglement of persons, non-human actors (such as microbes) and environments,[1] they can only be managed through a similar engagement between actors with diverse but complementary competences. This chapter explores the regulatory network responsible for the management of food-borne illnesses, illuminating the regulatory competences of the network and considering the roles that each network participant plays in the response to such illness.

The importance of networks in the governance of risk is a central theme of regulatory scholarship.[2] A monocentric model, where a single body is responsible for the management of risks of all types, is not feasible in a system as 'complex and dynamic' as that which ensures that consumers receive safe food.[3] Actors have different regulatory capacities, with different abilities to make rules, detect non-compliance with those rules and take action in order to change behaviour in the direction of compliance so that regulatory goals are achieved. Such capacities may flow from formal legal powers possessed by such a body, or from the factual position of the actor compared to the incident of food-borne illness.

Alongside the fragmented, polycentric governance network, centralised regulatory control through guidance and oversight by central regulatory actors is put in place in order to ensure that fast-spreading high-risk food-borne illnesses are managed appropriately.[4]

[1] Kezia Barker, Sarah L Taylor and Andrew Dobson, 'Introduction: Interrogating bio-insecurities' in Andrew Dobson, Kezia Barker and Sarah L Taylor (eds), *Biosecurity: the socio-politics of invasive species and infectious diseases* (Routledge 2013) 8.

[2] Julia Black, 'The decentred regulatory state?' in Peter Vass (ed), *CRI Regulatory Review 2006/2007* (Centre for the Study of Regulated Industries, University of Bath 2007), 253.

[3] Ibid, 259.

[4] Julia Black, 'Tensions in the Regulatory State' [2007] *Public Law* 58.

No one actor can have the expertise or information to manage the risk entirely. A polycentric network of actors with differentiated capacities is necessary to ensure that the risks of food-borne illness are managed. Therefore different actors must be enrolled into a regulatory network in order that the network can function to investigate food-borne illness and control its spread. Enrolment may be formal, with a particular role intentionally allocated to a particular actor in a particular network by another actor within that network, or may be informal, with ad hoc enrolment taking place in particular circumstance in order that the enrolling actor may achieve its regulatory aims.[5]

In the management of risks resulting from food-borne illness, the governance network involves a wide variety of participants, including: the EU; national and devolved governments, in both their legislative and executive capacities; national regulatory bodies, such as the Food Standards Agency and Public Health England; local regulatory bodies, particularly local authorities and the Environmental Health Officers (EHOs) that they employ; medical professionals, particularly those who practise in the public health field; law enforcement authorities, and particularly the police; non-governmental organisations, such as the Chartered Institute of Environmental Health, which may have responsibility for setting standards for other actors within the network; advisers, such as lawyers advising other network actors about their powers; food-business operators and their employees; other market actors that provide services to food business operators, such as insurers who provide public liability and product liability insurance; consumers; and the courts. Where the incident has multi-national scope, regulatory bodies in other countries will be enrolled in a multinational governance network.[6] In the UK the central actors in the governance of food-borne illness risks are local authorities, which have powers governing both food and public health. It is therefore with local authorities that a response to food-borne illness often begins, with other actors enrolled in the network as necessary to address the risk.

Whilst the network is often loose, there is a formal mechanism for coordinating it in circumstances where the incident rises to the level of an outbreak. An Outbreak Control Team (OCT) is formed to lead in the management of the spread of food-borne illness in such circumstances. Such OCTs involve

[5] Eg, where an employee blows the whistle on non-compliance by his or her employer, that employee is enrolled in the regulatory network as an information-providing actor, and he or she also enrols the regulator to achieve the aim of addressing the non-compliance notified (see Ashley Savage and Richard Hyde, 'The Response to Whistleblowing by Regulators: A Practical Perspective' (2014) *Legal Studies* (forthcoming), available at <http://www.dx.doi.org/10.1111/lest.12066>).

[6] A similar list of network participants appears, in the context of the governance of financial services, in Julia Black, 'Enrolling Actors in Regulatory Systems: Examples from UK Financial Services Regulation [2003] *Public Law* 63, 70.

participants from many of the various network actors, and meet and make decisions about the management of the outbreak; decide what information needs to be collected (although the manner of collection is left to EHOs); assess such information; and take decisions on necessary control measures, although measures are formally imposed by the local authority.[7] The OCT is also responsible for analysing the incident following successful control and making recommendations to be implemented by network actors to reduce the future risk of food-borne illness.[8] Outbreak Control Teams play no formal role in enforcement, although the discussions and reports of an OCT may form the basis of a decision to take enforcement action.[9] The regulatory capacity of the OCT is enhanced by the presence of each actor enrolled in the team. Where the incident is international in scope, an international 'Crisis Unit' will be brought together by the EU Commission, to ensure that the complementary capacities of actors within the multinational regulatory network are harnessed to investigate and control the incident.[10]

This chapter examines the central actors enrolled in the network, and considers the roles they play in achieving the network's goals of investigation, control and enforcement. The next chapter takes a closer look at the powers that these actors have to respond to incidents of food-borne illness, considering the regulatory capacity of the actors in respect of investigation, control and enforcement.

II. THE EU AND THE UK GOVERNMENT

The European Union (EU) and the UK Government primarily function legislatively as standard-setting actors within the regulatory network. National and supra-national standard-setting bodies have a responsibility to design regulatory frameworks to manage the risk resulting from food-borne illness. The standards apply to the food itself and to the conditions in which it is produced. They are considered in the next chapter, but have the goal of ensuring that food is free from agents that cause food-borne illness. Given the complexity of food flows within the EU (and more broadly throughout

[7] The terms of reference of an OCT can be found in Food Standards Agency, *Management of outbreaks of food-borne illness in England and Wales* (Food Standards Agency 2008) 15–16. Separate guidance applies in Scotland (Food Standards Agency and Scottish Health Department, *Guidance on the Investigation and Control of Outbreaks of Foodborne Disease in Scotland* (Food Standards Agency 2006)).

[8] Food Standards Agency, *Management of outbreaks of food-borne illness in England and Wales*, above n 7, 16, terms of reference 9 and 10.

[9] As in the *South-West Water* case, discussed in ch 6.V.A.ii.

[10] Regulation 178/2002, arts 56–57. Art 57 gives the Crisis Unit the power to 'request the assistance of any public or private person whose expertise it deems necessary to manage the crisis effectively', providing a formal basis for enrolling actors in the network.

the world),[11] these standards function to manage the risk of all food circulating within the EU. As legislators, these actors also seek to ensure legal preparedness, providing the networks actors, who are limited in their competences, with the capacity to investigate, control and enforce.[12]

When functioning in an executive fashion, the UK and EU have important, although rarely used, regulatory capacities that can be used to address incidents of food-borne illness with national or international scope. The powers possessed by the UK and EU have broad geographical reach, and enable the network to control unsafe products across the UK, or across the whole of the EU.

Within the UK, the Food Safety Act 1990, section 13 gives the Secretary of State power, through an order in council (known as an Emergency Control Order), to control products of a particular type or description where there is an 'imminent risk to health'. This power has been used six times since 1990, including for controlling beef at risk of infection with BSE. Most relevantly, the Executive chose to use an Emergency Control Order to control cheese produced by a particular food business, which was found to be contaminated with *E. coli* O157.[13] The UK Executive also has broad capacity to take action in an emergency under the Civil Contingencies Act 2004.[14] Emergencies include threats to human welfare from 'human illness or injury', giving a extensive capacity to set standards and enforce them in emergency situations.

The EU Commission has a similar power, which can be found in Regulation 178/2002, article 53. This provides that the Commission may take action to manage a serious risk to human health that cannot be controlled adequately by Member States. This action may include preventing the marketing of the food product in question, or 'any other appropriate interim measure'. This broad power functions to equip the Commission with the capacity to control food and food-borne illness in limited circumstances.

III. THE FOOD STANDARDS AGENCY

The Food Standards Agency ('the Agency') is the national regulator with responsibility for food. The 'main objective' of the Agency is 'to protect public health from risks which may arise in connection with the consumption of food (including risks caused by the way in which it is produced or supplied) and otherwise to protect the interests of consumers in relation to

[11] Of course, the Codex Alimentarius Commission is enrolled into the network as a body that sets international standards for food.

[12] Estair Van Wagner, 'The practice of biosecurity in Canada: public health legal preparedness and Toronto's SARS crisis' (2008) 40 *Environment and Planning A* 1647.

[13] Detailed in *R v Secretary of State for Health, ex p Eastside Cheese* [1999] 3 CMLR 123.

[14] See pt 2 of that Act.

food'.[15] It was created by the Food Standards Act 1999, and functions as a non-ministerial government department.[16] From April 2015 the role of the Food Standards Agency in Scotland will be taken over by Food Standards Scotland.[17] This body will play a similar role in the network to that currently played by the Food Standards Agency.[18]

The Food Standards Agency plays a key role where an incident has cross-authority scope. The capacity for the Agency to gather information about food-borne illness within different local authority areas and to coordinate the response to food-borne illness is important. The involvement of the Agency gives the network increased informational capacity, as actors (such as local authorities or food businesses) transmit information about food-borne illness risks to the Agency. It is responsible for sharing information with local authorities about risks that potentially exist within their areas, in order that they may use their powers to take the necessary action, or be aware of the possibility that action might be needed. In some cases an alert may trigger a local authority to take action to investigate and/or control a risk 'where the [Food Standards Agency's] risk assessment has identified urgent actions for local authorities (eg removal of products from sale)'.[19] Such an alert is known as a 'Food Alert for Action' (FAFA).[20] Food Alerts for Action may be supplemented by direct contact between the Food Standards Agency and the local authorities 'most likely to be affected' by the risk.[21] Investigations undertaken in response to a food alert may provide evidence used in an enforcement action.

In less urgent cases the Food Standards Agency may issue a Food Alert for Information (FAFI). A FAFI is issued when the local authority should take note but not action in respect of a food-borne illness. Where a 'company/manufacturer has already withdrawn/recalled a product or is in the process of withdrawing/recalling a product to the satisfaction of the [Food Standards Agency]',[22] this will be noted in order that authorities may advise concerned consumers. However, these alerts will not usually trigger investigation, control or enforcement, but do add to the capacity of the Food Standards Agency to take a long-term view of trends demonstrated by the shared information, enabling it to take action to prevent future risks.

[15] Food Standards Act 1999, s 1(2).

[16] Explanatory Notes accompanying the Food Standards Act 1999, para 10.

[17] See the Food (Scotland) Act 2015, pt 1.

[18] The objectives of Food Standards Scotland include protecting 'the public from risks to health which may arise in connection with the consumption of food' (Food (Scotland) Act 2015, s 2(1)(a)).

[19] PEN/JW/FSA.07245.

[20] For an example of a FAFA, see PEN/HL/SWP.00269.

[21] PEN/JW/FSA.07245.

[22] PEN/JW/FSA.07245.

IV. LOCAL AUTHORITIES

Local authorities are key players in the response to food-borne illness. They have the capacity to investigate, control and enforce, possessing both food and public health powers. Compared to the Food Standards Agency, they have the local manpower to carry out a resource-intensive investigation. They also have the regulatory capacity and experience to control the spread of illness, exercising formal and informal control powers. Local authorities are the proper enforcement body for breaches of food safety and/or food hygiene norms. Where a school is affected, the local authority has educational powers,[23] and enrols members of its education departments to use their expertise and powers to manage risk within the school.[24] The local authorities are central to empowering the regulatory network, and often function to enrol other actors into that network where necessary. They communicate with national bodies, medical colleagues and the food businesses, enrolling them into the network with the goal of enhancing regulatory capacity. They have the capacity to communicate with the public, including on risk reduction techniques, thereby enrolling consumers into the network working to reduce the incidence of food-borne illness.

Local authority responsibilities are divided between county- and district-level authorities.[25] County-level councils generally cover a larger area and are responsible for higher-level functions. District-level councils are geographically smaller, and perform lower-level or more localised functions.[26] Some areas are served by a single unitary authority,[27] which is responsible for all the functions assigned to local government.[28] London Borough Councils are functionally equivalent to unitary authorities.[29] Figure 2.1 illustrates the structure of local government in the UK.

District-level authorities are responsible for food safety and food hygiene. County authorities are responsible for food standards (for example, issues relating to labelling, packaging or advertising). This means that district-level authorities are the key local authority players in the response to food-borne

[23] Eg South Wales *E. Coli*, full details available at <http://wales.gov.uk/ecoliinquiry/?lang=en>.

[24] Where an academy or free school is a site of cases of food-borne illness, the academy trust has a governance role.

[25] Ignoring parish and town councils, which have no role to play in food law enforcement.

[26] District councils and borough councils operate at the same level. For the difference, see Local Government Act 1972, s 245.

[27] Authority A is a unitary authority. On unitary authorities, see Andrew Arden, Christopher Baker and Jonathan Manning (eds), *Local Government Constitutional and Administrative Law* (2nd rev edn, Sweet & Maxwell 2008).

[28] Unitary authorities may be 'County Councils', 'Metropolitan Borough Councils', 'City Councils', 'Borough Councils', or 'District Councils'; in this book they are collectively referred to as 'unitary authorities'.

[29] The Greater London Authority, created by the Greater London Authority Act 1999, does not function as a second tier of local government. It is more similar to a devolved central government department.

Local Authorities with responsibility for food, as defined by section 5 of the Food Safety Act 1990, are shaded.

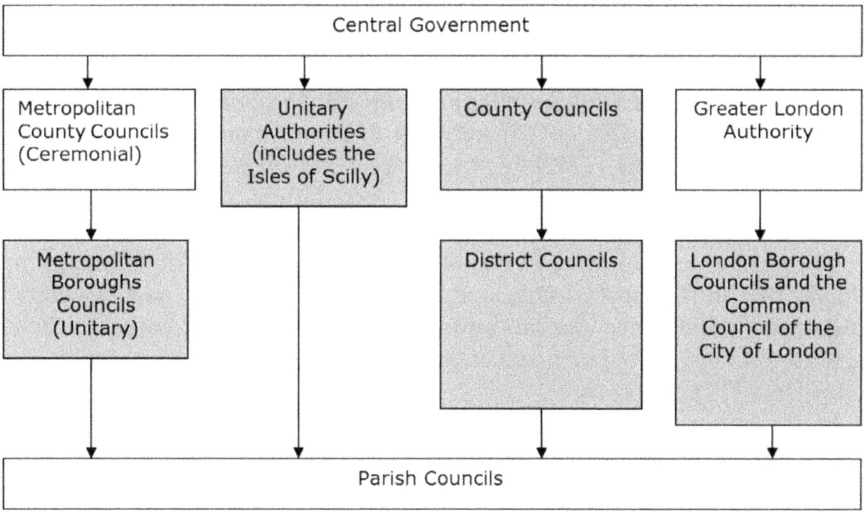

Figure 2.1: The arrangement of local government in England

illness, but county councils may be enrolled into the regulatory network on an ad hoc basis where issues of food standards arise during an investigation into an incident of food-borne illness.

Local authorities are statutory creations. This means that they must have the power to act, otherwise their actions will be quashed as being ultra vires. The principal provision that empowers local authorities in the area of food safety is section 6(2) of the Food Safety Act 1990. This provides:

> Every food authority shall enforce and execute within their area the provisions of this Act with respect to which the duty is not imposed expressly or by necessary implication on some other authority.

'Food authority' is defined in section 5 as 'the council of that borough, district or county'.[30] District and county councils may therefore concurrently enforce the Food Safety Act 1990.

Secondary legislation under the Food Safety Act 1990 sets out which body is responsible for enforcement.[31] The Food Safety and Hygiene (England) Regulations 2013 provide that local authorities are responsible for enforcement of the provisions of Regulation 178/2002,[32] with responsibility for

[30] Food Safety Act 1990, s 5(1)(a). Food authorities are shaded in Fig 2.1. This definition of food authority is incorporated by reference into the Food Safety and Hygiene (England) Regulations 2013, reg 2.

[31] Food Safety Act 1990, s 6(4).

[32] Food Safety and Hygiene (England) Regulations 2013, SI 2013/2996, reg 5(6).

execution and enforcement of the 'hygiene regulations'[33] being shared between food authorities and the Food Standards Agency.[34] Local authorities are responsible for enforcement in most food businesses, except those involved in primary production and processing of food of an animal origin (where responsibility is shared with the Food Standards Agency).[35] In Wales and Scotland, the General Food Regulations 2004 provide that food authorities shall be responsible for enforcement in circumstances where there is a breach of Regulation 178/2002,[36] and the Food Hygiene (Wales) Regulations 2006 and Food Hygiene (Scotland) Regulations 2006 empower local authorities to take action in respect of breaches of hygiene regulations.[37]

The public health powers of the local authority are primarily found in the Public Health (Control of Disease) Act 1984 (as amended) and associated regulations. These give local authorities the capacity to take control actions against persons, premises, products or environments. They are examined in more detail in chapter three.

Local authorities can only act in relation to breaches that have effects inside the boundaries of the authority.[38] However, when investigating breaches of food safety law committed within authority boundaries, officers may conduct inquiries, for example viewing premises and taking samples, at locations within other local authority areas.[39] This is useful where food suspected to be the source of food-borne illness is produced beyond the boundaries of the authority. Rather than conducting the investigation themselves, officers may enrol the EHOs employed by the local authority covering that area to undertake this task, geographically expanding the network.[40]

Local authorities may also be formally enrolled into the network as the home or primary authority of a food business. When acting as home or

[33] Regulation (EC) No 852/2004 of the European Parliament and of the Council of 29 April 2004 on the hygiene of foodstuffs [2004] OJ L139/1; Regulation (EC) No 853/2004 of the European Parliament and of the Council of 29 April 2004 laying down specific hygiene rules for food of animal origin [2004] OJ L139/55; Regulation (EC) No 854/2004 of the European Parliament and of the Council of 29 April 2004 laying down specific rules for the organisation of official controls on products of animal origin intended for human consumption [2004] OJ L139/206; Commission Regulation (EC) No 2073/2005 of 15 November 2005 on microbiological criteria for foodstuffs [2005] OJ L338/1; Commission Regulation (EC) No 2075/2005 of 5 December 2005 laying down specific rules on official controls for Trichinella in meat [2005] OJ L338/60; and the Food Safety and Hygiene (England) Regulations 2013.

[34] Food Safety and Hygiene (England) Regulations 2013, reg 5(1).

[35] Food Safety and Hygiene (England) Regulations 2013, reg 5(1). The Food Standards Agency has exclusive responsibility for enforcement in slaughterhouses, game-handling establishments and cutting plants (Food Safety and Hygiene (England) Regulations 2013, reg 5(2)).

[36] General Food Regulations 2004, SI 2004/3279, reg 6(1).

[37] Food Hygiene (Wales) Regulations 2006, SI 2006/31, reg 5; Food Hygiene (Scotland) Regulations 2006, SI 2006/3, reg 5.

[38] Although in relation to Trading Standards this position is modified by the Consumer Rights Act 2015, sch 5, pt 6.

[39] See, eg, *Walkers Snack Foods Ltd v Coventry City Council* [1998] 3 All ER 163.

[40] B/EHO1.

primary authority, the local authority will provide advice on the law that applies to the business, when requested to do so. In the event that enforcement action is contemplated following an incident of food-borne illness, contact will be made with the home or primary authority to ensure that the action of the business was not taken on the basis of regulatory advice given by the home or primary authority. However, given the nature of an incident of food-borne illness, advice given by the primary or home authority is unlikely to be a reason not to proceed with enforcement action.[41] Even so, a home or primary authority may provide important information about the business to other network actors.

Environmental Health Officers are the primary professionals through whom local authorities act in response to food-borne illness.[42] They provide the manpower that allows the regulatory capacity of the local authority to investigate, control and enforce to be operationalised. The regulatory capacity is vested in the EHOs through the authorisation to use the powers given by the Food Safety Act 1990 and the Food Safety and Hygiene (England) Regulations 2013.[43] Such authorisation is achieved through a formalised and documented process.[44] Once authorised, EHOs must carry a record of their authorisations when investigating incidents of food-borne illness, and will show it when requested by food businesses.

If there is not a specific authorisation procedure, local authority powers may be delegated to EHOs. Section 101(1) of the Local Government Act 1972 allows authorities to 'arrange for the discharge of any of their functions by a committee, a sub-committee or an officer of the authority'. Public health powers were often delegated to the 'proper officer' of the authority (for historical reasons often the Consultant in Communicable Disease Control (CCDC)) or to a senior EHO.[45]

However, EHOs have limited regulatory capacity in certain areas. They cannot set standards and rely on the actors with legislative powers to do so. However, the central weakness of local authorities as network participants is their information-gathering capacity. They are resource limited, and therefore cannot be present on the premises observing the practices of the

[41] Regulatory Enforcement and Sanctions Act 2008, s 28. The Coordination of Regulatory Enforcement (Enforcement Action) Order 2009, SI 2009/665 provides that the duty to consult does not apply where urgent action is necessary to prevent a serious risk to health.

[42] EHOs can specialise in a number of different functions, including food, or may work in many different areas. They are degree-educated and members of the CIEH. Their work is supported by other members of environmental health teams, who may not have the qualifications of an EHO. These individuals may include technical officers, sampling officers and placement students. All staff members play an important role in responding to incidents of food-borne illness.

[43] The General Food Regulations 2004, reg 6; and the Food Hygiene (Wales) Regulations 2006, reg 5 and Food Hygiene (Scotland) Regulations 2006, reg 5 in Wales and Scotland.

[44] Food Standards Agency, *The Framework Agreement on Official Feed and Food Controls* (5th amended edn, Food Standards Agency 2010) para 5.1.

[45] In all authorities examined in this book, the 'proper officer' was the CCDC.

food-business operators at all times. Therefore they cannot function to detect all cases of regulatory non-compliance, nor can they detect all cases of food-borne illness. In order to enhance their information-gathering capacity they must enrol other actors into the network, particularly consumers, food businesses and food business employees, with these enrolled actors functioning to provide information about incidents of food-borne illness and their causes.

V. MEDICAL ACTORS

Medical practitioners, whether public health specialists, accident and emergency doctors, or general practitioners, are an essential part of the regulatory network, working to reduce the incidence and spread of food-borne illness.

Non-specialist medical professionals are enrolled on an ad hoc basis, providing advice that attempts to control the spread of food-borne illness through simple barrier techniques, hand-washing and advice to remain away from work. They may also provide important information to other members of the network, functioning to detect (and confirm) food-borne illness through their contacts with patients, which may include taking samples, and providing this information to other network participants via formal reporting procedures or informal contacts with medical colleagues specialising in public health. Further, doctors may act to encourage consumers to enrol into the regulatory network by advising them to report their illness to EHOs, which enhances the information available to those officers. This increases EHOs' capacity to detect, and therefore investigate, food-borne illness.

Specialist medical professionals with an interest in public health are enrolled into the network more formally. Each local authority is affiliated with one or more CCDCs. A CCDC is a medical professional specialising in public health. The CDDCs are trained in both microbiology and epidemiology. They work alongside local authorities in managing all incidents of food-borne illness, and will provide advice and direction about investigation and/or control, as necessary. Acting upon the public health knowledge possessed by a CCDC allows the regulatory network to target the response most appropriately when taking action in connection with an incident (or suspected incident) of food-borne illness. The CCDC will provide medical information, which influences the shape of the response to an incident, and, as noted in section IV. above, may be nominated as the proper officer for the purpose of public health powers.[46] The CCDC may also act as an expert

[46] The proper officer will receive notifications of food-borne illness under the Health Protection (Notification) Regulations 2010/659, and prior to the 2010 reforms to the Public Health (Control of Disease) Act 1984 had responsibility for the exercise of many control powers.

witness, enhancing the regulatory capacity of the court by augmenting its knowledge of food-borne illness. Such assistance is provided in all incidents, where requested by local authorities.

Once an outbreak is formally declared, a CCDC plays a particular role in the response to it. The CCDC acts as chair of the formal OCT that coordinates the efforts to respond to and manage the outbreak.[47] He or she will also be responsible for the collation and dissemination of information necessary for control, and will lead discussion on the control efforts to be taken. The CCDC becomes the central actor in the investigation and control functions exercised by the regulatory network.

In England and Wales, Public Health England, an executive agency of the Department of Health,[48] and the Public Health Wales National Health Service Trust function to support local authorities and CCDCs in their response to food-borne illness. The Secretary of State for Health has a statutory responsibility to 'protect ... the public in England from disease', and may 'provide microbiological or other technical services' and 'information and advice'.[49] These duties are performed by Public Health England. The Public Health Wales National Health Service Trust has similar functions as part of its remit.[50]

Nationally, the Public Health England collates and evaluates data received from local public health units to assess whether there is a national rise in, inter alia, particular food-borne illnesses that merits a response. If such a trend is shown, appropriate local authorities will be alerted.

Public Health England is also responsible for maintaining the regional microbiological network, employing public health microbiologists who are available to provide microbiological advice and to commission microbiological analysis, where necessary. This microbiological capacity increases the capacity of the network to gain information about the food-borne illness.[51] Public Health England is also responsible for national reference laboratories responsible for testing and cross-typing samples obtained during an investigation into an incident of food-borne illness.[52] It may also coordinate (alongside the OCT) the medical response to national incidents of food-borne illness.

[47] Food Standards Agency, *Management of outbreaks of food-borne illness in England and Wales*, above n 7, para 3.4.

[48] During some of incidents examined in this book the Health Protection Agency had responsibility for many of the public health functions now carried out by Public Health England. However, the Health Protection Agency was abolished by the Health and Social Care Act 2012, s 56.

[49] National Health Service Act 2006, s 2A.

[50] See Public Health Wales National Health Service Trust (Establishment) Order 2009, SI 2009/2058.

[51] Where the risk is the result of contamination by an outside substance, a Public Analyst plays a similar role, providing analytical expertise that may contribute information to underpin control and enforcement actions.

[52] Eg Colindale is the national reference laboratory for *E. Coli*.

VI. THE POLICE

Where an incident of food-borne illness results in death,[53] or where there is suspicion that the contamination of food was deliberate (eg bioterrorism or extortion attempts), the police may become involved. In South Wales the police were responsible for the collection and assembly of information following the death of Mason Jones as a result of the *E. coli* outbreak in 2005. The OCT and the local authorities remained responsible for the control of illness, and collected information necessary for that purpose.

The powers the police have available during investigations are different from, and in some ways more extensive than, those possessed by EHOs.[54] The police also have greater manpower and financial resources than local authority environmental health departments. They also have greater experience collecting evidence for the purpose of prosecution, although they are not as experienced as EHOs in dealing with food-borne illness. When investigating food-borne illness, the police work alongside EHOs in order that this expertise and experience can be utilised. The expertise and powers of the police increase the enforcement capacity of the regulatory network.

VII. FOOD BUSINESSES AND THEIR EMPLOYEES

Food businesses often play a central role in the regulatory network's response to food-borne illness. Food businesses have a greater informational capacity than other actors in the network. They have information about the source and destination of food products, and about the processes undertaken by their employees. They are able to enhance the network's ability to respond to food-borne illness, both by providing information and by implementing steps to control the spread of illness. Cooperation between food businesses and other network actors can therefore be exceptionally beneficial in the response, as regulatory goals can be more easily achieved when food businesses are enrolled into the network.

However, in some cases the rational self-interest of the firm in not incurring costs (both directly and indirectly imposed) as a result of self-reporting prevents the disclosure of information to the regulator by the regulated entity.[55] Concern regarding cost may also lead to businesses' reluctance

[53] Where death results there will be a Coroner's Inquest, and information gathered by EHOs and the police will be forwarded.

[54] Eg, the police have a power of arrest under Police and Criminal Evidence Act 1984, s 24. However, the powers of entry, search and seizure possessed by an EHO are greater than those found in the 1984 Act.

[55] Sarah L Stafford, 'Should you turn yourself in? The consequence of environmental self-policing' (2007) 26 *The Journal of Policy Management and Analysis* 305.

as regards implementing control measures, particularly where these are voluntary.[56]

Where the business itself cannot be enrolled, network actors may seek to enrol its employees into the network. Employees have informational capacity beyond that possessed by other network actors, being present in the business more frequently and for longer than any other actor (including the upper management of the business, who will respond when the business is involved). Employees are able to provide information about the handling of food within the business, which may allow a likely source to be pinpointed and controlled, and to identify regulatory non-compliance.[57] They may either act with the encouragement of their employer, or may self-enrol without their employer's knowledge, blowing the whistle on regulatory non-compliance.

Whistleblowers are encouraged to self-enrol through the provision of protections in the event that they are subjected to detriment or dismissed on account of their whistleblowing. These protections are contained in part IVA of the Employment Rights Act 1996. In particular, disclosures to regulators, including local authorities and the Food Standards Agency, may fall within section 43F of the 1996 Act, provided that the employee can demonstrate that the disclosure was in the public interest, that he or she had a reasonable belief that the regulator could deal with the subject matter of the disclosure, that the disclosure falls within one or more of the categories set out in section 43B(1) and that the employee had a reasonable belief that the matters disclosed are substantially true. A breach of food safety or food hygiene requirements will normally fall within section 43B(1)(b) as a failure to comply with a legal obligation, or within section 43B(1)(d) as an action which may result in the health of an individual being endangered.

VIII. CONSUMERS

Consumers are enrolled into the regulatory network as the primary sufferers of food-borne illness. They can therefore provide information about an incident of food-borne illness, including their symptoms and food history. Such information would not be available to the network if it was not provided by consumers. They can also provide samples, both of food products that they have retained and of faecal matter, which can be analysed in order to provide information about the micro-organism responsible for the incident of food-borne illness.

[56] One EHO suggested that such reluctance stemmed from fear that liabilities would not be covered by insurers if voluntary action was taken (B/EHO1). It therefore may be necessary to enrol insurers into the network when considering control actions.

[57] For further consideration of the role of employees in regulatory networks, see Savage and Hyde, above n 5.

Consumers self-enrol into the network by contacting their local authority regarding the incident of food-borne illness. They may be encouraged to make contact by a medical professional, or may make contact of their own accord. By making contact consumers function to provide other network actors with information about food-borne illness and regulatory non-compliance that they might not otherwise possess, enhancing the capacity to investigate, and potentially the capacity to control and enforce. However, consumers can only provide a limited amount of information to the officers, and the quality of information may be limited by difficulties of perception (consumers may not be able to see the whole of the food preparation process and, of course, cannot visually perceive micro-organisms) and recall. These challenges will be explored in chapter six.

IX. CONCLUSION

Networked governance is essential to the management of the risks resulting from food-borne illness. Without a network of regulatory actors, it is unlikely that investigation, control and enforcement following incidents of food-borne illness could be undertaken successfully. Various actors are enrolled into the network. Each plays an important role in the networked response to food-borne illness. Local authorities are the central actor, as they have the greatest capacity to gather information, manage risk and change behaviour. However, they could not utilise their capacity without contributions from the other network actors, who play important roles in the network, enhancing the standard-setting capacity, the informational capacity, the control capacity and the enforcement capacity of the network.

In the next chapter the powers of the network actors, and the ways that can be used to manage an incident of food-borne illness, are considered.

3

The Regulatory Landscape

IN THE LAST chapter, the network actors that contribute to the control of incidents of food-borne illness were considered. In this chapter it is necessary to examine both the substantive law requirements that form the background to the response to food-borne illness and the powers that the network participants have to take action, both during an incident and following its control.

Food production is heavily regulated, which is appropriate given the grave risks of microbiological contamination during food production. Indeed, food is an area that has long been specially regulated beyond the requirements that apply to products through the General Product Safety Regulations 2005.[1] Such products are governed by standards that govern the final product. Whilst food products are required to be safe, for food businesses, regulatory requirements also extend to the methods of production adopted and the premises in which food is produced. The more extensive regulation applicable to food must therefore be examined (section I.).

The risks of an incident of food-borne illness also necessitate a wide suite of powers to control products, premises, people and environments. In order to prevent the spread of illness, regulatory actors may use a number of different tools. It is to these tools that the second half of the chapter turns, considering the capacity of the regulatory network to take action both during and after an incident of food-borne illness (section II.).

I. THE GOVERNANCE OF FOOD PRODUCTION

Substantive food regulations underpin local authorities' response to incidents of food-borne illness. The requirements placed on food businesses are extensive. A breach of these regulations is a strict liability criminal offence.[2] As well as being subject to specific regulations, a business is bound by the

[1] SI 2005/1803. Richard Hyde, 'Why Separate the Regulatory Regimes Applicable to Food Safety and Product Safety?' (2013) 33(4) *Legal Studies* 509.

[2] The use of strict liability in such offences has a long history. See Ingeborg Paulus, *The search for pure food: a sociology of legislation in Britain* (Martin Robertson 1974); *Fitzpatrick v Kelly* (1872–73) LR 8 QB 337; and *Roberts v Edgerton* (1873–74) LR 9 QB 494.

general criminal law, and may face prosecution for manslaughter in the event that a person dies from a food-borne illness traced to food manufactured or produced by that business.[3]

As will be demonstrated below, information collection and assessment are influenced by the content of the underlying norms.[4] Formal action premised on a regulatory breach must identify the regulatory breaches to which the action responds, and the investigation must therefore collect enough information to identify and prove the breach. Therefore, it is necessary to consider the regulations that bind food business, and which shape the response to an incident of food-borne illness.

A. Regulations Governing Food Products: Regulation 178/2002

Regulation 19 of the Food Safety and Hygiene (England) Regulations 2013[5] (in England) and regulation 4 of the General Food Regulations 2004 (in Wales and Scotland) make failure to comply with six provisions of Regulation 178/2002, laying down the general principles and requirements of food law, an offence.[6] An unlimited fine may be imposed upon conviction in the Crown Court.[7]

Article 14(1) of Regulation 178/2002 is particularly likely to be applicable following incidents of food-borne illness. The effect of these provisions is that it is a criminal offence to place unsafe food on the market. 'Unsafe' is defined by reference to article 14 of Regulation 178/2002, which provides three routes by which food is able to be judged safe or otherwise: food may be shown to be unsafe per se; or it may be deemed unsafe if it can be shown to be either injurious to health or unfit for human consumption.[8] Where

[3] Under either the Corporate Manslaughter and Corporate Homicide Act 2007, or the common law of gross negligence manslaughter (see *R v Adomako* [1995] 1 AC 171). However, such prosecutions have faced problems proving that negligence of the food business caused the death of the victim. This was clearly the case in the South Wales investigation.

[4] Paul Roberts, 'Law and Criminal Investigation' in Tim Newburn, Tom Williamson and Alan Wright (eds), *Handbook of Criminal Investigation* (Willan 2007), 95.

[5] SI 2013/2996.

[6] Regulation 178/2002, arts 12, 14(1), 16, 18(2), 18(3) and 19.

[7] In *R v McSweeney, Kaya and Mitchells and Butlers plc* (Snaresbrook Crown Court, 8 January 2015), a fine of £1.5 million was imposed on Mitchells and Butler for the offence of placing unsafe food on the market, following an incident where one person died and 33 were made sick as a result of consuming turkey contaminated with *clostridium perfringins*.

[8] These are alternative rather than cumulative. *Hazlewood Grocery Limited v Lion Foods Limited* [2007] EWHC 1887 [163] states that 'food can be unsafe either on the grounds specified in Art 14.2(a) or (b) … it can be unfit for human consumption even though it is not injurious to health'. It is submitted that *Hazlewood* is wrong in so far as it decides that 'unfit for human consumption' and 'injurious to health' are the only grounds on which food can be unsafe.

food is shown to comply with certain Community provisions it is deemed to be safe.[9]

'Placed on the market' is defined in article 3 of Regulation 178/2002 as meaning

> the holding of food ... for the purpose of sale, including offering for sale or any other form of transfer, whether free of charge or not, and the sale, distribution and other forms of transfer themselves ...

The Regulations are therefore aimed primarily at sellers of food products.

i. Unsafe Per Se

Whilst this route to showing that the safety requirement has been breached is often ignored by texts and practitioners, the drafting of article 14 of Regulation 178/2002 suggests that it is open to regulators to attempt to prove, through evidence, that food is unsafe despite being neither unfit for human consumption nor injurious to health. However, this is difficult. Defendants will be able to challenge a determination of (a lack of) safety, in contrast to cases where the deeming provisions apply. Whether food is unsafe is a question of fact. The open-textured nature of 'unsafe' is necessary, as food and food science are constantly developing, and regulatory regimes aimed at ensuring consumer safety must be able to cope with future developments.

The need to future-proof a definition of 'safety' means that it is unwise to attempt to adopt a definitive exposition. However, article 14(3) gives some guidance, providing:

> In determining whether any food is unsafe, regard shall be had:
>
> (a) to the normal conditions of use of the food by the consumer and at each stage of production, processing and distribution, and
>
> (b) to the information provided to the consumer, including information on the label, or other information generally available to the consumer concerning the avoidance of specific adverse health effects from a particular food or category of foods.

These matters are not determinative of the safety (or otherwise) of food.[10] Applying article 14(3)(a), where proper cooking would remove the risk to the consumer by killing bacteria that is present within the food, that food should not be seen as unsafe. The requirement in article 14(3)(b) is linked to the requirement to consider whether normal use by the consumer will

[9] Regulation 178/2002, art 14(7). Safe levels for microbial contaminants are set in Commission Regulation (EC) No 2073/2005 of 15 November 2005 on microbiological criteria for foodstuffs [2005] OJ L338/1; however, the approved level is mostly 0. Action to prevent the spread of food-borne illness may still be taken against food falling within the art 14(7) safe harbour.

[10] These factors must also be considered when deciding whether food is injurious to health or unfit for human consumption.

render the food safe. Cooking instructions set out on the label of the food will be good evidence of the normal conditions of use. If following instructions would reduce food safety risk to an acceptable level, then it is unlikely that the food is 'unsafe'. Given the nature of food safety risks, only a low level of risk should be seen as acceptable.

ii. Injurious to Health

Food that is injurious to health will be deemed unsafe. Article 14(4) of Regulation 178/2002 gives guidance on determining whether food is injurious to health:

> In determining whether any food is injurious to health, regard shall be had:
>
> (a) not only to the probable immediate and/or short-term and/or long-term effects of that food on the health of a person consuming it, but also on subsequent generations;
> (b) to the probable cumulative toxic effects;
> (c) to the particular health sensitivities of a specific category of consumers where the food is intended for that category of consumers.

These subparagraphs are not exclusive. A particular food may be injurious to health on the basis of matters not set out. Food that is contaminated with food-borne illness organisms is likely to be injurious to health in all cases.

Clearly, the primary consideration for the decision maker is the 'probable immediate and/or short-term and/or long-term effects of that food on the health of a person consuming it'. Immediate and short-term effects are likely to have occurred by the time a local authority is notified of food-borne illness. The illness suffered by the consumer is good evidence that a food was injurious to health, but it may be challenging to link the illness to a particular food. Where meat contains *E. Coli* O157 or *Salmonella* bacteria, the decision that the food poses a risk of injury to health, and therefore needs control, is clear.

Food may also be injurious to health where there are longer-term health consequences of consumption. Food-borne illness cases typically deal with food that gives rise to short-term injurious consequences,[11] and therefore questions of long-term consequences are not central to considerations by enforcement officers. Where it is necessary to consider long-term consequences, information will be obtained from medical participants in the regulatory network, such as the CCDC.

Adverse health effects need not relate to consumers or potential consumers. Health effects on subsequent generations must also be considered.[12] Food contaminated with a food-borne illness that has an effect on a foetus

[11] Although long-term consequences may also be caused.
[12] For example if the food is mutagenic.

in utero will be seen as injurious to health, even if it does not affect the mother-consumer.

Whether food is injurious to health is an initially objective test.[13] However, the vulnerabilities and characteristics of the consumer can be taken into account in particular circumstances.[14] For example, where illness is linked to baby food, it should be assessed whether this food is injurious to babies, who have particular vulnerabilities and are more likely to suffer illness when exposed to low numbers of microbes compared to adults. Food must be safe for the type of consumers at whom it is aimed. Similarly, particular vulnerabilities must be taken into account if food is intended for the sick or elderly.

iii. Unfit for Human Consumption

The question of whether food is unfit for human consumption is a question of fact.[15] In *Kyle v Laird*, which dealt with the meaning of the archaic phrase 'unfit for the food of man',[16] the Lord-Justice Clerk stated

> What makes milk unfit for the food of man seems to me to be very much a question of circumstances, and the way in which the problem is to be solved must also be very much a matter of circumstances, and these circumstances must be infinitely varied. Various tests were suggested but I do not think it possible to lay down any hard and fast test. This is the sort of thing to be looked at in a practical, common sense way.[17]

Similarly, the presence of foreign contaminants in food does not automatically render that food unfit for human consumption; it is merely a factor that the court can take into account when making a factual judgement.[18]

The decision whether food is unfit for human consumption is dependent on information. When dealing with a dynamic situation like food-borne illness, it is difficult to create a hard-and-fast test. Decision makers must exercise their professional judgement when determining whether food is unfit for human consumption. A microbiologist suggested that the key is to ask 'Would I eat this?' If the answer is no then the food is unfit.[19]

[13] See, eg (in a housing law context), *Oakley v Birmingham City Council* [2001] 1 AC 617, 634 and *Cunningham v Birmingham City Council* (1998) 30 HLR 158, 164.

[14] Regulation 178/2002, art 14(4)(c).

[15] Dominique Lauterberg, *Food Law: Policy and Ethics* (Cavendish 2001), 59.

[16] *Kyle v Laird* 1951 JC 65. The term has the same meaning as 'unfit for human consumption'; see *Guild v Gateway Foodmarkets Ltd* 1990 JC 277, 279, where the High Court of Justiciary stated 'that the meaning of the phrases "unfit for the food of man" and "unfit for human consumption" in terms of sec 8 (1)(a) of the Food and Drugs (Scotland) Act 1956 is identical'. Further, in *Kenn v Bell* 1910 SC(J) 13, 15, the Lord Justice-Clerk used 'unfit for human food' in an interchangeable matter with 'unfit for the food of man'.

[17] *Kyle v Laird* 1951 JC 65, 69.

[18] *Hazlewood Grocery v Lion Foods*, above n 8, [163].

[19] EXP/MIC1.

Regulation 14(5) sets out matters that may be taken into account when determining whether food is fit for human consumption:

> [R]egard shall be had to whether the food is unacceptable for human consumption according to its intended use, for reasons of contamination, whether by extraneous matter or otherwise, or through putrefaction, deterioration or decay.

The first consideration must be the 'intended use' of food. Likely processing by consumers should be taken into account before deciding whether food is unfit for human consumption. Whilst food in its raw state may be so unfit, after domestic processing and cooking it may be rendered fit. This is possible where food is microbiologically contaminated but the microbes will be killed by proper cooking. Putrefied, deteriorated or decayed food is unlikely to be rendered fit through processing by the consumer.

'Contamination' is not defined in the Regulation. It is likely to be interpreted widely[20] and as an ordinary word of the English language. The *Oxford English Dictionary* defines 'contaminated' as 'defiled, sullied, or infected', particularly by contact with foreign matter. Lauterberg suggests that the presence of foreign bodies, mould, pesticide residues, heavy metals, mites or other infestations, radioactive material or any other unauthorised material is likely to render food contaminated.[21] Expert evidence may be necessary in cases where food is alleged to be unfit by reason of microbiological contamination.

It seems clear that food need not be harmful (or potentially harmful) to human health in order to be unfit for human consumption.[22] This was also the case under the Food Safety Act. If it were necessary to show that the food posed a health risk, article 14(5) would be rendered otiose as the food would also be 'injurious to health'.[23] In a case under the Food and Drugs Act 1955, it was held that the question of unfitness must be looked at in a broad sense. For example, a mouldy piece of food is '*prima facie* unfit for human consumption whether or not there is any evidence as to whether there would be any injury to health if it were eaten'.[24] The mouldy bread would clearly be putrefied, deteriorated or decayed.

A piece of string in a loaf of bread and a clean piece of metal in a cream cake do not, in themselves, render food unfit for human consumption,[25] but they will amount to contamination. In such cases the question whether food is unacceptable for human consumption by reason of the contamination will

[20] Lauterberg, above n 15, 60.

[21] Ibid. Anything that would be seen as contamination under the Contaminants in Food (England) Regulations 2013, SI 2013/2196, is likely to be seen as contamination for the purposes of the Regulation 178/2002.

[22] See *Guild v Gateway Foodmarkets Ltd* 1990 JC 277, 280.

[23] See the dicta of John Behrens QC in *Hazlewood Grocery Limited v Lion Foods Limited*, quoted above, n 8.

[24] *David Greig Ltd v Goldfinch* (1961) 59 LGR 304, 305.

[25] *Turner & Son Ltd v Owen* [1956] 1 QB 49; *J Miller Ltd v Battersea BC* [1956] 1 QB 43.

arise. A loaf of bread containing a dirty bandage,[26] a roll containing part of a cigarette,[27] and a pork pie containing a black mould,[28] all are examples of food unfit for human consumption. Further, in *Meah v Roberts*,[29] a bottle that was sold as containing lemonade, but which in fact contained caustic soda, was held to be unfit for human consumption.

There is considerable overlap between regulation 14 of Regulation 178/2002 and section 14 of the Food Safety Act 1990, which makes it an offence to sell food that is not of 'the nature or substance or quality demanded by the purchaser'.[30] Where a product is unfit for human consumption or injurious to health, it is unlikely to be of the quality demanded. Therefore, it is likely that food contaminated with food-borne illness organisms will be seen as contravening section 14 of the Food Safety Act 1990 as well as regulation 14 of Regulation 178/2002.

When a description is applied to a food product by the seller, a failure to comply with the description means the product is not of the nature demanded. Lemonade that was actually caustic soda was held not to be of the 'nature … demanded'.[31] 'Minced beef' that contained 10 per cent pork mince and 10 per cent lamb mince was also found not to be of the nature demanded.[32]

Prosecutions alleging that a product is not of the substance demanded overlap with the contamination cases discussed above. In *Smedleys v Breed*,[33] a tin of peas containing a caterpillar was held not to be of the substance demanded; similarly, a beetle found in a can of strawberries was held to render the food not of the substance demanded.[34]

B. Regulations Governing Food Premises: Food Hygiene Requirements

The Food Safety and Hygiene (England) Regulations 2013, the Food Hygiene (Wales) Regulations 2006 and the Food Hygiene (Scotland) Regulations 2006 create strict liability offences of failure to comply with hygiene requirements[35] set out in EU regulations and directly applicable to food

[26] *Chibnall's Bakeries v Cope Brown* [1956] *Crim LR* 263.
[27] *Fisher v Barnett & Pomeroy (Bakers) Ltd* [1954] 1 WLR 351.
[28] *David Grieg v Goldfinch* (1961) 105 Sol J 307.
[29] *Meah v Roberts* [1977] 1 WLR 1187.
[30] When prosecuting this offence the prosecutor must be careful to avoid duplicity by making clear which limb of s 14 is relied upon.
[31] *Meah v Roberts* [1977] 1 WLR 1187. The lemonade was also held to be unfit for human consumption, see the text associated with n 28 above.
[32] *Shearer v Rowe* (1996) 84 LGR 196.
[33] *Smedleys v Breed* [1974] AC 839.
[34] *Greater Manchester City Council v Lockwood Foods Ltd* [1979] *Crim LR* 593.
[35] Food Safety and Hygiene (England) Regulations 2013, SI 2013/2996, reg 19 and sch 2; Food Hygiene (Wales) Regulations 2006, SI 2006/31, reg 17(1) and sch 2; Food Hygiene (Scotland) Regulations 2006, SI 2006/3, reg 17(1) and sch 2.

businesses.[36] All food businesses must comply with the requirements set out in the annexes to Regulation 852/2004.[37] Businesses processing products of an animal origin, in particular meat, must comply with the more onerous requirements of Regulation 853/2004.[38] The domestic regulations render failure to comply with all the hygiene requirements set out in these Regulations a criminal offence. Therefore, a large number of offences may be identified following an incident of food-borne illness.

Given the complexity of food hygiene law, if formal action is taken, the regulatory requirement alleged to have been breached must be specified carefully. Each regulatory breach must form the basis of separate formal action (unless action is taken under the general obligation to comply with food hygiene requirements).[39] Without careful drafting there is a risk that prosecutorial action may be dismissed as duplicitous.[40]

i. The General Obligation

Article 3 of Regulation 852/2004 requires that food businesses 'ensure that all stages of production, processing and distribution of food under their control satisfy the relevant hygiene requirements'. This imposes a general obligation on food businesses to comply with the 'hygiene requirements' laid out in Regulation 852/2004. Given the approach of criminalising all breaches of the regulations, this norm both duplicates and reinforces the requirements at a more general level. At least one hygiene requirement that has not been complied with must be identified.

This requirement may ground advisory action in situations where a food business has breached a number of food hygiene requirements, rather than requiring the taking of separate enforcement actions in respect of each breach. Serving a hygiene improvement notice on the basis of a breach of article 3 of Regulation 852/2004 may be particularly useful when managing incidents of food-borne illness, as a number of deficiencies in hygiene practices may have been identified. This more generalised action reduces the paperwork needed, but does not reduce the need to particularise breaches. Advice must clearly identify the hygiene requirements breached, in order that compliance can be achieved.

[36] They do not apply to domestic producers of food. However, where an incident has a domestic source, control action may still be necessary to manage the spread of illness.

[37] Regulation (EC) No 852/2004 of the European Parliament and of the Council of 29 April 2004 on the hygiene of foodstuffs [2004] OJ L139/1.

[38] Regulation (EC) No 853/2004 of the European Parliament and of the Council of 29 April 2004 laying down specific hygiene rules for food of animal origin [2004] OJ L139/55.

[39] See section I.B.i. below.

[40] See Criminal Procedure Rules 2014, r 14.2(1); *R v Greenfield* (1973) 57 Cr App R 849; and *R v Asif* (1986) 82 Cr App R 123.

ii. Temperature Control Requirements

Businesses must comply with temperature control requirements.[41] Failure to do so is a strict liability offence.[42] Regulatory compliance is confirmed by temperature records that businesses must keep. Incorrect cooking and storage are often factors in an incident of food-borne illness. Temperature controls require that food is stored at the correct temperature to prevent or slow development of potentially dangerous bacteria or toxins, and that food is cooked to a temperature at which bacteria are killed. The closer food is to ambient temperature, the faster the rate of growth of microbial or fungal contaminants.[43] The more inadequate the temperature control, the greater the risk to consumers. If food is kept above a maximum temperature, below a minimum temperature or outside the range of appropriate temperatures,[44] then the business will be guilty of an offence.

Temperature control requirements are especially important where food is particularly hazardous. Raw and cooked meat (or products containing raw and cooked meat), dairy products, seafood, and salads and fresh food products containing food in these categories (such as sandwiches) must be kept in a temperature-controlled environment. Whether food should be frozen, chilled or held hot will depend on the type of food at issue. Environmental Health Officers have experience and training in temperature controls, and can determine whether controls are adequate. They may be assisted by expert food scientists, where necessary.

iii. Microbiological Safety Requirements

Businesses must not provide products that contain unacceptably high levels of microbial contamination.[45] In particular, products must not exceed the maximum permitted levels of *listeria*, *salmonella* and/or *E. coli*. Due to the serious risk these present, the maximum number of microbes per product is often set at zero. Exceeding these levels is a strict liability criminal offence, and where non-compliant food is implicated in an incident, enforcement action may be taken. This is in addition to the food's being 'unsafe' as a result of microbiological contamination, and thus contravening article 14(1) of Regulation 178/2002.

[41] Regulation 852/2004, art 4(3)(c).

[42] Food Safety and Hygiene (England) Regulations 2013, reg 19 and sch 2; Food Hygiene (Wales) Regulations 2006, reg 17(1) and sch 2; Food Hygiene (Scotland) Regulations 2006, reg 17(1) and sch 2.

[43] See Thomas P Coultate, *Food: the Chemistry of its Components* (4th edn, The Royal Society of Chemistry 2002) 343–46.

[44] Details of the appropriate temperature control environment should be based on the hot and chill holding requirements found in sch 4 to the Food Safety and Hygiene (England) Regulations 2013.

[45] Regulation 2073/2005, art 3.

In order to show that the limits have been exceeded, scientific evidence is necessary. Such evidence will be provided by a food examiner acting in accordance with sampling plans and analytic reference methods for particular types of microbial contamination in particular foods, which are set out in Regulation 2073/2005.[46]

iv. Hazard Analysis Critical Control Point

Food businesses must manage food safety risks in accordance with a Hazard Analysis Critical Control Point (HACCP) plan. This plan sets out the steps that the business must take to ensure that the risks to consumers from food production are minimised. The principles to be adopted when drafting a HACCP plan are set out in article 5(2) of Regulation 852/2004. The HACCP plan is seen as the best risk management method for food production. It is required by both ISO Standard 22000 and the Recommended International Code of Practice on the General Principles of Food Hygiene, produced by the Codex Alimentarius Commission.[47] Where a business has no plan, or has a plan that is inadequate, it commits a strict liability offence under regulation 19(1) of and schedule 2 to the Food Safety and Hygiene (England) Regulations 2013.[48]

Food businesses design their own plans based on the HACCP principles, and create risk management interventions to suit the practices and procedures of their business.[49] Businesses need not take steps that are not relevant to the control of the risks of their business. Once a method for managing risk is identified, businesses must also identify a way of monitoring whether the risk management plan is being complied with, usually by testing characteristics of the product at so-called 'critical control points'. When innovative techniques are adopted by food businesses, the plan must be amended, future-proofing food hygiene regulation. If food preparation were governed entirely by command and control regulation, such techniques might slip through the gaps in regulation that failed to anticipate them.

The requirement to put in place a food safety management system applies to all businesses involved in the production, manufacturing or preparation of food, except those only involved in primary production.[50] Whilst the

[46] See Food Safety and Hygiene (England) Regulations 2013, reg 15(1)(b).

[47] Codex Alimentarius Commission, CAC/RCP 1-1969, *General Principles of Food Hygiene* (revised 2003), available at <http://www.codexalimentarius.org/standards/list-of-standards/en/>.

[48] It has been suggested that a small inadequacy in the plan does not render the business in breach of the regulatory requirement, but this does not appear to be supported by the statutory language.

[49] Laurian J Unnevehr and Helen H Jensen, 'The economic implications of using HACCP as a food safety regulatory standard' (1999) 24 *Food Policy* 625, 630.

[50] Primary producers are encouraged to design safety management systems based on HACCP, but are not mandated to do so.

HACCP plan was initially designed to be used in large-scale businesses,[51] it must also be adopted by small-scale catering enterprises. The Food Standards Agency has produced a precedent food safety management system, known as 'Safer Food, Better Business', for use by such businesses.[52]

The HACCP plan should be in place before the food business begins operations, and should be reviewed whenever 'any modification is made in the product, process, or any step'.[53] Following review, the business must make any necessary changes to the HACCP procedures previously in place. Failure to comply is a strict liability offence.

Turning the requirement to put in place a HACCP plan into a criminal offence has created major uncertainties for both food businesses and enforcement bodies. First, it seems clear that more than one offence has been created. Businesses are required to 'put in place, implement and maintain' a food safety management system based on HACCP principles. This appears to create at least three offences (one of failure to put in place; one of failure to implement; and one of failure to maintain). A charge or a notice of formal action must make clear to which failure it relates. It is also necessary to distinguish whether a HACCP plan has not been put in place, or whether the HACCP plan is alleged to be inadequate. If a plan is inadequate, it may be said not to be based on the HACCP principles. So there is, logically, a breach by failure to put in place a plan, and a breach by putting in place a plan but failing to put in place a plan based on HACCP principles. A HACCP plan may be inadequate in failing to accord with any one of the seven HACCP principles set out in regulation 5(2) of Regulation 852/2004. Therefore there are seven separate types of inadequacy, which may be broken down further as each of the HACCP principles imposes more than one requirement. This means that it can be a challenge to identify the right breach of the HACCP requirements when formal action is taken. If the breach is not identified, a business may be able to challenge the action. There are other, more straightforward breaches that can be used following an incident of food-borne illness, such as those relating to cleaning. These

[51] HACCP systems were initially developed in the 1960s, when NASA asked Pillsbury to make food for its astronauts and ensure food safety (see Richard Hyde, A Bryce Hoflund and Michelle Pautz, 'One HACCP, Two Approaches: Experiences with and Perceptions of the Hazard Analysis and Critical Control Points (HACCP) Food Safety Management Systems in the US and the EU' (2015) *Administration and Society* (forthcoming), available at <http://www.dx.doi.org/10.1177/0095399714548266>).

[52] Available at <http://www.food.gov.uk/business-industry/caterers/sfbb> (last visited 19 January 2015).

[53] Regulation 852/2004, art 5(2). It is not clear whether a directing mind of a corporate entity must be shown to be aware of a modification before a failure to review becomes a breach of regulatory requirements, or whether any modification, authorised or unauthorised, triggers a requirement to review and modify a HACCP plan. It is likely, however, that a business that did not know of a modification could take advantage of a due diligence defence if it had in place procedures to search for modifications.

can be drafted and proved simply, so may be seen as preferable for resource reasons.[54]

v. Condition

'Food premises are to be kept clean and maintained in good repair and condition.'[55] Lack of maintenance and cleanliness is often a factor in food-borne illness. Failure to maintain and/or clean premises where food is sold is an offence. Cleanliness is a contextual standard. What suffices for cleanliness in one context may not suffice in another. Further, cleanliness goes beyond the visible, and includes microbiological cleanliness.

vi. Notification

Under article 6(2) of Regulation 852/2004, businesses that operate an establishment involved in production, processing and distribution of food must 'notify the appropriate competent authority' of their operations. In most cases the competent authority will be the local authority. Notification forms are found in annex 8 to the Food Law Code.[56] Notified establishments are then registered. The competent authority must be told of any changes in registered details.[57] Failure to notify is a strict liability offence.

II. THE CONTROL, ENFORCEMENT AND ADVISORY TOOLBOX: POWERS AVAILABLE TO LOCAL AUTHORITIES

A range of powers is available to local authorities as they respond to incidents of food-borne illness. The use of each of these powers is based on information collected during responses to incidents of food-borne illness, with conclusions about both the need to take formal or informal action and the case supporting such action built from that information. Before considering how information is assembled, it is necessary to examine what powers are available, and the prerequisites that accompany them. The prerequisites may shape the investigation, just as they shape formal action. Powers can be conceptualised as 'control' powers, 'enforcement' powers or 'advisory' powers. Control and enforcement powers play the central role in response to food-borne illness.

[54] Those drafting charges or notices may be used to command and control regulation, and may not be confident in correctly identifying the breaches of the HACCP requirements in a formal document, despite being able to identify them in practice.
[55] Regulation 852/2004, annex 2, ch 1, para 1.
[56] Food Standards Agency, *Food Law Code of Practice for England* (Food Standards Agency 2008) (hereinafter 'Food Law Code').
[57] Regulation 852/2004, art 6(2) subpara 2. Changes to be notified include closure.

Control powers are those powers that are used whilst the illness is still spreading, to prevent further primary and/or secondary cases of the illness. They seek to prevent the mixing of the infected and uninfected, separating products, premises, people and environments contaminated with illness-causing micro-organisms, from those products, premises, people and environments that are not contaminated. Control powers are not premised on responsibility for the illness but are simply based on status as 'infected'. They can, of course, be used in relation to those businesses responsible for the incident. Contrary to the presentation of all powers to take formal action as sanctions in Macrory,[58] control powers should not be conceptualised as sanctions, as they do not respond to and punish a regulatory breach, and indeed may not be aimed at something that can be punished, but instead seek to limit the consequences of a status that may have been acquired unknowingly.

Enforcement powers, on the other hand, are premised on responsibility. They are used once the illness is no longer spreading, and against those responsible for an incident of food-borne illness. Enforcement powers require responsibility for a regulatory breach to be demonstrated by the information collected during the incident. Enforcement powers are true sanctions, responding to and punishing a regulatory breach. They do not necessarily require a mental element to be established, but they must be targeted at a regulatory actor.

Environmental Health Officers also have a power to advise, in order to reduce the likelihood of an incident's recurring. Advisory powers are closer to enforcement than control, as they are generally used following control of an incident, but they adopt techniques similar to control, seeking to minimise risk by changing premises or product. Advisory powers are, however, focused on the future, rather than the present. They look to prevent the next incident, rather than to reduce the extent of the current incident. The provision of advice is not central to the role of the EHO in responding to an incident of food-borne illness, whereas the desire for control and/or enforcement shapes the actions of EHOs during the response. However, post-incident actors in the regulatory network may work together to produce guidance that reduces the risk of future food borne-illness.

The delineation between powers is imperfect and less clear-cut than presented here. It is to some extent purposive, dependent on when and why EHOs deploy their powers. The separation nonetheless represents the usage of powers by EHOs, with powers used first to control, followed by different

[58] Richard Macrory, *Regulatory Justice: Making Sanctions Effective* (Better Regulation Executive 2006) E.12; see also Julia Black, 'A review of enforcement techniques' in Law Commission (ed), *Criminal Liability in Regulatory Contexts—Consultation Paper 195* (Law Commission 2010).

powers used to sanction and advise businesses.[59] However, control powers may be perceived as enforcement by regulated businesses.[60]

Control powers, powers of enforcement and advisory powers are considered in further detail in sections II.A–C below.

A. Four Species of Control Power Used During Incidents of Food-borne Illness

Control powers are used to manage risks arising from products, premises, people or environments. Different risks require different interventions, and it is necessary to examine the powers available to manage each type of risk in turn. First, however, we need to consider the risks that control actions seek to prevent: primary spread (infection by the source), and secondary spread (infection by a person or thing that is not the source).

Control first attempts to deal with the risk of primary spread by preventing further consumption of a contaminated product. Two types of control intervention are utilised in this regard: control of products, and control of places. With products, the food itself may be contaminated with food-borne illness. Control action will focus on removing the product from the market, and tracing the food up the chain of supply to discover the source of infection. Action may then be taken against this source. Premises that are unclean and contaminated with food-borne illness microbes may cross-contaminate all food produced within them. Individuals who consume the food produced will be primary sufferers. Control action may be taken against the premises, including prohibiting food-processing operations.

Environmental Health Officers work to reduce the risk of secondary infection, which means person-to-person spread of the food-borne illness. Their focus here is more on the control of people than on the control of the disease itself, given the role of people as vectors in the transmission of illnesses that originally were food-borne.[61] It is simpler to control people, who can readily be monitored, than to attempt to control microbes. Environmental Health Officers may also attempt to control the environments in which people work, to prevent illness being transmitted by person-food-person and person-surface-food-person mechanisms.

[59] See ch 5.

[60] BAR-2.

[61] In some cases other vectors, such as animals, may be subject to control by regulators. The Public Health (Control of Disease) Act 1984, s 45H ensures that a magistrate may order that an infected 'thing' is, inter alia, quarantined, decontaminated or destroyed. Extra-statutory guidance makes clear that 'thing' 'has a wide meaning and includes animals and plant material as well as inanimate objects' (Department of Health, *Health Protection Legislation (England) Guidance 2010* (Department of Health, 2010), 69).

i. Powers that Control Products

Seizure is the most widely used formal power that controls the marketing of products.[62] The most important power to seize and destroy unsafe food is set out in section 9 of the Food Safety Act 1990.[63]

The power of seizure allows local authorities to remove unsafe food (or food produced in an unsafe environment) from manufacturers or sellers, and to destroy the food so that it never enters the food chain. Seizure is about control of the primary spread of the illness; the power allows EHOs to reduce the number of consumers contracting the illness through consumption of contaminated food. Hazardous food is removed from the supply chain. The power is not based on whether destruction is 'deserved'; it is about preventing the hazard through destruction of the food product.

Environmental Health Officers may seize any food that fails to comply with food safety requirements,[64] or appears 'likely to cause food poisoning or any disease communicable to human beings'.[65] This determination may be based on the EHO's own information gathering, or on information obtained from other network actors, such as the Food Standards Agency, through a FAFI or FAFA, or from another authority. If the conditions in section 9 are satisfied, the EHO may immediately 'seize the food and remove it in order to have it dealt with by a justice of the peace'.[66]

If food has 'not been produced, processed or distributed in compliance with the Hygiene Regulations', an EHO must use section 9 powers to seize that food.[67] A certificate that food was produced in contravention of the hygiene requirements found in Regulations 852/2004 and 853/2004 allows EHOs to seize all food in the same batch, lot or consignment. This allows them to take action to manage the risk on the basis of a single certificate, although it must be accompanied by traceability information so that the batch can be followed. Seizure of a batch may be challenged if it can be shown that the production, processing and/or distribution environment

[62] The power under the Public Health (Control of Disease) Act 1984, s 45H may be used against a food product that 'presents or could present significant harm to human health', as such a product amounts to a 'thing' regarding which a magistrate may make an order. However, in food-borne illness cases, where the 'thing' is a food product, the specific food powers are preferable.

[63] There are a number of statutory instruments that contain specific seizure and destruction powers (eg the Contaminants in Food (England) Regulations 2013). However, these powers are given to county authorities and relate to food standards, and are therefore unlikely to be used in the response to incidents of food-borne illness.

[64] Food Safety Act 1990, s 9(1).

[65] Food Safety Act 1990, s 9(2); microbiological analysis may be required to demonstrate the likelihood of food-borne illness; in the interim, food will be detained.

[66] Food Safety Act 1990, s 9(3)(b).

[67] Food Safety and Hygiene (England) Regulations 2013, reg 29; Food Law Code, para 3.4.5.

complied with the Regulations, and the part of the batch tested was unfit for human consumption due to, for example, unique storage conditions.[68]

Once seized, food must be placed before a magistrate for condemnation. Any person who may be subject to prosecution in respect of the food, for example the manufacturer, the importer or the seller, must be informed, and may appear before the magistrate and call witnesses.[69]

If a magistrate decides that the food fails to comply with food safety requirements then the food must be condemned.[70] There is no residual discretion to allow food to be marketed once it has been demonstrated that the food satisfies the criteria set out in section 9.[71] Once condemned, food will be destroyed or disposed of in order to ensure that it will not be consumed by humans.[72] Incineration is the preferred method. Between condemnation and destruction the food may be dyed to prevent re-entry into the food chain.

Despite the mandatory nature of guidance in the Food Law Code, which provides that food must be seized and destroyed when it fails to comply with food safety requirements, agreement to destroy food voluntarily may be reached between an EHO and a business.[73] A business may offer in writing to surrender food voluntarily that fails to comply with food safety requirements, and this may be accepted by an EHO, who must explain the consequences of voluntary surrender to the business. Where food is surrendered, a receipt should be supplied.[74]

Alternatively, rather than seizing food that is unfit for human consumption, EHOs may agree that food can be treated or processed if the post-treatment food would be 'sound and wholesome' and 'satisfy food safety requirements'.[75] The food will be allowed to return to the market only if it poses no further risk of primary transmission and is 'wholesome,' which, in relation to food, has been defined as equivalent to 'fit for human consumption'.[76] Proposed processing and treatment must be made the subject of a written undertaking, which should be signed by the EHO and an authorised representative of the business.[77]

As well as seizing food, local authorities may also use the threat of criminal action to ensure the withdrawal of unsafe food. If a business is aware

[68] Food Safety and Hygiene (England) Regulations 2013, reg 29(3).
[69] Food Safety Act 1990, s 9(5)(a).
[70] Food Safety Act 1990, s 9(6).
[71] *R (Food Standards Agency) v Brent Justices* [2004] EWHC 459 (Admin).
[72] Food Safety Act 1990, s 9(6)(a).
[73] In most cases voluntary surrender is unlikely because insurance companies require formal seizure as a trigger for payments.
[74] Food Law Code, para 3.4.9.
[75] Ibid, para 3.4.5.
[76] Food Safety (General Food Hygiene) Regulations 1995, reg 2(1) (now repealed).
[77] Food Law Code, para 3.4.5.

that food that is unsafe has left its control, the business must initiate procedures to withdraw the food from the market and to 'inform the competent authorities'[78] of its actions. Failure to do so is an offence.[79] A retailer has a more limited obligation, and is required to remove products from its shelves ('within the limits of its ... activities')[80] and to cooperate with measures taken by the competent authorities or businesses higher in the supply chain. Where food has reached consumers then the business must accurately and effectively inform them of the withdrawal of the product and the reasons for its withdrawal.

Whilst seizure and withdrawal are important powers for controlling the risk of primary spread of food-borne illness, they are not powers of recall. Seizure relates solely to food held by a particular business, and therefore numerous seizures may need to be made in order to manage the risk. Seizure and withdrawal do not apply to food held in private hands. Where the risk to health is particularly severe, a decision to seize food or to order withdrawal must be accompanied by voluntary or mandatory recall action, in order to prevent further primary cases.

According to Regulation 178/2002 article 19(1), if withdrawal is not sufficient to ensure 'a high level of health protection', because the food is in wide circulation amongst consumers, then the business is obliged to 'recall from consumers products already supplied to them'. The failure to recall is rendered a criminal offence by the Food Safety and Hygiene (England) Regulations 2013 regulation 19. In contrast to the General Product Safety Regulations 2005, authorities do not have a specific power to carry out a recall if a business fails to do so.[81] However, authorities may use the threat of criminal punishment to encourage businesses to manage risk through recall.[82]

As noted in chapter two, section II., the Secretary of State may also play a role in control of products, using power under the Food Safety Act 1990, section 13 to make an order in council prohibiting, and criminalising, the marketing of food of a particular description. This power is used in particularly risky and urgent situations, where other steps of control will not

[78] Eg, local authorities and the Food Standards Agency.

[79] Food Safety and Hygiene (England) Regulations 2013, reg 19 and sch 2, rendering failure to comply with Regulation 178/2002, art 19 an offence.

[80] Regulation 178/2002, art 19(2).

[81] See Duncan Fairgrieve and Geraint Howells, 'General Product Safety—a revolution through reform' (2006) 69 *MLR* 59, 65–67. There have been calls to creates such a power, see Michael T Roberts, 'Mandatory recall authority: A sensible and minimalist approach to improving food safety' (2004) 59 *Food and Drug Law Journal* 563. It does appear, however, that the power under the General Product Safety Regulations 2005 can be used when the unsafe product is food, as there is no overriding specific power (see reg 3).

[82] It may be possible to obtain an injunction to enforce the criminal law requirement to recall if a business was refusing to comply with his obligations. See, eg, *Stoke on Trent City Council v B&Q (Retail) Ltd* [1984] AC 754.

be sufficient to manage the risk to consumers.[83] The power has been used to criminalise the supply of cheese from a particular manufacturer, where cheese contaminated with *E. coli* O157 had been found on the market.[84]

ii. Powers that Control Premises and Processes

When faced with an incident of food-borne illness seemingly due to poor conditions in food business premises, the key method of control is to ensure that food is not produced there until compliance with food hygiene requirements is demonstrated, thereby reducing the risk to consumers.

A Hygiene Emergency Prohibition Notice (HEPN) prohibits a person from producing food in an environment, or using a process, that creates risk to human health during the processing of food.[85] A notice of prohibition must be displayed, and failure to comply is a criminal offence. It is used as an immediate response to an urgent need to prevent production,[86] and aims to prevent the production of food that poses a risk to consumers' health. When premises no longer pose a threat, they may reopen.

A HEPN may be issued only if the EHO is 'satisfied'[87] that the 'health risk condition' is 'fulfilled'.[88] This must be based on information that the premises present a risk to health. The health risk condition is fulfilled if:

(a) the use for the purposes of the business of any process or treatment;
(b) the construction of any premises used for the purposes of the business, or the use for those purposes of any equipment; [or]
(c) the state or condition of any premises or equipment used for the purposes of the business...

presents a 'risk of injury to health (including any impairment, whether permanent or temporary)'.[89]

A prohibition must be appropriately tailored to terminate this risk. The notice will have a different prohibitory scope depending on whether processes, construction or conditions cause the health risk. The appropriate

[83] The making of a s 13 order must be necessary and proportionate in light of the risk to public health (see *R (Eastside Cheese) v Secretary of State for Health* [1999] 3 CMLR 123).

[84] Described in *R (Eastside Cheese) v Secretary of State for Health*, above n 80, 127–32.

[85] Food Safety and Hygiene (England) Regulations 2013, reg 8.

[86] The urgent nature of the emergency prohibition notice is shown by the exemption of the service of these notices from the requirements to consult the primary authority under the Regulatory Enforcement and Sanctions Act 2008 (see the Coordination of Regulatory Enforcement (Enforcement Action) Order 2009, SI 2009/655, art 3).

[87] In other regulatory areas the courts have construed 'satisfied' as leaving local authorities with significant discretion, provided that all relevant factors have been taken into account when considering the term (see *R v Brighton BC, ex p Bunch* [1989] COD 558 and *R (Maud) v Castle Point Borough Council* [2003] RTR 7).

[88] Food Safety Act 1990, s 12(1); Food Safety and Hygiene (England) Regulations 2013, reg 8(1).

[89] Food Safety Act 1990, s 11(2); Food Safety and Hygiene (England) Regulations 2013, reg 7(2).

prohibitions are set out in regulation 7(3) of the Food Safety and Hygiene (England) Regulations 2013:

(a) where the risk is caused by a process, 'a prohibition on the use of the process or treatment for the purposes of the business';
(b) where the risk is caused by construction, 'a prohibition on the use of the premises or equipment for the purposes of the business or any other food business of the same class or description'; and
(c) where the risk is caused by conditions, 'a prohibition on the use of the premises or equipment for the purposes of any food business'.

Premises should be prohibited only when it is 'reasonable, proportionate, risk based and consistent with good practice'.[90] However, the Food Law Code makes clear that emergency prohibition will be appropriate when the premises are 'implicated in an outbreak of food poisoning'.[91] An inspection in response to the report of an incident may expose an independent ground for prohibition, such as 'infestation', 'poor structural condition' or serious contraventions of food law.[92]

The Food Law Code and practice guidance encourage EHOs to seek out expert advice when determining whether to prohibit premises.[93] However, the final decision on prohibition rests with the EHO,[94] and he or she bears the 'burden of proof and the persuasive burden' of demonstrating that the premises pose a risk to health.[95] Therefore the EHO must have evidence implicating premises in the incident of food-borne illness.

In some cases a business may agree to close voluntarily during an incident to prevent further new cases. An EHO may choose to allow this in preference to taking formal action. Voluntary closure should be confirmed in writing, and include an undertaking not to reopen before consent has been given by an EHO.[96] The likelihood of the business's reopening will be considered, as voluntary closure is not as secure a method of control as prohibition, as there is no separate sanction if the business breaches this agreement.[97]

If a premises processes animal products, those premises must be approved.[98] It is a criminal offence to process animal products without

[90] Food Law Code, para 3.1.3.
[91] Ibid, para 3.3.2.2.1.
[92] Ibid.
[93] Ibid, para 3.3.8. Usually from the CCDC or OCT, who are already part of the regulatory network.
[94] Ibid, para 3.3.8.
[95] Food Standards Agency, *Food Law Practice Guidance (England)* (Food Standards Agency 2006) para 3.3.7.2.
[96] Ibid, para 3.3.2.4.
[97] Ibid.
[98] Regulation 853/2004, art 4(2). Approval applies to the establishment, which has been interpreted to mean the entire operation of the food business (see *Allan Rich Seafoods v Lincoln Magistrates' Court* [2009] EWHC 3391 (Admin)). Approvals cannot be transferred between businesses, even where a change of ownership is effected by share sale (*R (on the application of Allan Rich Seafoods Ltd) v West Lindsey DC* [2010] EWHC 1232 (Admin)).

approval. Enforcement authorities may withdraw or suspend an approval,[99] which will have the effect of stopping processing and preventing further risk of food-borne illness from products processed at the plant. Once approval is withdrawn, premises cannot be used for activities that require approval. A local authority must initiate proceedings to withdraw an approval if it identifies 'serious deficiencies', or if it has to 'stop production at an establishment repeatedly' and the business 'is not able to provide adequate guarantees regarding future production'.[100] Serious deficiencies may include breaches of hygiene requirements discovered when investigating an incident of food-borne illness. Once approval is withdrawn, animal products can be processed on the premises only if a new approval is applied for and granted by the local authority.

If the permanent removal of an approval is deemed unnecessary, approval may be suspended. Suspension allows food businesses time to put in place measures to manage microbiological risk (and therefore prevent food-borne illness), whilst preventing food processing until these measures are put in place. An approval should be suspended, rather than withdrawn, only 'if the ... [business] can guarantee that it will resolve deficiencies within a reasonable time'.[101] An approval may be suspended for any period an enforcement authority deems fit.

When molluscs are discovered to be the source of food-borne illness, the area from which they are harvested may be shut until water quality improves.[102] In cases of *norovirus*, molluscs may be the source when a harvesting ground is contaminated with sewage.[103] When a harvesting ground is closed, the food authority must liaise with the Food Standards Agency and consider whether molluscs harvested from the closed production area should be withdrawn from sale.[104] If it is necessary to prevent further primary cases then molluscs already harvested will be withdrawn.

iii. Powers that Control People

Local authorities may exclude ill individuals from particular places in a bid to prevent the secondary spread of food-borne illness. Whilst blanket quarantines are available,[105] these will be inappropriate in cases of food-borne

[99] Regulation 882/2004, art 31(2)(e), incorporated into English law by the Official Feed and Food Controls (England) Regulations 2009, SI 2009/3255, reg 3(3)–(6) and sch 5.
[100] Regulation 882/2004, art 31(2)(e).
[101] Regulation 882/2004, art 31(2)(e).
[102] Regulation 854/2004, annex II, ch II, para C1.
[103] Eg, A/I/16; Fat Duck.
[104] Food Law Code, para 5.3.6.
[105] Eg, through the Civil Contingencies Act 2004. Quarantines have been used as a response to incidents of non food-borne illness, such as SARS in Canada, discussed in Andrew Donaldson, 'Biosecurity after the event: risk politics and animal disease' (2008) 40 *Environment and Planning A* 1552.

illness, as those illnesses are imperfectly airborne and often require large infective doses. In order for secondary transmission to take place, close proximity to an infected person or cross-contamination of food by an infected person is usually required. Therefore, control is targeted at individual infected persons.[106] Under section 45G of the Public Health (Control of Disease) Act 1984, a local authority may apply for an order 'that [a person] be subject to restrictions on where [that person] goes or with whom [that person] has contact',[107] or 'that [a person] abstain from working or trading'.[108] An order may be made if a magistrate is satisfied that a person 'is or may be infected or contaminated', that 'the infection or contamination is one which presents or could present significant harm to human health', that 'there is a risk that [the person] might infect or contaminate others' and that 'it is necessary to make the order in order to remove or reduce that risk'.[109]

The magistrate must ensure that his or her order complies with the Human Rights Act 1998, section 6 and the requirements of the European Convention on Human Rights,[110] and must particularly ensure that the measure proposed is necessary and proportionate to the risk. Coercive measures may be justified more easily in relation to highly infective illnesses that pose serious risks to those who suffer them. Food-borne illnesses are usually sufficiently serious and sufficiently transmissible for a restriction on liberty to be necessary and proportionate. Of course, individuals suffering from a food-borne illness may voluntarily exclude themselves from work.

An order will specify the period for which it remains in force. This will not exceed 28 days.[111] An order may include a requirement for the local authority to compensate the excluded person.[112]

Where a school child is suffering from a transmissible illness, a local authority has the power to serve a notice on the child's parents, requiring the child be kept away from school.[113] An order from a magistrate is not required. The exclusion lasts for a specified period of up to 28 days, and consecutive exclusion notices may be served. The school should be kept informed of the actions taken by the local authority.

[106] As most food-borne illness microbes are not particularly well adapted to aerosol transmission, with bacterial illnesses in particular not being able to travel long distances and not being able survive for long once airborne, direct person-to-person transmission can be prevented through the implementation of procedures aimed at ensuring that microbes cannot pass between individuals.

[107] Public Health (Control of Disease) Act 1984, s 45G(2)(j).

[108] Public Health (Control of Disease) Act 1984, s 45G(2)(k).

[109] Public Health (Control of Disease) Act 1984, s 45G(1).

[110] Particularly art 5 (right to liberty and security), but also, eg, art 8 (right to respect for private and family life).

[111] Health Protection (Part 2A Orders) Regulations 2010, SI 2010/658, r 5.

[112] Public Health (Control of Disease) Act 1984, s 45K(7).

[113] Health Protection (Local Authority Powers) Regulations 2010, SI 2010/657, reg 2.

Authorities may also use informal actions to separate symptomatic and asymptomatic individuals. During the South Wales outbreak, communications from the OCT encouraged symptomatic individuals to exclude themselves voluntarily from their place of work. Parents were asked to ensure that symptomatic children stayed away from school. Parents were told, 'if your child has a tummy upset (diarrhoea and vomiting), for any reason, they should not go to school'.[114] This call was reiterated and developed in a letter of 4 October 2005, which stated, 'should your child develop vomiting/diarrhoea he/she should be kept off school and should not return until at least 48 hours have elapsed from the end of the symptoms'.[115] Voluntary compliance is more likely to be achieved if the circumstances in which exclusion is necessary are clearly explained.

iv. Powers that Control the Environment

Local authorities may take actions to ensure that environmental conditions are not those that assist the spread of food-borne illness. These actions are more often informal than formal. For example, local authorities may ensure that swimming pools are closed to prevent spread of illness through faecal matter in the water. Local authorities also have the power to disinfect premises when a request is made by the owner or tenant, and the power to disinfect articles when a request is made by the owner or a person who has custody of the article.[116] This may be used where an environment, such as a children's soft play area, poses a risk of secondary transmission. Further, they may also request that businesses or individuals take action to ensure that the environment is not conducive to the transmission of food-borne illness.[117]

In the South Wales case, children's play environments were modified to reduce the risk of secondary spread. Schools and nurseries were contacted and asked to prevent children from using sandpits and plasticine for the duration of the outbreak. Tuck shops were redesigned to prevent children from touching food then not buying it, and another child eating contaminated food. Staff were required to observe hand-washing by children aged five and under, to ensure that this was properly carried out. These actions attempted to make it more difficult for food-borne illness micro-organisms to be transmitted from person to person.

[114] PEN/EJD/BCC.07562, annexes 3–5.
[115] PEN/EJD/BCC.07599.
[116] Health Protection (Local Authority Powers) Regulations 2010, regs 4, 5, 6 and 7.
[117] Health Protection (Local Authority Powers) Regulations 2010, reg 8.

B. Two Enforcement Powers Used Following Incidents of Food-borne Illness

After the risk of primary and secondary spread has been controlled, action may be taken to sanction the regulatory breaches that caused or contributed to the incident of food-borne illness.

The two enforcement powers, prosecution and caution, are those that are perhaps most closely connected with enforcement in the eyes of both the public and EHOs. These powers are aimed at sanctioning those responsible for regulatory breaches leading to incidents of food-borne illness. Where the term 'enforcement action' is used below, it should be taken to refer to these powers.

i. Prosecution

Prosecution is the enforcement option most closely linked in the public mind with sanctioning regulatory infractions. For a corporate entity, the maximum sentence in the Crown Court is generally an unlimited fine.

Previous studies have suggested that regulatory authorities view prosecution as a response of last resort.[118] Environmental Health Officers do not work on an initial assumption that regulatory breaches should be enforced by prosecution, even if they arise in the context of an incident of food-borne illness.

Prosecutions may be brought by laying an information, in the magistrates' court, or on indictment, in the Crown Court. However, an explicit or implicit power to prosecute must be identified before a local authority can take any action.[119] If an authority has no power to prosecute, any action taken will be stayed.[120]

The primary source of local authorities' general power to prosecute can be found in section 222 of the Local Government Act 1972. This provides:

> (1) Where a local authority consider it expedient for the promotion or protection of the interests of the inhabitants of their area
> (a) they may prosecute or defend … any legal proceedings and, in the case of civil proceedings, may institute [proceedings] in their own name…

118 Keith Hawkins, *Law as Last Resort: Prosecution Decision-Making in a Regulatory Agency* (Oxford Univeristy Press 2002).

119 See, eg, *Attorney-General v Great Eastern Railway Company* (1879) 11 ChD 449, 484 per James LJ, which states, 'So far as [a statutory corporation] has compulsory powers it must not abuse them; so far as it has statutory duties it cannot delegate them; so far as it is under any statutory prohibition or direction it must not violate the one or neglect the other.'

120 See, eg, *Boddington v British Transport Police* [1999] 2 AC 143, 160, although in this case the action in question (a bylaw prohibiting smoking) was found to be within the powers of the public authority.

This section grants local authorities an extensive power to engage in legal proceedings. The power to prosecute is not limited to food safety regulation.[121] Whilst a prosecution must be 'expedient for the promotion or protection of the interests of the inhabitants of [the local authority's] area', courts are reluctant to disturb a decision to prosecute.[122] A wide margin of discretion is given when determining whether the test in section 222 is satisfied.

However, the power to prosecute under section 222 is limited to food businesses that are based in, manufacture in, or supply products to the local authority area. There must be some connection between an incident which forms the basis of a prosecution and the interests of the inhabitants of the authority. Given the resource and manpower limitations on investigations, it is unlikely that an authority would investigate or prosecute an incident of food-borne illness that appears to arise outside its area, although the realities of large incidents of food-borne illness mean that it is often difficult to identify the geographic scope of incidents when the initial report is made, meaning that an authority may engage in investigations of incidents that are centred outside their area, necessitating cooperation and information sharing with other local authorities.

Authorities also have a specific power to institute proceedings in the area of food safety. According to section 6 of the Food Safety Act 1990, a food authority may 'enforce and execute within their area the provisions of [the Food Safety Act 1990]'.[123] Enforcement includes the power to 'institute proceedings'.[124] An authority may lay informations and summons in its own name for offences within the food safety sphere.[125]

The types of conduct that could be subject to prosecution as breaches of food safety and hygiene norms are exceptionally wide.[126] Policy documents attempt to control food authorities' exercise of prosecutorial power. The Food Standards Agency's Food Law Code, in paragraph 3.1.10, lays down principles in accordance with which prosecutorial discretion should be exercised.

Decisions to prosecute must be taken at the 'earliest possible opportunity'.[127] The principles found in the *Code for Crown Prosecutors* ('the *Code*') apply to prosecutorial decisions made following incidents of food-borne

[121] In *R v Jarrett and Steward* [1997] Crim LR 517, the Court of Appeal held that the s 222 power was wide enough to encompass a prosecution for conspiracy to defraud.

[122] *R v Director of Public Prosecutions, ex p C* [1995] 1 Cr App R 136.

[123] Food Safety Act 1990, s 6(2).

[124] Ibid.

[125] *Monks v East Northamptonshire DC* [2002] EWHC 473 (Admin) [24]. The former practice of laying an information in the name of the enforcement officer is therefore unnecessary.

[126] See above text to nn 4 et seq.

[127] Food Standards Agency, Food Law Code, 47 and 51. Of course, the timing of the earliest opportunity will depend on the progress of information collection.

illness.[128] The evidential sufficiency and public interest tests must be satisfied. Further specific tests are found in the Food Law Code, which must be satisfied before prosecution is undertaken.

The two tests found in the *Code* are intended to be considered sequentially, with the public interest test being considered only once the evidential test is satisfied. However, a study of decision making by the Crown Prosecution Service (CPS) found some evidence that the two tests were in fact considered at the same time, with the public interest in prosecution influencing the evaluation of the evidential basis of a particular charge.[129] Such concurrent consideration was particularly prevalent in cases where consequences were serious, or where intense media interest was generated.[130]

The evidential test requires EHOs to consider whether a prosecution would offer a 'realistic prospect of conviction'.[131] A local authority must take a view of the merits of the case and decide whether it is 'more likely than not' that a properly directed jury or magistrates' court would convict the proposed defendant on the evidence that could be put before the court.[132]

Applying the evidential test requires the prosecuting authority to answer two questions: the availability question, and the admissibility question. Availability considers whether the information assembled during an investigation is sufficient to demonstrate a regulatory breach. This question must be addressed in all cases where formal action is contemplated, with the determination of the breach an important role of the EHOs.

Admissibility asks the EHO to consider whether particular evidence will be allowed before a court. This question is perhaps the more familiar to legal scholars, who often begin evidential consideration by assuming that there is information in existence that the party wishes to place before the court. If evidence is inadmissible, the EHO will not take it into account during decision making. Evidence may be inadmissible because it is irrelevant, or because it contravenes a rule of criminal evidence.[133] The policy of the CPS is to take into account evidence that *may* be excluded on application in cases where the result of such an application is not clear.[134] The policy of local authorities is perhaps more cautious.[135]

[128] Ibid, 51. The *Code* is issued by the Director of Public Prosecutions under s 10 of the Prosecution of Offences Act 1985 (Crown Prosecution Service, *The Code for Crown Prosecutors* (CPS 2010)).

[129] Allan Hoyano *et al*, 'A Study of the Impact of the Revised Code for Crown Prosecutors' [1997] *Crim LR* 556, 562.

[130] Ibid, 562.

[131] *Code*, above n 125, para 5.2.

[132] Ibid, para 5.3.

[133] See Paul Roberts and Adrian AS Zuckerman, *Criminal Evidence* (2nd edn, Oxford University Press 2010) ch 3, and particularly s 3.1 and the flowchart at 99.

[134] It is the position of the CPS that if 'the issue is not "clear cut" the case may be continued and the matter put before the court' (Andrew Ashworth and Julia Fionda, 'The New Code for Crown Prosecutors: Part 1: Prosecution, Accountability and the Public-Interest' [1994] *Crim LR* 894, 897).

[135] See ch 6.

The Food Law Code emphasises certain factors that the local authority should consider when assessing the evidential basis of a food law prosecution. In particular, under paragraph 3.1.10 'the likely cogency of any important witness' will be considered. Further, EHOs must consider any potential due diligence defence when assessing whether there is a realistic prospect of conviction. Statutory due diligence defences are found in the regulations that apply following incidents of food-borne illness.[136] An EHO must examine information about the practices and policies of the food business, and assess the likelihood of success of a due diligence defence. Where an EHO assesses that a due diligence defence will be successful, prosecution will not take place.[137] Other defences should also be considered, and paragraph 3.1.10 of the Food Law Code makes clear that the assessment of evidential sufficiency should take into account 'any explanation offered by the suspect', in so far as this has a bearing on the prospects of success of any proposed prosecution.

When considering strict liability offences, some commentators assume that a conviction can be obtained easily.[138] Indeed, ease of conviction is seen as a positive characteristic of strict liability offences.[139] Macrory asserts that there is 'no significant evidence that … issues of proof' impact on enforcement action by regulatory agencies.[140] Because of this, strict liability is perceived to create a large category of acceptable cases, where sufficient evidence can be gathered with ease and enforcement can take place. This 'leaves the prospect of criminal conviction to the discretion of enforcement officers'.[141] Without discretionary decision making, even businesses that have acted in accordance with the highest standards of good practice would be open to enforcement action,[142] including prosecution, if they breached regulatory requirements due to an isolated piece of bad luck.[143]

[136] See, eg, the Food Safety Act 1990, s 21.

[137] In particular, the existence of a HACCP plan (see section I.B.iv. above) will not be sufficient to amount to due diligence.

[138] This often forms part of a normative critique of strict liability offences (see, eg, many of the contributions to Andrew P Simester (ed), *Appraising Strict Liability* (Oxford University Press 2005)). See also Samuel L Bray, 'Power Rules' (2010) 110 *Columbia Law Review* 1172, 1187–88.

[139] See, eg, Anthony I Ogus, *Regulation: Legal Form and Economic Theory* (Hart Publishing 2004) 82.

[140] Richard Macrory, 'Reforming regulatory sanctions—a personal perspective' (2009) 11 *Environmental Law Review* 69, 72.

[141] Andrew P Simester, 'Is Strict Liability Always Wrong?' in Andrew P Simester (ed), *Appraising Strict Liability* (Oxford University Press 2005), 33. See also Simester, 'Preface' in Andrew P Simester (ed), *Appraising Strict Liability* (Oxford University Press 2005), vii (those who breach regulations are 'almost certain to be convicted'); and Kieron Reid, 'Strict Liability: Some Principles for Parliament' (2008) 29 *Statute Law Review* 173, 186, commenting on fixed penalty notices, 'in effect the police simply decide who has committed an offence'.

[142] According to the 'evidentially easy' critique, discretion must be restrained using policy documents, such as the Food Law Code, although due diligence defences are intended to address this.

[143] Such prosecutions were criticised by the House of Lords in *Smedleys v Breed* [1974] AC 839, 856.

The ease of proving strict liability offences is also assumed by courts[144] and in many texts that concentrate on core criminal law. For example, Simester *et al*, whilst rejecting efficiency as a proper rationale for strict liability, do not challenge the assumption that strict liability offences are easier, and require fewer resources, to prove than *mens rea* offences.[145] The argument that 'many guilty people would escape' without strict liability assumes that an *actus reus* element is provable, and that the only evidential challenge is proof of culpability (although the use of 'guilty' suggests that culpability is believed to exist).[146] The argument that strict liability is necessary for public protection presupposes that the only challenge to imposing criminal liability in strict liability cases is of proving *mens rea*.[147]

Ashworth argues that lawmakers believe that 'proving fault, particularly mens rea, invariably causes difficulties for the prosecution'.[148] On the other hand, strict liability offences 'make it easier to convict those who cause, threaten or risk harm'.[149] At least for government, *mens rea* offences are seen as difficult to prove, with strict liability viewed as being easier. One US author refers to strict liability as the 'easy proof' standard.[150]

It is submitted that these arguments concentrate on the metaphysical ease of proof.[151] The point may be well taken: assuming that information detailing all the elements can be gathered, it is less burdensome to prove the offence with fewer elements. It is harder to know a man's mind than his actions. However, critics use the lack of metaphysical difficulties of proof in strict liability offences to assert that there are no epistemic difficulties of proof.[152] This assertion is neither logically nor empirically sound. Epistemic difficulties arise from the challenges of assembling information to demonstrate that the elements of the offence are satisfied. Strict liability offences cannot be said to be epistemically easy, even if they may be seen as metaphysically easy.[153] Local authority decision makers may have a number of difficulties in satisfying the test of realistic prospect of conviction.

Even if a realistic prospect of conviction can be demonstrated, the enforcement authority must consider whether prosecution is in the public interest.

[144] Eg, in *Smedleys v Breed*, ibid.

[145] Andrew P Simester *et al*, *Simester and Sullivan's Criminal Law: Theory and Doctrine* (5th edn Hart Publishing 2013) 191–93.

[146] Herbert Wechsler, 'The Modern Penal Code' in John Llewelyn Jones Edwards (ed), *Modern Advances in Criminology* (Centre of Criminology, University of Toronto 1965), 73.

[147] David C Ormerod, John C Smith and Brian Hogan, *Smith and Hogan Criminal Law* (13th edn, Oxford University Press 2013) 178.

[148] Andrew Ashworth, 'Should Strict Liability be Removed from all Imprisonable Offences?' (2010) 45 *Irish Jurist* 1, 10.

[149] Ibid, 9.

[150] Daniel E Hall, *Criminal Law and Procedure* (5th edn, Cengage 2009), 57.

[151] Alvin I Goldman, *Knowledge in a social world* (Oxford University Press 1999) 277.

[152] Ibid.

[153] See ch 6.

The public interest test does not operate as a purely numeric exercise, counting factors for and against prosecution and doing whichever has the higher score.[154] Instead, it is a 'normative exercise, because it depends on the relative value placed on each particular factor'.[155] One factor in favour of prosecution may outweigh a number of factors against taking such action, or vice versa, because of the greater weight placed on the single factor as compared to the combination of factors taken together. The public interest test is a matter of judgement, and policy documents do not attempt to lay down strict guidance on the operation of the test. Instead, the *Code* sets out factors that make it more or less in the public interest to prosecute, and entrusts the balancing exercise to the prosecutor.[156]

The more serious the offence, the more likely that prosecution is in the public interest.[157] The emphasis on seriousness is repeated in the Food Law Code.[158] Food-borne illness poses a large risk to public health, and may result in severe illness or death, and is therefore treated as a serious regulatory breach. The Food Law Code requires that EHOs brief prosecutorial decision makers and legal representatives on the public health consequences of the breach,[159] in order that seriousness can be assessed.

Where formal or informal action has been taken against the business, against the particular premises, or where a previous incident has been linked to the premises, prosecution is more likely. This was clearly a factor that influenced the decision to prosecute in *R v South-West Water*.[160] Other *Code* factors may influence the decision. In particular, the decision maker should consider whether the offence was premeditated, or whether it was the result of mere thoughtlessness;[161] and whether the offence is likely to be continued or repeated, bearing in mind the history of compliance (or non-compliance) by the business.[162]

The Food Law Code provides that where an offence was 'committed as a result of a genuine mistake or misunderstanding',[163] a prosecution should be seen as less in the public interest than in cases where the breach was premeditated. If a breach results from incompetence rather than intention, this is a factor that weighs against prosecution. However, this factor is likely to

154 *Code*, above n 125, para 5.11.
155 Ashworth and Fionda, above note 131, 898.
156 *Code*, above n 125, paras 5.9–5.10.
157 Ibid, para 5.8.
158 Food Law Code, 52.
159 Ibid.
160 *R v South-West Water* (Bristol Crown Court, 16 September 1997). See Peter Jiggins and W Michael Waite, 'Cryptosporidium in England and Wales' in Paul R Hunter, W Michael Waite and Elettra Ronchi (eds), *Drinking Water and Infectious Disease: Establishing the Links* (CRC Press 2002).
161 *Code*, above n 125, para 5.9(g).
162 Ibid, para 5.9(o).
163 Food Law Code, 52.

be outweighed where serious consequences result from the breach. Further, cases where nominal penalties are likely should not generally be seen as in the public interest.[164]

The Food Law Code imposes two additional hurdles on the decision to prosecute. The prosecutorial burden is therefore more onerous than that imposed on the CPS. The authority must ensure that prosecution is the most appropriate enforcement response given the other food law enforcement options available (taking into account the control actions that may already have been taken). It should also consider whether to offer a caution (see section II.B.ii. below) as an alternative to prosecution.

As noted by Ashworth and Fionda, an extensive toolbox of enforcement options may allow a greater commitment to diversion from prosecution,[165] allowing prosecution to be used as a last resort,[166] rather than as a routine response.

A local authority must also comply with its own food law enforcement policy. An authority is required to have such a policy by the Food Law Code[167] and the Framework Agreement on Official Feed and Food Controls by Local Authorities.[168] The policy may be specific to food, or may be a global policy that covers all law enforcement functions.[169] It should be available to the population served by the local authority.[170] The policy will reflect and expand upon relevant national policy. Local policies provide EHOs with large amounts of discretion, in an attempt to avoid the consequences of the decision in *R v Adaway*,[171] even though the courts moved away from a strict interpretation of *Adaway* in later cases.[172]

ii. Caution

Local authorities may caution a food business in circumstances where they could prosecute. The evidential and public interest tests must be satisfied,[173] but the public interest would be better met by diversionary disposal. Cautions

[164] Ibid.

[165] Ashworth and Fionda, 'The New Code for Crown Prosecutors: Part 1: Prosecution, Accountability and the Public-Interest' above n 130, 898–99.

[166] Ibid

[167] Food Law Code, para 3.1.

[168] Food Standards Agency, *The Framework Agreement on Official Feed and Food Controls* (5th amended edn, Food Standards Agency 2010) ch 2, para 15.1.

[169] Food Law Code, 48.

[170] Food Standards Agency, above n 165, para 15.1.

[171] *R v Adaway* [2004] EWCA Crim 2831, where the Court of Appeal held that a prosecution of a trader for supplying goods with a false trade description which was commenced in breach of an enforcement policy adopted by Trading Standards Officers was an abuse of process which meant that the proceeding should be stopped.

[172] See, eg, *Sumal & Sons (Properties) Ltd v London Borough of Newham* [2013] 1 WLR 2078 [22]; and *Moss & Son Ltd v Crown Prosecution Service* [2012] EWHC 3658 (Admin).

[173] *Code*, above n 125.

aim to 'deliver swift, simple and effective justice' in cases of 'low level offending'.[174] Food-borne illness is unlikely to be seen as a low-level offence. A caution may deter individual food businesses from breaching food law in future,[175] but it is likely that improvement notices (see section II.C.i. below) will be seen as more appropriate.

Cautions themselves have no statutory basis.[176] The formal basis for the power of local authorities to administer them is found in section 111 of the Local Government Act 1972. This provides that 'a local authority shall have power to do any thing ... which is calculated to facilitate, or is conducive or incidental to, the discharge of any of their functions'. As local authorities are empowered to enforce food safety norms, the issue of cautions is incidental to this function.

A caution may only be issued where the offender has made a 'clear and reliable admission of the offence'.[177] A caution cannot be imposed; it must be accepted by the food business. The Food Law Code provides that cautions should be used in accordance with appropriate Ministry of Justice guidance.[178]

C. The Power to Advise

A third type of power is available to EHOs and other network participants. Environmental Health Officers have powers that facilitate the provision of advice to food businesses. Advisory powers are generally used after the incident of food-borne illness is controlled, and look to the future, rather than at a particular incident. They may be focused on breaches that are responsible for an incident of food-borne illness, but alternatively may focus on weaknesses identified during an investigation that have no connection with the incident. Advice may even be given to businesses unconnected with the incident that are initially implicated and then discounted. Advisory powers are not, therefore, either control powers or enforcement powers, although formal advice powers may perform a weak enforcement function by recording a regulatory breach in need of remedy.[179] Advice to businesses does not function to control an incident of food-borne illness due to the future focus and the time-lag from advice to implementation, but advice may be given to third parties in an attempt to separate infected from uninfected.

174 Ministry of Justice, *Simple Cautions for Adult Offenders* (MOJ 2014) 4.

175 Ibid, para 5.

176 Roger Evans, 'Challenging a Police Caution Using Judicial Review' [1996] *Crim LR* 104, 104.

177 Ministry of Justice, above n 171, para 43 and 59–62.

178 Food Law Code, para 3.1.10; Ministry of Justice, above n 171.

179 The possibility of formal or informal advice will be taken into account when considering whether prosecution is the most appropriate enforcement response (Food Law Code, para 3.1.10).

Whilst advice is seen as central to the role of enforcement officers on a day-to-day basis, and is particularly important in ensuring future regulatory compliance by businesses, it is not a central concern of EHOs when investigating food-borne illness. The need to advise businesses and improve future compliance is a side-effect of the investigation into the incident of food-borne illness, which focuses on control and enforcement. The positive effect of identifying areas where businesses need advice is a tertiary benefit of the investigation. The need to give advice does not, therefore, determine the investigatory steps taken by EHOs. Information upon which advice is based is produced by fact-finding actions taken for reasons of control and enforcement. However, it is necessary to consider improvement notices briefly, as they frequently appear in the cases examined, as EHOs attempt to ensure that an incident of food-borne illness will not be repeated in the future.

i. Improvement Notices

Businesses that are in breach of food hygiene requirements may be issued with an Improvement Notice or a Hygiene Improvement Notice (HIN).[180] Environmental Health Officers may issue such notices without resorting to the courts. Improvement notices may be issued when an EHO has 'reasonable grounds for believing that [a business] is failing to comply' with regulatory requirements.[181] Belief requires a 'more positive frame of mind'[182] than mere suspicion.[183] Applying this test, the EHO must have information that suggests that the business was 'failing to comply' with food safety norms as the only reasonable conclusion. The use of this test may prove to be an impediment to the issue of notices in cases where there is uncertainty over the factual circumstances.

Improvement notices set out the breaches and specify the steps the business must take to comply with regulatory requirements.[184] An EHO has wide discretion to determine these steps, but may only require compliance with the law. A notice must not require gold-plating with best practice. A time period for compliance must be specified. The period must be a minimum of 14 days. Failure to comply is an offence.

[180] Food Safety Act 1990, s 10; Food Safety and Hygiene (England) Regulations 2013, reg 6.

[181] Food Safety and Hygiene (England) Regulations 2013, reg 6(1).

[182] *R (Errington) v Metropolitan Police Authority* [2006] EWHC 1155 (Admin) [27], citing *R v Moys* (1986) 79 Cr App R 72.

[183] Claire Andrews, *The Enforcement of Regulatory Offences* (Sweet & Maxwell 1998) 70, argues that 'reasonable grounds for believing' should be construed with the aid of cases concerning the handling of stolen goods.

[184] Food Safety Act 1990, s 10(1)(b) and (c); Food Safety and Hygiene (England) Regulations 2013, reg 6(1)(b) and (c). A notice must be sufficiently clear to 'enable the recipient to know what is wrong and why it is wrong ... The requirement is that the notice should be clear and easily understood' (see Evans LJ in *The Borough of Bexley v Gardner Merchant Plc* (CA, 17 March 1993), cited in *BT Fleet Limited v McKenna* [2005] EWHC 387 (Admin) [14].)

Issuing an improvement notice does not preclude the enforcement authority from taking other formal action. In a situation of illness it may be appropriate to use an improvement notice alongside prohibition. Prosecution alongside an improvement notice may be appropriate where the breach of food safety law is 'serious'.[185] Where prohibition is not used, the improvement notice does not function as a control mechanism, as the business is able to continue preparing and supplying food until the period set out in the notice has expired.

Improvement notices are seen as having a 'problem solving character',[186] and should be used for dealing with breaches that are more 'specific and precise' than those dealt with by prosecution.[187] Improvement notices can be tailored to particular food business situations and actually get to the root of a food safety breach. They play an important role in explaining legal obligations to food businesses, and encouraging and enabling them to comply.

The Food Law Code provides that a HIN may be issued only when it is 'reasonable, proportionate, risk-based and consistent with good practice' to do so.[188] In particular, improvement notices should not be used where a letter of advice is (equally) likely to secure compliance within a reasonable time.[189] Neither a letter, nor an improvement notice is likely to achieve the desired result sufficiently quickly to, so each is likely to be used only once an illness is under control. Given the public health consequences of an incident of food-borne illness, a HIN is likely to be more appropriate than a letter of advice.[190]

III. CONCLUSION: THE POWERS OF THE NETWORK

During the investigation of food-borne illness it is likely that many regulatory breaches will be discovered. These are enforced through strict liability offences, which are much criticised and viewed, it is argued incorrectly, as easy to prove. The most important requirements are found in Food Safety and Hygiene (England) Regulations 2013 in England and the General Food Regulations 2004 and the Food Hygiene (Wales) Regulations 2006 or Food Hygiene (Scotland) Regulations 2006 in Wales and Scotland.

Environmental Health Officers have a number of formal and informal powers that they may use. These powers may be divided into control powers, enforcement powers and advisory powers. During an incident EHOs

185 Food Standards Agency, above n 92, para 3.2.2.
186 Hawkins, above n 115, 171.
187 Ibid.
188 Food Law Code, para 3.1.3.
189 Food Standards Agency, above n 92, para 3.2.2.
190 Ibid, 53, para 3.2.2.1.

use control powers to prevent further primary and secondary spread of food-borne illness. The powers allow them to control products, premises, processes, people and environments. Once the incident is controlled, they may use enforcement powers to sanction those responsible for the regulatory breach that caused the incident.

In order to use these powers, and to determine whether regulatory requirements have been complied with or breached, it is necessary for EHOs to assemble information. Control action cannot take place without information that identifies the products, places or people in need of control. Enforcement action cannot take place without evidence that is both available and admissible, and which demonstrates a realistic prospect of conviction for breaching regulatory requirements. The task of assembling information forms the core of the response to an incident of food-borne illness, and it is to this task that the next chapter turns.

4

The Investigation of Incidents of Food-borne Illness

THE REGULATORY NETWORK responsible for the control of food-borne illness must obtain information. This information forms the basis of decisions about what action should be taken to control the spread of the food-borne illness (chapter five), and whether the available and admissible evidence demonstrates that the regulatory requirements have been breached to a standard sufficient to justify taking enforcement action (chapter six).

The information necessary to make decisions about control and enforcement actions is usually obtained in two ways. First, a source may contact an authority to alert it to an incident. This will furnish the authority with some relevant information about the incident. Secondly, once notified, the authority will commence an investigation into the incident. The investigation will involve the collection of information in a variety of ways from a variety of sources. Such investigations will generally produce the bulk of information on which control and enforcement decisions are made.

I. NOTIFICATION

Authorities learn about incidents of food-borne illness from a number of different sources (PEN/DD/MCC.00003). Notification may come via communication from consumers, information from medical professionals, self-reporting or from another body.

In the files examined, communication from consumers was the most common form of notification.[1] Environmental Health Officers see it as a central function to 'respond to reports from members of the public ... [that] draw ... attention to suspected cases of food poisoning or other suspicious illnesses'

[1] Public health professionals have argued that over-reliance on public reporting may lead to under-reporting of cases of food-borne illness: see L Llewellyn, M Burtonwood and A Mukerjee, 'Non-notification of Food Poisoning—Whose Fault' (1995) 16 *Journal of Public Health Medicine* 368.

(PEN/DD/MCC.00004).[2] In a large outbreak, publicity may increase public reporting.[3]

Local authorities may be informed by medical professionals who are aware that one of their patients has a food-borne illness.[4] Medical professionals will see patients suffering from cases of food-borne illness, and EHOs are 'dependent upon ... medical professionals, whether GPs [or] A & E ... to alert [them] to instances of infectious diseases' (PEN/DD/MCC.00003). Such notification often comes directly from front-line doctors.[5] Notifications from medical practitioners are formally required to be given in writing, but in the Authority A and public files, oral notification is common (EHO-B1; PEN/DD/MCC.00004; Bradford *Salmonella*;[6] Lemon and Coriander Chicken Wrap),[7] and is now required in urgent cases by regulation 2(4) of the Health Protection (Notification) Regulations 2010.[8]

Public Health doctors employed by Public Health England, Public Health Wales or similar bodies in Scotland and Northern Ireland will notify local authorities where surveillance identifies a possible incident of food-borne illness (Cadbury *Salmonella*;[9] A/I/10). This is particularly the case where there is a spike in a specific type of illness within a local authority area. They are also responsible for notifying EHOs about incidents of food-borne illness connected to hospitals (B/I/1; Belfast *Listeria*).[10] This notification will

[2] 'In my experience, in most of the outbreaks it is the people who become ill that will contact us before anyone else does' (EHO-A2). See also EHO-A3; EHO-C1; A/I/11; A/I/20; A/I/21; A/I/25; Aberdeen Charlatans (Outbreak Control Team, *Outbreak of Norovirus Infection amongst Guests attending a Concert at the Music Hall Aberdeen May 2004* (OCT 2004)). Publicity around an incident increases public notifications.

[3] Health Protection Agency, *Foodborne illness at The Fat Duck restaurant: Report of an investigation of a foodborne outbreak of Norovirus among diners at The Fat Duck restaurant, Bray, Berkshire in January and February 2009* (HPA 2009) (hereinafter 'Fat Duck').

[4] 'The statutory notification of infectious diseases has been a crucial health protection measure in this country since the late 19th century' (Department of Health, *Health Protection Legislation (England) Guidance* 2010 *(Department of Health 2010)* 12).

[5] Doctors are under an obligation to notify the proper officer of a local authority when they have reasonable grounds for suspecting that a patient has a notifiable disease under the Health Protection (Notification) Regulations 2010, SI 2010/659. Some research has suggested that notification is incomplete, and not all cases that fall within the notification obligation are reported to proper officers (Stephen P Barrett and YK Lau, 'Incompleteness of statutory notification of bacterial gastro-intestinal infection' (1997) 111 *Public Health* 183, 184.)

[6] David Clapham, Angela Brindle and Jim Aveyard, 'Food Outbreak Response' in *Environmental Health Practitioner* (31 March 2006), available at <http://www.cieh.org/ehp/food_outbreak_response.html>.

[7] Qutub Syed, *Outbreak Report: National Outbreak of Vero cytotoxin-producing Escherichia coli O157 infection associated with lemon and coriander chicken wraps in England & Wales June–July 2007* (Health Protection Agency 2007).

[8] See Health Protection (Notification) Regulations 2010, reg 2(4) and Department of Health, above n 4, 26.

[9] Outbreak Control Team, 'National Increase in *Salmonella Montevideo* infections, England and Wales: March to July 2006' (2006) 16 (29) *CDR Weekly* (hereinafter 'Cadbury *Salmonella*').

[10] Outbreak Control Team, *The report of the Outbreak Control Team of the investigation of an outbreak of listeriosis in the Belfast Health and Social Care Trust during May to November 2008* (OCT 2009) (hereinafter 'Belfast *Listeria*').

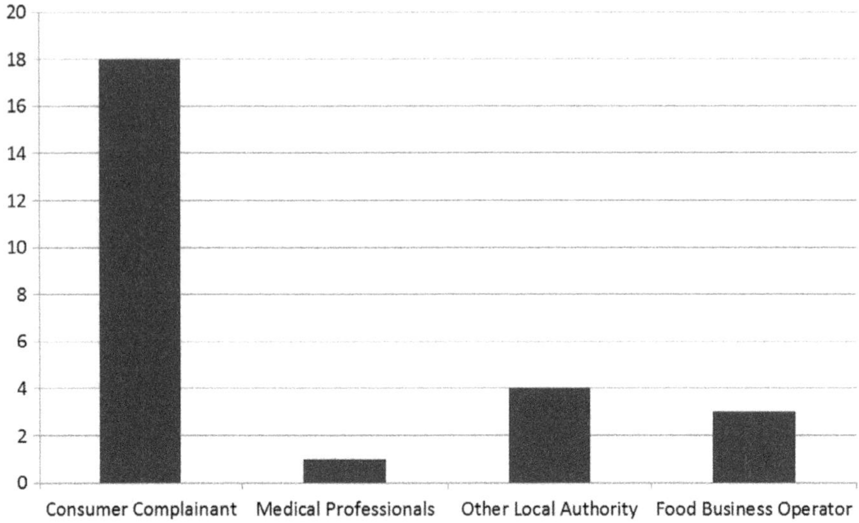

Figure 4.1: Sources of initial notification of the Local Authority A sample

contain information about the illness and a profile of those infected. The notification may set out suspected sources (as the Health Protection Agency may have conducted epidemiological interviews), or the task of identifying potential sources may be assigned to EHOs.

A business may self-report to the local authority information that indicates consumers are suffering from food-borne illness (A/I/6; A/I/12; Marathon Oil;[11] *Norovirus* in Oysters[12]).[13] Further, EHOs in one local authority may be informed by a colleague in the Food Standards Agency (eg through a FAFA) (PEN/JW) or another local authority. This notification may be formal (PEN/HL; A/I/24; A/I/17) or informal (PEN/EJD). An authority may also request assistance from another authority, for example with the collection of samples (PEN/HL; PEN/PP). The authority that provides information may have been notified by a consumer, a medical professional or a public health authority. Figure 4.1 sets out the sources of initial notification of the Local Authority A sample.

[11] Outbreak Control Team, *Outbreak of Norovirus Infection at Marathon Oil UK, Aberdeen March 2008* (OCT 2008)

[12] Baker K, *et al*, 'An outbreak of norovirus infection linked to oyster consumption at a UK restaurant, February 2010' (2011) 33 *J Public Health-UK* 205 (hereinafter *Norovirus* in Oysters)

[13] This is particularly likely where they have a continuing relationship with their customers: 'places like care homes tend to be a lot more open because the nature of their business. The relationship between care homes and their residents is slightly different to the relationship between restaurants and their customers' (EHO-A1). Similarly, where employees become ill in staff canteens, the employer is more likely to report the incident.

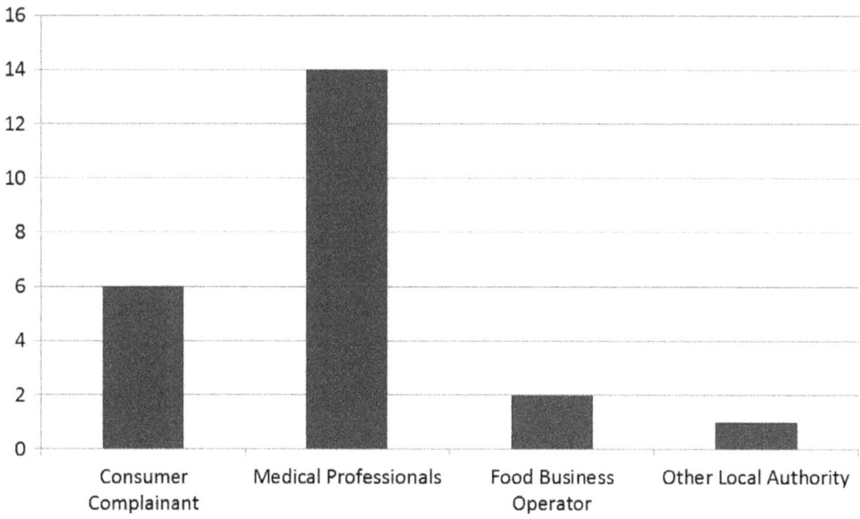

Figure 4.2: Notification in the public sample

The data presented in Figure 4.2 may not sufficiently represent the role of medical professionals in reporting food-borne illness to local authorities. Case A/I/17, classified as a referral from another local authority, was initially reported to the notifying local authority by the Health Protection Agency. Local Authority B was notified of B/I/1 by medical professionals. In 13 of the public cases, initial notification was received from medical professionals. Figure 4.2 sets out the sources of notification in the public sample.

Further, a number of the consumer complaints in the Authority A sample were prompted by medical professionals, who advised consumers to contact their local authority. This contact was often recommended following receipt of the results of faecal analysis, which disclosed that the individual was suffering from a food-borne illness. Medically prompted complaints appear particularly in cases where a consumer was suffering from bacterial food-borne illness, and in particular *campylobacter* (A/I/2; A/I/24).

For example, in A/I/2 the complainant contacted Local Authority A after he had attended his doctor's surgery with diarrhoea and vomiting, had a sample taken and received the results of analysis of the sample. These results disclosed that he was suffering from *campylobacter*. At this point, on the recommendation of his doctor, he contacted the local authority to inform it of his illness. Similarly, in A/I/24 the complainant contacted her local authority after she had been told by her doctor that she had *campylobacter*. The doctor had advised her to contact the local environmental health department. Her local authority, after preliminary investigation, then referred the matter to Local Authority A.

The pathways by which authorities are informed may work in tandem. 'It is quite usual … to receive both local sources of information and formal notification [from the medical profession] at much the same time regarding individual cases' (PEN/DD/MCC.00004). Multiple actors enrol into the regulatory network and provide information necessary to begin an investigation into the incident of food-borne illness.

Whilst a notification is necessary to begin the process of responding to an incident of food-borne illness, and the information provided may prove useful (and indeed necessary), this information is unlikely to be sufficient to make informed decisions about appropriate control and enforcement actions (although initial control actions may be taken, such as advising a notifying individual not to attend work until free of symptoms for 48 hours). The rest of this chapter focuses on the investigation performed by the authority to obtain information that will influence actions taken during and following the incident. The shape of the investigation is dictated by the content and timing of the notification. Depending on the information transmitted to the authority, some of the steps detailed below need not be taken, particularly if information necessary for decision making is already in the possession of the authority. Depending when the authority is notified, a regulator may decide not to take some investigative steps, as these would be unlikely to produce useful information.

II. INVESTIGATION OF INCIDENTS OF FOOD-BORNE ILLNESS

Once notified of an incident of food-borne illness, local authorities will commence an investigation into the people, food products and premises implicated in the incident.[14] The shape of this investigation will depend on what EHOs know about the incident. However, in all cases investigation is 'a matter of assembling really as much … useful information [as possible] at an early stage'.[15]

Generally, an EHO will be assigned to lead the investigative team. Decisions about the investigative steps may be decided in consultation with others in the regulatory network, in particular the CCDC and other medical professionals (CCDC2). Where an outbreak is formally declared, the OCT will take the lead in determining necessary investigative steps, coordinating the actions of the regulatory network. These decisions will be influenced by the needs of control, rather than enforcement, as an OCT has no formal enforcement role.

[14] EHO-A1; EHO-A2; EHO-B1; CCDC1. EHO-C1 noted 'if we get any outbreak sort of scenario, we investigate'.

[15] PEN/RS/LIVE-10-3-pg6line23.

The investigation will aim to produce information sufficient to draw conclusions about the outbreak and to inform control or enforcement action. It seeks to obtain necessary data so that action can be taken targeting both the source and carriers of the illness. The investigation must enable EHOs to rule out both false positives (things that look like something but are not) and false negatives (things which do not look like something but are) for sources and carriers, so that control and/or enforcement action is/are not taken unnecessarily. It aims to provide 'a plausible framework [of] how all these things would have—could have happened' (PEN/RS/LIVE-10-3-pg40line18). The goal of the investigation is 'to identify the source of an outbreak and [prevent] its further spread' (PEN/RS/LIVE-10-3-pg3line23). Information obtained is distributed to those involved in control and enforcement decision making, and may lead to further investigative steps.

Investigations tend to have three strands:

(a) epidemiological investigations;
(b) microbiological investigations; and
(c) environmental investigations (BAR-1).

A combination of information in each of these three areas is necessary to become informed about an incident of food-borne illness. Different network participants may be involved in each of these strands. Once informed about sources and carriers, the regulatory network can make decisions about necessary control and/or enforcement action(s).

III. EPIDEMIOLOGICAL INVESTIGATIONS

Epidemiological investigations focus on the spread of a particular food-borne illness, and examine the source and cause of such illness. Epidemiology is the process of identifying sources of food-borne illness and exposing the need to control them. Only as a secondary function might it expose those responsible for an incident through regulatory non-compliance. Epidemiological investigations examine information gained both from individuals who have been affected by the illness (cases) and individuals who have not been affected (controls). Epidemiological investigation is, at heart, 'a systematic investigation into commonalities between all cases' (PEN/HL/SWP.00262) and, conversely, the differences between 'cases' and 'controls'. By comparing the exposures of cases and controls to different potential sources of illness, it is possible to determine which potential source is likely to be the actual source of the illness (and therefore in need of control).

Potential sources include not only food and drink, but also exposure to animals and their faecal matter; to swimming pools and jacuzzis; and to potential person-to-person spread. Information about exposure to these potential sources is needed by those investigating food-borne illness, and therefore these potential sources are included in the standard list of exposures put to individuals suffering from suspected food-borne illness. The questions asked may be modified during an incident to focus on likely sources of a particular illness. In the investigation into the South Wales *E. Coli* O157 outbreak, information was obtained in the following way:

> [V]isits were made to all the known victims of the outbreak who fitted the case definition. There is a specific protocol for the investigation of cases of *E. coli* and this was used as the framework for the investigation and questioning of each case. This protocol specifies a questionnaire,[16] which should be used to investigate individual cases of illness. Issues such as food history, travel history and family details would be considered as part of this process. (PEN/HL/SWP.00263)

In these interviews,

> the practice is to ask about and document basic details about the person and their household. In addition details of the illness are collected noting in particular the date of onset of symptoms as well as details of potentially relevant 'exposures;' that is foods or activities that could potentially put someone at risk of verotoxin producing Escherichia coli O157 infection. (PEN/RS/NPH.00833)

Before epidemiological information can be obtained, cases and controls to whom these questions will be asked must be identified.

A. Identifying Cases and Controls

The first step in an epidemiological investigation is for EHOs to obtain names and contact details for 'cases' and 'controls'. For example, a list of attendees at an event may be obtained, or a list of reservations from a restaurant. Despite the important role played by this information in epidemiological analysis, the actions of EHOs in obtaining identity information are framed in terms of control, as preventing secondary spread requires EHOs to be aware of primary cases (A/I/5). The positive benefits to enforcement of high quality epidemiology are seen as a secondary benefit.

i. Case Definition

Having a case definition means that EHOs can decide whether a person is a 'case' or 'control'. If a person falls within the definition, he or she will be identified as a 'case'. Information must be obtained from these individuals. If they fall outside the definition they treated as 'controls' not infected by the food-borne illness being investigated, and therefore as less likely to have been exposed to the source of the illness. Obtaining information from them

[16] The questionnaire(s) can be found at PEN/EJD/BCC.02375 and PEN/EJD/BCC.02378.

is not a priority, as they will not need control,[17] and data supplied by them are unlikely to pinpoint the source of illness, except by elimination. Whilst the exposures of 'controls' may be compared to 'cases', this is not the priority of EHOs. A case definition attempts to 'bring some structure to the people that you take an interest in' (PEN/RS/LIVE-10-3-pg7line21).

In the majority of cases examined, a case definition was formulated by the EHO leading the investigation and control of the incident (A/I/5), with assistance from the CCDC if necessary (CCDC2). In general, the smaller the incident, in terms of geographical scope and number affected, the more informal the definition.[18] When an 'outbreak' is formally declared, the case definition is an important item on the agenda for decision at the initial meeting of the OCT (PEN/GL/NPH.00850).

Where a single EHO is responsible for investigation, he or she may mentally operate a consistent case definition without a formal written definition being adopted. In large-scale incidents, a formal definition operates to ensure consistency in identifying cases across multiple network actors. Once adopted, a definition may be amended on the basis of the continuing investigation.[19]

The definition adopted influences investigative decisions taken by EHOs. They use the definition to decide from whom to collect information. They also use this definition to determine whether to take control action. If a person is a 'case', according to the definition, the risk of secondary spread will be assessed and necessary measures taken to prevent it.

Where an incident is accompanied by publicity, a large number of potential 'cases' will self-report to a local authority (EHO-A3; EHO-B1; Fat Duck), seeking to enrol into the regulatory network. The case definition is used to distinguish those providing useful information from those who do not. A person with symptoms that do not fall within the definition may legitimately be left unpursued. If outside the definition, a person is unlikely to be connected to the incident, and the information provided is unlikely to contribute positively to control and enforcement. Information supplied by those outside the case definition may nevertheless contribute negatively by allowing sources to be ruled out. If a case definition is too wide, irrelevant data will be collected and considered, resources will be expended collecting these data, and unnecessary control action may be taken; if it is too narrow, those making control and enforcement decisions may be deprived of valuable information, so that necessary control action is not taken and data that would be obtained are not available for formal enforcement action.

[17] The movements of those who fall within a case definition may need to be controlled in order to prevent secondary spread.

[18] In smaller cases, a definition may be adopted that limits cases of interest to those within a single dining party (A/I/14).

[19] Lemon and Coriander Chicken Wrap, above n 7, 8.

In South Wales the initial definition was too wide, and irrelevance drowned out relevant 'cases'. Therefore, the definition was amended, from 'individuals suffering from diarrhoea' to 'individuals suffering from *bloody* diarrhoea'. This was intended to reduce false positive notifications within the 'cases' classification, as individuals suffering from diarrhoea as a result of, for example, Irritable Bowel Syndrome, were caught in the initial definition (PEN/PP/RCC.00329). After the definitional change, individuals who fell outside the new definition, but who would have fallen within the initial definition, were not questioned on exposures, not factored into epidemiological analyses as cases and not controlled to prevent the (non-existent) risk of secondary spread.

The case definition is generally based on the symptoms of a typical 'case', often the first case, linked to the incident.[20] Geographical, temporal or consumption-based limits may be placed on the case definition. For example, if an incident is confined to a geographic area, the case definition may include only people potentially exposed within that area. Narrowing the definition through these additional factors increases the quality of information available, allowing EHOs to draw better conclusions for the purposes of control and enforcement.

The following are examples of case definitions utilised in two of the public cases:

South Wales

This case definition was agreed as probable cases being persons resident within South Wales with bloody diarrhoea within the last 14 days and the confirmed case would be a microbiologically confirmed probable case. (PEN/AP/SWP.00489)

Fat Duck

Case: An individual reporting at least two of the following symptoms not more than seven days after eating at The Fat Duck restaurant: a. Nausea b. Vomiting c. Diarrhoea or loose stool.[21]

In some circumstances, microbiological tests will supersede the case definition and assist in determining whether a 'case' should be included in the analysis of data gained during the investigation. Whilst individuals will not be removed from the analysis in the event that a stool sample fails to confirm they are suffering from the same illness (as faecal samples may not always find microbiological evidence, for reasons discussed below),[22] they

[20] Often the 'case' who initially notifies.

[21] Fat Duck, above n 3, 7.

[22] The Merthyr *Cryptosporidium* OCT Report notes that 'an individual may be classified as a probable case for more than one reason, for instance: An individual reporting a history of symptoms may have recovered before being interviewed by officers, and a stool sample may not have been requested or provided. Standard laboratory tests used to identify *Cryptosporidium* from stool samples are not 100% sensitive. Occasionally, the test may fail to detect *Cryptosporidium* in a sample especially if the parasite is present in low numbers. Therefore

may be removed if analysis shows they are suffering from an unconnected illness that exhibits the same symptoms, as data collected will likely confound analysis. Microbiological tests may also be combined with any epidemiological information supplied to assist in deciding whether control is necessary (or continues to be necessary). Epidemiological information, such as reported symptoms, may lead to controls being imposed on a person; the results of microbiological tests may lead to a relaxation of control if no micro-organisms are detected, or further controls may be put in place if a 'case' is microbiologically confirmed.

ii. Snowballing from Consumers

Environmental Health Officers may obtain details of 'cases' from other individuals suffering from the food-borne illness. A consumer-complainant may have details of other individuals affected, and may be willing to supply these details to the local authority so that the EHO can contact them.[23] The process then repeats itself, with each consumer being contacted by EHOs and asked whether he or she is aware of other cases, until saturation point is reached and no new 'cases' are identified by those contacted. This is often the quickest way to identify potential cases so that relevant control can take place.

For example, in A/I/16 the complainant was able to identify cases and controls. Six individuals had eaten a meal together at Food Business K; four had subsequently become ill and two had not suffered any symptoms. The consumer-complainant was able to provide names, addresses and contact details for all those who ate the meal, and EHO-A4 was able to contact all these individuals to obtain epidemiological information.

In A/I/18 the complainant became ill, along with three others, after eating at Food Business H with four colleagues. The complainant provided contact details for three group members. Group members were contacted by EHO-A3 to obtain epidemiological information. Another member of the group was able to provide contact details for the final group member.

Alternatively, the consumer may be unwilling to provide names to the EHO. In such a case, the consumer may contact others and encourage them to contact the EHO.[24] This is more common in situations where the function is more formal in nature, such as a meal following a business meeting.

occasionally a negative test result may be obtained for someone who does indeed have *Cryptosporidium* infection' (Outbreak Control Team, *Outbreak of Cryptosporidium Infection in a swimming pool complex in Merthyr Tydfil South Wales Summer 2009* (OCT 2010) (hereinafter 'Merthyr *Cryptosporidium*')).

[23] Eg A/I/14.
[24] Eg A/I/3.

In A/I/3 seven work colleagues went out for a meal. Five became ill. The complainant was unwilling to provide the names of the dining party, citing 'data protection', but agreed to provide EHO-A3's details to other group members and ask them to contact him. This course of action was agreed to by EHO-A3 as it appeared to offer the quickest way of obtaining information, and therefore offered the quickest route to putting in place necessary control. This expedient does not guarantee full information, though. Some members of the party might resist the encouragement of the complainant, and might not contact the EHO. Therefore EHOs prefer complainants to provide as much detail as possible (EHO-A3). However, EHOs will utilise this route to enrol consumers into the network, where it swiftly allows information to be obtained, despite its non-ideal nature.

iii. Utilising the Business

A second method of identifying affected persons is by contacting a business implicated in an incident of food-borne illness. Businesses may retain contact details of individuals who complain about safety issues, and may therefore be able to provide details of affected individuals to the local authority.

In A/I/20, the food business provided details of individuals who complained about food eaten at its restaurant, and EHO-A5 contacted the individuals affected. In A/I/9, EHO-A2 and EHO-A6 visited a food business following a notification. The manager identified four additional parties who complained about illness following meals taken at the same time as the initial complainant. E-mail addresses were provided to EHO-A2, and he was able to contact the parties identified in order to obtain information necessary to progress the investigation. Lists of parties who have made bookings may be used to trace potential cases (Merthyr *Cryptosporidium*).

If the incident of food-borne illness is linked to a food business with a regular, defined population, such as a nursery,[25] school[26] or nursing home,[27] the food business should readily be able to supply a list of potentially affected persons by providing access to a register or similar.[28] Such businesses will have access to contact details for potential cases, or, in the case of children, their parents or guardians. For residential care homes, the 'case' will, of course, be contacted at that care home. Contact will be made once details have been obtained (EHO-A1; EHO-B1).

In A/I/5 the nursery concerned provided a list of all the children who had attended, contact details and details of the days on which they had

[25] Eg, A/I/5.

[26] Eg Feltham Hill Infants (Overview and Scrutiny Committee, *Report of the Scrutiny Review of the E. Coli O157 Outbreak at Feltham Hill Infant and Nursery School* (London Borough of Hounslow 2010)).

[27] Eg, A/I/12.

[28] Eg, PEN/PP/RCC.00322.

attended. A list of children who had been absent through illness was provided separately to the EHO. The parents or guardians of the ill children were contacted first, as absence is a possible indication of food-borne illness. Environmental Health Officers therefore managed their resources to investigate the most likely ill individuals first, in particular those that might require urgent control measures. Obtaining similar lists formed an important part of the South Wales investigation.

Obtaining information from a business may require delicate negotiations. In the *Norovirus* in Oysters case:

> Restaurant records identified approximately 300 diners who ate at the restaurant over the weekend period from 5 to 7 February 2010. The restaurant management agreed to provide contact details of diners in parties which included at least one person who consumed oysters, however they declined to provide further information on other parties.[29]

Here, the local authority balanced the continued cooperation of the food business, which was prepared to disclose details of those most likely to be affected, with the need to contact all people who had eaten at the restaurant to rule out other causes. The EHO made the choice that obtaining the information should be prioritised, as urgent control measures could have been necessary. The information that the business agreed to provide identified those most likely to cause secondary spread. Therefore, the disclosure proposed was agreed, despite the information's presenting an incomplete picture.

By choosing to take the information in the form presented by the food business, the EHO preserved the working relationship, which might assist later in the investigation or in future dealings with the food business. The need to obtain information quickly to enable control militates against complex, lengthy negotiation, and accepting any disclosure by the business is 'better than nothing'. Environmental Health Officers appear to operate with an acceptance of limitations on their ability to obtain the maximum amount of information, and instead operate in accordance with non-ideal conditions to achieve their goal—controlling the spread of food-borne illness.

iv. Utilising the Event Organiser

Affected individuals may be identified through information possessed by the organiser of an event. This is an important source of information where the incident appears linked to a particular function or event, such as a conference or wedding. Organisers of these events will have a guest list. This list allows the EHO to contact potentially affected individuals and obtain

[29] Kezia Baker *et al*, 'An outbreak of norovirus infection linked to oyster consumption at a UK restaurant, February 2010' (2011) 33 *Journal of Public Health* 205.

information necessary to progress the investigation. In some cases organisers are willing to provide a list of attendees.[30]

However, in other cases organisers may be less willing. There are two reasons for this. The first is embarrassment (EHO-A1). Organisers of an event may blame themselves for an incident of food-borne illness, and do not want to add to the inconvenience of the guests by allowing them to be contacted by the local authority.

The second reason is confidentiality. In A/I/2, Business Z, the organiser of the event, declined to provide a list of the individuals who attended, citing the Data Protection Act 1998. Further, Business Z expressed concern about the commercial confidentiality of the list, as invitees included a number of 'target clients'. The EHO (EHO-A3) considered the possibility of using Business Z to ask the invitees to contact the enforcement authority, but this was rejected. Two hundred and fifty individuals from across the UK and beyond attended the event. In consultation with CCDC1 and EHO-A1, EHO-A3 considered that the information-gathering process would only be effective if he had details of all the attendees and could contact them. Here, the non-ideal situation contemplated was not seen as a legitimate method of achieving the aims of the investigation, as an incomplete list of guests would pose a high risk of uncontrolled secondary spread, and might not allow the primary source to be identified. Therefore, Local Authority A used its power under the Public Health (Control of Disease) Act 1984 to compel Business Z to provide information about the guests who attended the event.[31] The imperative of control here outweighed the desire of EHO-A3 to retain an informal and cooperative relationship with the business.

v. Identification by Medical Professionals

Medical professionals may be well placed to identify cases that are linked to an on-going incident. Professionals dealing with an incident will contact doctors, enrolling them into the network and asking them to report any cases consistent with the case definition (CCDC2). If individuals attend doctors' surgeries reporting symptoms that match the case definition, investigators will become aware of it, and will commence investigations into food

[30] A/I/15; New Deer Scout Camp (Outbreak Control Team, *The Outbreak of E. Coli O157 at New Deer Millennium Scout Camp May/June 2000* (OCT 2000)).

[31] The Public Health (Control of Disease) Act 1984, s18 (now repealed) provided: 'On the application of the proper officer of the local authority for any district, the occupier of any premises in the district in which there is or has been any person suffering from … food poisoning shall furnish such information within his knowledge as that officer may reasonably require for the purpose of enabling measures to be taken to prevent the spread of the disease or, as the case may be, to trace the source of food poisoning.' Failure to comply with a notice issued under s 18 was an offence. This section has been replaced by s 45I, which allows a magistrate to order disclosure.

history. This allows investigators to obtain information about cases that are not identified by the means examined above. In particular, cases infected by secondary spread often cannot be identified by consumers, businesses or organisers. Unless these cases self-report, they are often not brought to EHOs' attention, and further spread is possible as control cannot be put in place. Therefore, enrolment of medical professionals to report such cases is necessary to achieve control.

B. Questioning Affected Persons

Once potential 'cases' are identified, EHOs will contact these individuals to 'obtain a detailed history of the illness and of possible sources of the infection, in order to identify factors which are common to some or all cases'.[32] This must often be done quickly so that necessary control measures can be put in place and spread of the disease prevented as soon as possible. The need to control, and therefore the need for information, was so urgent in South Wales that, on a Friday evening following the first OCT meeting, it was agreed that EHOs should proceed 'immediately ... to collect information from the hospital cases' (PEN/GL/NPH.00875). The speed required when collecting information means that the information is not initially collected in the form of witness statements, although those giving the information are asked to sign any forms that are completed and any notes taken by the EHO.

Environmental Health Officers complete a prepared questionnaire, the goal of which is to 'obtain a detailed movement history and food consumption history of the [case], [and] also to attempt to locate the source of the [food-borne illness]' (PEN/HL/SWP.00264). Questions usually focus on four areas:

(a) personal information about the case;
(b) the illness, and in particular the symptoms and onset;
(c) food histories, seeking to identify what a person ate and where it was eaten during the possible incubation of an illness; and
(d) the individual's exposure to other possible sources of illness.[33]

The questions are tailored according to the initial information obtained. If the organism is known, questions will be asked that concentrate on likely exposures.[34]

[32] Food Standards Agency, *Management of outbreaks of foodborne illness in England and Wales* (Food Standards Agency 2008) para 5.7.
[33] PEN/AP/SWP.00489; PEN/RS/NPH.00833; Merthyr *Cryptosporidium* 9.
[34] PEN/RS/LIVE-10-3-pg6line19.

In some cases the affected person will be unable to respond to questions asked by enforcement officers. This may be because he or she is a child; is suffering from a condition that means he or she is unable to respond to the questions (such as Alzheimer's) (EHO-A3; PEN/PP/RCC.00322); is unable to answer the questions due to incapacitation by the food-borne illness; or is dead. In these cases, enforcement officers will attempt to obtain information from others familiar with the individual. Even if the incapacitation is temporary, EHOs will not wait until the affected person is able to answer questions, due to the urgent need to obtain information in order to facilitate control. In the case of a child, an EHO may ask a parent or guardian to provide the information, either by filling in a questionnaire or by answering questions orally.[35] However, this often does not produce the detail necessary to draw conclusions about the source of the illness. Whilst some information is better than none (EHO-A3), EHOs take steps to enhance the level of information available, and therefore secondary documentation, such as menus or records held by schools or nurseries, may also be used to provide the detail required. Similarly, for non-child 'cases' who are unable to answer questions, information will be collected by questioning partners, friends or carers. Nursing homes and hospitals often retain records of food eaten by residents, and this can be used to draw up food histories of those who are unable to recall the history themselves (EHO-A3).

i. Information about the Case/Control

Information about the identity of the 'case' and demographic details relating to that person will be the initial details gathered in an investigation. Such details are necessary for both control and epidemiological reasons. By obtaining such information, EHOs can select 'controls' that closely match the attributes of the ill person, and control statistically for demographic characteristics. This minimises the risk that factors other than those explored in the epidemiological questioning will be responsible for the food-borne illness. For example, if the 'case' is a child who attends a particular school, an asymptomatic child of the same age who attends the same school will be selected as a control (South Wales).

However, EHOs focus much more on the possibility of controlling secondary spread as the rationale for obtaining personal data. Details of potential exposures to environments where there is a high risk of secondary transmission are necessary (EHO-A3). If a person who is, or has recently been, symptomatic works in a high-risk occupation, such as in a kitchen, then the EHO will take action to ensure that that person refrains from working until tested, to ensure that he or she is not shedding food-borne illness organisms.

[35] See A/I/6; PEN/CE/SWP.01061; PEN/CE/SWP.01064; PEN/PP/RCC.00323; PEN/PP/SWP.00313; PEN/PP/SWP.00316; PEN/PP/SWP.00319; PEN/HL/SWP.00264.

This is initially an informal request, but if the request does not succeed, the EHO may apply to exclude the person from work formally under the Public Health (Control of Disease) Act 1984, section 45G.

Information will also be obtained about a person's relationship (if any) with other symptomatic cases. Has that person eaten with another 'case' at any time within the incubation period of the illness? Has he or she spent a significant period of time with another 'case' in the period leading to the illness? These questions are asked for two reasons:

(a) If two cases have shared only one period of time together during the incubation period of the illness, this strongly implicates this period as the time when at least one of the individuals became infected (A/I/14). If this time period is a shared meal, the meal will warrant further close investigation. Such questioning narrows the scope of the investigation.
(b) If the cases spend a significant period of time together, there is a greater likelihood that the illness has been spread person-to-person.

More potential sources may be implicated if individuals work together: snacks served in the office, water coolers and office equipment (which may not be managed in a hygienic manner) must be considered as possible sources (A/I/3; A/I/19). If 'cases' live together, meals they have eaten at home will come under suspicion. The investigation will widen as shared exposure between 'cases' increases.

ii. Information about Symptoms

The Food Standard Agency management guidance provides that local authorities should seek to obtain information about the following:

— Date and time of first symptoms
— Nature of initial and subsequent symptoms
— Severity and duration of symptoms
— Hospital admission and/or antibiotic or other treatment
— Outcome of illness[36]

People who self-notify their illness to a local authority will be asked about their symptoms during the initial conversation.[37] They will then be asked to repeat their answers in response to the epidemiological questionnaire, which will either be administered by an EHO or sent to a 'case' for self-completion. Potential 'cases', known either to have eaten at a food business implicated in an incident, or to have suffered from symptoms similar to those of the initial complainant, will also be asked to complete a questionnaire to ascertain which (if any) symptoms they have suffered. This allows

[36] Food Standards Agency, above n 30, para 5.35.
[37] In the file notes examined, symptoms were described in all initial interactions.

an EHO to compare symptoms to the adopted case definition, and to decide whether the potential 'case' forms part of the incident. This enables the EHO to disregard information on food history if it is unlikely to be linked to the incident. It also allows an EHO to decide whether control is necessary. If symptoms are no longer present and ceased more than 48 hours previously, control will generally not be needed.

In A/I/8 a notification suggested that three people were ill following a meal at Food Business V. One 'case' (Person 1) had vomiting and no diarrhoea; the other two 'cases' (Person 2 and Person 3) had diarrhoea and no vomiting. By comparing the symptoms of the 'cases', it appeared to EHO-A3 that Person 1 and Persons 2 and 3 might have been suffering from different illnesses. This suggested that the illnesses were not connected to the same food source, and therefore there was more than one source. Person 1 did not fall within the case definition presented by Persons 2 and 3, and vice versa.

Information about symptoms allows EHOs to hypothesise about the illness suffered by the 'case'. If EHOs can identify the illness, they can utilise medical knowledge about its progression. In particular they can use the likely time between infection and onset of symptoms to work backwards and identify likely sources, delimiting inquiries made about food histories.

Onset time of illness is, therefore, an important piece of information that EHOs obtain during an investigation. Once it is clear from which illness the 'case' is suffering, calculations based on the onset time may narrow both the investigation and the potential need for control. If the likely exposure time is known, the onset may allow an EHO to pinpoint a source, or rule out particular potential sources as either too distant or too recent to be at the root of the symptoms suffered by the 'case'. For example, *cryptosporidiosis* has an average onset time of seven days, with a range between two and 10 days. With a confirmed case of *cryptosporidiosis* with a known onset time, potential sources to which the individual was exposed less than two days before becoming symptomatic can be disregarded, allowing the EHO to narrow his or her investigation in relation to that case.

In large outbreaks, assessment of symptoms will also allow the EHOs to highlight those cases that are most likely to provide valuable information. This allows the prioritisation of limited investigative resources on the basis of this probable value. For example, in the South Wales outbreak:

> Several EHOs including myself worked through the list, to find out more about the symptoms in each case. On the advice of Dr Sarah Hayes, if a case reported 3 or more episodes of diarrhoea in 24 hours, or any bloody diarrhoea, we would treat it as a presumptive case and arranged to interview and deliver a sample pot. (PEN/PP/RCC.00322)[38]

Such filtering is based on the case definition adopted by the investigative team.

[38] See also PEN/PP/RCC.00323; PEN/PP/RCC.00327.

iii. Food History

Obtaining food histories is a central and ubiquitous part of an EHO's role in investigating food-borne illness. In every case within the public and local authority samples, EHOs obtained information about the food consumed by 'cases' and 'controls'. The data contained in such histories are compared to those relating to food eaten by other 'cases' in order to discover commonalities. Such commonalities suggest the source of the food-borne illness, which will be the focus of both control and enforcement action.

a. Why Compile a Food History?

A food history provides a comprehensive record of the food and drink consumed by the individual over a period of up to two weeks prior to the onset of symptoms (PEN/GL/NPH.00878). This period may be varied based on the information held by the EHO;[39] however 14 days is generally used, as it is the maximum incubation period of the common gastro-intestinal illnesses encountered by EHOs.

When responding to an incident, resources will be allocated to obtaining histories from those most likely to be 'cases'. A statement made by Patricia Pritchard to South Wales Police illustrates this:

> I tried to visit to interview the mother of [redacted] and [redacted] who both attend [redacted] Primary School but there was no one home. I decided that in light of the information about the food served that it was unlikely that these children had *E. Coli* O157 poisoning. Therefore I decided not to pursue an interview unless their [sample] results came back positive. (PEN/PP/SWP.00321)

Decisions allocating resources are based on the case definition adopted by those investigating the incident, or on partial food histories and knowledge of likely sources. If the reported symptoms fall outside the case definition then obtaining a food history is not a priority, because control is unlikely to be necessary, and the information will not positively contribute to building a case for enforcement action.

b. How are Food Histories Compiled?

Pro forma questionnaires exist to assist with the collection of food history. Food histories are generally represented in a grid, with dates listed in the left vertical column, and the three main meals, snacks and drinks located in the top horizontal column. Food history should include food eaten in the home, although consumers frequently are unable to recall this. The consumer should list all the food eaten and identify the source of food as fully as possible (eg, chicken breast bought from food business X, tin of baked beans

[39] Eg, if the illness is known due to sample analysis, the time period may be shortened.

	Breakfast	Lunch	Dinner	Snacks	Drinks
Monday	Corn Flakes, Semi-Skimmed Milk, Apple	Cheese Sandwich (white bread, Red Leicester Cheese, Margarine, Tomato), Strawberry Yogurt	Fajita Kit (Spice, Salsa and flour tortillas), free-range chicken breasts, Onion and Peppers.	Peach yogurt. Orange.	Tap Water x 4 glasses, Lemon squash diluted with tap water x 2 glasses, Cola x 2 Cans, orange juice x 1 glass

Figure 4.3: Example food history

produced by food business Y), the preparation method (if known), the location where the food was eaten (eg, spaghetti bolognese eaten at food business Z) and the quantities that were consumed (in order that dose/response relationships can be investigated). If the consumer has further information or documentation about the products in the food history, such as packaging, the EHO will ask for this in order to, for example, identify the batch from which the product comes. An illustration of a food history grid for one day, completed by the author, is shown in Figure 4.3.

Food histories may be completed by the EHO during a face-to-face or telephone interview (PEN/GL/NPH.00875; PEN/PP/SWP.00316; PEN/AC/SWP.00115), or may be self-completed. Environmental Health Officers show a weak preference for completion in the presence of an EHO (EHO-A3; EHO-C2), as this allows the officer to clarify and probe items within the food history, and to offer informal control advice aimed at preventing the spread of secondary infection, whilst the food history is being completed. Taking the information in person also means that EHOs become aware of information more quickly, and therefore can respond more swiftly. However, where large numbers of individuals have been affected, and there is no significant risk of secondary infection that justifies a visit from an EHO in order to put in place or advise upon preventative measures, the food history may be self-completed, either in hard copy form or online. In large incidents, online completion may be preferred by enforcement officers, as soft-copy data are more easily manageable and may be directly analysed, whereas answers to hard-copy questionnaires will need to be transcribed prior to analysis. Soft-copy information can therefore be dealt with more quickly, allowing decisions about the objects that need to be controlled to be made rapidly.

When it is clear from the notification that a particular event or food business is implicated in the incident, questions about food history can be narrowed down. For example, where a large number of guests who have attended a function, and who have no other common exposures, are suffering from the same illness then it is clear that the function is the source of the incident, even though the exact cause at that function (be it a product used in the food served, unhygienic practices in the kitchen or an ill food handler) cannot be identified. Questions will be limited to food that was consumed at the event or from the food business. This may allow the food source at the event or within the business to be isolated. Isolating the food source within the business is necessary to properly particularise any enforcement action alleging breach of Regulation 178/2004, article 14. It may be necessary to trace other parts of a batch that are unfit for human consumption and take them off the market.

Where food histories are to be obtained from children, EHOs may have to use innovative methods. One potential method is to use pictures, and to ask children to point to the food they had eaten. However, this will work only where there is a limited menu. Such an approach is likely to be taken where a nursery or child-minding business is implicated in an incident (as it is likely that a limited menu will exist) and that business is unable to say precisely what each child had eaten (EHO-A3).

c. Businesses and Food Histories

In some cases food histories may be compiled with the assistance of information obtained from implicated premises (PEN/AP/SWP.00489; PEN/PP/RCC.00318; PEN/AC/SWP.00117; PEN/HL/SWP.00266; PEN/CE/SWP.00159). Information may be used for two purposes: narrowing inquiry; and filling gaps in recall. Menus obtained from food premises allow EHOs to draft tailored food history questionnaires, which ask specifically about the food available within implicated premises (A/I/20; Fat Duck).

The creation of tailored questionnaires is encouraged by the Food Standards Agency management guidance, which advises that 'a data collection form should be designed for each individual outbreak to ensure all necessary and relevant information is assembled in a uniform way'.[40] The use of a tailored questionnaire narrows the investigation, and makes identification of the source more likely.

In A/I/2 a postal questionnaire was created using the set menu that was available at the function implicated in the outbreak. Individuals were asked to indicate whether they had eaten all, some or none of each of the three courses served, as well as which of the available drinks they had consumed.

A tailored questionnaire was used in the investigation of the Fat Duck Outbreak.[41] Environmental Health Officers created a questionnaire that allowed individuals to answer whether they had eaten all, part or none of the dishes on the 13-course tasting menu, or to indicate that they did not know. If the individuals stated that they ate only part of a particular course,

[40] Food Standards Agency, above n 30, para 5.35.
[41] Fat Duck, above n 3, 29–36.

they were asked to indicate the part or parts of the dish that they did not eat. Similarly, those who had eaten from the *a la carte* menu were asked to indicate which of the dishes they ordered, and whether they ate the whole, part or none of the dishes, or did not know. Again, individuals who had eaten only part of the dish were asked to indicate separately which parts of the dish they did not eat.

In a hospital-based incident of food-borne illness, a greater range of sources may be accessed in order to compile a food history. Menus and 'hospital clinical records' may be relevant.[42] Similar records may assist the investigation of incidents in nursing homes. Where extra sources of information about the food consumption of a 'case' are available, they will be utilised in order to create the most accurate food-history record possible. Initially, however, reliance is placed on the individual to recall the food he or she ate, which may lead to incomplete or inadequate information, or to information of dubious reliability.[43]

Receipts or other documentation held by the food business may contain information about the food eaten by particular parties. Harvesting this information may allow an EHO to assemble a more complete food history than is possible from using interviews and/or self-report questionnaires. In the South Wales case a detailed food history for some consumers was obtained from canteen swipe cards:

> I established that food is paid for at the canteen using a swipe card system. Basic details of each pupil's purchases from the canteen can be retrieved; however, vending machine purchases are not included. The cook-supervisor provided me with a printout of purchases since the beginning of term. (PEN/PP/SWP. RCC.00318)

iv. Information about Other Risk Factors

Illnesses associated with food may be spread from person to person as well as in food. This is, of course, the reason that control may be necessary to prevent secondary spread. Environmental Health Officers will ask questions in order to assess whether the illness suffered by investigated cases may itself be a result of spread from person to person. Other questions will focus on exposure to potential non-food sources during the incubation period of the illness.

a. Animals

Questions were asked about exposure to animals. Animals carry food borne-illness organisms in their gut, and these may be transmitted via the faecal-oral route if appropriate hygiene practices are not adopted by both

[42] Belfast *Listeria*, para 40.
[43] See ch 6.II.

consumers and businesses where humans and animals interact.[44] Questions will therefore be asked about the domestic pets and farm animals with which the consumer has come into contact.

More general questions about visits to the countryside will be asked, even if a visit did not involve contact with animals. If a person walks through a field, he or she is walking where large animals may have defecated. Some bacteria are able to survive for a significant period outside the intestinal tract. Particularly in muddy conditions, soil, contaminated with micro-organisms contained in animal faeces, may become attached to a consumer, and enter that person's mouth if proper hygiene practices are not adopted. This is particularly likely if individuals are engaged in outdoor pursuits, as people may be unable to wash their hands properly prior to eating.[45] If animals are implicated as the source, EHOs may wish to take action to control access to them, or to enforce proper hygiene procedures.[46]

b. Swimming Pools

Swimming pools may become contaminated with faecal matter and hence food-borne illness organisms. Bacteria survive in swimming-pool water if the pool is inefficiently filtered and chlorinated. Consumers may become infected by contaminated water through accidental ingestion or, in some cases, contact between open wounds and contaminated water. Control action must therefore be taken if a swimming pool is found to be the source of an outbreak (Merthyr *Cryptosporidium*).

'Cases' will be asked to indicate whether they have been swimming during the incubation period of the illness and, if so, the location of the swimming pool. If a swimming pool is implicated in an outbreak, more detailed questions may be asked, such as in which of the pools within the complex the person swam, and whether he or she used any pool furniture, such as slides or water features (Merthyr *Cryptosporidium*). This allows control action to be targeted appropriately.

c. Untreated Water

Untreated water is a known source of *Cryptosporidium* and *E. coli*.[47] Untreated water becomes contaminated through exposure to human or animal

[44] Godstone Farm (Independent Investigation Committee, *Review of the major outbreak of E. coli O157 in Surrey, 2009* (IIC 2010)); A/I/5.

[45] Outbreak Control Team, *The investigation of an outbreak of diarrhoeal illness in participants of the Builth Wells Mountain Bike Marathon July 2008* (OCT 2008).

[46] See, eg, the measure taken at petting zoos following the Godstone Farm incident, detailed in Independent Investigation Committee, above n 42.

[47] Outbreak Control Team, *Outbreak of E. coli O157 infection Auchinclech, Aberdeenshire August 2008* (OCT 2009).

faecal matter. Environmental Health Officers ask questions about the exposure of 'cases' to untreated water, through both drinking and bathing, whether from private water supplies or natural water sources. They will ask about the location of the source of the untreated water, and compare the exposures to untreated water reported by 'cases'. If 'cases' are exposed to the same untreated water source then that source will be implicated in the incident, and control measures may be necessary.

d. Travel

Environmental Health Officers will often ask whether a person has travelled abroad during the incubation period of the illness. Overseas infection with Typhoid is a known risk.[48] If a sporadic notification of food-borne illness is made by a person with a recent history of travel abroad, where no other common risk factors are disclosed in the food history, EHOs may decide that the source of the illness was most likely abroad, and therefore decide not to investigate further. This decision is based on a determination that there is no further risk of primary spread of the illness. The investigation will go as far as is necessary to establish that there is little or no risk, and no further. This does not, however, mean that control measures will not be imposed on an individual suffering from a food-borne illness contracted abroad (CCDC1). An individual may be excluded from work if he or she works in a high-risk occupation.

C. Analysing Epidemiological Information

Once information has been obtained from 'cases' and 'controls' it must be analysed. The goal is to indicate to which potential sources those suffering from illness have been exposed more than those who are not suffering from illness. The aim is to compare 'cases' to see if common risk factors are disclosed.[49] Something common between 'cases' is likely to be a source of the illness, and therefore in need of control and, if responsibility can be established, enforcement.

In general a specialist epidemiologist (usually the CCDC or others within Public Health England) must be enrolled into the regulatory network for the analysis of epidemiological data, 'as training in epidemiology is required to ensure effective collection of data and interpretation of results; for example, in the identification of confounding factors and the avoidance of bias'.[50]

[48] CCDC1; EHO-C1.

[49] Guidance suggests that a response rate of at least 60% (and preferably 80%) should be achieved. A lower response rate will result is less robust results.

[50] Food Standards Agency, above n 30, app III, para 1. Analysis will usually be undertaken by computer (PEN/EJN/RCC.00235).

In smaller incidents examined, descriptive epidemiology was undertaken by EHOs,[51] particularly where there was a small, tightly defined group suffering from the food-borne illness. In such circumstances, EHOs felt capable of performing such epidemiology.[52]

'Descriptive epidemiology' is usually the first method of testing the hypothesis. However, in order to give a realistic representation of the likelihood that a particular source was responsible for the illness, it is necessary to use analytic epidemiology techniques. The goal of analytic epidemiology is to test whether 'there is a statistically significant difference between those eating and those not eating the suspect food'; if so, 'this gives support to the theory that the food was contaminated'.[53] The two most common analytic techniques are case control studies and cohort studies. A significance level (usually 95 per cent or 99 per cent, depending on whether a single food item is or a number of food items are being tested)[54] will be set, and hypothesis testing will take place. Environmental Health Officers generally view analytic epidemiology demonstrating a likely relationship as necessary for enforcement action to take place, but are prepared to take control action on the basis of a descriptive relationship between a particular food and food-borne illness.

i. Building a Hypothesis

As epidemiology has a statistical basis, the first step in testing the relationship of possible sources with the illness is the creation of a hypothesis. The default null hypothesis is that there is no relationship between a particular source and the illness, and the default alternative hypothesis is that there is such a relationship.

An investigation may suggest an alternative hypothesis that a particular food business or a particular food is responsible for the incident of food-borne illness. The possibility of this food business being the source is tested through descriptive and analytical epidemiology. The development of the hypothesis in South Wales is detailed below:

> By the time of the outbreak control meeting on Saturday 17th September (17/09), 3.30pm (1530) I had received reports from EHOs for 7 cases who had been interviewed. All of the cases were school children who ate school meals, 5 were associated with Aberdare swimming pool, 5 had eaten at McDonalds (although they had not eaten at the same outlet), and 3 had eaten at Kentucky Fried Chicken. The four of these links could not be ruled out at this stage and warranted further investigation … By the next outbreak control meeting which took place on Sunday 18th September at 10am, I had received reports for 19 cases. All had eaten school

[51] Eg, A/I/16; A/I/ 18.
[52] EHO-B2.
[53] Food Standards Agency, above n 30, app III, para 6.
[54] Ibid, para 5.41.

> meals but the other links did not have any further cases associated with them … I reported my findings to the outbreak control team and it was agreed that Aberdare swimming pool, and the fast food outlets were unlikely to be the source of the outbreak. This conclusion was drawn not only from my feedback but also because all but one of the cases were in school. It would be expected that there would be more adult cases if one of the other links was the source. Additionally, the only adult case was associated with school meals as she was a dinner lady who ate the school meals. (PEN/HL/SWP.00272)

Information received from 'cases' (and epidemiological and microbiological investigations) may suggest that somewhere or something is the source of the food-borne illness. This will form the basis of the alternative hypothesis, which will then be tested.

ii. Testing a Hypothesis

a. Descriptive Epidemiology

Descriptive epidemiology seeks to describe patterns within the data collected from 'cases'. These patterns suggest the source of food-borne illness by a rational process of elimination. This result can then be compared with the hypothesis. Descriptive epidemiology does not provide a probability that a particular business or food is the source of the illness. It is 'unmeasurable'.[55] In South Wales, epidemiological conclusions were reached by Heather Lewis, an EHO, through a two-stage process:

(a) first, 'as so many schools were affected I knew that the contamination must be associated with a supplier as opposed to anything that happened at the individual school' (PEN/HL/SWP.00273); and
(b) secondly, 'by systematically analysing all the menu choices in the affected schools during the first week of term and cross referencing to see whether all affected schools had used similar products, I was able to make a link to cold, sliced meat delivered by Tudors of Bridgend' (PEN/HL/SWP.00274).

Descriptive epidemiology at its most simple was used in A/I/16. After obtaining food histories from all members of a group of six, from which four individuals had become ill after eating at Food Business K, EHO-A4 drew up a grid setting out which individuals in the group ate what, and which individuals were symptomatic. A simplified version of the grid is reproduced at Figure 4.4. From the grid it was clear that all the members of the group suffering from symptoms had eaten Food A at the restaurant. One hundred per cent of the symptomatic individuals within the group had eaten

[55] John M Cowden, 'Investigating outbreaks of infectious intestinal disease: How, why and when do you take action?', speech given to Health Protection Scotland and NHS Scotland, Glasgow (19 November 2007).

Person	Food A	Food B	Food C	Drink D	Symptoms – D+V
U	x		x	x	x
V		x		x	
W	x		x	x	x
X	x	x		x	x
Y	x	x		x	x
Z			x	x	

Figure 4.4: Cross-tabulation of food history

Food A, and no one who had not eaten Food A was ill. Only 50 per cent of the symptomatic cases had eaten Food B or Food C. One hundred per cent of the cases had drunk Drink D, but so had 100 per cent of the controls. Two-thirds of the Drink D drinkers were suffering from illness. This suggested that the source of the food-borne illness was Food A.

b. Mapping

A second form of descriptive analysis is to use maps. By mapping the distribution of cases, EHOs may be able to determine whether the incident has a point source, or whether the source is distributed in a more diffuse manner, and draw inferential conclusions about the source.[56]

Mapping is particularly useful when dealing with an incident of *cryptosporidium*. There are two major pathways by which people may become infected with this illness: drinking contaminated tap water, or using a contaminated point source such as a swimming pool. By mapping the home addresses of 'cases', it is possible to draw preliminary conclusions about which pathway is responsible for the incident. Where a swimming pool is responsible, a map will show a cluster of cases in a fairly small area (Merthyr *Cryptosporidium*). Those who attend a swimming pool may be expected to live within a limited catchment area. Where cases appear in a small cluster, businesses in that area will be the primary focus of investigation.

Where the mains water supply is contaminated, cases will be distributed throughout the area served by the supply from a particular source. For example, in the 1995 Torbay *Cryptosporidium* outbreak the cases were distributed throughout the area served by water from the Littlehempston reservoir and water treatment plant.[57] Whilst there may be

[56] These maps must be distinguished from crime maps, which attempt to make predictions about future crime events from the location of crime. See Kate J Bowers, Shane D Johnson and Ken Pease, 'Prospective hot-spotting—The future of crime mapping?' (2004) 44 *British Journal of Criminology* 641.

[57] W Michael Waite, *Assessment of Water Supply and Associated Matters in relation to the Incidence of Cryptosporidiosis in Torbay in August and September 1995* (DWI 1997). A similar pattern appeared in the North-West Wales *Cryptosporidium* outbreak (Outbreak Control Team, *Outbreak of cryptosporidiosis in North West Wales, 2005* (OCT 2006)). When plotted on the map, cases were clustered within the area served by the Llyn Cwellyn Reservoir.

outliers,[58] this may be due to consumption of tap water during a visit, or the person may be a secondary case.

Similar, maps can be used to draw conclusions about the likely source of an incident of food-borne illness. Where a single outlet is the source of an incident, the cluster of cases will be relatively tight, given the geographically limited customer base of most single food businesses.[59] In the South Wales case, mapping suggested that Tudors, a local catering butcher, rather than a national distributor, was the source of contamination: 'if [the suppliers] had been the source of the problem the outbreak of *E. coli* would have been much wider spread. It would not have been limited to an association with schools in the South Wales valleys' (PEN/HL/SWP.00270).

Where a supplier or primary producer, with a large sphere of distribution, is the source of contamination, the cases will be more widely dispersed, potentially on a national scale. In the Cadbury *Salmonella* case,[60] a map of the cases showed widely dispersed instances, suggesting the source was a food with nationwide distribution. Where a supplier is implicated, a map of the premises where affected food was bought should correlate to premises supplied by the business.[61]

c. Cohort Study

A cohort study is a key method of assessing the likely source of food-borne illness. 'Cohort studies are more commonly used than case-control studies in foodborne outbreaks because they fit the circumstances of a group of people, who have eaten together, with illness becoming recognised relatively soon afterwards.'[62] A cohort study aims to pinpoint a source when there is a known food business operator or event implicated in an incident.

According to the Food Standards Agency management guidance, a cohort study is used 'when a group of people who have been exposed to a particular risk have been identified eg have attended a wedding function'.[63] It involves getting data from all the individuals who attended that food business operator or event, and comparing the type and amount of food eaten by those who are ill and by those who are not. Controls do not have to be selected in cohort studies. They are self-selecting within the group that attended the event. In A/I/2 a cohort study was used to investigate which

[58] Eg, the holiday-makers in the Torbay outbreak.

[59] Although this does not hold true for every food business—in the case of the Fat Duck outbreak, the restaurant attracted customers from across the UK and beyond due to its reputation as one of the world's best restaurants.

[60] See above n 9.

[61] In South Wales, 'the distribution of cases correspond[ed] to the distribution network of Tudors' (PEN/HL/SWP.00274).

[62] Food Standards Agency, above n 30, app III, para 2.

[63] Ibid, para 5.40.

dish served at a business banquet was likely to have caused the illness. The difference between food consumed by the ill individuals and the individuals who are not ill should be tested for statistical significance.[64]

d. Case-control Study (Paired-sampling)

Another method of analysing epidemiological information is via a case-control study, described by Roland Salmon, a regional epidemiologist, in his oral evidence to Pennington:

> For every case of the illness, howsoever defined, you choose, one, two, three otherwise healthy people with which to compare them and you compare them precisely in respect of the sort of exposures that we've talked about. What foods have they eaten? Do they eat school dinners? Where have they visited? What recreational activities have they undertaken? Then you simply statistically look at the percentage in the group of cases against the percentage in the group of controls, and there are various statistical tests you can add to that to refine your analysis of that comparison, but conceptually, as I say, it was a rather obvious idea. (PEN/RS/LIVE-10-3-pg17line4)

A case-control study is used

> when the 'at risk' population is unknown or so large in relation to the number of people ill that it is impracticable or uneconomical to include them all in a study. An example might be when a nationally distributed food is thought to be responsible for an outbreak.[65]

Where it is not clear what the source of the food-borne illness is, or where the group exposed cannot be defined, a case-control study is used.

'Controls' should have had the same opportunity to consume the source. For example, in the event that there is an incident centred on a school, names of 'controls' can be selected at random from those on the roll who had not been reported to be suffering with illness.[66] Alternatively, 'controls' may be selected randomly (Lemon and Coriander Chicken Wrap[67]), or matched in respect of important demographic characteristics. Questionnaires identical to those administered to 'cases' would then be administered to 'controls'. The results of these questionnaires would then be compared with those of the questionnaires given to the 'cases', to assess which risk factors are represented more among the 'cases' than the 'controls'. Such analysis will be carried out statistically.[68]

[64] Ibid, app III, para 6.
[65] Ibid, para 5.40.
[66] See, eg, PEN/RS/LIVE-10-3-pg24line7.
[67] Lemon and Coriander Chicken Wrap, above n 7.
[68] Food Standards Agency, above n 30, app III, para 6.

IV. MICROBIOLOGICAL INVESTIGATIONS

Microbiological investigations seek to discover food-borne illness organisms. Samples taken from humans, food or food businesses are the subject of such investigations. Identifying a food-borne illness organism in any sample may assist EHOs in identifying the organism causing the incident, and may lead to control measures to prevent spread of the organism from the sampled object (human; food; premises).

Whilst one positive sample is helpful in establishing a need to control, in order to support enforcement action EHOs often require microbiological investigations to link a 'case' to a food vehicle, a component of a food vehicle, or the environment in which the food vehicle or component was processed.[69] The link is established by finding two genetically indistinguishable organisms in samples taken from a 'case' and a food or the environment. Finding two linked samples allows EHOs to understand how a person became infected and, if samples taken from the staff of the food business or from the environment are positive, how the food became contaminated with the micro-organism.

Time is of the essence in microbiological investigations. Delay can damage the prospects of obtaining microbiological information from humans, food or the environment.[70] Therefore, obtaining samples and swabs that can be submitted for analysis assumes a high priority in an investigation into an incident of food-borne illness. In the South Wales case, 'it was decided to inspect the premise at the earliest convenience and take appropriate samples and swabs' (PEN/EJD/BCC.00924).[71]

Guidance on sampling is offered by the Food Law Code[72] and the LACORS *Guidance on Sampling for Microbiological Purposes*.[73] A local authority may have its own specific sampling guidance that applies to EHOs within that authority. One microbiologist noted that such guidance may cause problems if it is too complex, as EHOs may fail to follow it, resulting in the exclusion of information obtained from analysis of the sample by a court adjudicating on subsequent enforcement action (EXP-MIC1).

A. Human Samples

Micro-organisms that cause food-borne illness are excreted in faeces. If faeces are sampled[74] and analysed, the microbiological cause of the illness

[69] Cowden, above n 53.
[70] See ch 7.I.F.i.
[71] See also PEN/EJD/RCC.00218.
[72] Food Standards Agency, *Food Law Code of Practice for England* (Food Standards Agency 2008).
[73] LACORS, *Guidance on Food Sampling for Microbiological Purposes* (LACORS 2006).
[74] EHOs investigating an incident of food-borne illness will not be concerned with other types of human samples.

can be identified.[75] People with micro-organisms present in their stool may require control. This control may be as simple as advice on hand hygiene, or it may involve exclusion from work.

i. From Consumers

Analysis of stool samples taken from 'cases' is central to the investigation of food-borne illness.[76] A sample from the index 'case' allows EHOs (with the assistance of microbiologists) to identify the organism responsible for the incident.

Without a faecal sample, other samples (staff, food or environment) cannot be linked definitively to the incident, and cases cannot be microbiologically confirmed to be connected. A faecal sample forms the basis for showing microbiological linkages. Therefore, obtaining a sample from a 'case' is a priority. It may result in the reclassification of a person as a suspected 'case' to a 'control', as the sample may show that the person from whom the sample was collected is not suffering from the illness at the centre of the investigation.[77]

In all incidents examined, EHOs sought to obtain samples. In the South Wales outbreak, 'at each visit [to a 'case'] faecal pots would have been left with the cases and their families so that they could submit a faecal sample' (PEN/HL/SWP.00263). Samples are generally taken by 'cases' themselves. Sampling equipment (a 'pot') is left with consumers, and they are asked to place faeces in the pot, using the spoon provided. Only a small amount of faeces is required.

'Potting', or the delivering of sample pots to notified 'cases' of food-borne illness, is a ritualistic part of the investigation of food-borne illness. Along with obtaining a food history, delivering a sample pot and obtaining samples is the standard response to a notification of food-borne illness. Maintenance of a 'potters list' of submitted samples, and chasing up cases who have not 'potted' or submitted a sample, are a routine parts of the investigation. Samples will be labelled with information to allow the laboratory and EHOs to identify the 'case' to which they relate.

Once the sample has been provided by the 'case' it must be analysed. Environmental Health Officers may collect the samples, or 'cases' may be asked to deliver the samples to their doctors or to the appropriate microbiological laboratory. The EHOs expressed a weak preference for collection, as this allows more control over timing and, therefore, potentially quicker access to analysis, but this is often not possible in large outbreaks. In some cases doctors will arrange for samples to be taken prior to EHOs' becoming

[75] The species and phage type of the micro-organism will be exposed by analysis.

[76] PEN/HL/SWP.00271; PEN/PP/RCC.00315; PEN/PP/RCC.00316; PEN/PP/RCC.00317; PEN/PP/RCC.00319; PEN/PP/RCC.00320.

[77] PEN/PP/RCC.00315.

aware of an infected individual.[78] Further samples need not be taken. In many cases examined in the book, enforcement officers were unable to obtain a faecal sample.

Where illness can be transmitted person-to-person, EHOs often request faecal samples from close contacts of the 'case'.[79] These samples are taken for the purposes of control. Sample analysis allows EHOs to see whether household contacts are asymptomatic excretors posing a risk of secondary spread. If they are, they may be subject to control action. Sample analysis may also enable identification of pre-symptomatic cases, enabling prompt treatment and control. Further, household contacts may have similar food histories, and microbiologically establishing the contact as a 'control' allows comparisons between food histories, enabling descriptive epidemiological conclusions to be drawn.

Where an incident is linked to a closed environment, where a fixed population exists in close proximity, samples may be requested from a wider range of contacts.[80] The purpose of such blanket sampling is control. Such sampling is intended to assist in preventing secondary spread of the illness. For example, in the Abercynon outbreak,[81] which occurred concurrently with the *E. coli* outbreak in South Wales, all pupils of a school were sampled after bloody diarrhoea, which could not be linked to a particular pupil, was found in a school toilet. Pupils were excluded from school until a negative sample had been provided. The risk of person-to-person transmission by an undiagnosed school child was sufficiently high that closing the school and screening to identify the 'case' was seen as an appropriate control measure. The EHOs could not optimally respond, by excluding the affected pupil, so the next best option, excluding all pupils to prevent contact between the unknown case and others, was taken.[82]

ii. From Employees

As part of their investigation, EHOs will often ask for stool samples from employees of businesses linked to the illness.[83] Such samples are obtained for the purpose of control. Analysis of such samples will expose whether someone involved in food processing is suffering from food-borne illness. If an analysis is positive for food-borne illness organisms, even if the

[78] PEN/PP/RCC.00319; PEN/PP/RCC.00328; PEN/PP/RCC.00329; PEN/CE/SWP.00165.

[79] PEN/PP/RCC.00313; PEN/AC/SWP.00115; PEN/AP/SWP.00489.

[80] Examples of such environments include nurseries and nursing homes (A/I/6; A/I/12).

[81] Detailed in the South Wales E. Coli documentation, available at <http://wales.gov.uk/ecoliinquiry/?lang=en>.

[82] See also the Feltham Hill Infants case, above n 24, where all staff and pupils were excluded until a negative sample had been provided.

[83] PEN/EJD/RCC.00231; PEN/JD/RCC.00258; PEN/AL/RCC.00342; PEN/AL/RCC.00346; PEN/EJD/RCC.00233.

employee is asymptomatic, it may be necessary to exclude that employee from work. The risk of cross-contamination is very high, and exclusion is one step towards controlling the risk. Exclusion removes the risk that the employee will contaminate food that is being processed, preventing further cases. Alternatively, EHOs may give informal advice on controlling the risk of cross-contamination.

Environmental Health Officers do not have the power to compel employees to provide samples, so must obtain such samples by consent, and often enlist the cooperation of the employer in obtaining these. Employee samples are less commonly requested where it appears there is no on-going risk of transmission, because the need for control is lessened. In viral cases, EHOs might choose not to obtain samples since the analysis offers less reliable results (EXP-MIC1).

An employee sample may also be taken for diagnostic and explanatory purposes. If a sample provided by an employee is positive, it will be compared with other positive samples from 'cases' or food. This will confirm whether the samples are contaminated with the same organism. This does not demonstrate causation. However, this information, allied with other information obtained from, for example, an interview with an employee, may be used to explain how the food, eaten by the consumer, came to be contaminated with food-borne illness organisms.

If it can be shown that the employee brought the organisms onto the premises, EHOs will be able to provide a fuller picture of the process that led to an incident. They must bear in mind that the reverse process may be true, that the employee was infected by food produced on the premises. If a sick individual is identified as the source of the incident, this may suggest weaknesses in the hygiene and employee sickness procedures operated by the food business, which EHOs should address by giving advice using formal or informal powers.

As with 'cases' and their household contacts, self-sampling is the preferred method for obtaining a sample from employees. Sample pots are generally provided to the business, to distribute to employees at their place of work.[84] The employees then take a sample of their faeces and return the sample to an EHO or medical professional for submission for analysis. The EHOs will generally maintain a separate potting list of employees, and indicate on the list when a sample had been provided and when an analysis result is returned.

B. Food Samples

Analysis of food samples is necessary for control purposes and for explaining the incident. Environmental Health Officers take samples from food in

84 PEN/AL/RCC.00342.

order to link implicated food to the illness suffered by individuals. Food samples may also be taken to assess whether food should be removed from the marketplace. In the event that food is shown to be contaminated, EHOs will use the power to seize and destroy available under the Food Safety Act 1990, section 9.

Samples may be obtained either from the consumer (in the case of food purchased from a retailer and eaten at home), or from a business. If a supplier is implicated in an incident, a sample may be taken from food held by a business below that supplier in the supply chain. Once samples are obtained they will be analysed.

Environmental Health Officers have the power to take samples from a food business under section 29(b) of the Food Safety Act 1990. This provides:

> An authorised officer of an enforcement authority may…
>
> (b) take a sample of any food, or any such substance, which—
> (i) appears to him to be intended for sale, or to have been sold, for human consumption; or
> (ii) is found by him on or in any premises which he is authorised to enter by or under section 32…

Section 29(c) allows an EHO to 'take a sample from any food source, or a sample of any contact material, which is found by him on or in' a premises which he or she is entitled to enter under section 32. Similar powers are given to EHOs under the Food Safety and Hygiene (England) Regulations 2013.[85] Samples may also be provided by consent, and any samples obtained from consumers must be obtained by consent. A receipt should be provided for samples taken by EHOs.[86]

Samples should be taken in a manner that ensures that they reach the laboratory in 'a microbiologically unchanged condition from that existing when the sample was taken'.[87] Temperature control should be maintained where necessary.[88] Sampling techniques should ensure that samples are not cross-contaminated by the EHO, equipment used during sampling, sample containers or the environment.[89] This would mean that more micro-organisms would be present when the sample was analysed, and therefore the results of analysis would be unreliable. For this reason, equipment that local authorities use to take samples should be sterilised between uses, or supplied sterile by the manufacturer.[90] This prevents the introduction of micro-organisms

[85] Food Safety and Hygiene (England) Regulations 2013, SI 2013/2996, reg 14(b) and (c).
[86] LACORS, above n 70, 4.6.
[87] Ibid, 4.1.
[88] Ibid, 4.1 and EXP-MIC1.
[89] LACORS, above n 70, 6.
[90] Ibid, 4.2. Authorities maintain records of sterilisation in order to rebut suggestions of potential cross-contamination (EXP-MIC1).

during the sampling process. Evidence bags with a tamper-evident seal should be used for all samples to ensure that cross-contamination does not take place between sampling and analysis.[91] Guidance attempts to ensure that the analysis provides accurate information for the purposes of control and enforcement.

If an implicated food product is found intact then the entire package should be taken for analysis.[92] The package should be placed in a sample container and submitted to the food examiner, enrolling him or her into the regulatory network. At least 100g of a product should be taken for sampling purposes.[93] This will allow the food examiner to perform all the necessary analyses. In some cases, there will not be 100g of an implicated food available for sampling. In such cases, sampling the smaller amount is permissible, but an EHO should consult the food examiner about steps that should be taken to enhance the ability of the examiner to perform the necessary analysis.

When samples are taken, it is advisable for the business to observe the sampling process.[94] If this is the case, it should be recorded by EHOs. If samples are taken by the business for parallel analysis, this should also be recorded by EHOs, as should the way in which the samples were taken (PEN/PP/RCC.00324-00325).

The centrality of sampling is demonstrated by the South Wales case, where a large number of food samples were taken both from Tudors' premises[95] and from schools supplied by Tudors.[96] These were all analysed, with the results being used both as the basis for action controlling other meat supplied by Tudors and as a central plank of the evidence explaining the source of the outbreak during the subsequent prosecution. Despite the importance of food sampling to the investigation of incidents, in many of the cases examined in this book there was no food available to sample.

C. Environmental Samples

During an investigation EHOs may attend premises implicated in an outbreak and take samples from the premises itself.[97] Analysis will show whether microbiological organisms, linked to the incident, are found on the premises. Such information has control and explanatory uses. Such samples

[91] LACORS, above n 70, 11.2.
[92] Ibid, 5.2.
[93] Ibid, 4.3.
[94] Ibid, 4.5.
[95] PEN/JD/BCC.01030; PEN/JD/RCC.00263; PEN/EJD/BCC.00937; PEN/EJD/RCC.00244; PEN/PP/RCC.00314; PEN/PP/RCC.00324.
[96] PEN/JD/BCC.01032; PEN/AL/RCC.00360; PEN/AL/RCC.00341; PEN/CE/SWP.00160; PEN/HL/SWP.00271; PEN/HL/SWP.00267.
[97] PEN/JD/BCC.01029; PEN/JD/BCC.01029; PEN/JD/BCC.01032; PEN/EJD/RCC.00234.

may take the form of physical items from the premises, or, more likely, swabs taken from the premises. Section 29(d) of the Food Safety Act provides:

> An authorised officer of an enforcement authority may …
>
> (d) take a sample of any article or substance which is found by him on or in [premises which he is entitled to enter under section 32] and which he has reason to believe may be required as evidence in proceedings under any of the provisions of this Act or of regulations or orders made under it.

A similar provision appears in regulation 14(d) of the Food Safety and Hygiene (England) Regulations 2013. Environmental samples may also be taken by consent.

Environmental Health Officers may take swabs from surfaces such as walls, ceilings or floors, or from processing or cutting equipment. During swabbing, care will be taken to avoid potential cross-contamination.[98] A sterile template will generally be used to define the area to be swabbed. Once swabbing is completed, the swab will be placed in a sterile container. The swabs will be submitted for analysis. A detailed note must be taken of the location from which the swabs were taken,[99] and the container must be labelled with that location. It is good practice to take a photograph of the area swabbed, and to mark the location on a sketch plan of the premises (PEN/JD/RCC.00292).

In the event that the analysis of swabs discloses microbial activity, this may suggest that there is a risk of cross-contamination. This may require control action, and in particular emergency prohibition. An EHO may also encourage voluntary action, such as a deep clean, to remove microbes from surfaces.

Positive environmental samples may suggest that the incident was caused by microbes on surfaces or equipment, often due to inadequate cleaning practices. This is important information that enforcement officers can use to demonstrate the non-compliance of a business with regulatory cleaning requirements.

D. Testing and Analysis of Samples

Samples are submitted to a food examiner for microbiological examination. The food examiner plays an important part in the gathering of information

[98] PEN/AC/SWP.00118.

[99] Examples of the detail can be found at PEN/JD/RCC.00272, eg Swab from Bottom of Inside of Vac Packer—left hand side, Swab from Bottom of Inside of Vac Packer—right hand side and Swab from Inner Lid Surface to main body of Vac Packer (where the lid meets main body of unit).

for the regulatory network. The analysis process is conveniently set out in the evidence given to the Pennington Inquiry:

> Samples were received into the laboratory Specimen Reception Area. The samples arrived with a request form which gave patient information and details of the investigations required. One part of this form remained in the Reception where the sample was checked in and date and time stamped. The second part of the form remained with the sample. The patient information from the sample request form was logged into the laboratory computer system. Once all the necessary tests had been performed, a report was generated and sent to the EHO who had referred the sample ... The faecal samples were received directly from EHOs. The samples arrived in a sample pot with a request form attached and were given a laboratory sample number. The samples were introduced on to plates of culture media (also known as Petri dishes). These culture plates have specific media in them according to the sample and tests to be carried out. The culture medium used for the isolation of *E. coli O157* is Sorbitol MacConkey medium. The culture plates are used to grow the bacteria so that the bacteria are visible to the naked eye. It takes 18–24 hours for the bacteria to develop to the necessary level. In order to grow the bacteria, the culture plates were placed into an incubator which was set at 35–37 degrees Celsius. The temperature, batch number and the incubation period were logged. Once incubation had taken place, the sample was tested for *E. coli* O157. If these initial tests proved positive, confirmatory tests were undertaken. (PEN/AP/NPH.00668-00669)

Food samples, faecal samples and environmental samples may be submitted to the same laboratory, or may be submitted to separate laboratories. Large outbreaks will be assigned a reference number by the food examiner (PEN/AP/NPH.00668). An examiner will deal with a large number of samples, submitted at different times by different people. The reference number for the incident should be placed on the samples, in order that all the microbiological information about the incident is collated in the same place and can be analysed together.

The analysis will take place in accordance with a protocol in order to ensure that each sample is analysed in the same manner (PEN/AP/NPH.00669).[100] Once the analysis has taken place, results will be forwarded to the EHO or other network participant who requested the samples.[101] In large outbreaks, microbiologists may attend OCT meetings and report findings in person.[102] In urgent cases results will be communicated by phone, in order to allow control to take place.[103] The results from faecal samples are then compared with positive food or environmental samples. If the samples match, the EHO

[100] PEN/NPH.00740 and PEN/NPH.00686.

[101] Results will be forwarded in the form of a certificate under s 30 of the Food Safety Act 1990.

[102] PEN/EJD/RCC.00238.

[103] PEN/HL/SWP.00268.

may be able to explain the source of the illness. The EHO (in consultation with others) will then take investigation, control and enforcement decisions.

After a sample is initially found to be positive for a particular food-borne illness, further testing, including DNA analysis and phage-typing,[104] will be undertaken in order to specifically identify the organism found in the sample.[105] This allows samples to be linked at a more precise level. During the South Wales outbreak, some cases of *E. coli* were found to be of a different strain from the one causing the outbreak.[106] Isolates from samples may have to be submitted to specialist laboratories in order for this analysis to take place.[107]

In the South Wales case, analysis showed that 'the *E. Coli* found in the meat was indistinguishable in terms of DNA from that found in the faecal samples from the cases' (PEN/HL/SWP.00269).[108] This was important evidence in the prosecution, linking Tudors to the incident and ruling out other sources.

Environmental Health Officers may attempt to identify the initial source of food-borne illness, by identifying, for example, the primary meat suppliers to a business, and taking faecal samples from the live animals in order to discover whether the particular strain of illness implicated in the incident is present (PEN/HL/SWP.00270). This allows EHOs to provide an explanation as to how the bacteria or virus initially arrived on the premises, which, combined with analysis of the environmental conditions of the premises, may allow them to provide a 'life history' of the outbreak, from 'farm to fork'. Such a complete narrative of the incident may be useful in the event of formal action. The ability to provide a formal narrative means there is less doubt about the source of the illness, and as a consequence arguments offered by businesses resisting enforcement action arising out of the incident may be less compelling. It may also suggest the need for animal controls.

V. ENVIRONMENTAL INVESTIGATION

The goal of environmental investigation is to discover the 'physical or procedural faults compatible with, or likely to have caused, the outbreak'.[109] If faults are continuing, this may require urgent control action, including

[104] Phage typing is a form of analysis that identifies the particular strain of bacteria responsible for an incident of food-borne illness. It utilises bacteriophages (viruses which attack only particular forms of bacteria), and by assessing which phage is successful in attacking the bacteria, it allows analysts to identify the type of bacteria involved in the incident.

[105] PEN/HL/SWP.00270; PEN/AP/NPH.00669.

[106] PEN/PP/RCC.00315.

[107] PEN/SB/NPH.00726.

[108] See also PEN/HL/SWP.00275; PEN/SB/NPH.00726.

[109] Cowden, above n 53.

prohibition. Environmental investigations play a central role in EHOs' conclusions about whether a business is in breach of food safety or food hygiene requirements, and therefore whether enforcement action should be taken. A file note in A/I/8 by EHO-A3 reads 'I could find no evidence at the Hotel which would help to prove that the illness was caused by the meal', and the EHO therefore concluded that there was insufficient information to take formal enforcement action.

The EHOs examine the food production environment and assess whether problems with the premises may have contributed to or been responsible for the incident of food-borne illness. This allows them to offer a fuller narrative of the factors leading to an incident, and to make decisions about the likely cause(s) of an incident, which may require control action. If food is produced in a hygienic environment, this may indicate that it is necessary to trace food further up the chain of supply, as contamination within the examined food business premises appears unlikely. In A/I/16, the hygienic state of the kitchens at Food Business K was one important factor in the assessment that the implicated food was contaminated when it reached the business, and that investigation up the supply chain was necessary. In A/I/23 the good hygiene practices observed in the kitchens of Food Business N influenced the conclusion that the illness suffered by the complainant and her dining companion was likely to have been spread person-to-person rather than through food. Control was not needed for those businesses, as they did not pose a risk of further primary or secondary cases.

Further, environmental investigations are central to the detection of failures to comply with hygiene requirements. Businesses must comply with a wide range of hygiene regulations in establishments where food is produced. Epidemiological and microbiological investigation of food-borne illness is insufficient to discover whether a food business is acting hygienically. Therefore environmental investigations are required in order to obtain information for the purposes of enforcement of hygiene requirements.

In order to undertake environmental investigations, EHOs must attend food premises. They may enter those premises with the consent of the business. This is the preferred route of EHOs,[110] who believe that a cooperative stance is more likely to obtain the information necessary for control in a timely manner.[111] They believe that the explanatory value of information obtained during consensual premise visits is higher than that of information obtained during non-consensual visits, as businesses are more willing to cooperate, both in environmental examinations and in interviews.[112] If an entry is made without the consent of the business, EHOs believe that a relationship is created that is not conducive to the information gathering necessary to

[110] EHO-A3; EHO-C2.
[111] EHO-A3.
[112] EHO-A2; EHO-A3; EHO-C2.

achieve their goal of preventing further cases as soon as possible.[113] Non-consensual entry is a confrontational step, and is seen as potentially damaging to the relationship between businesses and EHOs, which may need to be preserved so that the businesses remain within the regulatory network for control purposes.[114]

In the event that consent is not forthcoming, EHOs have the power 'to enter any premises within the authority's area for the purpose of ascertaining whether there is or has been on the premises any contravention of the provisions of this Act, or of regulations or orders made under it',[115] 'to enter any business premises, whether within or outside the authority's area, for the purpose of ascertaining whether there is on the premises any evidence of any contravention within that area of any of such provisions'[116] and, 'in the case of an authorised officer of a food authority, to enter any premises for the purpose of the performance by the authority of their functions under this Act'.[117] Entry is available to establish whether offences have been committed and whether defences are available.[118] Entry must take place at a reasonable hour, and EHOs must produce authority if requested. An authorised EHO may take with him or her such other persons as he or she considers necessary.[119] This may include other members of the regulatory network, for example food technicians, or, if resistance to entry is anticipated, members of the police force.

The power applies to both business premises and dwellings. The power to enter dwellings extends only to dwellings situated within the local authority area.[120] Before a dwelling is entered 24 hours' notice must be given.[121] Environmental Health Officers wishing to enter dwellings will usually do so by consent. This will be quicker and will foster better relations with those living in the dwelling, who are likely to be victims rather than perpetrators, and will be more successful in enrolling the individuals into the regulatory network.

[113] EHO-A3; EHO-B2.

[114] EHO-A3.

[115] Food Safety Act 1990, s 32(1)(a).

[116] Food Safety Act 1990, s 32(1)(b). EHOs have different powers to enter business premises inside and outside their local authority area. The power of entry is more restricted outside the area. EHOs 'enter only for the purpose of ascertaining whether there "is" any evidence of contravention'. See *Walkers Snack Food v Coventry CC* [1998] 3 All ER 163, 170.

[117] Food Safety Act 1990, s 32(1)(c). The Food Safety and Hygiene (England) Regulations 2013, reg 16 is to similar effect as s 32(1) of the 1990 Act. In the cases examined, the power to enter under warrant was used very rarely, seen as even less conducive to co-operation compared with warrantless powers.

[118] *Walkers Snack Food v Coventry*, above n 112, 170.

[119] Food Safety Act 1990, s 32(4); Food Safety and Hygiene (England) Regulations 2013, reg 16(5).

[120] Compare s 32(1)(a) and (b), and see *Walkers Snack Food v Coventry*, above n 112.

[121] Food Safety Act 1990, s 32(1).

A. Contacting the Food Business

Once particular food business premises are implicated in an incident of food-borne illness, EHOs will contact that food business as soon as possible to inform it of this fact. The EHOs will try to arrange a convenient time for a consensual visit to the premises to investigate (PEN/AC/SWP.00116). A time will be arranged when the owner of the business or a senior staff member is available, so that as much information as possible can be obtained. This is likely to lead to more efficient control actions, as these individuals are more likely to have access to information that EHOs require.

Inquiries will be made of the food business during this initial contact. In particular, EHOs will ask whether the business is aware of any other cases of food-borne illness linked to its premises, often through customer complaints. This information may be used to obtain epidemiological information from further 'cases'.

In A/I/23, the food business implicated in an incident by a consumer complaint was contacted. The head chef was spoken to by EHO-A3, who informed him of the details of the notification. A convenient time to visit was arranged by EHO-A3; that afternoon, after the lunch service. The head chef was asked by EHO-A3 whether he was aware of any other cases of illness, whether any staff had been off sick and whether there were any problems in the kitchen, particularly with pests or drains. The chef stated that he had been ill, but had waited until he was 48 hours symptom-free before returning to work, and was not aware of any other illness amongst customers, staff sickness or any hygiene problems within the kitchen.

In some cases it may be necessary to make an unannounced visit. Generally, such visits will be made where there is a risk that information central to the investigation of the incident will be disposed of. In the Authority A cases examined, unannounced visits were not undertaken. The EHOs suggested that they were not as likely to produce useful information as announced visits. In South Wales, the initial visit was unannounced, but consensual access was negotiated on arrival.[122] In that case, the need for urgent information to facilitate control demanded an unannounced visit.

B. Physical Inspections of Premises

The central component of the environmental investigation of an incident is a visit to an implicated food business,[123] for example a shop, a restaurant, a processing plant or a primary producer. All types of vehicles used to transport food may be inspected if they are implicated in the incident.

[122] PEN/EJD/RCC.00219.
[123] PEN/AC/SWP.00120.

A physical inspection of the premises involves a visit to the business and a visual inspection of the areas where food is processed, sold and served, as well as to connected areas, such as toilets and washing facilities. Other senses, in particular smell and touch, may be utilised in the inspection. A visit took place in all the cases in the sample apart from A/I/1. In this case the food business was due for inspection within a week of notification of an incident. The illness concerned did not appear to need control, as the three affected persons were all members of the same party, had all recovered and there had been no reports of any further illness associated with the food business. Therefore, it was agreed that an inspection of the premises would be deferred until the normally scheduled visit the following week, where matters raised by the notification would be followed up.

The physical condition of the premises will be a central concern of EHOs during an inspection. In particular, the cleanliness of the premises will be examined. It is a requirement of Regulation 852/2004 that food business premises be 'clean'.[124] Whilst this may be difficult to assess in borderline cases (EXP-MIC1), non-compliance may be discovered from a simple visual inspection. Two examples from South Wales may be given:

> The ceiling was dirty throughout ... The ceiling mounted cooler units were dusty and dirty ... Cobwebs, spiders and insects were noted to the light units. The walls throughout this area were dirty and discoloured, especially at high level. The wall surrounding the power supply box to the steriliser unit was also dirty. (PEN/AL/BCC.01093)

> The light covers were dirty with flies and insects, whilst numerous insects and woodlice were noted on the floor behind the large stainless steel table. The stainless steel table was also dirty. (PEN/AL/BCC.01094)[125]

'Unclean' material may be seized by an EHO and retained as potential evidence. For example, droppings from pests discovered on the premises will be retained. In one case discussed by EHO-B1, a decomposing mouse was found on the premises and retained in evidence. The mouse was photographed *in situ*, placed and tagged in an evidence bag, stored and produced as evidence in the prosecution of the food business for failure to put in place a proper pest control system. It proved to be good evidence of the failure of the business to comply with the requirement to prevent the presence of pests in an establishment where food processing is being carried out.

The lay-out of the premises will also be examined during the visit to assess whether it helps or hinders the hygienic processing of food. In the best laid-out premises food flows, so that raw and cooked products do not co-exist in

[124] Regulation (EC) No 852/2004 of the European Parliament and of theCouncil of 29 April 2004 on the hygiene of foodstuffs [2004] OJ L139/1, annex II, ch 1, para 1.

[125] See also PEN/AL/BCC.01094; PEN/EJD/RCC.00239; PEN/AP/SWP.00491; PEN/AP/SWP.00492.

the same space. This minimises the risk of cross-contamination. Observing the premises, particularly during service, may allow EHOs to identify sites of potential cross-contamination. If the risk is serious, control may be necessary and premises (or processes) prohibited. Alternatively, advice (either formally, in the form of improvement notices, or informally) may be given on reducing the potential for future cross-contamination. Such observations may also provide explanatory information about an incident of food-borne illness.[126]

The equipment used in processing and cleaning is also scrutinised during an inspection. This inspection will usually be conducted visually. Visual inspection will disclose obvious breaches of the requirement to maintain equipment in a clean condition.[127] For example, in South Wales, 'the band saw machine was heavily dirty and congealed debris was noted on the upper external surfaces'.[128]

The storage of food on the premises will also be a matter of interest during an inspection. Is the food stored sufficiently well to prevent the risk of cross-contamination? Is it stored in appropriate chillers or freezers?[129] Is it stored in airtight containers to prevent decomposition? In South Wales, the disorganised nature of storage in freezers and chillers provided information about the lax hygiene practices of Tudors,[130] which demonstrated the need for control, was an important part of the story of the outbreak and provided important information demonstrating non-compliance with hygiene regulations.

In some cases EHOs may leave equipment on the premises to monitor their condition. In particular, where there is suspected pest infestation, posing a risk of cross-contamination, traps and glue boards may be left. This has both control and investigative purposes. By catching pests, EHOs can obtain evidence that they are present. Monitoring devices may also function to control pests by capture and reduce the risk of cross-contamination. However, the implementation of such measures is unlikely to be acceptable as the only control measure where a continuing risk of primary infection exists.

Environmental Health Officers will record the findings of their visual inspections in pocket-books[131] and by taking photographs of the premises.[132] Information obtained during the inspection will allow EHOs to assess,

[126] PEN/EJD/BCC.00928; PEN/AL/BCC.01093.

[127] Eg, PEN/AL/BCC.01093; PEN/AL/BCC.01094; PEN/EJD/BCC.00926; PEN/AP/SWP.00492.

[128] PEN/AL/BCC.01094.

[129] PEN/AC/SWP.00118.

[130] Eg, 'There were numerous instances where cooked chicken portions were found amongst raw chicken pieces. Boxes of uncovered chickens were also found which were badly frozen up and encased in ice in parts.' (PEN/JD/RCC.00269)

[131] PEN/EJD/RCC.00232; PEN/JD/RCC.00304.

[132] PEN/JD/RCC.00269.

first, whether there is a continuing risk of primary infection and, secondly, whether hygiene requirements are being complied with. It may also allow them to understand a cause of the outbreak of food-borne illness. Notes will record contraventions of regulatory standards.[133]

The notes may later be converted into a witness statement, which will set out the observations made by the EHO during his or her inspection of the premises. Within the local authorities examined, contemporaneous notes were converted into formal statements complying with section 9 of the Criminal Justice Act 1967 only when enforcement action was seriously contemplated. In other cases, contemporaneous notes were often typed and inserted into the file as file notes.

Officers frequently carry digital cameras on inspections.[134] These cameras are set up to date-stamp photographs digitally. Hard-copy photographs are printed and placed on file. Where EHOs still use film cameras, hard-copy photographs and negatives will be retained. Photography plays a number of roles in the investigation, and is one of the key methods of detailing environmental investigations. Photographs may be used by EHOs in three ways:

(a) to document the investigation;
(b) to describe the premises and processes implicated in the outbreak; and
(c) to provide the basis for analysis by experts.[135]

The documentary function of photographs is 'the simplistic recording of items, people and scenes using photography as a source of documentation'.[136] An example is the recording of the fact that an emergency prohibition notice (a control measure) has been placed on a piece of equipment or premises implicated in an outbreak.[137] They may also be used to document contents of premises, such as Tudors' meat chiller in South Wales.[138] The descriptive function of photographs attempts to provide 'a narrative of the situation the photography is attempting to record'.[139] An example of a narrative may be a series of photographs that seek to demonstrate the level of cleanliness of a piece of processing equipment or premises.[140] The photographs taken by Alexis Pierris in the South Wales case (PEN/AP/SWP.00492-00494) attempt to narrate the condition of Tudors' premises. Further, photographs may have an analytic function in both control and enforcement decisions. Control decisions may be made by regulatory actors, such as the OCT or a senior EHO, partially on the basis of information presented

[133] PEN/JD/BCC.01029.
[134] PEN/JD/BCC.01030; PEN/AL/BCC.01094; PEN/AP/SWP.00492.
[135] Glenn Porter, 'A new theoretical framework regarding the application and reliability of photographic evidence' (2011) 15 *Evidence and Proof* 26.
[136] Ibid, 44.
[137] PEN/EJD/RCC.00227.
[138] PEN/EJD/RCC.00239; PEN/EJD/RCC.00241.
[139] Porter, above n 131, 44.
[140] PEN/AP/SWP.00490.

via photographs. In enforcement situations expert witnesses may be asked to base reports (partially) on photographs taken during an investigation.[141]

Sketch plans of the premises may be drawn up (PEN/JD/RCC.00300). These serve two purposes. The first is descriptive, showing how the premises are laid out and describing the actions of enforcement officers during the inspection. For example, the area(s) shown in photographs may be marked on the plan. This assists more senior enforcement officers, who may take decisions about what control and enforcement actions should be taken based on the photographs, and future judicial decision makers, to understand what and where is being shown by photographs.[142] Secondly, the plan may seek to narrate breaches of hygiene regulations. By detailing flows of raw and cooked food, a plan can show the risk of cross-contamination present in the lay-out of the premises. This may have control functions, may form the basis of advice or formal action that prevents further cross-contamination (and therefore further primary cases), and may allow EHOs to demonstrate breaches of hygiene regulations.

C. Examination of Documentation Retained at Premises

A second important part of a visit to a business's premises during an investigation into food-borne illness is the examination of documentation relating to the food business.[143] By examining documentation an EHO may be able to discern procedural weaknesses that contributed to the incident.[144] For example, documentation sets out the food safety management systems in place to ensure compliance with food safety and food hygiene regulation.[145] Weaknesses in this system may be a factor in an incident of food-borne illness.

The EHOs seek to examine such documentation by consent so as not to jeopardise cooperation between the food business and the officers. In the event that such consent is not forthcoming, EHOs have the power to examine such documentation under the Food Safety and Hygiene (England) Regulations 2013. Regulation 16(6) provides:

> (6) An authorised officer entering premises by virtue of this regulation, or of a warrant issued under it, may inspect any records (in whatever form they are held) relating to a food business and, where any such records are stored in any electronic form—

141 See, eg, Colin Houston's expert report in South Wales (PEN/CH/RCC.03672).

142 PEN/JD/RCC.00300.

143 PEN/DG/SWP.00571. In *R v McSweeney, Kaya and Mitchells and Butler plc* (Snaresbrook Crown Court, 8 January 2015) unreported, two staff members employed by a food business were convicted of perverting the course of justice and jailed for falsifying documentation following an incident of clostridium perfringens which led to the death of one customer and 33 other cases of illness.

144 PEN/AC/SWP.00118.

145 PEN/AC/SWP.00117; PEN/EJD/RCC.00221.

> (a) may have access to, and inspect and check the operation of, any computer and any associated apparatus or material which is or has been in use in connection with the records; and
> (b) may require any person having charge of, or otherwise concerned with the operation of, the computer, apparatus or material to afford him such assistance as the officer may reasonably require.

The EHOs may also take away such documentation for later examination,[146] but will seek to obtain copies by consent. In either case, a receipt should be issued.[147] If documentation essential to the running of the business, such as the Hazard Analysis Critical Control Point (HACCP) plan, is removed, EHOs should ensure that the business retains copies, in order that it can continue to operate. Original documentation should be retained in secure storage, and copies placed on file for the EHO to use.

Documentation may be more readily available in soft copy, and in this case EHOs may take copies of files, and examine these on computers when they return to their office. Regulation 16(7) of the Food Safety and Hygiene (England) Regulations 2013 provides:

> Any officer exercising any power conferred by paragraph (6) may—
> (a) seize and detain any records which the officer has reason to believe may be required as evidence in proceedings under any of the provisions of these Regulations; and
> (b) where the records are stored in any electronic form, require the records to be produced in a form in which they may be taken away.

Section 32(5) and (6) of the Food Safety Act 1990 give EHOs a power to inspect and take away documents in substantially similar terms.

i. Food Safety Management System Documentation

The first thing that an EHO will ask to see during an inspection is the HACCP documents.[148] These documents, inter alia, set out the procedures in place to ensure that the food is microbiologically safe, and the steps taken to monitor compliance with these procedures. Documents will be assessed to determine whether they adequately control the risk of food-borne illness. Copies of these documents will be placed on file. These documents may be forwarded to an expert for an assessment of the adequacy of a food safety management system (EXP-MIC1; South Wales). Where they do not disclose adequate systems, control action may be necessary to ensure the business does not operate until proper systems are put in place.

[146] PEN/EJD/RCC.00221.
[147] PEN/EJD/RCC.00224.
[148] PEN/EJD/RCC.00221. Note that the documentation may be in a standard form, based on the Food Standards Agency 'Safer Food, Better Business' package, available from <http://www.food.gov.uk/business-industry/caterers/sfbb>.

ii. Temperature records

In most cases EHOs examine temperature control records kept by businesses implicated in an outbreak.[149] Creating and retaining temperature records is a requirement of HACCP plans where heating and chilling form a key part of the food business.

In A/I/16, copies of the temperature control sheets relating to the chiller where the oysters implicated in the outbreak were stored were examined, copied and placed on file. In A/I/23, EHO-A3 examined the temperature records relating to the fridge where ingredients of the dish implicated in the food-borne illness were stored.

Examination of temperature records kept by food businesses plays a central role in the investigation of food-borne illness. Identifying a failure to cook or chill food to the correct temperature may provide an explanation for the existence of micro-organisms within the food. Temperature records are important evidence in enforcement actions taken against businesses over non-compliance with refrigeration requirements, hot and chill holding requirements, and their HACCP plan.

iii. Preparation Instructions

If a particular dish is implicated in an incident, EHOs will obtain instructions for preparing the dish. In some cases instructions may disclose a process that offers the chance for food to become or remain microbiologically contaminated. If so, the process may be prohibited.[150]

In A/I/16, the procedure that set out how the dish should be prepared, cooked and presented was copied and placed on file. Shellfish were to be served raw. Therefore, micro-organisms present within the shellfish would not be killed during preparation. Similarly, other dishes for which the preparation does not involve heating to 83°C (eg, steak tatare, carpaccio, liver parfait) disclose a risk that organisms within the food will not be killed during preparation (EHO-A2).

In A/I/12, preparation instructions required the meat to be cooked, left to cool overnight at ambient temperature then served without reheating. The EHOs concluded that this created a situation where the presence of micro-organisms in the meat was likely. Examining the preparation instructions allowed them to provide a likely explanation of the incident, involving deficiencies in the method of preparation. Advice was given about future preparation. Preparation instructions were placed on file.

[149] Similar actions were taken in public cases; PEN/EJD/RCC.00222; PEN/AP/SWP.00491.

[150] In some situations experts may instructed to give an opinion on whether the preparation method adopted is adequate to destroy any microbiological contamination, as in the case of *R v Kashioulis t/a Oakwood Deli* (Wood Green Crown Court, 2000) discussed in David Hetherington and Slim Dinsdale, 'Successfully defending food prosecutions' (2001) 12 *International Food Hygiene* 5, 7.

In the South Wales case, the preparation of school meals that involved not heating cooked meat exposed consumers to the risk of *E. coli* present in the meat when delivered, whereas preparation instructions that involved heating significantly reduced that risk. By accessing preparation instructions, EHOs were able to explain why children in some schools that received cooked meat from Tudors became ill, while children in other schools did not.

iv. Absence and Sickness Records

Details of staff sickness and/or absence are accessed by EHOs in order to identify (or rule out) the possibility of contamination by ill food handlers during food preparation. Records of staff sickness and absence will be examined by EHOs. Sickness records may also identify people who need control.

In A/I/20, staff absence records were obtained from Food Business G. Fourteen members of staff had been absent from work in the six weeks prior to the notification of an incident of food-borne illness. The majority had reported diarrhoea and vomiting as the reason for their absence. The records also showed that one staff member had been sent home after vomiting on the premises. Examination of these records suggested that viral gastro-enteritis, probably norovirus, had been present in the staff, and had been introduced into the food by cross-contamination in the food preparation areas. The incident of vomiting on the premises, which would have led to the virus's becoming airborne, was identified as the most likely cause of cross-contamination.

In A/I/23, the sickness records of the business were obtained. Procedure required that those staff members who reported sick were required to be clear of symptoms for 48 hours prior to returning to work. The records showed that one staff member had been ill, but that he had been properly excluded from work in accordance with policy. Records demonstrating compliance with sickness procedures tended to suggest that the food was unlikely to have become cross-contaminated by ill food handlers.

v. Other Documents

Other documents, such as cleaning schedules, delivery records, employee training records, personal hygiene policies and the business's sickness procedures, may be of interest to EHOs.[151] Copies of documents of interest will be placed on file.

[151] PEN/EJD/RCC.00248; PEN/CE/SWP.00166.

D. Questioning Businesses

A key part of the visit to premises implicated in an incident of food-borne illness is asking questions of businesses. Answers obtained provide a fuller picture about the extent and causes of the incident. Questions may be asked under caution or without a caution (see below), although both EHOs and files demonstrated a preference for asking questions without a caution. This preference is based on a perception that businesses will be more forthcoming with information necessary to control the spread of illness if they are questioned informally.

i. Under Caution

The requirement, found in the Police and Criminal Evidence Act 1984 (PACE) and associated Codes,[152] to caution those questioned who are suspected of committing a criminal offence, applies to EHOs conducting interviews following outbreaks of food-borne illness. A person charged with the duty of investigating offences must conduct interviews in accordance with PACE Code C.[153] This 'is a question of fact in each case',[154] considering the context of the inquiry and the role played by EHOs.

It may be argued that EHOs are investigating and controlling outbreaks of food-borne illness rather than 'charged with the duty of investigating offences', and therefore that the obligation to caution does not apply. However, the investigation and control of food-borne illness cannot be seen as separate from the investigation of whether offences have been committed, and the two roles may exist concurrently.

In *R v Gill*,[155] Special Compliance Officers employed by the Inland Revenue interviewed the appellant as part of a civil investigation into the non-payment of tax. No caution was administered, and subsequently the Revenue sought to use the answers given in interview as part of the evidence in a criminal trial, arguing that civil enforcement officers were not charged with enforcing criminal law. The court rejected this argument, holding that 'The [Special Compliance Officers] were charged with investigating serious fraud and, since serious fraud inevitably involves the commission of an offence or offences, it seem to us to follow that they were charged with the duty of investigating offences.'[156] It seems that this can be applied by analogy to EHOs investigating incidents of food-borne illness, since such incidents

[152] The PACE Codes apply to local authority EHOs. See *Dudley MBC v Debenhams* (1994) 159 JP 18, which discussed the application of PACE Code B to inspections by Trading Standards Officers.

[153] Police and Criminal Evidence Act 1984, s 67(9).

[154] *R v Seelig* [1992] 1 WLR 148.

[155] *R v Gill* [2004] 1 WLR 469.

[156] Ibid, para 38.

(almost) inevitably involve the commission of an offence or offences under the exceptionally broad law of food safety and food hygiene. It seems to follow that EHOs charged with investigating these incidents are also charged with the duty of investigating offences.

Paragraph 10.1 of PACE Code C provides:

> A person whom there are grounds to suspect of an offence ... must be cautioned before any [answers to] questions about an offence ... may be given in evidence to a court in a prosecution.

Paragraph 10.1 does not prevent EHOs from asking questions not under caution for purposes other than being 'given in evidence to a court in a prosecution'. Therefore, EHOs may ask questions necessary for controlling food-borne illness without administering a caution. However, the answers may not be admissible in a prosecution.

Note for Guidance 10A to PACE Code C provides that 'grounds to suspect of an offence' means that 'there must be some reasonable, objective grounds for the suspicion, based on known facts or information which are relevant to the likelihood the offence has been committed and the person to be questioned committed it'. The objective nature of the test was confirmed in *R v Nelson and Rose*.[157] The EHO need not be able to identify a particular offence that he or she suspects has been committed, but must merely suspect that *an* offence has been committed.[158]

The required suspicion will not necessarily be present in offences requiring *mens rea*, where an EHO has objective grounds to suspect that the *actus reus* of an offence had been committed but has no objective grounds to suspect that the interviewee has the *mens rea* necessary for the offence. Therefore, an EHO may ask questions intended to establish suspicion of *mens rea* before he or she is required to administer a caution as required under Code C, paragraph 10.1. However, when investigating incidents of food-borne illness, EHOs are faced with strict liability offences. Therefore, the objective grounds need only relate to the *actus reus* of an offence.

When there has been a notification of food-borne illness and EHOs attend an implicated food business, it is likely that there will be reasonable, objective grounds to suspect that an offence or offences under food safety and/or food hygiene law has or have been committed (although it may be unclear exactly what offence).[159] When there are a number of reported illnesses, with a common business identified as the source, there is likely to be suspicion that the offence of selling food unfit for human consumption

[157] *R v Nelson and Rose* [1998] 2 Cr App R 399.

[158] *R v Rodger* [2002] EWCA Crim 660 [29]–[32].

[159] Eg, is the HACCP plan inadequate, or is it adequate but has not been followed? Have temperature control requirements been breached, or has the business failed to comply with the cold chain?

or injurious to health has been committed.[160] The law of food hygiene is so all-encompassing, and breaches of food hygiene law so closely associated with incidents of food-borne illness, that in most situations where premises are epidemiologically, microbiologically or even anecdotally associated with an outbreak, there will be an objectively reasonable suspicion that there has been a regulatory contravention on those premises.

Other procedural requirements apply when an interview is conducted under caution. Environmental Health Officers understand that interviewees must be informed of the nature of the offence in respect of which they are being interviewed,[161] that the interviewees 'are not under arrest and are free to leave if they want to',[162] and that they may obtain legal advice and may have a solicitor present during the interview (EHO-A3; EHO-B1). However, *McNamara v Television Licensing Region Centre* appears to suggest that an interviewee need not be informed of his or her freedom to leave and of his or her right to a solicitor in circumstances where the officer does not have a power of arrest, or where the interview is conducted on premises controlled by the individual being interviewed.[163] This reflects the situation in which EHOs often find themselves when investigating incidents of food-borne illness, where the EHO does not have a power of arrest (other than a citizen's power of arrest)[164] and is conducting the interview on the premises of the business. However, in all cases included within the sample, where an interview under caution was conducted, the EHOs ensured that the voluntary nature of the interview and the entitlement to legal advice were stressed,[165] suggesting that *McNamara* does not reflect the practice of EHOs investigating incidents of food-borne illness.

It is clear from the files examined that where the business is a company, a representative of the company will be questioned. Environmental Health Officers express a preference for the person questioned to be sufficiently senior to be able to answer on behalf of the company, and to have broad knowledge of the company's activities and practices.

In most cases the caution that should be administered when questioning the food business on the premises will be the pre-inferences caution, as the food business will not have access to legal advice prior to questioning. This ensures that inferences could not be drawn, and the inferences caution should not be given. The form of the caution is prescribed in PACE Code C:

> You do not have to say anything. But it may harm your defence if you do not mention when questioned something which you later rely on in Court. Anything you do say may be given in evidence.

[160] PEN/EJD/RCC.00244.
[161] PACE Code C, para 11.1A.
[162] PACE Code C, para 10.2.
[163] *McNamara v Television Licensing Region Centre* [2002] EWHC 2798 (Admin) [21].
[164] Police and Criminal Evidence Act 1984, s 24A.
[165] PEN/AL/RCC.00344. See also PEN/JD/RCC.00258.

In the South Wales investigation, William Tudor was interviewed under caution twice. When the interview was conducted by Jane Donagh, she noted that 'being satisfied of a breach of [food safety requirements] ... I would be cautioning him'.[166] Here, the caution appears to be issued on the basis of satisfaction that a breach has been committed, rather than on reasonable, objective suspicion of an offence. It appears that EHOs are using a higher threshold to decide whether a caution is appropriate in a particular case. This may be because of EHOs' reluctance to damage the cooperative relationship between them and a business by cautioning the business, which EHOs believe places the relationship on a confrontational level, removing the business from the regulatory network.[167]

Most interviews under caution conducted on the premises of the business will be recorded using contemporaneous notes, rather than tape-recorded. This is because of the situation of urgency in which the questions arise. Following such interviews, the interviewee will be given the opportunity to read the contemporaneous notes and to make any necessary additions or corrections. The interviewee will sign the contemporaneous notes to indicate that they represent an accurate record.[168]

Food businesses may also be invited to a voluntary interview under caution at the offices of the local authority. Such an interview is likely to take place after the incident of food-borne illness has been controlled and there is no further risk of primary or secondary cases (CON-1; EHO-A3). In these cases, interviews will not seek information required for control purposes. Such interviews are tape-recorded, and will often be conducted with a legal adviser present. Often food businesses refuse to attend these interviews under caution (EHO-A3; Cadbury *Salmonella*).[169]

ii. Not Under Caution

Interviews under caution were rare in the cases examined. In many cases EHOs asked questions of businesses without cautioning them first, even where, in most cases, there were objective, reasonable grounds to suspect that an offence had been committed.[170] This appears contrary to the requirements of PACE.

Questions are asked not under caution because of the need to obtain information necessary to control the incident of food-borne illness. The EHOs found businesses more willing to cooperate with their investigations into an

166 PEN/EJD/BCC.00931.
167 EHO-A3; EHO-C2.
168 PEN/AL/RCC.00347.
169 Above n 9.
170 See, eg, PEN/EJD/RCC.00223.

incident if they asked questions without a caution.[171] Cooperation is important in obtaining information about products, places or people that require control. By cautioning a business, EHOs feel that they may damage their rapport, often built over significant periods of interaction through annual inspections and advice.[172] This EHO–business relationship may contribute to the ability of EHOs to obtain information regarding the food-borne illness. This concern was expressed by EHO-A3:

> Because we want to try and find out what happened, and stop it, we wouldn't want to do something which would prevent people from giving us as much information as possible. If we started PACEing people straight away, then they might not tell us information. They have a right not to say anything, so they might not say anything until they have got a lawyer there and that could stop us from controlling the outbreak. So we do, I suppose, lose a little bit in the evidence gathering, but gaining in knowledge for investigation and control.

Environmental Health Officers view interviews conducted under caution as confrontational, creating an antagonistic relationship between the individual and the EHO. This is because, as noted by the Court of Appeal in the context of an investigation by the police, a 'caution informs the suspect that he is the suspect and that the [officer], in speaking to him, [is] not treating him simply as a witness to assist [the officer] in [his] enquiries but [is] looking for evidence against him'.[173] Once the interviewee becomes aware of this, there is unlikely to be as cooperative a relationship between him and EHO, whereas if a caution were not administered, the business (as witness) would be likely to want to help, self-enrolling into the regulatory network.

The practice of EHOs' choosing not to caution in order to obtain better information is the antithesis of the police practice, examined by the Court of Appeal in *R v Shillibier*,[174] to caution witnesses even where there were no reasonable grounds for suspecting that they had committed an offence. This practice was adopted 'in order to improve the chances of the interview being admitted in evidence should it later be held that the person concerned ought to have been treated as a suspect'.[175]

In the event that a caution is administered, businesses may not be willing to answer questions, at least without consulting a lawyer, disrupting the flow of information necessary for the control effort. Delay in obtaining information may (perhaps temporarily, perhaps permanently) prevent necessary control measures being put in place, leading to further primary or secondary cases. This is unacceptable to EHOs, who see their key role as preventing the spread of food-borne illness.

171 EHO-A3.
172 EHO-A3.
173 *R v Rodger* [2002] EWCA Crim 660 [34].
174 *R v Shillibier* [2006] EWCA Crim 793.
175 *R v Shillibier* [2006] EWCA Crim 793 [69], per Richards LJ.

Environmental Health Officers wish to obtain information quickly and cooperatively, rather than under caution, so that control can take place. By advising the witness of his or her right to silence and the right to consult a lawyer, the relationship between the interviewee and the EHO is framed in confrontational terms from the start, with consequences for the quality of evidence that can be gathered. By using a tool associated with criminal investigation, EHOs feel that businesses will be deterred from assisting with control.

In South Wales, the initial questioning of William Tudor on the first visit following notification took place without a caution's being administered. This was despite the fact that the food business was implicated in an outbreak of *E. Coli* O157 by initial epidemiology. This was likely to give rise to a suspicion that an offence under the food safety and/or food hygiene regulation had been committed.[176] Questions were asked about the supplies to and from the business, the operations of the business on the premises, the use and cleaning of the vacuum-packing machine, the preparation and (lack of) amendment of HACCP documentation and stock rotation.[177] A caution was administered only later. Even after the interview under caution (specifically about the vacuum-packer) had taken place, EHOs from Bridgend County Borough Council questioned William Tudor without a caution:

> In relation to the use of the vac packer, I questioned Mr W Tudor what packaging was used. Mr W Tudor showed me into a small room off the raw meat area [containing] boxes of plastic packaging which he advised were used for the vac packing. When asked whether the same packaging was used for the cooked products he advised 'no' and took me to the delivery area where he showed me more plastic packaging which he confirmed was used for the cooked products. (PEN/EJD/BCC.00937)

Once Mr Tudor had instructed a solicitor, the relationship between the EHOs and Tudors became less cooperative. This demonstrates that the perception of a restricted information flow following caution may have some basis in fact:

> Mr Hennah [Solicitor for Tudor] advised that he would be recommending that his client not be interviewed more than once and that he should be presented with all the evidence against him prior to the interview ... At approximately 3.30pm (1530) that day I spoke to Mr William Tudor's solicitor, Mr Hennah. I explained to him ... the possible need to interview Mr William Tudor under caution. He advised that he would be recommending that his client not answer any questions under PACE. (PEN/EJD/RCC.00237 and PEN/EJD/RCC.00240)

[176] Eg, an offence under Food Safety and Hygiene (England) Regulations 2013, reg 19, of supplying food injurious to health.

[177] PEN/EJD/BCC.00925-00926; PEN/EJD/RCC.00219-00221; PEN/AP/SWP.00491.

After this point, all further questioning of Mr Tudor was conducted by the police under caution, due to the inquiry's evolving into an investigation into suspected manslaughter.[178]

E. Questioning Employees of Food Businesses

An EHO may wish to question individuals about offences under the food safety and food hygiene legislation.[179] In the cases examined, EHOs tended to approach employees of businesses and ask questions with the consent of the employers. The employees most often questioned were the kitchen staff directly responsible for preparing implicated food.[180] If a particular dish was implicated, the employee responsible for that dish was of particular interest to EHOs. The head chef, or other person responsible for the kitchen, was also often questioned, because he or she was the person best placed to explain the practices and procedures adopted. How was the food prepared? How was the food stored? How was equipment cleaned? Employees may be better placed to answer these questions than the business (or, in reality, senior officers and managers), particularly in large organisations. Other staff, such as delivery drivers[181] or serving staff, may also be questioned.

In A/I/12, EHOs questioned the cook employed by Nursing Home A about the methods used to prepare the beef implicated in the incident of food-borne illness. Similarly, in A/I/16, the chef who prepared the shellfish that was epidemiologically linked to the illness was questioned about the preparation methods adopted.

Whilst EHOs have the power to compel employees to answer questions,[182] a cooperative stance is taken. The EHOs will attempt to build a rapport between the employees and themselves. They try to make it clear that they are looking for information, not looking to apportion blame, and seek to enrol employees into the network engaged in the control effort, stressing the importance of the information they can provide. This information may lead to control action(s).

[178] The transcripts of the police interviews can be found at <http://new.wales.gov.uk/ecolidocs/sourcematerial/JTS/sourcematerialjtsswptranscpt.pdf?lang=en> (last visited 19 January 2015).

[179] It is likely that victims of food hygiene incidents will give statements voluntarily.

[180] PEN/AC/SWP.00118; PEN/PP/RCC.00321; PEN/PP/RCC.00322.

[181] PEN/EJD/RCC.00236; PEN/AP/SWP.00495.

[182] Food Safety Act 1990, s 33; Food Safety and Hygiene (England) Regulations 2013, reg 17(1)(b). If an answer given by an employee might tend to incriminate him or her, the employee may refuse to answer.

F. Observation of Working Practices

An EHO may ask the business, or an employee, to demonstrate processes used in the business.[183] This allows the EHO to gain an understanding of day-to-day practices. These practices may demonstrate weaknesses responsible for contamination of food with food-borne illness micro-organisms. This may suggest a cause of the outbreak, and a need for control action. It may also demonstrate food business failure to comply with food safety or food hygiene requirements or documented practices, particularly HACCP plans.

In A/I/16, the chef at Food Business K was asked to prepare the oyster dish implicated in the outbreak in front of the EHOs, in order that kitchen practices could be assessed. Similarly, in A/I/23, the chef was asked to prepare the noodle dish eaten by both people suffering from symptoms: EHO-A3 observed the preparation of the dish, and found it to be prepared in a hygienic manner. Nothing observed in either of these cases suggested a need for control or enforcement action.

In A/I/27, EHO-A3 asked to observe the preparation of a burger, as the food safety management system and preparation instructions did not demonstrate that the burger would reach a sufficient temperature to destroy microbes in or on the item. The chef prepared the burger, and EHO-A3 used a probe thermometer to check its temperature. This showed that the internal temperature of the burger was above 83°C, adequate to kill the organisms that might cause food-borne illness. This suggested that urgent control action (possibly by way of prohibition) was not necessary to prevent further cases of food-borne illness. The need for temperature control was stressed by way of advice.

As well as food preparation, enforcement officers may ask for cleaning practices to be demonstrated, in order that they can ensure that these are adequate to minimise the risk of cross-contamination.[184] Observation may demonstrate that cleaning practices are inadequate, or that documented cleaning practices are not being complied with. If cleaning does not appear adequate to remove the risk of food-borne illness, it may be necessary to take control action. Observation may also be good evidence of breaches of hygiene requirements, providing information that may be used during enforcement action.

VI. SUPPLY CHAIN INVESTIGATIONS: TRACING

Tracing the source of food implicated in an incident of food-borne illness is an important part of the role of an EHO responding to notifications of

183 PEN/JD/RCC.00280; PEN/EJD/BCC.00935.
184 PEN/EJD/BCC.00926; PEN/EJD/RCC.00228.

food-borne illness. Identifying where particular food comes from, and to where it has been dispatched, is essential in the event that enforcement officers wish to put in place control measures to prevent the occurrence of further primary cases. Withdrawing the product from the market requires that EHOs trace other food businesses that use or sell the food product (other retailers), and identify food businesses that may be responsible for the contamination of the product (manufacturers and producers). Control may necessitate identifying food businesses below, above and level with an initially implicated business in the supply chain.

Tracing is also necessary when building an enforcement case. In order to take enforcement action against, for example, a primary producer, it is necessary to establish the linkage between that producer and the product implicated in the incident of food-borne illness. Tracing sampled products through the supply chain allows this linkage to be established.

Tracing requires enforcement officers to access information from businesses. The business must identify the organisations that supplied them with the food ('upwards traceability') and the organisations to which they have supplied food ('downwards traceability'). Tracing should also include businesses that handle food, such as logistical contractors. Regulation 178/2002[185] imposes a requirement that food businesses retain documentation allowing tracing by enforcement authorities. Failure to retain traceability information is a criminal offence.[186] Businesses are required to have both upwards and downwards traceability.

Article 18(2) of Regulation 178/2002 provides that a business must be able to 'identify any person from whom they have been supplied with a food … a food-producing animal, or any substance intended to be, or expected to be, incorporated into a food or feed'. This requires upwards traceability, with businesses expected to keep records of their suppliers and to be able to show these on demand to those investigating an incident of food-borne illness. An EHO investigating such an incident should therefore be able to request copies of traceability documentation, and use these to track food through the food chain. Often documents retained for the purpose of establishing traceability are invoices and delivery notes. Packaging may also be retained to indicate the source (and batch) of the product. These documents will identify the supplier of the food, and allow the EHO to contact the supplier to continue the investigation and to take control action if necessary.

Article 18(3) of Regulation 178/2002 provides that businesses must 'have in place systems and procedures to identify the other businesses to which

[185] Regulation (EC) No 178/2002 of the European Parliament and of the Council of 28 January 2002 laying down the general principles and requirements of food law, establishing the European Food Safety Authority and laying down procedures in matters of food safety [2002] OJ L31/1.

[186] Food Safety and Hygiene (England) Regulation 2013, reg 19.

their products have been supplied'. This requires downwards traceability. Documents such as order forms, invoices and delivery notes may be retained to assist in this. Environmental Health Officers may request these in order to identify businesses lower in the supply chain that may need investigation, for example to establish whether they retain products requiring seizure and destruction. The downwards traceability requirement applies only to business-to-business transactions. It does not apply require a business to identify consumers to whom it has sold food products.

Whilst the regulatory obligations relate to external traceability, it is necessary to have internal traceability procedures in place to comply with such regulations, so that a food business can be sure which food relates to which supply. In a business with a large turnover of stock, systems must be in place to ensure that it is possible to say which batch of stock was allocated to a particular business further down the chain of supply. It is not enough merely to know that, for example, turkey was delivered to a business on the Xth day of a particular month. More detail must be provided: Who supplied the meat to you? When? What identifying marks does it have on it?

The availability of traceability information should facilitate the control of outbreaks of food-borne diseases by allowing actors within the regulatory network to swiftly narrow down the source of the outbreak, and to enable identification of products that may pose a risk to consumer safety. These products can then be controlled.

Gathering information about the sources and destinations of food is standard practice during the investigation of an incident. Suppliers may not be contacted during the investigation in the event that hygiene practices within the food business are clearly to blame for the incident, but in cases where a product is implicated, tracing through the supply chain will prove central to the inquiry. European Union legislation on traceability was implemented in part in order to 'ensure correct product identification in the event of a … recall for health and safety reasons'.[187] Figure 4.5 illustrates the traceability requirements of Regulation 178/2002.

In A/I/16, it was necessary to trace the suppliers of shellfish following an incident of *norovirus*, which affected four diners in a party of six who had eaten at Food Business K. Epidemiological investigations pinpointed shellfish as the food vehicle carrying *norovirus*, and initial investigations at Food Business K indicated that the shellfish had not been contaminated on the premises. It was necessary to trace the shellfish up the chain, in order to discover the source of the *norovirus*, and to prevent further primary cases from

[187] Cliff Morrison, 'Traceability in Food Processing: An Introduction' in Michèle Lees (ed), *Food Authenticity and Traceability* (Woodhead Publishing 2003), 478. From the point of view of manufacturers, traceability is important 'to substantiate any on-pack marketing claims, for example "Organic"; to provide due diligence in the event of a Public Enforcement challenge [and] to minimise the quantities involved in the event of a recall' (ibid, 477).

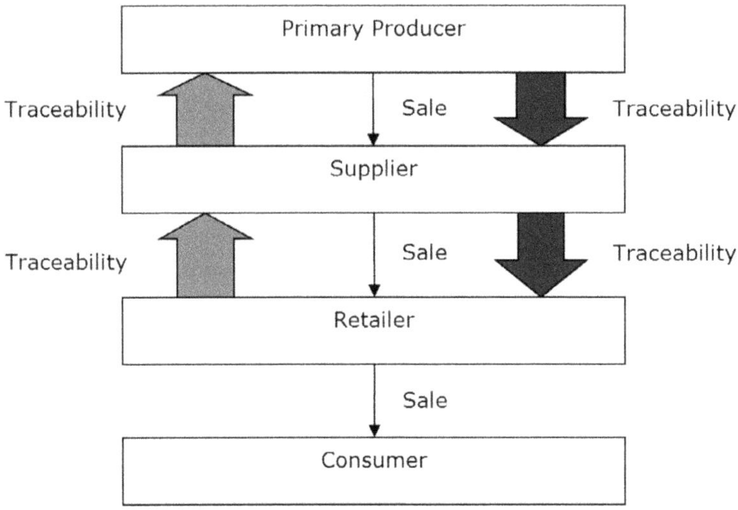

Figure 4.5: Traceability requirements of Regulation 178/2002, article 18

the implicated batch of shellfish in other food businesses. As shellfish are generally served uncooked, it was particularly urgent and important to trace other potentially affected shellfish, as consumers would not have the protection of cooking to destroy contamination. Therefore, Food Business K was asked to identify its suppliers. It did so, voluntarily identifying Supplier H as the source of the shellfish, and providing the invoice for the batch involved in the incident.

Supplier H, situated in a suburb of A, was contacted by EHO-A4. A visit was made, which did not suggest that the shellfish had been contaminated on the premises of Supplier H. Therefore, Supplier H was asked to identify its suppliers and any other food businesses to which the batch had been supplied. Supplier H confirmed that no other food businesses had been supplied with shellfish from the batch implicated in the incident, and that the shellfish were obtained directly from a primary producer. Supplier H identified Primary Producer C as the source of the shellfish. Primary Producer C was situated in a different EU state. The EHOs obtained copies of invoices for the batches of shellfish purchased from Primary Producer C.

Primary Producer C was then contacted by EHO-A4. The producer was unaware of any incidents of *norovirus* associated with shellfish in the batch supplied to Supplier H. The last water sample taken from the beds disclosed no contamination, but this sample had been taken a month previously. The shellfish beds had been closed in the past due to contamination by sewage outfall. The central food safety authority of the EU state where the primary producer was based was then contacted by EHO-A4. A new sample

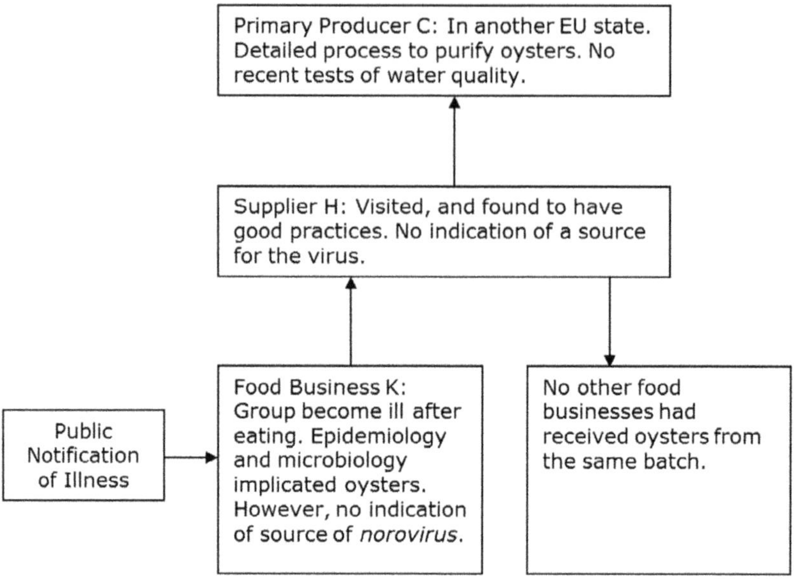

Figure 4.6: How EHOs traced up the supply chain in Case A/I/16

of water was taken for analysis, disclosing contamination in the water, and the shellfish beds were closed voluntarily until two analyses disclosed that the water was free from *norovirus*. The tracing process used in A/I/16 is represented diagrammatically in Figure 4.6.

In A/I/8, Food Business V was asked to provide information about the source of salmon, which had been eaten by three members of a party of seven diners, who had fallen ill. The details of the supplier were provided to the enforcement officers, in the form of an invoice for the batch of salmon from which the dish had been made. However, a decision was made that it was not necessary to contact the supplier, as many others had eaten salmon dishes made from the same batch at Food Business K without falling ill, suggesting that it was not the salmon itself that was the problem but that it had either become cross-contaminated in the kitchens of Food Business V, or the complainants had become ill via person-to-person spread.

In A/I/10, the storage of spices in unlabelled containers was criticised by EHOs. Whilst the containers were airtight, and therefore adequate to prevent cross-contamination, the fact they were unlabelled impeded the ability of the EHOs to trace the manufacturer and the particular batch of spices concerned. The food business was advised that transferring spices to such containers would constitute a breach of traceability requirements unless a written record was kept, identifying the source of each spice and its batch number.

VII. CONCLUSION: INVESTIGATION OF INCIDENTS OF FOOD-BORNE ILLNESS

Environmental Health Officers have a wide range of investigative techniques available them to gain information about a suspected incident of food-borne illness. Collecting all potential information about an incident is a time-consuming and resource-intensive task, particularly when EHOs are faced with an incident involving a large number of potential victims. A network of specialists will work alongside EHOs to assist (and guide) the investigation. In some cases an OCT coordinates the network, whereas in other cases the network may be less formal, with specialists consulted on an *ad hoc* basis.

Investigations provide enforcement officers with a large amount of information about incidents of food-borne illness. A wide range of methods is available to obtain it. Information is primarily sought to enable EHOs to control the spread of food-borne illness. They seek information that will allow them to identify contaminated products and places, and infected individuals. They are prepared to accept incomplete information if this gives them the chance to prevent the primary and/or secondary spread of illness. Generally, the investigation consists of epidemiological, microbiological and environmental inquiries.

Information may form the basis of an enforcement action against a business following an outbreak of food-borne illness. However, such information must be marshalled to ensure that the regulatory breach alleged can be demonstrated to the standard required. Information is often not sought for its value in enforcement. This presents significant challenges for EHOs, who, as discussed in chapter six, may find that investigation does not produce the evidence required to prove that regulations were breached ('availability challenges'), or that information is not admissible as evidence ('admissibility challenges'). These challenges may be caused by the conduct of investigations, which may sacrifice the case-building rigour necessary for enforcement in order to achieve swift control of the spread of illness. The reluctance to conduct interviews under caution is a valuable example of this.

5

The Key Goal: Control of Food-borne Illness

I. INTRODUCTION

CONTROL IS SEEN by EHOs as the key objective when dealing with an incident of food-borne illness (EHO-A3; EHO-B1). They perceive their actions as responding to and managing food-borne illness, inhibiting its spread from infected products, places or people ('objects') to uninfected products, places or people. Preventing further individuals from suffering from illness (and possibly dying) is the key goal; anything else that may be achieved during a response to food-borne illness is secondary.

Biosecurity, which can briefly be defined as 'making life safe',[1] is the central objective following an incident, with EHOs seeing their primary role as quickly taking measures to preclude the spread of illness once an infected object has been discovered. They aim to prevent two types of transmission: primary spread, where 'cases' contract the illness from the original source of the infection (the food product or premises); and secondary spread, where 'cases' are infected by existing 'cases'.[2] Formal or informal control of products, premises, people or environments may be used to achieve the prevention of primary or secondary spread. Control is generally secured through small-scale practices of authorities in relation to localised outbreaks of illness. This chapter explores these practices and places them within a biosecurity frame.

Control actions may be viewed as part of the process of managing the risks presented by an incident of food-borne illness. The investigation allows the EHO to identify, characterise and assess hazards, and calculate likelihood and consequences if the hazards eventuate (ie the risks). The EHO perceives

[1] Steven Hinchliffe, 'Biosecurity' version of 1 January 14, available at < http://www.biosecurity-borderlands.org/sites/default/files/research_outputs/biosecurity_web_copy.pdf>, downloaded 7 May 2014.

[2] This has been conceptualised as risk management, 'reducing the likelihood of a given population becoming infected, [as] reducing risk in this (limited but pertinent) sense' (Andrew Donaldson, 'Biosecurity after the event: risk politics and animal disease' (2008) 40 *Environment and Planning A* 1552, 1556).

the main risk as further cases of the illness. An intervention should then be made to reduce all risks to an acceptable level. The intervention may then be communicated to the public, in the event that it requires their action. Formal or informal control actions are the usual form of intervention when managing the risks of an incident of food-borne illness.

The response to food-borne illness is therefore aimed at the discovery of risky objects in need of control. Information illuminates the objects of control, and without information action cannot be taken. Control is therefore intimately linked to the collection and analysis of data about an incident of food-borne illness. In chapter four, the way in which that information is collected was presented. Investigative decisions are influenced by the need to discover objects of illness in need of control.

Whilst both formal control and enforcement actions are shaped by the extensive data gathered during responses to food-borne illness,[3] these data similarly are shaped by the need to control and enforce. This iterative process of information collection and control and enforcement is an important finding of this book. However, the need to control the spread of food-borne illness is the primary shaper of the investigation, as control is the primary objective of the investigators.

The imperative of controlling incidents is not new. Control of illnesses has long been an area of government intervention into the behaviour of private citizens.[4] Since at least the Black Death, preventing the spread of illness has been seen as a key responsibility of government.[5] Much historic public health intervention focused on prevention of illness.[6] Control of illness already present in the population has also been seen as an important role of government, and a key site of intervention into citizens' lives. Further, the traditional role of government in controlling illness has meant that illness has become a metaphor for other areas that call for intervention.[7]

Control of illness as a regulatory imperative has not been subject to significant consideration in the literature. Much of the socio-legal literature has focused on regulatory responses to one-off incidents, or on the routine

[3] Paul Rabinow, 'Episodes or incidents: Seeking significance' in Andrew Lakoff and Stephen J Collier (eds), *Biosecurity Interventions: Global Health and Security Questions* (Columbia University Press 2008).

[4] Simon Carter, 'Disease and Infection in the City' in Gary Bridge and Sophie Watson (eds), *The Blackwell Companion to the City* (Wiley Blackwell 2011).

[5] Ibid. The 'Black Death' was the name given (from the 16th century) to the plague, both pneumonic and bubonic, that arrived in and spread through Europe between 1348 and 1351, with devastating results.

[6] Eg, the power under Public Health Act 1936, s 83 to clean filthy or verminous premises. See further Joanne Fozzard and Gai Murphy, 'Public Perception of the Local Authority Pest Control Service in the UK' (2014) 14 *Journal of Environmental Health Research* 17.

[7] See Jonathan Simon, *Governing through crime: how the war on crime transformed American democracy and created a culture of fear* (Oxford University Press 2007).

interactions of regulators and businesses.[8] Incidents of illness caused by regulatory breach do not fit easily into either of these two categories, and control is particularly important in motivating regulatory action following incidents of illness. Techniques and possibilities of control of biological risks have become important objects of study over the last decade, with increased awareness of biological threats to modern life spurred on by increasing incidences of human and animal disease risk.

Why is control particularly important in a situation of food-borne illness? With food-borne illness, there are continuing consequences that need to be dealt with. Such continuing consequences do not arise in other regulatory contexts. An accident at work is generally a one-off event. Changes may be required to avoid a similar breach in future, but the breach that caused the accident is unlikely to continue to have consequences. Products that do not comply with safety regulations may be present on the market, but injurious consequences do not spread from product to product. Removal from the marketplace, which is an aspect of control, may be necessary, but the complexities of control involving products, premises and living people are not present.

Control is generally exercised on a small scale, in terms both of the numbers affected and of the geographical scope of the incident. Even the South Wales outbreak,[9] which involved 157 *E. coli* sufferers, only affected people attending schools within a relatively small geographic area. The median number of people suffering from illness in incidents detailed in the Local Authority A files was four.[10] The incidents detailed in the public documents were larger, but the sufferers generally numbered in the tens. In a small number of cases more than one local authority was involved, but no incident was truly nationwide.

Therefore, response to food-borne illness is primarily an exercise in managing primary and secondary spread of illness, and preventing further cases, on a relatively small-scale. The EHOs interviewed saw this control as their primary function, with a central goal of reducing the number of people ultimately affected by the incident.

II. BIOSECURITY: THE THEORETICAL FRAMEWORK

Humans, non-human entities and inanimate objects constitute a dynamic network that functions to construct the lives we lead and are able to lead.

[8] Eg, Ross Cranston, *Regulating Business: Law and Consumer Agencies* (The Macmillan Press 1979); Keith Hawkins, *Law as Last Resort: Prosecution Decision-Making in a Regulatory Agency* (Oxford Univeristy Press 2002); Bridget M Hutter, *The reasonable arm of the law?: the law enforcement procedures of environmental health officers* (Clarendon 1988).

[9] Full details available at <http://wales.gov.uk/ecoliinquiry/?lang=en>.

[10] Mean = 8.36. Mode = 2. The range of people affected was between 1 and 46.

Within the complex network, individual entities may pose a risk either to the human actors, or to something valued by the human actors (such as animals and plants, and particularly those animals and plants that provide an economic gain to humans). These entities may be the subject of intervention by humans, who attempt to control the risk within the *bios* engendered by the risk actors through techniques of securitisation. These techniques seek to interrupt the circulation of the risky actor within the complex system of interactions between humans, non-humans and the environment, through monitoring and control, particularly through the separation of the risky thing from the rest of the system, either by initially preventing the thing from entering the system or by removing it once it is within the system. To take a simple example, where a non-native species is seen as harmful to the natural *bios* of a particular locality then a biosecurity response would be to take steps to prevent the non-native species entering into the *bios* and removing any members of the non-native species already within it.

Of course, when concerned with illness, the potential harm to the network must be modelled in terms of risk. However, the inherent uncertainty in planning a biosecurity response sufficient to ensure that risky things are excluded from the *bios*, particularly given the dynamism of microbiological threats, which may evolve and adapt to security measures introduced, means that surveillance and monitoring forms a central part of a biosecurity response, identifying the objects against which the securitised response must be directed. The circulation of actors within the complex *bios* means that there are multiple entry points for unwanted food-borne illness entities. They may come from overseas, evading border controls through the mobility of migrating species, or be brought in by asymptomatic human carriers. The may exist in the environment, but enter into the food system only through the act of a human or non-human. They may have been within the system all along, with security measures to prevent them infecting food. It is necessary to identify when they have entered into the system and to take action to control spread. The way that control was operationalised in the cases studied, and how the food system was secured, is considered in the rest of this chapter.

III. CONTROL IN ACTION

Both interviews and documents demonstrated that the control of food-borne illness is central to the practise of EHOs. A response to food-borne illness will almost always involve some form of formal or informal control action.[11] As a biosecurity action this will generally involve a pathogen-based

[11] The exception is where the illness is no longer spreading by the time the authority is informed. In particular, where the illness is sporadic, and there is no further risk of either primary or secondary infections, control measures will not be necessary. If all the food that has been identified as the source of the infection has been eaten or otherwise disposed of, and there

precautionary approach to control.[12] Depending on the characteristics of the incident, the action may need to target particular premises, particular products, particular people or particular environments in a bid to reduce the risk of primary and secondary spread of food-borne illness. Primary infection is that illness caused by the product or premises that are the centre of the incident. Secondary infection is illness caused by transmission from a person suffering from the illness,[13] who may be either a primary or secondary 'case'. As control focuses on the 'infected' rather than the 'responsible', more than one product, location or person may need to be targeted.

Files examined and EHOs interviewed demonstrated the central role of control in their response to incidents of food-borne illness. Every EHO interviewed saw preventing primary and secondary spread of illness as their principal responsibility during the response to an incident. They expressed this in different ways, both expressly, stating that prevention of further cases was prioritised (EHO-A3; EHO-B1), and impliedly, through actions that favoured the prevention of further cases, such as the interviewing of implicated food businesses without caution[14] and agreeing to incomplete disclosure of information[15] where this would enable preventative control actions to be taken.

In almost every Local Authority A file there were numerous examples of control action. Products were controlled: in A/I/10 an ingredient suspected of contamination with *salmonella* was voluntarily destroyed; in A/I/16 all oysters sourced from a particular production location and harvested between particular dates were withdrawn from the market; and in A/I/17 food was seized and condemned by a magistrate. Premises and businesses were controlled: in A/I/26 a business voluntarily agreed to stop producing food. People were controlled: in A/I/5 and A/I/6 employees and customers were both formally and informally excluded. The environment was controlled: in A/I/11 advice was given on hand-washing practices.

Similarly, control played a central role in the public cases. In South Wales, meat held by schools was collected and destroyed. Meat held by Tudors was prevented from entering the market, although it was not seized, as the emergency prohibition notice meant there was no risk that the food could leave Tudors' premises; Tudors' premises were prohibited, and a school

is no secondary transmission risk, then the EHO will have no need to impose control measures. (In A/I/2, the food vehicle containing *campylobacter* had been consumed and there was little risk of secondary transmission, and therefore a decision was taken that control measures were unnecessary (EHO-A3).)

[12] Hinchliffe, above n 1.

[13] Different mechanisms may be responsible for spread, ie person-person, person-food-person or person-surface-food-person.

[14] See above, ch 4.V.D.

[15] *Norovirus* in Oysters, discussed in ch 4, in the text associated with n 27.

was closed when an unexplained bloody stool was discovered; children and adults suspected of suffering from food-borne illness were subject to voluntary and mandatory exclusion; and the school environment was altered to lower the risk of secondary transmission, by altering the operation of fruit tuck shops and preventing children from playing in sandpits and with plasticine. In the Merthyr *Cryptosporidium* case,[16] the swimming pool implicated was closed in order to allow thorough cleaning; similarly, the Fat Duck was closed voluntarily to allow decontamination;[17] in Marathon Oil, workers were encouraged to stay away from work until symptom-free for 48 hours;[18] in Feltham Hill School,[19] children were prevented from attending school until they had given two clear samples.

For EHO-B1, control action is central to the response to food-borne illness because it saves lives. The actions are necessary to reduce the likelihood that a person will die from the food-borne illness involved in the incident. In any incident, there is a chance that a person affected by food-borne illness may die, but the odds increase along with the number of 'cases'. By taking control action to prevent the spread of the illness, and therefore reduce the number of 'cases', EHO-B1 expressed the opinion that those actions reduce the likelihood that a person will die. Only control actions can reduce this likelihood, and therefore were central to the EHOs' role.

Of course, other EHOs do not see their role in quite such dramatic terms. They see it in terms of preventing harm, and do not reference the chance of death when justifying taking control action (EHO-D2). These EHOs make reference to the reduction of risk of illnesses due to their actions, rather than the reduction of the risk of death. In controlling food-borne illness, EHOs work closely with the CCDC and other healthcare professionals, in order to ensure that the action taken is adequate to prevent further cases from a medical viewpoint.

Actions taken during an investigation of food-illness are viewed by EHOs through the lens of control, and are justified by the effect they may have on preventing the spread of food-borne illness. Without information, EHOs cannot determine the identity of objects of formal or informal control, and therefore investigation is oriented towards identifying these objects. For example, EHOs talk about the need to obtain traceability information in

[16] Outbreak Control Team, *Outbreak of Cryptosporidium Infection in a swimming pool complex in Merthyr Tydfil South Wales Summer 2009* (OCT 2010).

[17] Health Protection Agency, *Foodborne illness at The Fat Duck restaurant: Report of an investigation of a foodborne outbreak of Norovirus among diners at The Fat Duck restaurant, Bray, Berkshire in January and February 2009* (HPA 2009).

[18] Outbreak Control Team, *Outbreak of Norovirus Infection at Marathon Oil UK, Aberdeen March 2008* (OCT 2008).

[19] Overview and Scrutiny Committee, *Report of the Scrutiny Review of the E. Coli O157 Outbreak at Feltham Hill Infant and Nursery School* (London Borough of Hounslow 2010).

terms of preventing further primary cases by removing the food from the market (through, for example, seizure), rather than in terms of tracing the responsible food business to take enforcement action. Similarly, EHOs seek to obtain details of all affected individuals quickly, in order to take exclusionary action (or at least give advice) to prevent secondary spread, before considering the probable epidemiological advantages of obtaining contact details. Even when these advantages are considered, they are considered in the light of the importance of quickly identifying the source in order to take control action to prevent further primary cases, perhaps through prohibition, rather than in terms of the advantages of high quality epidemiological evidence when taking formal enforcement action.

Control and information-gathering are in a symbiotic relationship. The investigation of a food-borne illness allows an EHO to assess the need to take control measures. In order to achieve the aim of preventing primary and secondary spread, the investigation must identify the products, premises or people that must be controlled by formal or informal action. The investigation must establish the source of the illness, whether the source is a product or a particular food business, and identify any individuals who may be affected; control measures can then be taken. This need to control the spread of the illness drives the information that is gathered, and the information that is gathered drives the formal and informal control action taken by EHOs, in consultation with the OCT (if any) and other professionals.

In contrast, the need for enforcement has less of an influence on the information that is gathered by EHOs during an investigation of an incident of food-borne illness. Examples of investigative decisions shaped by the need for control are seen in chapter four; in particular the decision to question a food business without a caution in order to maintain the cooperative relationship necessary for control may be identified.[20]

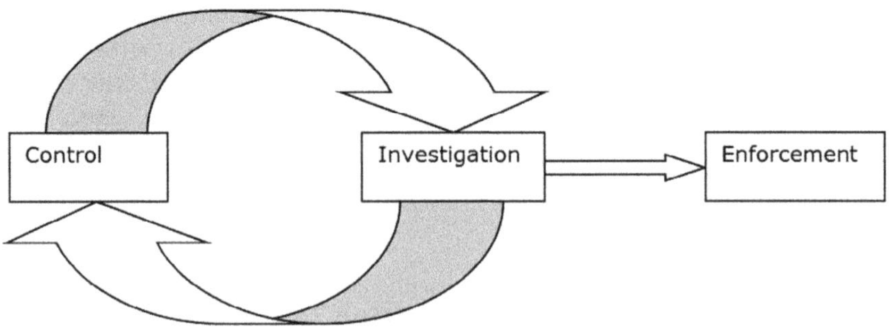

Figure 5.1: The relationship of investigation, control and enforcement

[20] Above, ch 4.V.D.ii.

Control could not take place without information gained during an investigation; it is likely that different information would be gathered if it were not necessary to control the spread of food-borne illness. Gaining information for the purposes of control is prioritised over gaining information for the purposes of enforcement. According to EHO-A3:

> When we're out there doing that initial visit after an outbreak has been reported, the most important thing on our minds is stopping it. The most important thing on our minds is not securing a conviction; it's stopping the disease from spreading and making sure that we are not going to get any further cases. I'm not saying that we compromise on evidence gathering, but it's not the first thing that we are doing.

This dynamic is not present in other regulatory investigations carried out by local authorities.

As well as prioritising information needed for control, it is clear that the level of information that EHOs require before action is taken is different for control and enforcement purposes. The level of information that justifies control action may not justify later enforcement action. Environmental Health Officers are prepared to take control actions on a precautionary basis when information is present that suggests a link between a product, place or person and the incident of food-borne illness. They are not prepared to take enforcement action on such a basis.

This is a precautionary approach,[21] and may be expressed as follows: where there is a risk to human health because of a food-borne illness, uncertainty about the source of that risk should not prevent a decision maker from taking action aimed at abating that risk.[22] Control action is be taken on the basis of information that suggests, without proof on a balance of probabilities or beyond a reasonable doubt, that a person, place or foodstuff poses a risk of primary or secondary spread; the importance of control is such that the evidential checks and balances that must be satisfied are fewer than those required before formal enforcement action can be taken.

For example, in A/I/5, an incident of *E. Coli* O157, Local Authority A took a precautionary approach to excluding a member of staff from work at the affected nursery. Information was obtained that the staff member had loose stools and frequent bowel movements. The staff member did not present with all the symptoms of *E. coli* O157, had an explanation for experiencing loose stools and frequent bowel movements (these were

[21] Local authorities are not required to take a precautionary approach (in contrast to the General Product Safety Regulations 2005, SI 2005/1803, reg 10(5)), but this approach is most likely to be successful in preventing further primary or secondary spread of food-borne illness.

[22] For a formulation of the precautionary principle that mirrors this, see Elizabeth Fisher, 'Is the precautionary principle justiciable?' (2001) 13 *Journal of Environmental Law* 315, 316. See also Per Sandin, 'The Precautionary Principle and the Concept of Precaution' (2004) 13 *Environmental Values* 461.

known side-effects of medication the staff member was taking) and was not a microbiologically confirmed case. However, the decision was taken by EHO-A3, in consultation with CCDC2, to exclude the staff member from work until he had given two negative samples 48 hours apart. The risk of infection justified exclusion, because of the relative ease of transmission of *E. coli*, particularly in a nursery environment. It was more prudent to exclude than to take the risk that the staff member was suffering from *E. coli*. Controlling the risk, however slight, by taking formal control action was seen as of primary importance in the response to this incident of food-borne illness.

Similarly, during the Merthyr *Cryptosporidium* outbreak, the investigation suggested that there was a small risk that all pools were infected with *Cryptosporidium*, but this was not thought to be likely. However, the actions of the OCT demonstrate the importance of controlling small risks, with formal control action being taken. The OCT 'decided to close all the pools in the centre as a *precautionary measure*',[23] and '*as a precautionary measure* the main pool remained closed until work that the OCT had agreed was essential to reopening was carried out'.[24]

The investigation is designed to produce information that identifies products, premises or people that may pose a risk to the public. Control action may then be taken as a precaution. Stronger proof may be produced, but it is not the goal of the process, as information showing risk is sufficient to justify such precautionary control action. A food-borne illness investigation, with the goal of obtaining information to enable control, may not produce information that is capable of demonstrating regulatory breaches at the standard of proof required for enforcement actions, damaging the ability to bring successful enforcement actions.

IV. TWO TECHNIQUES OF CONTROL

In the empirical work conducted, it was observed that EHOs sought to achieve control in a number of distinct and competing ways. These sometimes competing, sometimes complementary methods of control were either explicated by EHOs, or implicit in the control actions taken by them. All of these strategies—of spatial separation, market management and punishment—can be seen as aspects of a biosecurity approach to the response to an incident of food-borne illness. Whilst biosecurity literature focuses on spatial separation, it is argued that market management and punishment can play a key role in reducing risk to consumers, and therefore play a role in a biosecurity response to food-borne illness. These regulatory technologies are utilised,

[23] Merthyr *Cryptosporidium* OCT Report, above n 16, 34 (emphasis added).
[24] Merthyr *Cryptosporidium* OCT Report, ibid 35 (emphasis added).

alone or together, to prevent primary and/or secondary spread.[25] It is necessary to explore these different regulatory technologies, including how each works, to achieve the EHOs' primary goal of control.

A. Control Through Spatial Separation

Environmental Health Officers most commonly saw control as creating safe spaces in which the majority of uninfected individuals might go about their daily lives without the chance of contracting food-borne illness. By preventing contact between uninfected people and infected products, places or people, those who are not afflicted with the illness should not become ill. This spatial separation emphasis reflects the predominant biosecurity approach to management of incidents of illness, 'constructing and then protecting a system of spaces wherein disease is kept out',[26] although Hinchliffe *et al* argue that the utility of such an approach is limited, as the permeability of spatial barriers to microbiological forms of life prevents the achievement of 'safe' spaces and give rise to a false sense of security.[27]

Beginning with Foucault, the biosecurity literature, which examines control of illness,[28] demonstrates that the advent of illness has perennially been 'met with order; its function is to sort out every possible confusion'.[29] Foucault shows that in the seventeenth century, in response to an outbreak of plague, strict regulations were put in place to ensure that the government could undertake surveillance and assess which of the townspeople were suffering from illness.[30] Those who were ill were subject to regulation, preventing their mixing with individuals who were not ill. Outbreaks of illness result in 'the penetration of regulation into even the smallest details of everyday life'.[31] This is evident in the cases examined in this book. The spread of illness is prevented through the application of formal and informal powers that affect a wide range of people, including those not afflicted by the illness.

The use of control through spatial separation may in particular be discerned from the use of powers to control people under the Public Health (Control

[25] Stephen J Collier and Andrew Lakoff, 'The Problem of Securing Health' in Lakoff and Collier (eds), above n 3, 12.

[26] Hinchliffe, above n 1.

[27] Steven Hinchliffe *et al*, 'Biosecurity and the topologies of infected life: from borderlines to borderlands' (2013) 38 *Transactions of the Institute of British Geographers* 531, 535.

[28] As opposed to bioterrorism, or the battle to prevent colonisation by non-native species; see, eg, Kezia Barker, 'Flexible boundaries in biosecurity: accommodating gorse in Aotearoa New Zealand' (2008) 40 *Environment and Planning A* 1598; Kathleen M Vogel, 'Biodefence: Considering the Sociotechnological Dimension' in Lakoff and Collier (eds), above n 3, 227.

[29] Michel Foucault, *Discipline and punish: the birth of the prison* (Penguin 1979) 197; see also Carter, above n 4.

[30] Foucault, above n 29, 195.

[31] Ibid, 198.

of Disease) Act 1984, preventing interaction until a person no longer poses a risk.[32] The powers seek to create safe spaces, where the risk of infection is minimised. This reflects the classical operation of control presented in Foucault's work,[33] where the ill (and potentially ill) are separated from the well, in a bid to prevent cross-infection. The UK response to foot and mouth disease in cattle, and the worldwide response to SARS, both of which involved enforced separation of the ill from the well through regulatory action, have led to increased interest in the subject.

The separation of biological entities is viewed as the key characteristic of a biosecurity response to an incident of illness. Control attempts to create a safe space, where the uninfected are kept separate from the sick. This spatial conception is the foundation of much of the biosecurity literature that examines animal illnesses (such as foot and mouth and avian influenza), where emergency action to prevent the spread of outbreaks often includes the creation of exclusion zones to prevent the mixing of infected animals with those that are not infected.[34] Illnesses in chickens,[35] cattle,[36] pigs[37] and ostriches[38] are all discussed in the existing literature, which examines large-scale measures to control their epidemic and pandemic spread. Control measures aimed at illness on a national and international scale, such as border controls and 'legal preparedness', form the focus of much academic commentary.[39] As noted above, the incidents of food-borne illness are not at this epidemic or pandemic level,[40] but separation is still identified as a key goal of control, and as an important technique for preventing the spread of illness.[41] Formal control action taken in response to incidents of food-borne

[32] Further, failure to separate the ill and the well may be a criminal offence. A business must not allow a 'person suffering from, or being a carrier of a disease likely to be transmitted through food … to handle food or enter any food-handling area in any capacity' (Regulation 852/2004, annex II, chapter VIII, para 2).

[33] Foucault, above n 29.

[34] Nick Bingham and Steven Hinchliffe, 'Mapping the multiplicities of biosecurity' in Lakoff and Collier (eds), above n 3, 173.

[35] Ibid.

[36] Donaldson, above n 2, 2.

[37] Charles Mather and Amy Marshall, 'Biosecurity's unruly spaces' (2011) 177 *Geographical Journal* 300.

[38] Charles Mather and Amy Marshall, 'Living with disease? Biosecurity and avian influenza in ostriches' (2011) 25 *Agriculture and Human Values* 153.

[39] See, eg, Estair Van Wagner, 'The practice of biosecurity in Canada: public health legal preparedness and Toronto's SARS crisis' (2008) 40 *Environment and Planning A* 1647.

[40] Indeed, a control measure can target just one person in order to prevent the spread of illness. A typical situation in which a single person is targeted is that of a food handler presenting with typhoid following travel abroad (CCDC2). In this case it is necessary to prevent that person from having contact with food in order to manage the risk of secondary spread.

[41] Whilst transnational outbreaks of food-borne illness, such as the incident of *E. Coli* O104 in Europe in May and June 2011, do occur, the number of individuals affected is smaller than in international pandemics such as influenza or SARS.

illness reflects the techniques of biosecurity at a micro level,[42] with limited and discrete formal control measures.

Food safety has been identified as a key focus of biosecurity, where biosecurity interventions are used by governmental agencies in the practice of control of food-borne illness.[43] The creation of a space for consumers that is free from food-borne illness is part of the goal of EHOs who respond to an incident (EHO-B1, CCDC2). By creating a safe space for consumers, the risk of transmission is minimised. The characteristics of food-borne illness, with their imperfectly aerosol nature, mean that spaces from which the well are excluded, and within which the disease is confined, may be smaller than those studied in pandemic-focused biosecurity literature.

Hinchcliffe and Bingham note that 'the practices [of biosecurity] involve *both* a defining of territorial units, designating disease-free areas from those that are disease carriers, *and* a regulation of the flows and movements of living … matters'.[44] In the sphere of food-borne illness, both processes are evident. Whilst the space defined as 'infected' may be small in food-borne illness cases, perhaps limited to a site occupied by a food business or a residence of an infected person, EHOs attempt, using formal or informal control action, to prevent flows from such areas to those that are disease-free. Techniques adopted to prevent such flows include prohibiting the use of particular space for the carrying out of food business until it is rendered disease-free, and confining infected persons within delimited spaces where they cannot mix with the general population.

Biosecurity measures, implemented through control actions, attempt 'to monitor, regulate, and/or halt the movements of various forms of life',[45] from the microbes that cause illness to the humans suffering from the illness. Measures preventing those suffering from illness from entering 'clean' spaces, and separating the ill from the well, form a central concern of the literature. The use of control action by EHOs can be seen as an attempt both to regulate and to halt the movement of forms of life, human and microbial.

The safe spaces created in the response to food-borne illness need not be created through the use of physical restrictions on the movement of infected foods or infected persons. The creation of a safe space may also be based on the implementation of processes aimed at making transmission of food-borne illness difficult. This is possible because of the need for contact between individuals, or individuals and food, to transmit the disease.

[42] See further, and more prosaically, Nick Bingham and Stephanie Lavau, 'The object of regulation: Tending the tensions of food safety' (2012) 44 *Environment and Planning A* 1589, who examine the operation of biosecurity in a single meat inspection.

[43] Collier and Lakoff, above n 3, 11.

[44] Steven Hinchliffe and Nick Bingham, 'Securing life: the emerging practices of biosecurity' (2008) 40 *Environment and Planning A* 1534, 1535.

[45] Nick Bingham, Gareth Enticott and Steven Hinchliffe, 'Biosecurity: spaces, practices, and boundaries' 40 *Environment and Planning A* 1528, 1528.

In South Wales,[46] the implementation of environmental measures aimed at restricting the opportunity for microbes to be passed from person to person could also be characterised as micro-biosecurity responses aimed at creating safe spaces.

Biosecurity measures may operate on a voluntary level. Self-exclusion can classically be seen as a voluntary biosecurity measure, separating the ill from the healthy. However, in incidents of food-borne illness, voluntary exclusions tend to turn into mandatory exclusions in the event that illness is confirmed, due to the desire of EHOs for tight control on the spread of illness.[47] Whilst communications to parents urging voluntary exclusion during the South Wales outbreak set out good practice in the event that a child suffered from diarrhoea and vomiting,[48] more formal exclusion was used once a child became a confirmed 'case'. Once positive sample results were returned, EHOs required two clear samples before the child could return to school. Informal biosecurity actions of advice change to formal biosecurity actions of exclusion and control of movements when the risk is crystallised through microbiological analysis.

The control actions seen in the cases analysed fit within the biosecurity paradigm advanced above. They seek to make the uninfected safe, by reducing the risk of contamination by the infected. In order to assess these risks, investigation must be carried out. Biosecurity literature examines the collection and analysis of information about an incident of illness, and the processes by which such information is translated into formal action. These processes form an important part of the biosecurity practice of local authorities. The collection, analysis and use of information about food-borne illness is a central strand of this book.

Viewing the response to food-borne illness as a type of biosecurity, with a desire to control interactions between the infected and uninfected and extensive collection of information, fits with much of the empirical data. It also provides a useful frame through which to consider the response of local authorities when confronted with food-borne illness.

B. Control Through Market Management

Environmental Health Officers acknowledge that certain risks cannot be controlled through the separation of the infected and uninfected (EHO-A3). Control may be viewed as aimed at ensuring a safe marketplace, with formal powers used to achieve a market free from food contaminated with food-borne illness. This may be justified in accordance with economic

[46] South Wales *E. Coli* above n 9.
[47] Donaldson, above n 2, 1555.
[48] See ch 4, nn 110 and 111.

rationales for regulation, and can be seen as underlying the use of powers that control food products and food business premises. By managing the market to inhibit consumer access to products that pose a risk of food-borne illness, EHOs seek to prevent further cases of food-borne illness, and allow consumers to purchase food without risk of exposure to illness as a result.

Of course, removal of particular foods from the marketplace can be seen simply as another technology of separation, creating safe spaces through market exclusion rather than geographic exclusion. Indeed, market exclusion functions as a facet of a micro-biosecurity approach, but it should be analysed separately, as it focuses on food as an inanimate commodity rather than as a habitat of (micro-) biological entities.

Applying economic principles, it might be assumed that a perfect market would prevent incidents of food-borne illness.[49] Consumers are able to make informed choices about the food that they purchase, and would (presumably) not purchase food that placed them at significant risk of suffering from food-borne illness. Any food that was contaminated would not be purchased; and restaurants would not be visited if the kitchens posed a risk of contamination. Businesses would need to take precautions to prevent food's becoming contaminated with micro-organisms, or would risk being forced out of the market. Barring unavoidable accidents, food would be safe, and consumers would not risk food-borne illness when they purchased it.

However, the market is patently not perfect. The most significant imperfection in the market for food safety is the provision of sub-optimal information regarding the hazards and risks presented by food. The perfect market model assumes that consumers have all the information they need regarding the safety of the food they are purchasing and the terms on which they contract to purchase it.[50]

Imperfect information about the safety of food takes two main forms. In the first, neither buyer nor seller knows pertinent transactional information. In the second, one party, usually the seller, has more information than the other, usually the buyer. Antle argues that a lack of information about food safety risks is often a symptom of the first form of imperfection.[51] Lack of

[49] The qualifications for a perfect market are as follows: 'Numerous buyers and sellers operating in the market; Free entry to and free exit from the market; Product homogeneity, that is, products in the market have the same features; Perfect information about the product; and Transactions that only affect the parties to those transactions; that is there are no externalities.' Iain Ramsay, *Rationales for Intervention in the Consumer Market Place* (Office of Fair Trading 1984) para 3.3.

[50] London Economics, *Consumer Detriment under Conditions of Imperfect Information (OFT Research Paper 11)* (Office of Fair Trading 1997) 38.

[51] See John M Antle, 'Economic Analysis of Food Safety' in Bruce Gardner and Gordon Rausser (eds), *Handbook of Agricultural Economics*, vol 1 (North Holland Publishing Co 1999), 1085, 'in many cases … sellers may not have better information about the safety attribute of a product than a consumer'.

information is particularly prevalent regarding microbiological contamination. Pathogens are not visible, and are therefore difficult to detect without detailed scientific analysis. Sellers such as supermarkets or restaurants may not be in possession of sufficient information about food safety risks to enable them to give information to the buyer; and if they were in such a position, responsible retailers would presumably withdraw contaminated products from sale.

In addition, certain types of food safety information are asymmetrically distributed between buyers and sellers (the second form of imperfection identified above). For example, consumers are not generally aware of the standards of hygiene and the cleaning procedures that restaurants use in their kitchens, whereas restaurateurs clearly possess such information. Further, a seller may not provide information to consumers regarding the methods of production, such as food safety management systems, but this information would naturally be accessible to sellers themselves.

Deficiencies in information affect consumers' decisions about whether food is safe to purchase. Food safety often cannot be assessed until after the transaction has taken place between the seller and the consumer. Where food may be contaminated with microbial pathogens, safety is an experience good.[52] Experience goods are those products in which the deficient quality of the good cannot be assessed prior to purchase, but which enable assessment of food safety characteristics shortly after the consumption of the good. Where the food leads to food poisoning soon after it has been eaten, the quality (or lack thereof) of the food safety that has been purchased becomes palpable. Once the safety characteristic is assessed then future transactional decisions can be made on this basis. Of course, this may be cold comfort to the unfortunate person who has had to suffer an acute food-borne illness.

Control mechanisms are therefore used to reduce the risk arising from the informational imperfections, with infected products, about which consumers cannot be expected to know, removed from the market. Through the use of controls that restrict the ability of businesses to market their products, regulators attempt to increase the efficiency of market mechanisms for consumers attempting to purchase safe food. A safe marketplace is created, preventing the flow of infected products to consumers, and therefore precluding further primary cases. After any control intervention the market should produce more optimal results than the market prior to the intervention, with products presenting a risk of food-borne illness removed from the marketplace. Primary cases of food-borne illness should fall.

Control measures aimed at securing safe marketplaces view control as an economic concept, allowing consumers to achieve more optimal transaction

[52] Spencer Henson and Bruce Traill, 'The Demand for Food Safety: Market Imperfections and the Role of Government' (1993) 18 *Food Policy* 152, 157.

results. By preventing the marketing of food that is contaminated with food-borne illness, for example through seizure or through closure of a business using an HEPN, a consumer is not exposed to the risk that arises if he or she attempts to judge the safety of a product using inadequate information.

V. ENFORCING BIOSECURITY

The spectre of punishment is used to enforce the separation necessary to ensure biosecurity, to enable the achievement of safe spaces and marketplaces.[53] Punishment both sanctions the failure to comply with the biosecurity techniques adopted, and functions beyond those techniques, sanctioning a failure to control the spread of unwanted organisms through the interaction of products, peoples and places. Punishment has the goal of preventing the spread of micro-organisms through penal threats to those who may spread them.

Foucault contends that the control of illness historically took two punitive forms,[54] each focused on infected individuals,[55] which should be distinguished from preventative measures. Both forms were disciplinary in effect. Exclusion was the method commonly employed to combat the spread of leprosy. Confinement was the typical response to the plague. Both exclusion and confinement mechanisms feature in the control response to incidents of food-borne illness, with the EHOs, responsible for protecting the public from food-borne illness, acting to discipline those suffering from illness, to prevent those not suffering from becoming ill.

Historically, exclusion involved preventing a person from entering a particular place. Classically, the writ *de leproso amovendo* required a parish to remove a leper to a leper colony.[56] Lepers could also be stripped of their rights of citizenship. Whilst responses to food-borne illness are not quite so extreme, the exclusion of individuals from places where they may infect others, on pain of penalty, is a standard response to those individuals' being infected with a food-borne illness.[57]

When a town was infected with plague, all inhabitants were 'inserted in a fixed place', usually their houses, to prevent contact with others.[58] Distance

[53] Eg, the offence of selling food in contravention of a prohibition notice under Food Safety and Hygiene (England) Regulations 2013, SI 2013/2996, reg 8(6).

[54] Foucault, above n 29.

[55] Rather than focusing on infected products and places, which are also key areas of control. It will be argued later that the focus on people is to take a spatial approach to control, whereas the focus on places and products is to take an economic approach.

[56] Bryan A Garner (ed), *Black's Law Dictionary* (9th edn, West 2009) 326. Carole Rawcliffe, *Leprosy in Medieval England* (Boydell & Brewer 2006) casts some doubt on the frequency of the use of the writ.

[57] Eg, Public Health (Control of Disease) Act 1984, s 45O.

[58] Foucault, above n 29, 197.

was created between the illness and those not infected. By controlling people, the aim was to prevent the spread of the illness.[59] A similar impulse may be discerned in the guidance that applies to response to food-borne illness.[60]

Both exclusion and confinement regulate contact between people. By reducing contact the spread of illness may be retarded, reducing the number of individuals affected by illness. Contact is limited by forcible action of the state to ensure that individuals do not mix. These reflect the objectives of biosecurity to create safe spaces, considered above, but become a penal response through the common law of public nuisance, which turns illness from an object of regulation into an object of punishment.

In Britain, the nineteenth-century concern for public health was partly aimed at the control of illness, and at the creation and cleansing of contaminated spaces. Early efforts at control utilised the common law of public nuisance in an attempt to deter infected members of the public from mixing with uninfected individuals, and to punish those who were not so deterred. In *R v Vantandillo*,[61] a mother took her infant son, who was infected with smallpox, to a doctor for diagnosis. The indictment alleged that the exposure of the child within a narrow cul-de-sac led to the infection, and subsequent death, of two children who attended a school situated on that road. It was held that Vantandillo had committed the offence of public nuisance by incautiously exposing members of the public to a contagious, infectious and dangerous disease.[62] Similarly, *R v Burnett* confirmed that the crime of public nuisance is committed when a person incautiously 'expose[s] persons infected with contagious disorders, and therefore [risks] communicat[ing] the ... [illness] to the public, in a public place of resort'.[63]

These cases concerned smallpox, although the reasoning is equally applicable to other diseases.[64] There was no need to wish to expose others to the illness, and indeed in *Vantandillo* the court accepted that the mother had perfectly good reasons for taking her child to the doctor. It seems likely that the common law offence remains in existence. *Vantandillo* and *Henson* were cited without adverse comment by the House of Lords in the more recent case *R v Rimmington*.[65]

[59] The classic British example of isolationist control, although a self-regulatory exercise rather than a governmental command, is the (possibly exaggerated) story of the quarantine of the small village of Eyam to prevent the spread of bubonic plague: see Patrick Wallace, 'A Dreadful Heritage: Interpreting Epidemic Disease at Eyam, 1666–2000' 61 *History Workshop Journal* 31.

[60] Food Standards Agency, *Management of outbreaks of foodborne illness in England and Wales* (Food Standards Agency 2008) para 5.44.

[61] *R v Vantandillo* (1815) 4 Maule and Selwyn 75; 105 ER 762.

[62] A similar result was reached in *R v Henson* (1852) 1 Dears 24; 169 ER 621 in relation to a mare infected with a 'contagious, infectious and dangerous disease.'

[63] *R v Burnett* (1815) 4 Maule and Selwyn 272; 105 ER 835, per Le Blanc J.

[64] William Hawkins, *Treatise of the Pleas of the Crown* (7th edn, G. G. Robinson 1795) suggests that spreading the plague is an offence at common law.

[65] *R v Rimmington* [2005] UKHL 63; [2006] 1 AC 459.

By enforcing separation through criminal prohibitions, the court attempted to ensure that 'no person having a disorder … ought to be publicly exposed … endangering the health and lives of the rest of the subjects'.[66] By criminalising individuals suffering from particular illnesses, the difference (and distance) between the ill and the well is emphasised, despite the lack of any distinguishing moral characteristics. The ill often become ill by chance, and to punish them due to their illness, rather than to attempt to assist with management in order to ensure that they become well (and able to mix with the uninfected), does not reflect the approach of most EHOs to the management of food-borne illness.

Hinchcliffe and Bingham note that biosecurity has historically involved a 'curtailing of civil liberties',[67] with the state asserting its police power against the ill. Indeed, as detailed by Van Wagner, the public health response to illnesses (and particularly SARS) in Canada, involving quarantine and forced treatment, has been subject to challenge on human rights grounds.[68] Operating control in such a manner throws up questions of the balancing of rights and interests between the ill and the well.

However, control should not be seen simply, or indeed largely, as effected through punishment. Whilst control of illness can be viewed as an area where states attempt to assert disciplinary power over biological entities, enforced separation through criminal prohibition is no longer the preferred regulatory response to food-borne (or other types) of illness. Spatial biosecurity, with its geographically separated biological populations, ensures separation in a less punitive manner. Regulators tend to use a more varied toolbox, focusing on the management of spaces and marketplaces, using powers to support the public in avoiding illness, rather than punishing those who are unlucky enough to suffer.

VI. CONTROL IN A REGULATORY CONTEXT

Control is a regulatory exercise. The three methods examined above, spatial separation, market management and punishment, are used to diminish the potential for uninfected consumers to be infected by food-borne illness. Environmental Health Officers place controls on products, places or people. But control is also a regulatory objective, a reason for EHOs to take action in a particular case. Control is invoked as the purpose of particular steps taken by EHOs.

The identity of regulatory objectives, and the role that they play in the decision making of street-level enforcement officers, has been an important

66 *Vantandillo*, above n 62, 764.
67 Hinchliffe and Bingham, above n 44, 1546.
68 Van Wagner, above n 39, 1653–55.

area of study by regulatory scholars. The balance between the desire to punish and the desire to ensure future compliance has proved a particularly fruitful area of scholarship, with tensions between these goals influencing decision making across the regulatory spectrum.[69] With the identification of control as a goal of EHOs responding to incidents of food-borne illness, it is necessary to explore what role it may play in this balancing exercise.

Formal and/or informal control action starts to be taken at an earlier point in the regulatory timeline of an incident than formal enforcement action. It takes place against the background of an on-going investigation into an incident of food-borne illness, and spread may be controlled by the time consideration is given to formal enforcement action, on which much of the study of regulatory decision-making is focused. The need to prevent food-borne illness does not influence decisions at the latter point, having influenced decisions made much earlier, whilst the illness was still spreading. Instead of influencing enforcement, the need for control informs the collection and analysis of data, and formal or informal control interventions. Therefore, control as a motivation underlying regulatory decision making may not be apparent in studies that focus on enforcement.

Control should not be seen as 'compliance by another name'. Control measures do not appear in Ayers and Braithwaite's famous pyramid of sanctions,[70] which has the goal of encouraging compliance against a background of sanctions of escalating severity. The compliance goal of regulatory action relates to the generalised future compliance of food businesses with food hygiene regulation, whereas control relates to a specific incident. Control seeks to minimise the consequences of, and the risk to the consumer from, a failure to comply with regulations in a particular situation. Whilst suspension and/or withdrawal appear at the top of the pyramid,[71] as an an awesome power present, in the main, for deterrent effect, this does not take into account the possibly important role (particularly) of suspension in the response to an incident of food-borne illness. Here, the power is used in a way that is less about past non-compliance and more about present risk, in a way that focuses less on the business and more on the consumers who might suffer from food-borne illness.

The need for control urges regulatory intervention in circumstances where the food-borne illness is not attributable to a particular breach. For example, where a food handler returns from holiday with a food-borne illness, control action may be taken to prevent secondary spread (CCDC2). Whilst the result may be compliance with regulations requiring the exclusion of

[69] See, eg, Ian Ayres and John Braithwaite, *Responsive Regulation: Transcending the Deregulation Debate* (Oxford University Press 1992).
[70] Ibid, 35.
[71] Ibid.

food handlers infected with transmissible diseases, this is a secondary result of the desire to control the spread of food-borne illness.

Whilst compliance is general, control is specific. Whereas action aimed at ensuring compliance may arise out of a range of regulatory activity, action aimed at ensuring control arises only out of incidents of food-borne illness. Control is limited in timescale, while compliance is unlimited in time. Control actions are therefore not motivated either by a desire to ensure compliance with regulatory requirements, or by the need to sanction a breach of regulations.

Environmental Health Officers do not see control as an interest to be balanced against other regulatory goals (EHO-B1).[72] Control is seen as the overriding objective, which should be achieved prior to consideration of whether actions promote other regulatory goals such as compliance. A balancing exercise between public interest factors favouring the taking or not taking of control actions does not occur. Control action will always be taken where deemed necessary, and will not be outweighed by countervailing factors.

Other regulatory objectives are disregarded in order to achieve the goal of control. For example, the interest in taking formal enforcement action in respect of past behaviour, or deterring future breaching behaviour or ensuring compliance in the future, is overridden by the need to control the spread of food-borne illness.

The precedence of control is founded in EHOs' self-perception as guardians of human health and, in some cases, life. They see their key role as preventing avoidable illness. This approach sees the preservation of life and health as *the* objective that EHOs should seek to achieve.

The well-being of every individual who may suffer from food-borne illness is seen as an end in itself. A person's illness or death, if avoidable, should not be condoned in order to achieve another desirable regulatory objective. A deontological approach detectably underpins the primacy of control, and the unwillingness to balance control against other regulatory objectives. Indeed, from an intrinsic moral perspective, an EHO is impelled to take actions that prevent avoidable harm to individuals. The EHOs place an exceptionally high value on human life and health, which cannot be displaced by calculations that weigh the consequences of particular actions. No matter what the consequences, the action that achieves control of the illness should be taken. Therefore, control action aimed at avoiding illness or death should take place in all circumstances, no matter what the effects are on the

[72] Control, however, does involve a balance between one person's intrinsic interest in health and another (perhaps infected) person's freedom of movement. In general, the balance of rights by EHOs favours the uninfected person, with the right of a person to exist in a disease-free environment favoured over the rights of an infected person. (Of course, in both the European Convention of Human Rights and the Treaty on the Functioning of the European Union, public health concerns provide a justification for the restriction of many of the protected rights. Action taken must, however, be necessary and proportionate.)

ability to achieve other regulatory aims. The proportionality required from EHO responses is satisfied, as the risk is seen as so great that every step is justified where it reduces that risk.

This stance may be criticised from an instrumental perspective. If action taken to achieve control prevents action that may generally deter future breach of regulation, or that will ensure future compliance, in the long run greater suffering may be caused, although suffering will be minimised in the short term. If many businesses would comply with hygiene requirements due to the prosecution of one business for a breach of food hygiene regulation, and such prosecution is prevented due to EHOs' taking control action aimed at ensuring that a small number of individuals do not suffer illness, consequentialists may argue that the greatest value to the population as a whole is not being achieved by the prioritisation of control. Further, if consideration is given to the maximisation of economic value, it may be argued that the action that reduces incidence of illness in the long term is the most economically beneficial, because whilst control now will reduce short-term absence from work with illness, in the long term greater compliance with hygiene regulations should raise workplace attendance, increasing productivity.

The choice between balancing control with other objectives and seeking to prevent as many cases as possible can also be understood as a contrast between macro and micro perspectives. Environmental health practitioners are dealing with an incident of food-borne illness at close range. Describing a serious incident as a 'nightmare scenario' (EHO-B1), EHOs see their primary role as stopping the spread of the illness (EHO-A3; EHO-C2). They do not look at the long-term, macro view, judging the consequences of their actions for future compliance. They are focused on the now, preferring current benefits to potential reductions in numbers of future incidents.[73]

Longer-term control actions, such as import controls, emanating from central government may take a more strategic view of the balance between control and other objectives. With greater distance between the decision makers and the illness, decisions can be made to balance control against other goals. Much of the biosecurity literature suggests that central government

[73] Regulators also may focus on controlling *immediate* spread, rather than more distant regulatory goals, in order to avoid the negative publicity that may accompany the occurrence of preventable cases. Hinchliffe argues that regulators 'assert their sanitary agency over the living processes they organize ... such that, should the worst happen, guilt cannot be linked to the actions of the institution' (Hinchliffe, above n 1). Such publicity-based decision making is an acknowledged determinant of regulatory action (see Hawkins, above n 8, 237). Future non-compliance due to regulatory actions during the management of an incident is far less visible than current illness, and regulators may not appear credible and legitimate if they do not achieve these visible, short-term goals. However, there is also a possibility of publicity risk if enforcement action is not taken (see Anon, 'E.coli family's manslaughter call', *BBC News Website* (13 September 2007), available at <http://news.bbc.co.uk/1/hi/wales/6993508.stm>), and this must be balanced against other publicity risks.

action is driven by desire to reform the work practices of non-compliant businesses in order to increase homogeneity in the agricultural sector, and therefore to manage incidents of illness better in future.[74] Therefore, a balance is being struck between this goal and the goal of preventing further cases, which would be alien to enforcement officers.

VII. CONCLUSION

Control involves the collection and sorting of information, using this information to illuminate those products, places or people that must be controlled in order to minimise the spread of the illness. It has two facets: control of primary spread, and control of secondary spread. Different tools are used to prevent primary and secondary spread. Regulatory techniques concentrate on securing safe spaces and safe marketplaces. Different formal and informal control powers will be used.

Control is the central goal of EHOs involved in the response to food-borne illness. They see the aversion of preventable cases of food-borne illness as key in the response to such illness. This goal is clearly the correct one for the EHOs to have, and their determination to achieve safety for the public reflects their consumer orientation and their focus on risk prevention, and also a common humanity shared by EHOs, who do not wish to see individuals suffer with food-borne illness where this could be prevented by taking of one or more control actions.

This chapter suggests that the analysis of practices of biosecurity, which often focus on large-scale pandemic outbreaks, can fruitfully be turned to the analysis of efforts to control the spread of food-borne illness. Biosecurity examines regulatory attempts to deal with '"out of place" biological entities',[75] and this description may be applied to the practices of enforcement officers. Microbiological contamination is clearly 'out of place' in food, and enforcement officers seek to remove it from spaces inhabited by uninfected humans. Micro-biosecurity, as practised by EHOs, warrants further investigation.

[74] Bingham and Hinchliffe, above n 34.
[75] Ibid, 174.

6

Enforcement Following Incidents of Food-borne Illness

I. INTRODUCTION

ONCE INFORMATION HAS been gathered during an investigation into an incident of food-borne illness, and the illness is no longer spreading, EHOs must assess the information obtained and decide whether to take formal enforcement action against a food business implicated in the incident.[1] Once illness is controlled, EHOs perceive that they have fulfilled the minimum requirements of their role but nonetheless recognise that enforcement is something that may be desirable following an incident. The empirical work conducted demonstrates that EHOs face evidential difficulties in showing that regulatory requirements have been breached. Information that demonstrates that a regulatory requirement had been breached either is not available, or is available but would be inadmissible in enforcement action. This, rather than an exercise of prosecutorial discretion, is the principal reason formal enforcement action often is not taken.

The primary obstacles to EHOs' demonstrating breaches are evidential. Evidential weaknesses were apparent in a large number of cases examined in this book, with file notes or letters to consumer-complainants setting out the view of the EHO that the investigation produced insufficient information to allow the officer to come to a conclusion about the incident of food-borne illness and to determine whether there had been a breach of food safety or food hygiene requirements. Two separate but linked epistemic challenges can be discerned. First, officers may have insufficient information to identify the source of the illness (whether food or otherwise) or breaches that led

[1] If an investigation has identified weaknesses in compliance with regulations, EHOs will usually give formal or informal advice on remedying the weakness. Whilst EHOs' ability to give advice is bounded by the strictures of the Food Law Code and Practice Guidance, they are more willing to take action in this area than to take formal enforcement action. The less dramatic consequences for the business, particularly with informal advice, mean that EHOs are willing to intervene in order to seek future compliance. In all cases examined in this book, some form of advice was given following the control of food-borne illness. Most commonly, informal advice was given about temperature controls or sickness policies, which were routinely found to be weak during investigations into food-borne illness.

to contamination.[2] Secondly, EHOs may be certain of the source of the illness, through information and intuition, but have insufficient admissible evidence to prove this to the required criminal standard.[3] These two challenges roughly correspond to difficulties regarding availability and admissibility, with insufficient information usually caused by unavailability[4] and insufficient evidence caused by inadmissibility.[5]

It is clear that proving a food safety offence is epistemically challenging, contrary to the traditional view of strict liability offences.[6] Six key evidential difficulties may be discerned from the data examined in this book:

(a) failure to obtain epidemiological evidence;
(b) failure to obtain food sample evidence;
(c) failure to obtain faecal sample evidence;
(d) medical confidentiality;
(e) inadmissibility of OCT reports;
(f) inadmissibility of information gained from conversations with businesses.

Difficulties (a) to (c) are availability challenges, meaning that officers have insufficient information to identify the source of food-borne illness. Difficulties (d) to (f) are admissibility challenges, meaning that officers may be able to identify the source, but will not be able to prove a regulatory breach beyond a reasonable doubt.

Control decisions, based upon the information gathered during an investigation, are taken on a precautionary basis in situations of uncertainty.[7] The difficulties described above therefore do not prevent EHOs from achieving their primary, control-orientated goal. However, these challenges do prevent the fulfilment of the secondary goal of enforcement, as EHOs often refuse to act without a belief that a prosecution will be successful.

[2] Eg, 'It is very difficult to prove exactly what's happened in outbreaks a lot of the time. There are a lot of outbreaks where we don't know a lot at the end of it, and we can only guess. There are some cases where we are pretty sure that we know what happened ... but in the majority we have to say "we're not sure exactly what happened there"' (EHO-A3); 'it is difficult to prove' (EHO-D3); 'a speculative explanation is ...' (Incident Management Team, *An Outbreak of Food-borne Botulism in Scotland, November 2011* (IMT 2012) 18–19).

[3] Eg '[W]e're as sure as we can be how that outbreak was caused, but are in no position to prove it' and '[W]e are as certain as we ever can be of what happened in relation to them. But it will become clear just how difficult it is even to consider pursuing a prosecution even when you are that certain.' (EHO-A2)

[4] Eg, 'Insufficient evidence to show that there was any food borne illness' (File note, A/I/8); 'It is not possible to ascertain the source of the outbreak' (File note, A/I/10); 'I cannot say with any certainty that the illness suffered was food poisoning or where it originated ... I do not intend to take further action in this case' (Letter to Food Business Q, A/I/25).

[5] Eg, 'There is insufficient evidence for me to prove beyond a reasonable doubt that your illness was caused by deficiencies at [Food Business P]' (Letter to complainants, A/I/24).

[6] See ch 3.II.B.i.

[7] See above ch 5.III.

II. UNAVAILABILITY OF EPIDEMIOLOGICAL EVIDENCE AND ITS IMPACT ON ENFORCEMENT

The first difficulty EHOs face is a lack of epidemiological information. Food history information is particularly difficult to obtain. In a file note, EHO-A3 explained, '[i]t was difficult to obtain an accurate list of food eaten as the hotel did not keep detailed records and delegates had difficulty remembering what they had eaten' (A/I/15). Similarly, in the Belfast *Listeria* incident, 'food history was incomplete in the majority of cases'.[8] Three reasons for are suggested for this lack: 'source fixation'; incomplete memory; and the special features of buffets. These are explored in further detail below.

Whilst shortage of epidemiological information poses some problems for control (and may lead to over-control as well as under-control), it is not fatal to these efforts. Environmental Health Officers are prepared to take control measures against products, places or people they suspect of posing a risk to consumers, unconfirmed by epidemiological findings. For enforcement, however, EHOs feel that they cannot demonstrate a realistic prospect of conviction without solid epidemiological linkage between the illness and the business against which enforcement action is contemplated.

A. Information Limited by Consumers' 'Source Fixation'

The first reason for the failure to obtain complete food histories is 'source fixation'. In this context, this refers to a person's focus on a particular meal as the source of food-borne illness, and a corresponding unwillingness or inability to give details about other possible sources. Source fixation may be seen as being similar to availability, a noted behavioural trait.[9] Whilst availability is a cognitive bias that influences future decision making, source fixation inhibits consumer recall of information about the past.

Consumers are often convinced about where they contracted their food-borne illness, believing that they can identify the meal responsible for their symptoms. When contacted by EHOs, consumers communicate the identified source to the exclusion of other possible sources. Robust epidemiology requires a food history that is as full as possible. The fixed focus on a particular source compromises the ability of EHOs to obtain a full food history, and therefore the availability of complete epidemiological information. Without

[8] Outbreak Control Team, *The report of the Outbreak Control Team of the investigation of an outbreak of listeriosis in the Belfast Health and Social Care Trust during May to November 2008* (OCT 2009) 16.

[9] Amos Tversky and Daniel Kahneman, 'Judgment under Uncertainty—Heuristics and Biases' (1974) 185 *Science* 1124, 1127.

complete information, demonstrating a linkage between the illness and a business beyond a reasonable doubt may be impossible.

The general form of consumer complaint is 'I've eaten from so and so, and I've been ill, it must have been that premises that has made me ill' (EHO-C1).[10] The identified source is often the last meal before the consumer became symptomatic,[11] or is food that is perceived as 'risky' by the consumer, for example shellfish or late-night food. This presents a particular problem where the illness has a long onset time,[12] as a large number of potential sources are ruled out by the consumer prior to investigation by the EHO, and the EHO is never alerted to these. This is the case even where microbiological evidence suggests that the source of the illness was consumed before the consumer ate the supposed source identified by him or her.

An example of the investigations necessary to avoid source fixation was given by EHO-A3:

> A lot of people, when they phone up, they think they know where they have picked it up, and it's not always necessarily going to be the case … I can remember this file where a number of work colleagues became ill after eating at [Food Business X], and they pointed the finger there, but they had also stopped at a couple of pubs beforehand, and they all had cream cakes together in the office, so there were other factors that it could have been. It wasn't necessarily going to be [Food Business X]. They could have picked something up in a pub, either in the drink or in ice; or it could have been environmental contamination; or it could have been the cream cakes they had all had for somebody's birthday that day; or it could have been the water that they use in the office. There were other factors that we had to investigate. (EHO-A3)

'Source fixation' also damages EHOs' ability to control food-borne illness. They fear that fixation will prevent them from (quickly) finding the 'true' source, which requires formal control action to prevent further spread. Here EHOs are concerned about the 'false negative', controlling the fixated source rather than the actual source. With enforcement the converse is the fear: without full information, EHOs fear an epidemiological 'false positive', where the incorrect business is identified as the source of food-borne illness.

The source upon which consumers become fixated tends to be food eaten outside the home. Consumers are typically unwilling to accept domestic

[10] EHO-C1 characterises this form of complaint as 'the "I had this and thought it was dodgy" attitude' (EHO-C1).

[11] SOL-1; 'What people tend to think is that the last meal they had before they were poorly is what has made them poorly.' (EHO-C1)

[12] 'A lot of people phone up and say "I've got food poisoning from so-and-so, I ate there last night". But everybody else is alright, and you say "what did you have the day before". And they respond, "what's that got to do with it?" There is a lack of understanding of how long food poisoning can take' (EHO-C2). EHO-C2 argued that the media portrayal of food-borne illness may influence 'source fixation'.

food as a source, potentially inhibiting the detection of contaminated domestic products through the focus on food businesses. Members of the public are especially reluctant to contemplate that their own home cooking may be responsible for their illness. A case of campylobacter was recalled by EHO-A3, where a member of the public admitted domestically consuming under-cooked chicken, whilst insisting that his illness was a result of the meal he had eaten at a restaurant the night before. In such cases EHOs will investigate the food business, but also always bear in mind the possibility that illness resulted from home cooking. The likelihood of a domestic source will, of course, influence control decisions, but may also influence enforcement decisions. If the inspection discloses breaches of hygiene regulations unconnected with the illness, the likelihood that the business was not responsible for the incident of food-borne illness will influence the decision not to take action. However, it is likely that advice will be given (either formally or informally) in order to bring the business into future compliance.

Allied with memory difficulties,[13] the fixation on the last meal compromises EHOs' ability to obtain information and make judgements about the source of an illness. They are pushed towards a particular business or food as a source, even where this is not the most plausible explanation of the incident. If partial food histories are constructed due to source fixation, epidemiological evidence may be seen as lacking robustness, leading to reluctance to take enforcement action based on such histories.

Source fixation is a particular problem in smaller incidents, confined to a group of individuals known to each other, where consumers notify the local authority of illness. Complainants focus on particular meals eaten prior to symptoms, reinforced by conversations with other group members that provide spurious mutual corroborations. Investigations arising out of notifications received from medical authorities (eg A/I/10; Cadbury *Salmonella*;[14] Lemon and Coriander Chicken Wraps[15]) tend not to encounter source fixation. Consumers do not trigger the investigation and are therefore less assertive about a particular source. They are less likely to reach premature, or indeed any, conclusions about possible sources and pass these on to EHOs. This means that consumer opinions on likely sources have less influence over the quality of food histories obtained by EHOs.

[13] See ch 6.II.B below. Where children suffer from food-borne illness, their parents may become fixated on potential sources, further compromising the ability of EHOs to produce robust food history.

[14] Outbreak Control Team, 'National increase in *Salmonella* Montevideo infections, England and Wales: March to July 2006' (2006) 16 (29) *CDR Weekly*.

[15] Qutub Syed, *Outbreak Report: National Outbreak of Vero cytotoxin-producing Escherichia coli O157 infection associated with lemon and coriander chicken wraps in England & Wales June–July 2007* (Health Protection Agency 2007).

B. Information Limited by Consumers' Incomplete Memory

Consumers often have difficulty recalling their food history (of up to 14 days) in sufficient detail to allow EHOs to compare 'cases' relative exposure to different foods.[16] Further, some consumers may never be cognisant of certain useful information, such as the ultimate source and batch number of ingredients of home-prepared food, and therefore will not be able to report it when asked.

In A/I/10, the 'cases' suffering from illness were not able to recall (except in the most general terms) all the meals they had eaten over the previous fortnight, particularly when those meals had been eaten in the home. Likewise, in A/I/25, the consumer-complainant was unable to recall the location of a food business from which he purchased a snack identified in his food history. The EHOs investigating the South Wales case[17] faced difficulties with consumers unable to recall the food they had consumed in the days prior to becoming symptomatic.[18] In another case, even when the source was narrowed to a conference held at a particular hotel, 'delegates had difficulty remembering what they had eaten'.[19] This was despite the requested food history's being limited to meals eaten at the hotel over a four-day period, although this limited ability to recall was exacerbated by the service of certain meals in the form of a buffet, the effect of which is considered at section II.C. below.

Young children have particular difficulty recalling the food they have eaten over the previous 14-day period. In A/I/6, a child was unable to recall what she had eaten, or was unable to express her recall, and therefore the mother of the child suffering from *E. coli* was asked to provide a food history on behalf of her child, but there were gaps in this history from times when the mother was not with the child, such as when the child was with grandparents or at nursery. The child's grandmother and the nursery were asked to fill in the gaps, but the account of the child's food consumption remained incomplete. Similar difficulties were present in South Wales, where a large number of the 'cases' were young children. As noted by the CCDC, 'many of the children were between the ages of 3–6 years and were unable to say what they had eaten and very often their parents had no idea as to what their child had eaten' (PEN/GL/NPH.00881).[20] Where parents are asked to

[16] Eg, 'when you start going back through food history, that in itself is quite difficult—it's quite hard to remember every meal that you have eaten for the last five or six days' (EHO-C1); '[o]nce the questioning turns to food history, consumers often struggle to remember what they have eaten' (EHO-C2).

[17] For full details of the South Wales case see <http://wales.gov.uk/ecoliinquiry/?lang=en>.

[18] Eg, '[Redacted] couldn't remember an exact food history' (PEN/PP/RCC.00313). See also PEN/PP/RCC.00317; PEN/PP/RCC.00328; PEN/PP/RCC.00321; PEN/PP/RCC.00320; and PEN/PP/RCC.00319.

[19] File note, A/I/15.

[20] See also PEN/RS/NPH.00839.

fills gaps in food histories, they may, as noted above, fix on certain meals (particularly those they have consumed outside the home), and therefore fail to provide a complete food history. Source fixation is not confined to one's own meals.

One method of obtaining a quasi-food history from children is to ask them (or their parents) what food they like, and to infer from this that they would have eaten the food that they preferred. This is a second-best approach, which is used pragmatically to obtain missing information. These data will then be used to assess which preferred foods are common to 'cases' and do not appear in the 'control' preferences.[21] This approach suffices for control, where preferences are potentially valuable in determining which foods must be controlled (ruling out true negatives), and EHOs (in consultation with other network participants) may be prepared to take control action if a product, place or person is commonly preferred by affected children. Conversely, EHOs recognise that preferences cannot form the basis of enforcement action, as evidence based on such studies is insufficiently robust to rule out false positives.

Obtaining full food histories is also a problem with older people. Older consumers have a higher likelihood of suffering from problems with short-term memory loss, or more serious conditions such as Alzheimer's disease. This problem particularly manifests itself in incidents traced to locations where food is provided incidentally to health care, such as nursing homes. According to EHO-A3, when faced with patients in such locations, who are often suffering from dementia, 'You have no chance of being able to interview them, so you rely on the nursing home; some nursing homes now write down what people have had to eat every day, but not all of them.' Even if menus are kept by the institution, this may be insufficient, as such information will not include food brought in from outside, perhaps by family members or other visitors, and will not allow assessment of a dose–response relationship, as a history constructed from menus will not show whether, or how much of, a food was consumed by a person who is unable to provide a food history in a conventional manner.

When food histories are compromised by memory difficulties, the ability of EHOs to draw conclusions from those histories is also compromised. This impairs both control and, especially, enforcement efforts. Capturing a consumer's food history is essential to robust epidemiology. Compromises, such as settling for a partial food history or basing epidemiological analysis on preferences, may produce some information, but this is not seen as being as high quality as required for the construction of robust epidemiology. This information will be used to take control decisions, but is seen by EHOs as being insufficient for enforcement purposes. They are reluctant to take

[21] See PEN/RS/NPH.00842.

enforcement action on the basis of epidemiology constructed from the incomplete information that results when consumers cannot recall their food history fully and accurately.

C. Information Limited by the Special Features of Buffets

In the cases examined, incidents regularly arise where buffets are implicated as a source of food-borne illness. This is unsurprising, as buffets present a high risk of secondary transmission of illnesses due to cross-contamination of the buffet food by infected individuals, particularly where food is taken by consumers using their fingers.[22] Epidemiological information is difficult to obtain in such cases, limiting the possibilities for enforcement.

Buffets present peculiar, but significant, problems for the collection of epidemiological information by EHOs. The problems they pose are akin to those caused by memory problems, but more acute. Presented with a list of foods included in a buffet, consumers are unable to recall whether particular foods were eaten. They may fixate on a particular buffet offering. They cannot remember how much of a particular food was consumed.[23] These difficulties are exacerbated by the style of presentation and service of the food. Dishes in buffets are often not labelled, and even if interviewees know what they ate, they may not know what a particular dish was called. An incident centred on a buffet means that 'throughout the investigation it [is] difficult to obtain an accurate list of foods eaten' (EHO-A3 on A/I/14).

In A/I/7, individuals became ill after eating a selection of foods from different ethnic food businesses, but could not recall which dishes they ate except through vague description. Likewise, in A/I/3, a group consumed tapas-style food, sharing a number of dishes. The food business was contacted by EHO-A3, who obtained the group's receipt. This indicated the food ordered, which had formed part of the 'buffet'. The EHO attempted to obtain individual food histories, using a questionnaire setting out the dishes indicated by the receipt. However, the affected consumers had difficulties recalling which dishes they had consumed and (if eaten) the amounts. Similarly in A/I/4, viral gastro-enteritis affected a number of people who attended a two-day conference. On both days, lunch consisted of a buffet. The EHOs found it difficult to obtain food history, as interviewees could not remember which dishes they ate. To compound the difficulties, the buffet lunch on both days contained the same dishes, and consumers who could recall eating a particular dish had problems identifying on which day it was eaten.

[22] Colin Caywood, 'Buffets and Cross-Contamination' *Food Safety News* (20 July 2010), available at <http://www.foodsafetynews.com/2010/07/buffets-and-cross-contamination/>.

[23] This inhibits the ability of EHOs to investigate a possible dose–response relationship between buffet items and the illness suffered by cases.

When a single business appears to be the source of an incident, EHOs may rely on the business to provide information about food eaten by consumers. Ordinarily a business should (electronically) retain information about the food consumed by particular parties, particularly till receipts. Environmental Health Officers cannot use this method for obtaining food histories where a buffet is implicated. A business, when serving a buffet, will not record the food eaten by individuals or, in the case of buffet-style restaurants, a single party. The business may be able to provide information about the dishes that made up the buffet, but it cannot provide details to narrow down the dishes that may have been eaten by a particular 'case'. In A/I/15, a carvery restaurant was unable to provide information about the food consumption of ill consumers, 'as records were not kept, there was no written menu anyway and staff recollections of food items were very vague' (EHO-A3).

In buffet cases, EHOs often have the stark choice of controlling the premises or doing nothing. Buffets are often one-off events, and incidents are often caused by cross-contamination, either by consumer themselves or by staff. Therefore, control of the premises may not be necessary, as there is no continuing risk. The epidemiological information that can be uncovered does not allow implicated food to be identified. Information deficiencies may mask incidents that are linked to particular products and need control. Further, the information does not provide sufficient grounds to allow an EHO to take enforcement action, particularly where no obvious hygiene breaches are evident. However, advice will generally be given on practices that reduce the risk of cross-contamination (A/I/3; A/I/15).

D. The Effect of the Limitations on Enforcement Decisions

For the reasons detailed above, EHOs have difficulties obtaining food history information. The consumer cannot provide useful information about the possible source(s) of food-borne illness. Without this information, it is difficult to examine the commonalities in food (or exposure to other risk factors) that are shared between suspected 'cases', and both descriptive epidemiology and analytical epidemiology are compromised. Whilst analysis of incomplete food histories allows partial comparisons sufficient for control, ruling out potential sources with the remaining sources subject to control (if a partial history shows that no cases ate a particular food, but many 'controls' did, it is likely that this food is not the source of the incident, and is therefore not in need of control), these comparisons do not positively identify sources to a criminal standard.

Failure to obtain food histories may also mean that the basis for aggregated epidemiological analysis is weakened. If a full food history cannot be recalled, it may be that the case will be classified as a non- or partial response, and information supplied may be removed from epidemiological analysis. This may lead to epidemiological results not reaching the threshold of statistical significance, and/or the risk of false positive results in the epidemiological analysis.

Environmental Health Officers are unwilling to use such information in enforcement decision making, and particularly in taking the decision to bring a prosecution, as they do not believe that it demonstrates regulatory breaches to the 'beyond a reasonable doubt' standard. Whilst control may be undertaken on the basis of such information, and advice aimed at ensuring compliance may be given, formal enforcement action will not be taken.

Even where additional information is available, methodological difficulties with food history surveys may result in compromised epidemiological evidence. Often in consultation with the CCDC and other network participants, EHOs consider whether the methodology that underpins evidence is robust, focusing on data collection and data analysis (CCDC1).

A key problem with reliance on food history is the inability of EHOs to collect data sufficient to produce valuable epidemiological information. Two problems result from insufficient data, low response rate and incomplete responses, which lead to missing epidemiological data. A low response rate to surveys, particularly where they are distributed by post or over the Internet, means that analysis does not build a robust explanation regarding an incident of food-borne illness. Similarly, missing epidemiological data, for reasons of source fixation, incomplete memory or the structural problems arising out of buffets, means that EHOs cannot be sure that the comparison is capturing all the relevant similarities and differences between the histories that are compared. Incomplete or missing data compound the problems of source fixation, and may skew the results towards the last meal, potentially generating false positives and failing to expose potential linkages between the risk factors to which individuals are exposed. Whilst one response could be to disregard incomplete food histories, this compounds problems arising from low response rates. Particularly where a cohort analysis is carried out, EHOs tend to require a response rate of 60 per cent before they see epidemiological analysis as valuable. Whilst EHOs will chase responses in order to drive up a response rate (eg Fat Duck;[24] A/I/15), if the response rate remains low, or where only incomplete returns are made, the results will be disregarded for the purpose of enforcement, although the incomplete data may still provide valuable information for the purposes of control.

Epidemiological evidence collected in a way that is seen as methodologically unsound is not considered by EHOs when taking enforcement decisions (EHO-A1; EHO-D1). These data are perceived as unsuitable as the basis for

[24] Health Protection Agency, *Foodborne illness at The Fat Duck restaurant: Report of an investigation of a foodborne outbreak of Norovirus among diners at The Fat Duck restaurant, Bray, Berkshire in January and February 2009* (HPA 2009).

enforcement action (EHO-A3), as they do not demonstrate a breach beyond a reasonable doubt. Lack of robust data matters less for control: EHOs are willing to take action on a precautionary basis, if a risk is apparently shown by epidemiological data.

III. UNAVAILABILITY OF FOOD SAMPLE EVIDENCE AND ITS IMPACT ON ENFORCEMENT

The collection and analysis of food samples are central to the response to food-borne illness. Samples are primarily collected for the purpose of control. A sample that analysis shows is contaminated with food-borne illness micro-organisms will be controlled, through seizure and destruction and/or withdrawal from the marketplace of an affected batch, to prevent further primary cases. However, EHOs will take control action in the absence of food samples, relying upon circumstantial information that implicates the food (such as an epidemiological linkage),[25] or by relying on provisions that allow seizure if the food was produced in premises that breach the hygiene regulations.[26]

In contrast, food samples can play an essential role in enforcement action following an incident of food-borne illness. An analysis that shows the food eaten by the consumer-complainant (or retained by the food business from the same batch as the food eaten by the consumer) to be contaminated with a food-borne micro-organism is central (and perhaps sufficient) to demonstrating that food is unfit for human consumption or injurious to health.[27] Food samples were described by EHO-A2 as the 'smoking gun'. Without microbiological analysis, EHOs feel that success is unlikely in a case brought under food safety provisions (EHO-A3). Epidemiological evidence may also be adduced, but is not as valuable. Sample evidence illustrates the linkage between food and illness more clearly (EXP-MIC1).[28]

Environmental Health Officers are often unable to collect food samples.[29] The primary reason for this is obvious. Samples of food cannot be collected

[25] Subject to the challenges of obtaining epidemiological information, see section II above.

[26] Food Safety and Hygiene (England) Regulations 2013, SI 2013/2996, reg 29 and Food Safety Act 1990, s 9.

[27] 'As the laboratory did not examine any samples, I am unable to say with any certainty whether the illness suffered was food poisoning, although this is a possibility' (Letter to complainant, A/I/26); 'I cannot say with any certainty that the illness you suffered was caused by a food poisoning organism' (Letter to complainant, A/I/27); 'In the absence of any leftover foods, we will never be in a position to state categorically that either the hotel, or its staff, were responsible' (Letter to complainant, A/I/2).

[28] See, eg, the charges in the South Wales case (above n 17), where the General Food Regulations 2004, SI 2004/3279, charge of placing on the market food that was unsafe was based on specimens held by the local authorities.

[29] This section is concerned with unavailability of sample evidence. Sample evidence may be inadmissible where it is collected in contravention of the detailed procedures that govern

when the food no longer exists.[30] There are two reasons for this. First, the product under investigation is destroyed when it is eaten by the consumer.[31] This method of consumption contrasts with that occurring in product safety or health and safety investigations, where an implicated product exists, albeit in a possibly damaged state, to be examined following an incident. Whilst waste products resulting from consumption may be examined,[32] such examination gives little indication of the state or quality of the product before it was placed in the mouth, and therefore the waste products of a particular food (if indeed these waste products can be identified) are little substitute for the food itself. Secondly, unused food may be destroyed by a business (in accordance with stock rotation procedures)[33] or by consumers. In general, a hot dish will either be consumed entirely within one service period, or will be thrown away unused after the end of that period.[34] With domestic food products, the presence of durability dates less than the onset time of some food-borne illness means that these products may be discarded by consumers.

The likelihood of destruction (particularly of freshly produced food)[35] is increased as the delay between infection and notification increases.[36]

the collection of samples. Evidence will be excluded under the Police and Criminal Evidence Act (PACE) 1984, s 78, where the failure to follow procedure governing collection or analysis of samples is substantial and serious (see *Focus (DIY) Ltd v Hillingdon LBC* [2008] EWHC 1152 (Admin). Irregularities in the collection and/or analysis of sample evidence may also lead to an application to strike out the proceedings as an abuse of process (see, in general, Andrew LT Choo, *Abuse of process and judicial stays of criminal proceedings* (2nd edn, Oxford University Press 2008). In *Leatherland and Pritchard v Powys CC* [2007] EWHC 148 (Admin), proceedings were stayed where, in an animal welfare prosecution, a representative sample of carcasses were not retained for examination by the defendant, in breach of the applicable policy. However, PACE s 78 has been endorsed as the preferred vehicle by which a sampling processes should be challenged, by the High Court in *R (Environment Agency) v Drake* [2009] EWHC 1344 (Admin). (See also the judgement of the Privy Council in *Warren v Attorney-General of Jersey* [2011] UKPC 10 [77].) See further Slim Dinsdale, 'Microbiological results from foods—their use and abuse in food safety prosecutions' [2000] *New Law Journal Expert Witness Supplement* 771.

30 File note, Case A/I/3, 'No food left, so no samples could be taken.'

31 Nicole Coutrelis, 'Product Liability in the Food Sector' (2000) 28 *International Business Lawyer* 222, 224.

32 See section IV. below.

33 Food businesses are required to include polices governing the rotation of stock in their HACCP plans.

34 File Note, Case A/I/8, 'No food left for sampling—all consumed by the end of the day.'

35 However, in *R v Muriel Morris* (Birmingham Magistrates Court, 8 December 2010), the short onset time of the illness (a matter of hours), combined with the sensitive category of the individuals affected (police officers), meant that the sandwiches supplied by Morris were collected by EHOs before they could be eaten or thrown away. In contrast to the challenges for epidemiology, the focus on the least meal eaten worked positively here. However, if the illness had had a longer onset time, it is probable that the food would not have been available for sampling and analysis.

36 The chance that there will be food available for sampling increases when microbiologically stable or frozen food is implicated. In Cadbury *Salmonella*, above n 14, some long-dated chocolate bars were recovered for sampling; in South Wales, above n 17, schools had stored cooked meat supplied by Tudors in their freezers, and the meat was sampled from there by EHOs (PEN/DG/SWP.00569).

In A/I/14, EHO-A3 reported that samples of food eaten by the party were not available 'due to the time lapse between the group eating ... and the initial notification'.[37] Delay will inevitably result from the nature of food-borne illness, with consumers unaware that they are infected until they become symptomatic. With onset times varying between 24 hours and 14 days, delay is a structural feature of response to food-borne illness. Beyond the inevitable hiatus, further delay often exists because the consumer, understandably, waits until he or she has recovered before reporting the illness to the local authority.[38] The challenge for EHOs is to find implicated food items prior to their destruction. Because of delays, with the window to obtain the food for sampling generally smaller than the onset time of the illness, EHOs are frequently too late to procure samples; the rotation of an implicated batch of products through the supply chain and within the food business is shorter than the time between consumption and notification. Similarly, delay may mean that any food sampled has degraded (naturally or due to poor storage practices, etc), meaning that an EHO cannot demonstrate, beyond a reasonable doubt, that the food was in the condition shown by analysis at the time of consumption, and that any microbial contamination was present at the time of consumption and had not been introduced thereafter.[39]

Lack of food samples gives rise to an inability to decide whether the illness suffered by complainant-consumers was food-borne.[40] Without food samples it is difficult to conclude whether the source of an illness (particularly a viral illness) was food, or whether the incident was a result of person-to-person spread. In A/I/20, without samples the evidence assembled showed 'little to indicate if the illness was food-borne or was spread from person to person'.[41] Were consumers infected by food, or by another person? Lack of information generates reasonable doubt, and enforcement action will not therefore be brought.

Even where EHOs are certain that the illness is food-borne, the informational deficit compromises their ability to prove regulatory breaches. A positive microbiological analysis of the exact product thought to have caused the illness, or from products produced in the same batch,[42] is the simplest method of demonstration that food is unfit for human consumption or injurious to

[37] See also PEN/AC/SWP.00117 ('all food is disposed of after use, rather than keeping to a later date').

[38] EHO-A3.

[39] Where frozen food is implicated this problem is less severe, as frozen food will often be retained for periods longer than the onset times of food-borne illnesses.

[40] See A/I/21, A/I/23, A/I/26.

[41] EHO-A3. Similarly 'As the laboratory did not examine any samples, I am unable to say with any certainty whether the illness suffered was food poisoning, although this is a possibility' (A/I/26); 'Without any samples of the actual food which your party ate we could not analyse this food to identify any causative organism' (A/I/21).

[42] Defined to mean food product produced at the same time by the same method (EHO-A3).

health under the Food Safety and Hygiene (England) Regulations 2013.[43] Samples of other food demonstrating microbial contamination do not satisfy EHOs that they can prove breaches to the standard necessary for enforcement action, although they may be used for the purpose of control.

As well as damaging the ability to prove food safety charges, the lack of samples undercuts EHOs' ability to particularise charges under regulation 19 of the Food Safety and Hygiene (England) Regulations 2013 (BAR-1; BAR-2).[44] Without samples of food for analysis, particular food vehicles cannot be directly implicated in an incident of food-borne illness. For example, in A/I/2, both the starter and the dessert had a statistically significant relationship with the outbreak of *campylobacter*. Despite knowledge about the disease suggesting that the starter of chicken liver was responsible, both EHO-A2 and EHO-A3 noted the difficulties of particularising a potential charge to the satisfaction of the local authority lawyers. A charge that particularised one possible cause of the illness would risk an acquittal on the grounds that the other cause could not be ruled out.[45] In South Wales, food safety prosecutions were particularised based on specimens held by the prosecuting authorities.[46]

IV. UNAVAILABILITY OF FAECAL SAMPLE EVIDENCE AND ITS IMPACT ON ENFORCEMENT

We have seen that taking faecal samples is central to responses to food-borne illness. Samples may identify those people suffering from food-borne illness who pose a risk of secondary transmission and may therefore be made the subject of control actions.[47] Such samples are less useful in the control of premises and products, as decisions about control action may need to be taken before the production of test results. Further, faecal samples are often the only definitive way of identifying the type of illness affecting individuals. The type of illness identified may inform strategic decision making in ongoing investigations, and the control measures put in place.

In addition to their importance for control, faecal samples are a key part of any enforcement decision. They identify that the consumer has suffered a

[43] A/I/2; EHO-A2.

[44] An information or indictment, respectively, must include 'such particulars of the conduct constituting the commission of the offence as to make clear what the prosecutor alleges against the defendant' (Criminal Procedure Rules 2014, rr 7.3(1)(b) and 14.2(1)(b)).

[45] Similar to the problems identified in Michael Hirst, 'Guilty; but of what?' (2000) 4 *International Journal of Evidence and Proof* 31.

[46] South Wales *E Coli* above n 17.

[47] Faecal samples most readily play this role in bacterial cases, as viral excretion (and therefore the risk of secondary transmission) greatly diminishes when a person becomes non-symptomatic. In viral cases, therefore, exclusions can be based on symptoms; in bacterial cases, screening through sampling is necessary to ensure that a post-symptomatic case no longer presents a risk.

food-borne illness. This plays a central role in the decision making of EHOs, who are often unwilling to bring a prosecution without evidence that there was food-borne illness, with the effect of the regulatory breach forming a key part of the public interest test. Whilst a causal connection between food-borne illness and a breach of food hygiene is not necessary in law to bring a successful prosecution, EHOs like to be able to demonstrate this linkage. Faecal samples can also provide an important linkage between micro-organisms discovered environmentally and food-borne illness where food samples are not available (although such linkages do not demonstrate the causal mechanism, as the food may have contained the environment, the environment contaminated the food, or both food and environment may have been contaminated by a third person or object).

It is therefore damaging to both control and enforcement that, in the cases examined, EHOs were often unable to obtain faecal samples, or, in the event that samples were obtained, the analysis did not disclose the food-borne illness responsible for the symptoms. However, when taking control action, EHOs were still prepared to proceed without the linkage demonstrated through samples. Advice on improvements in hygiene practices may also be given without a definitive linkage, as such advice looks to the future rather than to the past breaches.

The central reason for the unavailability of samples is the time lapse between the consumption of contaminated food and notification of the illness to the local authority. This delay is caused by a combination of the onset time from consumption to the 'case's' becoming symptomatic, and the delay between the person's becoming ill and the local authority's becoming aware of this.[48] 'Few food poisoning outbreak investigations manage to positively identify cause because the [EHO's] intervention is usually too late.'[49] When investigation is (unavoidably) delayed, samples become fruitless, as a person who has recovered may no longer excrete food-borne illness micro-organisms in his or her faeces. Nigel Emery, in evidence to the House of Lords Science and Technology Committee, provided one example. In this case, members of a football team became ill. There was a delay in taking faecal samples, which meant that it was too late to be able to identify the cause and assess whether it was viral. Analysis of samples was undertaken, but no bacteria were found. Further delays ensued when other members of

[48] Eg, notifications are likely to be made once a person has recovered from illness, meaning that faecal samples are unlikely to contain microbes.

[49] Nigel Emery, 'The Role of the Environmental Health Officer in Fighting Human Infectious Disease' *Memorandum to the House of Lords Select Committee on Science and Technology* (8 October 2002), available at <http://www.parliament.the-stationery-office.co.uk/pa/ld200203/ldselect/ldsctech/23-vi/2121002.htm>, para 10.

the team became ill, despite advice on the need for prompt action so that samples could be tested for viruses. The result was that

> the investigating authority was left with little evidence that anything untoward had happened. Naturally the club management found this difficult to believe particularly as the episode had resulted in disruption to their training programmes during the build-up to the start of the new football season.[50]

Notification is often received by EHOs after the time when a viable sample could be taken. Viral gastro-enteritis in particular was identified by EHO-A3 as posing this problem: 'when people ring up and they say they've been ill they are usually better so it's hard to get any viable virus from stool samples, which makes it very difficult to investigate'.[51] Viruses generally remain in the body for a shorter period than bacteria. Whereas individuals can continue to excrete *E. coli* or *salmonella* for a significant period following recovery from the symptomatic phase of illness, this is not the case with viral illnesses. Once symptoms clear up, viral organisms generally cease to be found in faecal matter. Therefore, analysis of faecal samples will not function to discover the biological source of the outbreak, which EHOs often see as fatal to enforcement action.

In cases consistent with a viral source of food-borne illness, EHOs will often not distribute sample pots to post-symptomatic 'cases', as faecal samples are unlikely to yield worthwhile results (A/I/11; A/I/22). This contrasts with the normal investigative practice of EHOs to distribute 'pots' to all 'cases', with the practice altered as sampling is unlikely to produce information valuable for either control or enforcement purposes. Where samples are not taken on this basis, the likelihood of enforcement action is reduced, as the information potentially available to EHOs is diminished.

It is particularly difficult to isolate viral particles within faecal samples.[52] This may create doubt over whether an incident is one of food-borne illness at all. In A/I/23, EHO-A3 was unable to conclude whether the illness was food-borne due to the lack of positive sample results.[53] In cases where food-borne or person-to-person transmission is possible, a faecal sample, which corresponds to an environmental sample, is 'invaluable in linking into premises'.[54] Without samples of faeces or food to analyse, EHOs have

[50] Ibid, para 12.

[51] Likewise, EHO-C1 stated, 'With emergent things like *norovirus*, if you don't get a sample within the first few hours of a person being ill, you are not going to get a positive sample anyway.'

[52] See, eg, EHO-A3 ('Viral gastro-enteritis is very difficult to test for. Even if the person is still excreting you don't always find the virus in the stool samples') and EHO-A9 ('Viruses are extremely difficult to identify, and it may be that the laboratory was unable to isolate the causative organism'). EXP-MIC1 notes that techniques of analysis are improving, and detection of viruses in stool samples is on the increase.

[53] See also A/I/21.

[54] EHO-C1.

difficulty in concluding that an outbreak is attributable to a food source.[55] Even where a positive sample is obtained, this does not provide evidence of how the person became infected.

An illustration is provided by A/I/15. An individual reported illness following attendance at a conference staged by Food Business L. However, the report was initially made to the consumer-complainant's local authority, and was referred to Local Authority A following identification of Food Business L as a likely source. Once this referral was made, Local Authority A contacted the complainant and her employer, Business X, who had organised the conference. Business X provided the names of the conference delegates, and Local Authority A contacted them. However, by the time the complainant contacted her local authority she was recovering from her illness. This meant that when EHO-A3, on behalf of Local Authority A, contacted the delegates, only two remained symptomatic, despite 17 reporting that they had suffered from illness. Therefore, faecal samples were obtained from these two individuals only.

Even if delay does not prevent productive sampling, consumers may be reluctant to provide faecal samples. They may feel embarrassed and may not wish to give such intimate bodily products to EHOs. It was noted by EHO-C1 that consumers often 'don't want to give personal samples ... in terms of faecal samples people are like "actually, I'm feeling better" as soon as you say that a faecal sample would be really useful to isolate something'. Environmental Health Officers suggest that faecal samples are seen as something disgusting, because they require interaction between a person and his or her own bodily waste products (EHO-A2; EHO-C1). Therefore consumers may not provide such samples, even where they may still be excreting useful information in the form of micro-organisms, and EHOs are unable to obtain information about the illness affecting a person and link it to a product or to premises. The chances of a successful enforcement action are damaged (A/I/18).

Parents may also be reluctant to provide faecal samples from their children, particularly in incidents in childcare settings, where the decision has been taken to screen all children (A/I/5; A/I/6). In these situations, EHOs attempt to explain the importance of screening to parents (stressing the potential for asymptomatic excretors to infect other individuals, particularly in settings, such as childcare, where poor hygiene practice is the norm), emphasising that all children are to be screened. This information, combined

[55] Difficulties also arose where samples were obtained but were insufficiently identified to allow EHOs to link them to particular epidemiological evidence supplied by consumers (see Outbreak Control Team, *Outbreak of Norovirus Infection amongst Guests attending a Concert at the Music Hall Aberdeen May 2004* (OCT 2004) and Overview and Scrutiny Committee, *Report of the Scrutiny Review of the E. Coli O157 Outbreak at Feltham Hill Infant and Nursery School* (London Borough of Hounslow 2010)).

with personal phone calls and visits, was sufficient to obtain faecal samples from most children in the cases examined in this book, but some parents were still unwilling. In the latter cases, the child in question was excluded to reduce the risk of infection for other children. This practice attempts to prevent the spread of food-borne illness, and is an important control step, but does not produce evidence that can be used in enforcement action. The EHO is prepared to accept less information in return for a lower risk of secondary spread.

It is challenging to build a case when there is an absence of faecal samples, or of any positive analytical results from those samples. Indeed, EHOs see the difficulties with obtaining faecal samples as a serious obstacle to taking formal enforcement action following an incident of food-borne illness (EHO-A3; EHO-B1), although the absence of food samples is often seen as even worse. The sample cases examined in this research suggest that the absence of faecal samples is one of the most common reasons for the decision to take no further action.[56] In A/I/18, CCDC2 dismissed the chances of successful enforcement in his advice to EHO-A3: 'If we had found something wrong at the premises, or had a swab which could be linked to a faecal sample result through phage-typing, then we could have proceeded.' The failure to obtain a faecal sample was clearly a major factor in the decision not to take further action.[57] Likewise, a letter to the consumer in A/I/21 stated: 'A number of faecal samples were collected from your party but no pathogenic bacteria or virus particles were identified … as a result … we are unable to proceed further with our investigation' (EHO-A9).

Without being able to establish a direct causal linkage between the food business and the illness suffered by the consumer, EHOs feel that it becomes difficult to show, beyond a reasonable doubt, that the food business was selling food that was unfit for human consumption or injurious to health (EHO-A2; EHO-B1). This difficulty may be countered by the suggestion that EHOs should focus on food hygiene offences, rather than food safety crimes.

Despite these challenges, positive results may be obtained. However, a positive result is often confined to a single individual, even though more than one person is symptomatic. Following such results, EHOs have strong suspicions about the cause of particular food-borne illnesses, but 'concretising these is tough'.[58] According to EHO-A3, 'if we do get something, it's one person, and it's hard to build a case around one person'. Reasonable doubt may be raised surrounding the source of the infection of a single person, with the defendant arguing that its business was not responsible for the

[56] A/I/20; A/I/21; A/I/26.

[57] Letter EHO-A3 to complainant: 'It was not felt that there was a strong case to be able to prove beyond a reasonable doubt that the infection was caused by poor practices at [Food Business H], although this does remain a possibility.'

[58] EHO-A3.

incident and that the person was infected by another business, another person or at home. Only when there were a number of positive faecal samples, provided by individuals who can only be linked through one food business, would EHOs be confident that this doubt had been erased (EHO-A3).

Difficulties in obtaining both faecal and food samples essentially boil down to problems of delay. Delay compromises the ability of local authorities to obtain samples, which form a crucial part of the evidence showing a regulatory breach, fatally damaging the chances of successful prosecution in the eyes of the EHOs. The investigation becomes limited, and ceases to obtain material necessary to build an enforcement case. Control remains the focus, but the perception is that enforcement action could not be taken in any event. This pessimistic conclusion focuses heavily on the offences of placing unsafe food on the market, contravening the requirement of article 14 of Regulation 178/2002, and fails to consider the possibility of hygiene offences, which can be more easily proved by witness evidence given by the EHOs themselves, backed up by other information gathered during environmental investigations.

V. 'INADMISSIBILITY' DUE TO 'MEDICAL CONFIDENTIALITY' AND ITS IMPACT ON ENFORCEMENT

Assertions of confidentiality by the medical participants in the network responding to food-borne illness, may have the effect of depriving other network participants of information necessary to construct a case for enforcement action. The problems were recognised by the House of Lords Science and Technology Committee in its report *Fighting Infection*. The Committee noted that 'EHOs can have difficulty accessing information from doctors concerned about patient confidentiality'.[59] This is a problem as regards both control and enforcement. Without information, control and enforcement action cannot be taken. As control is the primary goal of EHOs, they act to ensure that control is possible. This may mean recognising medical confidentiality, and undertaking not to break confidentiality to the extent of using the information in court, in order to gain access to important information.

The rationale for privileging confidentiality over disclosure during enforcement action is expressed by Gwen Lowe, CCDC for South Wales: 'We need people to help us find the source or sources of the outbreak and we are more likely to get this help if we respect their privacy.'[60] The priority of

[59] *House of Lords Science and Technology Committee, Fourth Report—Fighting Infection* (House of Lords 2003) para 4.21.

[60] Gwen Lowe, quoted in Anon, 'Legionnaires' Outbreak: "We Are Giving Enough Informa-tion"—Health Bosses', *South Wales Argus* (17 September 2010), available at <http://www.southwalesargus.co.uk/news/8397721.LEGIONNAIRES_OUTBREAK_We_are_giving_enough_information_health_bosses/>.

control over enforcement is implicitly acknowledged in this statement. The need for cooperation is used as a reason for obtaining information on a confidential (or at least restricted use) basis, reducing its utility in enforcement action. Environmental Health Officers are reticent about taking action that conflicts with an assertion of medical confidentiality, in case this interferes with the flow of information, hindering control efforts.

Incidents investigated by Authority A did not disclose particular problems with medical confidentiality. However, two public incidents highlight problems that may be caused by assertions of medical confidentiality.

A. Two Case Studies

i. Cadbury Salmonella

In early 2006, Cadbury Schweppes released chocolate contaminated with *Salmonella Montevideo* on to the market. When discovered, Cadbury was jointly prosecuted by Birmingham City Council, Cadbury's home authority, and Herefordshire County Council, the food authority responsible for the processing plant identified as the source of the outbreak. Charges were brought under General Food Regulations 2004[61] (based on samples of chocolate obtained during the outbreak) and the Food Hygiene (England) Regulations 2006.[62] Medical confidentiality affected the evidential base available for the prosecution. The Health Protection Agency (HPA) was reluctant to release information about consumers suffering from illness linked to Cadbury chocolates, asserting medical confidentiality, and conceded that 'the need to protect patient confidentiality can conflict with the provision of evidence necessary to prosecute'.[63] In the particular investigation, the 'provision of evidence for prosecution presented major issues regarding the HPA's duty to maintain confidentiality and the need for evidence to conduct a criminal prosecution'.[64] As Cadbury chose to plead guilty to the charges, the assertion of confidentiality was not tested in court. The information was not required for the purposes of the prosecution, and the HPA was not required to disclose.

ii. R v South-West Water *(1997)*

In this case,[65] the defence sought the names of 'cases' in order to investigate the outbreak, but they were told that medical confidentiality prevented the

[61] SI 2004/3279.
[62] SI 2006/14.
[63] Richard Elson, 'A National Outbreak of Salmonella Montevideo Infection June 2006' (copy on file with author).
[64] Ibid.
[65] *R v South-West Water* (Bristol Crown Court, 16 September 1997).

disclosure of identities. During the control phase of the outbreak, South-West Water was provided with anonymised information about individuals suffering from cryptosporidiosis, with locations provided to assist its investigations, but did not receive identifying details. At trial, the prosecution were unwilling to identify the sufferers. Instead, they proposed placing into evidence an OCT report containing analysis of the anonymised data, which did not breach medical confidentiality.

The judge was critical of the stance regarding confidentiality, rejecting the assertion that medical privilege existed in criminal proceedings.[66] The assertion of confidentiality was not made by the prosecution but by the medical authorities, which did not wish to supply the Drinking Water Inspectorate (DWI) and local EHOs with information provided to them by patients for fear of breaching their professional obligations.[67] The alternative option, with the medical authorities asking the patients to contact the DWI and give consent to the use of medical data in the prosecution (including disclosing the information to the defence), was rejected. The sheer number of people affected by the outbreak meant that this would have been time-consuming and expensive, and would likely have resulted in an incomplete set of usable data, damaging the robustness of the epidemiological analysis.

Medical confidentiality was not accepted by the judge as a valid consideration in the exercise of the court's discretion to admit the OCT report as hearsay evidence under the Criminal Justice Act 1988, sections 24 and 25.[68] Whilst the court was required to have regard to 'all the circumstances', the assertion of 'so-called' medical confidentiality did not outweigh the right of the defence to test the case against it properly.[69] The difficulties for prosecutors caused by medical confidentiality could not be overcome and the case collapsed.

B. Three Legal and Ethical Reasons Offered for the Inadmissibility of Medical Information

i. 'Medical Privilege'[70]

As stated by the judge in *South-West Water*,[71] there is no rule of medical privilege in the English law of criminal evidence.[72] A doctor is both competent

[66] The judge made it clear that only legal professional privilege and (maybe) priest–penitent privilege were reasons for withholding documents from a criminal court at common law.

[67] Transcript Day 1, para 24.

[68] Now replaced by s 117 of the Criminal Justice Act 2003.

[69] Transcript Day 1, para 17.

[70] See broadly Jean McHale, *Medical Confidentiality and Legal Privilege* (Routledge, 1993).

[71] *R v South-West Water*, above n 65.

[72] See, eg, *Duchess of Kingston's case* (1776) 20 St Tr 355, 472, and *R v Gayle* [1994] Crim LR 679, CA. These rulings were followed by HHJ Bursall in *R v South-West Water*, above n 65.

and compellable to provide information about his or her patients, and the court may compel the production of documents created by doctors in the course of examining patients. However, a judge has discretion to allow a doctor to refuse to answer a question where that answer would involve a breach of confidence.[73]

The existence of a professional duty of confidentiality is only one factor in the exercise of the discretion by the judge. Whilst '[c]ourts have an inherent wish to respect … doctor and patient [confidentiality] … the court may have to decide, in particular circumstances, that the interest in preserving this confidence is outweighed by other interests to which the law attaches importance'.[74] In a criminal case arising out of an incident of food-borne illness, the most important interest that the court must balance with confidentiality claimed by a doctor is the defendant's right to a fair trial. Medical privilege cannot be asserted as a blanket ground for refusing to produce documents, and a court cannot be expected to accede to this course of action where this would deprive the defendant of an opportunity to test the case against it properly. In the event that the prosecution fail either to disclose or to produce documents owing to a plea of medical confidentiality, a court may refuse to continue with the proceedings, striking them out as an abuse of process.

ii. Data Protection

Medical confidentiality protects the privacy of patients. Privacy interests are, in part, protected by the Data Protection Act (DPA) 1998. Both doctors and the HPA have a duty to comply with the Act. Under the DPA 1998, the HPA and enforcement authorities are able to keep, maintain and use detailed filing systems. Such data retention is a necessary part of the architecture of control and enforcement. It facilitates the sharing of data obtained during an investigation between different bodies and different EHOs within the same authority. This information transfer must be in accordance with the statute.

However, in collecting, storing and sharing information, the data protection principles must be complied with.[75] Personal data, which means data that identify living individuals,[76] must be 'processed fairly and lawfully'. Processing is defined broadly in section 1, to include obtaining, recording, holding and disclosing information. Data should not be processed unless one of the schedule 2 conditions is met. Schedule 2 is satisfied where the

[73] *Hunter v Mann* [1974] QB 767, 775.

[74] *British Steel Corp v Granada Television Ltd* [1981] AC 1096, 1168–69, per Lord Wilberforce.

[75] DPA 1998, sch 1, pt 1.

[76] DPA 1998, s 1. A significant amount of information generated by medical professionals and enforcement authorities in their investigation of incidents of food-borne illness will fall within the definition of personal data.

processing is necessary for 'the exercise of any other functions of a public nature exercised in the public interest by any person'; 'for the exercise of any functions conferred on any person by or under any enactment' (for example the enforcement of food safety legislation conferred on food authorities by section 6 of the Food Safety Act 1990); or 'for the administration of justice'.[77] Data controllers also have a general right to process where 'the processing is necessary for the purposes of legitimate interests pursued by the data controller or by the third party or parties to whom the data are disclosed'.[78] This may apply here, as protection of public safety, and ensuring compliance with legislation, are legitimate interests of a food authority.

Where data are 'sensitive personal data', which includes information on 'physical ... health or condition', the data controller must demonstrate that one of the conditions in schedule 3 is satisfied before engaging in the processing of the data. A medical professional will have details of the physical health or condition of a person affected by an incident of food-borne illness. In order to disclose such data, it must be necessary 'for the exercise of any functions conferred on any person by or under an enactment' or for 'the administration of justice'.[79] In situations where authorities are dealing with incidents of food-borne illness this is likely to be satisfied. Therefore, the 1998 Act should not prevent medical authorities from transferring information obtained from patients for use in the enforcement of food safety and food hygiene law.

iii. Ethical Obligations of Confidentiality

Network participants, including EHOs, offer medical confidentiality as an important interest to be protected.[80] 'It is well settled that there is an abiding obligation of confidentiality as between doctor and patient.'[81] The Hippocratic Oath obliges doctors to keep information received from patients as 'sacred secrets'.[82] Guidance from the General Medical Council provides that patient information should be disclosed only where disclosure is required by law, where there is consent from the patient or where disclosure is in the

[77] DPA 1998, sch 2, para 5.

[78] DPA 1998, sch 2, para 6.

[79] DPA 1998, sch 3, para 7.

[80] Nick Lowe, 'Learning From Major Incidents: Cadbury Salmonella Outbreak', available at <http://www.google.co.uk/url?sa=t&rct=j&q=&esrc=s&source=web&cd=1&ved=0CCIQFjAA&url=http%3A%2F%2Fwww.sharpsafe.co.uk%2Fmedia%2Fuploads%2F02ff780cfb226210037a5913a58267d8b4e7463e.ppt&ei=jacJVfTAIaiR7AaguYDABg&usg=AFQjCNHqCl3b9UJRKCvfkI0UYIxvUlL3gg&bvm=bv.88198703,d.ZGU&cad=rja> (last visited 18 March 2015).

[81] *Ashworth Security Hospital v MGN* [2000] 1 WLR 515, 527.

[82] Quoted in Jonathan Herring, *Medical law and ethics* (5th edn, Oxford University Press 2014) 222.

public interest.[83] This is narrower than the range of circumstances contemplated in the DPA 1998. Notification of infectious disease under the Public Health (Control of Disease) Act 1984 (as amended) is specifically provided for as an exception to the obligation of confidentiality.[84] However, these disclosures may not be sufficient for enforcement purposes. Whilst disclosure in compliance with a court order is contemplated, doctors are advised that they 'must not disclose personal information to a third party such as a solicitor, police officer or officer of a court without the patient's express consent, unless it is required by law or can be justified in the public interest'.[85]

Disclosure in the public interest will be made only in exceptional circumstances, and should not be made where the disclosure will cause harm to the patient or to the relationship between doctor and patient.[86] Where information is released it must be anonymised, if possible.[87] This may be sufficient where epidemiological information is required to identify products or premises in need of control. Anonymised information will not be sufficient to identify people in need of control to prevent secondary spread, neither is it suitable for enforcement action, as defendants will be unable to confront consumers alleged to have been made ill by their products and explore alternative mechanisms through which they may have suffered food-borne illness.[88]

C. Policy Reasons for the 'Inadmissibility' of Medical Information

In *South-West Water*, DWI officers appeared to believe that medically confidential information was inadmissible as evidence.[89] However, the exigencies of criminal proof demand that this information is placed before the court in some cases involving food-borne illness. As demonstrated above, such information is admissible as evidence, and in some cases non-production may be an abuse of process, although there is discretion to refuse applications for production where the information is not necessary. Further, EHOs argued that the withholding of information was required both by the ethical obligations of doctors and by data protection obligations.[90] However, the ethical

[83] General Medical Council, *Confidentiality: Guidance for Doctors* (GMC 2009) para 8.

[84] Ibid, para 17.

[85] Ibid, para 22.

[86] Ibid, para, ss 36–37.

[87] Ibid, para 9.

[88] The argument that succeeded in *R v South-West Water*, above n 65, considered below ch 6.VI.A.

[89] Peter Jiggins and W Michael Waite, 'Cryptosporidium in England and Wales' in Paul R Hunter, W Michael Waite and Elettra Ronchi (eds), *Drinking Water and Infectious Disease: Establishing the Links* (CRC Press 2002) 123.

[90] At the time of *R v South-West Water* the relevant legislation governing data protection was the DPA 1984.

obligations of medical professionals and the DPA 1998 both allow disclosure where the information is necessary in the public interest. Therefore, the decision to proceed without confidential information is often a choice made by EHOs, with confidentiality claims emphasised and deferred to.

The medical profession (particularly the HPA and the responsible CCDC) work closely with EHOs as part of the network involved in the investigation and control of food-borne illness.[91] Doctors are often the first people to receive information that an outbreak is taking place, particularly where the illness is not confined to a single dining party. The EHOs need access to this information, which has been disclosed to medical authorities, to investigate and control outbreaks properly. The quality of the working relationship between medical and environmental health professionals is therefore essential to effective regulation.

Medical professionals have refused to release any information about infected individuals to EHOs where it might be publicly disclosed in court actions. This threatens the ability of EHOs to take action to control further spread, encouraging them to ensure that information supplied will not be used in a prosecution, where it would be publicly disclosed and tested. As this information forms the basis of much of the epidemiological and microbiological evidence for enforcement action, a case cannot be built.

However, medical confidentiality is not a legal justification for withholding disclosure. Environmental Health Officers have the power to compel 'any assistance or information which [the EHO] may reasonably require of [a person] for the performance of [the EHO's] functions'.[92] They use these powers in contexts other than medical information,[93] so are well aware of the possibilities. Why not use these powers to obtain information from the medical authorities?

Environmental Health Officers do not wish to challenge the assertion of medical confidentiality. Supporting confidentiality is necessary to enable them to obtain the information needed to secure control of the food-borne illness. Therefore they act in a way that facilitates control, supporting the assertion of medical confidentiality through a decision not to obtain the information using the powers available. The choice between control and enforcement is starkly presented. Either medical professionals' desire to retain the confidentiality of material is supported, or the opportunity to use that information for control is lost; and the availability of further medical information may be compromised in the future.

It is argued that challenging the assertion of medical confidentiality would be likely to damage the relationship between EHOs and the medical

[91] Lowe, above n 80.

[92] Food Safety Act 1990, s 33 and Food Safety and Hygiene (England) Regulations 2013, reg 17.

[93] Eg, A/I/2.

profession, who are part of the same network responding to incidents of food-borne illness.[94] The desire to preserve the relationship with the public health medical professions (formerly represented institutionally by the HPA and now by Public Health England), which is crucial to securing control in (particularly large) outbreak investigations,[95] trumps the desire to take enforcement action in particular cases. In the Cadbury case, the HPA provided 'essential support for the investigation', 'key [expert] witnesses', and the route of contact between the EHOs and the 'cases'.[96] Without the HPA, control efforts by the network would have been hindered. Environmental Health Officers decide not to proceed with enforcement action where the prosecution would rest on confidential medical information, in order to forestall conflict between the evidential needs of the EHOs and on-going relationships with the medical profession.[97]

If information is disclosed for the purposes of control, medical professionals may feel uncomfortable using this information for a different purpose in a public forum like a criminal trial. Even if not used a part of the prosecution case, materials used for the purpose of control might constitute 'unused material' that would need to be disclosed under the Criminal Procedure and Investigations Act 1996. Once a prosecution begins, the disclosure of the material is no longer controlled by medical professionals and EHOs. In order to retain command of the information and ensure that it remains confidential, EHOs utilise a bright-line rule and treat information as inadmissible, rendering enforcement action impossible. This ensures that the intra-network relationship between environmental health and medical professionals remains untarnished by disputes about the use of medically obtained information. The lack of information due to medical confidentiality, and its negative impact on case-building, is therefore largely self-imposed.

Environmental Health Officers could access the information if they chose to use the powers available to them, or take action and leave it to the court to decide whether the information should remain confidential. However, a deliberate decision is taken not to use the information for enforcement purposes in order to maintain relationships necessary for future control in impending incidents, privileging the obtaining of information necessary for the control of future incidents over obtaining information necessary for formal enforcement action following a past outbreak. The relative importance to EHOs in particular, and the network in general, of control compared to enforcement is clearly demonstrated in their attitude to medical confidentiality. Preserving confidentiality, to ensure the flow of information regarding

[94] EHO-CON3, explaining, whilst not necessarily agreeing with, the stance of the DWI in *R v South-West Water*.

[95] Lowe, above n 80.

[96] Ibid.

[97] EHO-CON3.

incidents, from consumers self-enrolling into the network and between established network actors, leads to a choice to support medical confidentiality, or at least treat the uses to which information can be put as limited.

One EHO stated that the key to resolving disputes surrounding confidentiality was improved communication between the enforcement and medical authorities.[98] By making the medical authorities feel part of the enforcement process, rather than being shut out from the process, there were likely to be fewer disputes surrounding confidentiality. This would suggest that the network built to control an incident of food-borne illness should also have responsibility for enforcement following such incidents, rather than the enforcement responsibility being hived off as a responsibility only of those who have formal powers to bring enforcement action. It was argued by EHO-C2 that, by building trust between the enforcement and medical authorities, concerns surrounding the sharing of medical information might be alleviated.

However, this study's findings suggest that this approach is likely to lead to EHOs' supporting assertions of confidentiality. As the relationship between medical and environmental health professionals becomes closer (as co-participants in the network of control) the more reluctant EHOs will be to damage this relationship (and the possibilities for control in the present and future)[99] by challenging medical professionals over confidentiality.[100] This approach is therefore unlikely to lead to more information being available to EHOs for case building.

VI. INADMISSIBILITY OF OUTBREAK/INCIDENT CONTROL TEAM REPORTS AND ITS IMPACT ON ENFORCEMENT

Investigations into incidents of food-borne illness produce significant amounts of information that will not, in enforcement action, be given as oral evidence but are relied upon in the investigation (and in subsequent enforcement action) as evidence of the truth of the matter stated. A key example is food histories. These are generally obtained by questionnaire.

In most cases, the individuals who supply those histories will not give oral evidence in enforcement proceedings. In large incidents, with great numbers

[98] EHO-C2.

[99] Lowe, above n 80. Interestingly, the HPA's review of *R v Cadbury* notes that '[p]rosecution of food businesses is a deterrent and ultimately contributes to the aims of outbreak investigation', and therefore that disputes over medical confidentiality do not, ultimately, benefit control of disease on a broader scale.

[100] Whilst this may appear reminiscent of regulatory capture, where the regulator supports the goals of the business rather than performing its regulatory function, the relationship here is of two regulators, rather than a regulator and regulated business, with the EHOs acting to best perform their functions. It is therefore perhaps better that EHOs favour shared regulatory goals, thereby minimising the tension between the regulators.

of people affected, the resources required to prepare those individuals to give live evidence on their food history deters EHOs from bringing enforcement actions. Whilst statements prepared in accordance with the Criminal Justice Act 1967, section 9 could be used, and admitted by agreement between the parties, food history questionnaires are often not prepared in accordance with the requirements of that section, for fear that the presence of formalities might deter symptomatic individuals from cooperating (EHO-B1).

Following the successful control of an incident, a report will be produced detailing the response. It will detail the investigations performed, and contain results of epidemiological and microbiological analyses which formed the basis for control. The report brings together all the information collected during the investigation, and draws conclusions from it. Such a report has both a backward-looking function, explaining how the incident happened, and a forward-looking function, setting out lessons to prevent similar incidents in the future. The report could be used by EHOs to introduce epidemiological and microbiological information into enforcement action, without the need for oral evidence to be given by affected consumers.

Attempts have been made to present these OCT reports as evidence in criminal proceedings, in order that the epidemiological and microbiological information contained within them may be placed before the court and relied upon as evidence. Most notably, the *South-West Water* prosecution relied on an OCT report.[101] The difficulty with using these reports is that the information contained in them is hearsay. Hearsay evidence is only admissible if allowed by section 114(1) of the Criminal Justice Act 2003. This provides:

(1) In criminal proceedings a statement not made in oral evidence in the proceedings is admissible as evidence of any matter stated if, but only if—

- (a) any provision of this Chapter or any other statutory provision makes it admissible,
- (b) any rule of law preserved by section 118 makes it admissible,
- (c) all parties to the proceedings agree to it being admissible, or
- (d) the court is satisfied that it is in the interests of justice for it to be admissible.

This is a major challenge faced by EHOs. Outbreak Control Team reports provide the best overview of a particular incident. They therefore could play a central role in enforcement action taken following the control of an incident. These reports are admissible if it can be demonstrated that they fall with one of the categories set out in paragraphs (a)–(d) above.

It is therefore illuminating to examine *R v South-West Water* in detail to consider whether OCT reports may be admitted into evidence, and therefore whether an EHO can consider them when deciding whether a contemplated prosecution has a reasonable prospect of success. If an OCT

[101] Jiggins and Waite, above n 89, 123.

report cannot be used, the resource implications for preparing a prosecution would be extensive, and worthwhile only in the most important cases, given the secondary importance of enforcement following incidents of food-borne illness.

A. Case Study: *R v South-West Water* (1997)—The (In)Admissibility of OCT Reports on Hearsay Grounds

On Friday, 11 August 1995, four microbiologically confirmed cases of cryptosporidiosis were reported to the CCDC responsible for South-West Devon. By the next day, 28 'cases' were known to the authorities. In a normal August in South-West Devon, the CCDC would expect to receive reports of around 16 cases of cryptosporidiosis. The increase suggested that an outbreak was in progress.

An OCT was convened and a preliminary meeting held. A map of the cases was created, and it was found that all could be connected to locations supplied by tap water from the Littlehempston Reservoir. South-West Water, the statutory undertaker with responsibility for Littlehempston, was alerted and joined the OCT, enrolling into the network aiming to control the outbreak. Samples were taken from service reservoirs containing treated water supplied from Littlehempston. On Sunday, 13 August, two samples were found to be positive for *Cryptosporidium* oocysts.

The initial hypothesis of the OCT was that the source of the outbreak was tap water, based on the geographic and demographic data about the cases, and the microbiological data from the samples of the treated water. When cases were reported to a doctor with symptoms suggesting cryptosporidiosis, a faecal sample was taken and dispatched for microbiological analysis. If the analysis was positive, information about the 'case' was passed to the OCT, which ensured that he or she was visited by an EHO and asked to complete a questionnaire. The data collected included demographics, a description of the symptoms suffered and details of exposure to potential sources, including animals, untreated milk and other food, rivers, swimming pools and drinking water from a variety of sources (mains water supplies, private water supplies and bottled water).

The OCT decided to put in place a number of precautionary control measures aimed at adjusting the use of the suspected mains waters by consumers and the way that the water was produced. On Monday, 14 August, consumers supplied by Littlehempston Reservoir were advised to boil their water on a precautionary basis until further notice. The message was distributed by local media, and leaflets were delivered to all households supplied from the Reservoir. A helpline was set up to deal with inquiries from consumers. Consumers were given advice on preventing infection, with particular emphasis on the need to boil water before use (including for washing cuts and burns) and follow strict personal hygiene. Advice was given to businesses on the additional precautions that they needed to take when using mains water supply.

Changes were made to the water treatment system at Littlehempston Reservoir and the connected water treatment works, in order to ensure that the procedures operated in accordance with the recommendations for best water treatment practice. Procedures were put in place that went beyond standard industry practice in order to minimise the risk of *Cryptosporidium* in the water supplied from Littlehempston. Abstraction from the River Dart was suspended when *Cryptosporidium* was detected in the river.

By mid-August, the OCT had determined 'on the balance of probability' that the outbreak was associated with mains water consumption.[102] This conclusion was reached on the basis of epidemiological data, in the form of questionnaires, collected by EHOs, which, when analysed, suggested that no other factor linked or could account for the 116 'cases' that had been reported to the OCT. Further, although the 'cases' were geographically distributed over a large area, they were all linked to locations supplied with mains water from Littlehempston. The large area suggested that there was no single point source of the outbreak, such as a swimming pool. As further microbiologically confirmed 'cases' were reported to the OCT, questionnaires continued to be completed, and descriptive epidemiology was revised to take into account new results.

The 'boil water' notice was lifted on Friday, 8 September 1995, once criteria agreed by the OCT had been met by South-West Water. The water company demonstrated a decline in new cases of cryptosporidiosis towards normal levels of incidence; that the water treatment works at Littlehempston were operating in optimal conditions; and that water quality monitoring had demonstrated that water supplied by Littlehempston had been free of oocysts for three consecutive days. Monitoring remained in place following the lifting of the boil water notice.

In total, 575 individuals in the Torbay area suffered cryptosporidiosis. Based on epidemiological and microbiological evidence gathered from these 575 individuals, the investigation concluded that the source of *cryptosporidium* oocysts was tap water supplied by the statutory water undertaker, South-West Water, from Littlehempston Reservoir. The geographical distribution of cases supported this conclusion.

Following the outbreak, a lengthy report was drafted by the OCT. It was created for the purpose of recommending steps to be taken in the management of future outbreaks within the area covered by the OCT and elsewhere. It describes 'the background to the epidemiology of cryptosporidiosis in the district and describes the water treatment process in the affected area. The

[102] Torbay 1995, OCT Report, 20.

methods used to investigate, control and monitor the outbreak are described and relevant results reported.'[103]

i. The Enforcement Decision

Once the outbreak was controlled, the DWI became involved. The DWI had not been part of the network responsible for controlling the incident. It is responsible for prosecuting offences under the Water Industry Act 1991, and particularly section 70(1), which, in 1995, provided:

> Subject to subsection (3) below, where a water undertaker supplies water by means of pipes to any premises and that water is unfit for human consumption, the undertaker shall be guilty of an offence.

Section 70(3) provides a defence if the water undertaker either 'had no reasonable grounds for suspecting that the water would be used for human consumption', or 'took all reasonable steps and exercised all due diligence for securing that the water was fit for human consumption on leaving its pipes or was not used for human consumption'.

The DWI decided to bring a prosecution against South-West Water for breach of section 70(1). Applying the evidential test, the Inspectorate believed that, on the evidence, a prosecution had a realistic prospect of success. Enforcement officers concluded that the company was unlikely to be able to demonstrate that it had exercised all due diligence, as there were aspects of the operation of the treatment process that could be criticised and did not conform to best water treatment practice.[104]

Applying the public interest test, officers considered that in 1992 there had been an outbreak in the same area epidemiologically associated with Littlehempston water, although the association was not robust.[105] Due to doubts about the epidemiology, enforcement action had not been taken. However, the history of the company's operations at Littlehempston and the scale of the outbreak led the DWI to conclude that it would be in the public interest to prosecute.

ii. The Prosecution

South-West Water was charged with six counts of supplying water unfit for human consumption contrary to section 70(1) of the Water Industry Act 1991. One charge related to the outbreak in general, and to supplying unfit water to all those served by the Littlehempston Reservoir. Specimen charges were advanced based on five water samples, which had been

[103] Torbay 1995, OCT Report, 1.

[104] Which at the time was set out in Department of Environment and Department of Health, *Cryptosporidium in Water Supplies* (HMSO 1990) (known as the 'Badenoch Report').

[105] Jiggins and Waite, above n 89, 123.

microbiologically analysed and shown to contain *cryptosporidium* oocysts. The case was committed to the Crown Court for trial.

The DWI proposed to rely on the report produced by the OCT as the primary evidence in the case. As we have seen, this report contained details of the epidemiological investigation, which established, using descriptive epidemiological methods, a linkage between drinking tap water and 'cases' within the definition adopted by the OCT. 'The OCT report and, in particular, the epidemiological study were not produced for the purpose of prosecution, but solely as part of managing and understanding the outbreak', but they formed the central piece of evidence in the prosecution, as the DWI enforcement officers 'believed that the report could be presented in evidence, as it was scientifically sound and reached very clear conclusions'.[106] The DWI was not a member of the OCT, and therefore relied upon the members of the OCT and their employees to collect information contemporaneously with the outbreak.

Once the case reached the Crown Court it became clear that there were substantial evidential issues between the prosecution and the defence. A pre-trial hearing before Judge Bursell was held to resolve the issues. Over the three-day hearing, the admissibility of the OCT report (and epidemiological evidence more generally) was canvassed, covering questions of relevance and hearsay.

The arguments and the decision of Judge Bursell are summarised below. It will then be necessary to consider whether changes to the law since 1997 would lead to a different decision if a similar case were to be heard today.

iii. The OCT Report

a. Relevance

At the pre-trial hearing, the defence argued that the probabilistic nature of the conclusions reached in the OCT report meant that the report was not relevant to determining whether the defendant was guilty of the section 70(1) offence beyond a reasonable doubt. However, the judge refused to exclude the report on this ground, holding that 'merely because something purports to reach a conclusion on the balance of probabilities, logically it does not exclude its actually proving something at the criminal standard of proof'.[107] This contrasts with the evidence of Roland Salmon to the Pennington Inquiry, who noted that some found probabilistic evidence unsatisfying when considering whether regulatory requirements had been breached.[108] The OCT report clearly states that it 'makes no claim to identify liability',

[106] Ibid, 123.
[107] Transcript Day 3, para 29.
[108] PEN/RS/LIVE-3-10-pg36line17.

saying that this is the 'responsibility of others'. This disclaimer does not prevent the report from providing evidence to those 'others' who do bear that responsibility.

b. Hearsay

Both the prosecution and the defence accepted that the OCT report would constitute hearsay if admitted in the criminal proceedings. It was a statement made outside of court that was being adduced in court for the purpose of proving the truth of its contents. It would therefore be prima facie inadmissible at common law,[109] unless it fell within an inclusionary exception to the hearsay rule.[110]

The prosecution argued that the OCT report fell within the inclusionary exception then contained in section 24 of the Criminal Justice Act 1988. The defence argued that the OCT report did not fall within section 24; alternatively, if the court held that the report was admissible under section 24, it should be excluded in the exercise of the judge's discretion under section 25(1). (A third submission was made, but not pursued, that the OCT report should, in any event, be excluded under section 78 of PACE 1984.) At the time of the outbreak, section 24 of the Criminal Justice Act 1988 provided, in material part:

> (1) [A] statement in a document shall be admissible in criminal proceedings as evidence of any fact of which direct oral evidence would be admissible, if the following conditions are satisfied—
>
> (i) the document was created or received by a person in the course of a trade, business, profession or other occupation, or as the holder of a paid or unpaid office; and
> (ii) the information contained in the document was supplied by a person (whether or not the maker of the statement) who had, or may reasonably be supposed to have had, personal knowledge of the matters dealt with.

Section 25 provided:

> (1) If, having regard to all the circumstances—
>
> (a) the Crown Court ...

[109] The rationales for the exclusion of hearsay were set out in the speech of Lord Normand in *Teper v R* [1952] AC 480, 486: Hearsay 'is not the best evidence and it is not delivered on oath. The truthfulness and accuracy of the person whose words are spoken to by another witness cannot be tested by cross-examination, and the light which his demeanour would throw on his testimony is lost.'

[110] *DDP v Myers* [1965] AC 1001 is a leading example of the operation of the prohibition against hearsay at common law, demonstrating the exclusion of evidence that could not be formalistically fitted into narrowly tailored exceptions.

is of the opinion that in the interests of justice a statement which is admissible by virtue of section 23 or 24 above nevertheless ought not to be admitted, it may direct that the statement shall not be admitted.

(2) Without prejudice to the generality of subsection (1) above, it shall be the duty of the court to have regard—

(a) to the nature and source of the document containing the statement and to whether or not, having regard to its nature and source and to any other circumstances that appear to the court to be relevant, it is likely that the document is authentic;
(b) to the extent to which the statement appears to supply evidence which would otherwise not be readily available;
(c) to the relevance of the evidence that it appears to supply to any issue which is likely to have to be determined in the proceedings; and
(d) to any risk, having regard in particular to whether it is likely to be possible to controvert the statement if the person making it does not attend to give oral evidence in the proceedings, that its admission or exclusion will result in unfairness to the accused or, if there is more than one, to any of them.

The judge held, after argument, that the information contained in questionnaires completed by 'cases' and returned to EHOs, and set out on labels applied to sample pots, identifying from whom the sample was procured, was initially supplied by a person with first-hand knowledge, and received by each person in the informational chain between the declarant and the court either as an office holder or the course of a business. Therefore, epidemiological questionnaires and microbiological sample labels prima facie fell within the scope of section 24.[111]

However, the argument was not primarily about the admissibility of this underlying information. Indeed, the defence were denied access to the questionnaires for reasons of medical confidentiality, and the prosecution would not (or could not) adduce this evidence at trial.[112] Instead the data from these questionnaires were aggregated and anonymised, and presented in the OCT report after epidemiological analysis. Therefore, argument focused on the OCT report itself. The prosecution contended that as the details that formed the basis of the analysis on the report were received by the OCT (or

[111] A literal reading of s 24 renders all documentary hearsay admissible, as it will be received (at some point) by an enforcement officer, a legal adviser or the court (see further Mark Ockleton, 'Documentary Hearsay in Criminal Cases' [1992] *Crim LR* 15). This does not appear to have been the intention of Parliament, as it would allow inadmissible hearsay to be made admissible by placing it in a document and passing the document to someone who receives it in the course of a business. The possibility of such laundering is deprecated, and expressly rejected, by Judge Bursell in *South-West Water*, mirroring the decision in *R v McGillivray* (1993) 97 Cr App R 232, 236.

[112] See the discussion above ch 6.VI.A.ii.

EHOs) as office holders,[113] and that at some point in the chain information had been supplied by a declarant with personal knowledge, the OCT report should therefore be admissible under section 24. The defence argued that admitting the OCT report under section 24 would be contrary to the intention underlying the provision, which was to allow business documents into evidence where they could speak for themselves, as this was more forensically valid than calling an individual to give live evidence to that effect.[114]

During argument, the judge expressed concern about the ability of the defendant to check the accuracy of the information in the OCT report. With reliance placed on the report, and the information used in calculations not disclosed (even as unused material), the defendant was, in the eyes of the judge, significantly disadvantaged if it wished to check the information used or the statistical calculations performed. The defence argued that this disadvantage meant that it would not be in the interests of justice to admit the report, and therefore the court ought to exercise its section 25(1) discretion and refuse to admit it.

During argument over the exercise of the section 25(1) discretion, the judge raised the possibility that article 6 of the European Convention on Human Rights (ECHR) entitled the defendant to information about the cases underlying the microbiological and epidemiological analysis on the OCT report.[115] In particular, Judge Bursell raised the question with the prosecution as to whether the ECHR bolstered the argument that the failure to allow the defence access to affected individuals was a breach of natural justice. However, as the ECHR was not directly applicable at the time of the hearing, this argument was not pursued further, and does not form part of the judgment.

Further argument was addressed to the question of whether the OCT report was a document prepared for the purpose of criminal proceedings or investigations. If so, under sections 24(4) and 26 of the Criminal Justice Act 1988, the document could not be admitted without the leave of the court. In considering whether to give leave, the court must consider whether admitting the statement would be in the interests of justice, with particular regard to the following statutory factors:

(a) the contents of the statement;
(b) any risk, having regard in particular to whether it is likely to be possible to controvert the statement if the person making it does not attend to give oral evidence in the proceedings, that its admission or exclusion will result in unfairness to the accused or, if there is more than one, to any of them; and
(c) any other circumstances that appear to the court to be relevant.

113 Transcript Day 1, para 41.
114 See Paul Roberts and AAS Zuckerman, *Criminal evidence* (2nd edn, Oxford University Press 2010), 410–12.
115 Transcript Day 2, paras 10–11.

Whilst the OCT report was prepared at a point where an investigation potentially leading to criminal proceedings was continuing, it was argued by the prosecution that the OCT report was separate from the criminal proceedings, notwithstanding the fact that it was adduced in evidence in such proceedings.

Judge Bursell refused to admit the OCT report. His ruling states that 'by anonymising the persons involved and therefore the [epidemiological and microbiological] analyses subsequent to the alleged outbreak [the prosecution] has prevented the defence, as it is entitled so to do, from sufficiently testing the case against it'.[116] Therefore, the judge exercised his discretion under section 25(1) to exclude the OCT report. It would be

> contrary to natural justice to cut out the defence from the possibility, if only through unused material, of checking how the samples were taken and the analysis of those samples … [I]t would be quite wrong for me to allow the placing of the OCT report before the jury when the defence have been cut out from what seems to me to be their fundamental right.[117]

Whilst the defence are prevented from cross-examining the declarant in all cases when hearsay is admitted, in this case, where the declarant was anonymous, the defence were further prevented from attacking the information supplied by the declarant collaterally, either by reviewing the information supplied by the declarant or by seeking out the declarant and challenging the information provided. Although this portion of the ruling appears to focus on samples, it is clear from the context that the judge is referring to all data obtained from individuals suffering from food-borne illness, including epidemiological information in the form of food histories.

Through the process of anonymisation (which was based on the OCT's perceived obligation of medical confidentiality), the defence were deprived of the names of those individuals who contributed data forming the basis of the analyses in the OCT report. The defence were unable to perform their own inquiries in order to assess whether the data gathered were sufficient to support the conclusions advanced in the report. The judge made it clear that

> it would be entirely inappropriate for a prosecution to be brought against any defendant if the only evidence to be placed before the jury against the defendant was a report such as this. It seems to me that it would, in effect, evidentially shift the burden of proof to the defendant in an entirely unfair way.[118]

For the sake of completeness, the judge then considered whether the report would be admissible in the event that his ruling on section 25(1) was incorrect. Initially considering the section 26 point, Judge Bursell accepted the prosecution submission that the OCT report was prepared apart from

[116] Transcript Day 3, para 32.
[117] Transcript Day 3, para 33.
[118] Transcript Day 3, para 36.

pending or contemplated criminal proceedings,[119] with the purpose of both analysing the control of the Torbay outbreak and assisting with the management of future outbreaks of *Cryptosporidium*. Unlike data stored on police databases,[120] the OCT report was not produced for the prosecution (despite the subsequent central role it assumed in evidence), but would have been produced even in circumstances in which enforcement action was not contemplated.[121]

The judge accepted that the OCT report fell 'fair and square' within the provisions of section 24.[122] The information contained in the report was received by holders of a paid office, and was initially provided by someone with first-hand knowledge of the information. However, the judge expressed considerable doubt about the ability of the prosecution to demonstrate that all the information was passed along the chain of people receiving the evidence 'in the course of a trade, business, profession or other occupation, or as the holder of a paid or unpaid office'. In respect of 10 per cent of the questionnaires and faecal samples underlying the OCT report, the EHOs who had received these could not be identified. The judge was not satisfied that, in respect of this information, the prosecution could demonstrate that it had been received by 'the holder of a paid or unpaid office', although some question may be raised as to who, other than office holders, would have been involved in the response to food-borne illness. However, even if the prosecution could satisfy section 24, for the reasons given, the judge would have exercised his exclusionary discretion to prevent the OCT report entering into evidence.[123]

iv. After the Ruling

Following the ruling, the DWI applied for an adjournment to allow the Inspectorate to collect further evidence, in the form of statements from all affected 'cases', but this application was refused. South-West Water was consequently acquitted of the charges brought. Even if the application had been granted, the DWI may have been unable to produce the evidence required by the judge, as much of the information on which the epidemiological report was based was subject to medical confidentiality, and the medical professionals involved made it clear that they would not consent to

[119] Ibid.
[120] *R (Wellington) v DPP* [2007] EWHC 1061 (Admin).
[121] Similar to the reasoning in *R v Bedi and Bedi* (1992) 95 Cr App R 21.
[122] Transcript Day 3, para 36.
[123] The changes to the hearsay regime in the Criminal Justice Act 2003, s 114 onwards are unlikely to have altered the position, as the rights of the defence, which, according to Judge Bursell, would have been compromised by the admission of the OCT report, remain an important consideration for the court when deciding whether to admit hearsay evidence under the inclusionary exceptions in the Act.

the use of such information.[124] The DWI was unable to pursue an appeal from this pre-trial ruling.[125]

The ruling meant that the DWI had great difficulty bringing prosecutions in respect of contaminated water supplies (CON-EHO4). Immediately following the ruling in *South-West Water*, the Inspectorate decided not to pursue a similar case involving Three Valleys Water, in which 32 people became ill with cryptosporidiosis after being supplied with water contaminated with *Cryptosporidium* oocysts.

In response to the difficulties exposed by the *South-West Water* case, the regulatory regime was amended to require management of the risk of *Cryptosporidium* in public water supplies, notification of such management steps to the DWI and monitoring of the levels of *Cryptosporidium* in water.[126] These rules were implemented in order to ensure that it was easier to take enforcement action following future outbreaks of *Cryptosporidium*. They have since been amended to cover other water-borne microbes. In future DWI cases, it will therefore be unnecessary to rely on OCT reports as the evidential basis for showing a section 70(1) offence, since other 'hygiene' offences may be prosecuted instead.[127] However, in food-borne incidents, EHOs may need to adduce an OCT report as evidence in a prosecution for a breach of food safety requirements, in particular of the requirements to provide food that is fit for human consumption and not injurious to health.

B. The Effect of Inadmissibility of OCT Reports on Enforcement Following Food-borne Illness

Environmental Health Officers are aware of the ruling in *South-West Water* that OCT reports cannot form the basis of enforcement action. All members of the Chartered Institute of Environmental Health were alerted to this decision, which was placed in the Institute's library. The EHOs interviewed in this study were aware of the doubtful admissibility of evidence presented in

[124] The question of medical confidentiality and decision making is examined above, ch 6.V.

[125] An Attorney-General's Reference may have been possible, but is only available in very limited circumstances, where a point of law arises that would benefit from a decision from the Court of Appeal before entering into circulation in the lower courts (see Criminal Justice Act 1972, s 36 and *Attorney-General's Reference (No 1 of 1975)* [1975] 3 WLR 11). It is unlikely that these circumstances would have been present here, where the judge made a discretionary decision to exclude evidence that was open to him, notwithstanding the prosecution's disagreement with that decision. An interlocutory appeal would now be possible under the Criminal Justice Act 2003, s 58, as the judgment of Judge Bursell would constitute a terminating ruling.

[126] See Water Supply (Water Quality) Regulations 2000.

[127] Indeed, the processes that must be put in place under the Water Supply (Water Quality) Regulations 2000, SI 2000/3184, are somewhat reminiscent of the requirement to put in place HACCP plans under Regulation (EC) No 852/2004 of the European Parliament and of the Council of 29 April 2004 on the hygiene of foodstuffs [2004] OJ L139/1 art 5, discussed above ch 3.I.B.iv.

OCT reports (EHO-A3; EHO-B1). They treat an OCT report as presumptively inadmissible when building a case for enforcement action following an incident of food-borne illness. Other information, which may or may not be available, must be used to show that hygiene or safety requirements have been breached.[128]

As an OCT report is *de facto* inadmissible and not to be considered when making an enforcement decision, food history questionnaires, which form the basis of epidemiological evidence, may be adduced to show that 'cases' ate a particular food while 'controls' did not. By placing such evidence before the court, the EHO seeks to demonstrate a link between a food and an illness suffered by the 'cases'. This information is adduced for the purposes of showing that particular food was eaten by a person, and is therefore hearsay in law.[129]

Hearsay is admissible if it falls within one of the categories set out in the Criminal Justice Act 2003, section 114(1)(a)–(d).[130] Following the *South-West Water* decision, food histories will be seen as business documents, created or received by EHOs in the course of their profession or as holders of an office.[131] Therefore they may prima facie be admitted under sections 114(1)(a) and 117 of the 2003 Act. The decision in *South-West Water* that an OCT report, and the information therein, was not created for the purposes of a criminal investigation (given the primary control purpose of investigations into incidents of food-borne illness) would seem to apply under the 2003 Act.[132] Therefore the requirements of section 117(5) of that Act do not apply.

[128] The status of *South-West Water* as authority for the proposition that OCT reports are inadmissible provides an interesting illustration the nature of precedent in this area. There are very few decided cases which touch directly on the issues raised in the cases that EHOs deal with. Therefore, a well-known case which decides issues relevant to EHOs' practise is treated as determining a legal issue, despite having no formal precedential value.

[129] US cases have held that survey evidence constitutes hearsay when adduced for the purposes of proving the truth of a proposition. See *Schering Corp v Pfizer, Inc* 189 F 3d 218, 225 (2d Cir 1999).

[130] Set out in the introductory paragraphs of section VI. above.

[131] It appears that EHOs believe that the changes to the law of evidence brought in by the Criminal Justice Act 2003 have not altered the admissibility of OCT reports. Given the similar drafting of s 24 and s 117, it seems likely that similar analyses would apply. Officers do not appear to have considered the possibility of attempting to utilise the 'safety valve' provision in s 114(1)(d) to admit an OCT report ('the court is satisfied that it is in the interests of justice for it to be admissible'). However, it is unlikely that this would be successful, as the courts have discouraged the use of s 114(1)(d) where this would evade the safeguards provided by other sections of the Act (see *R v Z* [2009] 1 Cr App R 34, where, discussing the use of s 114(1)(d) in circumstances in which evidence would not be admitted under s 116, the Court of Appeal stated that 'section 114(1)(d) is to be cautiously applied, since otherwise the conditions laid down by Parliament ... would be circumvented').

[132] The pre-2003 Act decision in *Bedi and Bedi*, above n 109, which mirrors the decision in *South-West Water* by holding that documents with a primary purpose other than criminal proceeding are not criminal process statements even though they may play an important role in criminal proceedings, has been followed in the post-2003 era—see *West Midlands Probation Board v French* [2009] 1 WLR 1715, paras 48–50.

However, the argument that admitting such evidence would be unfair to the defence, which was advanced in *South-West Water*, is likely to apply equally in a case arising today, and therefore it is unlikely that hearsay survey evidence will be admitted under section 117, although Judge Bursell's central objection to the admission of such evidence could be countered by identifying the symptomatic individuals to whom the data relate.

However, a food history may be admitted attached as an exhibit to a statement made by a 'case' or 'control', where that person is available to be cross-examined on the information contained in the survey. Such statements may be admitted in evidence without the necessity for the person to attend court, under the provisions of the Criminal Justice Act 1967, section 9, if the defendant agrees. For this reason, EHOs collecting food history evidence may ask individuals to sign a statement containing a declaration that the food history is true to the best of their knowledge and belief. It was the normal practice of EHOs in Local Authority A to collect information in this manner, with individuals being asked to confirm that they were prepared to attend court, if necessary, in connection with the matter. Whilst the primary purpose of collecting this information is control, by collecting it in this way, evidential value is preserved for enforcement. However, even if affected individuals are unwilling to attend court, information will still be collected. This will be accompanied by an assurance that the information will not be used in a prosecution. This cannot assist where the person from whom the food history is collected is not the person who consumed the food, for example where the food was consumed by a child or a person with memory difficulties, as the consumer's reported statements will be hearsay.

In some cases reported by legal professional informants, EHOs sought to include the food history of 'cases', or information about food preparation reported by employees, in their witness statements. It was said by BAR-1 that, in initial case files that come to him for appraisal, hearsay is often included in EHO witness statements. He advises EHOs to amend their statements, and, if possible, to collect admissible statements from 'cases' covering the inadmissible matters set out in the draft statements. If admissible evidence cannot be procured, the case may need to be dropped if the sum of the admissible evidence does not show a realistic prospect of success. He attributed these inclusions to a focus on control and, therefore, a lack of awareness of evidential rules amongst EHOs, allied to a desire to present information efficiently. Inexperience in drafting statements that comply with evidential requirements may lead to the inclusion of hearsay. Whilst trainee EHOs are informed about the hearsay rules, and how they restrict the information that can be included in statements (ACD-1; EHO-B2; BAR-1), without repeated practical experience, details of the rule become lost and inadmissible statements are drafted.

Where the inadmissible hearsay information—whether contained in an OCT report, an EHO's statement or a food history questionnaire—is essential for pursuing a prosecution, and cannot be supplied by other means, enforcement action will not be taken. If the information could potentially be made available in an admissible form but not without major resource implications, EHOs may choose not to expend time, money and energy making evidence admissible, preferring not to take enforcement action. This is not due to information being literally unavailable or inadmissible. The decision reflects the calculation that presenting information obtained during the control phase of enforcement action in a way that satisfies evidential requirements in a particular case is not worth the expenditure of resources, given the fulfilment of the primary goal of control of the spread of food-borne illness.

VII. INADMISSIBILITY OF INFORMATION GAINED FROM CONVERSATIONS WITH BUSINESSES AND EMPLOYEES AND ITS IMPACT ON ENFORCEMENT

We saw in chapter four that, when responding to an incident of food-borne illness, EHOs ask questions of food businesses without administering a caution.[133] They perceive food businesses as reluctant to engage with EHOs where the information provided might be used for the purposes of enforcement.[134] They fear that a business will not enrol into the control network if it is cautioned. Businesses are more willing where the informational exchange is focused on achieving control of the food-borne illness. The goals of EHOs and businesses are aligned in relation to control, with both parties wishing to halt the spread of illness. Conversely, the parties' goals conflict in relation to enforcement. Environmental Health Officers are reluctant to jeopardise a relationship with a business that is necessary for control by seeking to obtain information the business is reluctant to supply, for fear of restricting the flow of information that would otherwise be forthcoming. The primary goal of control will not be impeded in order to achieve the secondary goal of enforcement.

Information obtained from interviews not under caution is treated as if it will be inadmissible in criminal proceedings. A bright-line 'working rule' of evidence operates, with all evidence obtained in interviews with businesses not under caution treated as inadmissible. *De facto* inadmissible evidence will not be considered in applying the evidential test, reducing the chances that contemplated enforcement action will have a realistic prospect of success.

Information from employees may also not be forthcoming. Employees could theoretically act as witnesses, circumventing the need to interview the business under caution. However, employees are often unwilling to talk to EHOs, because of their weak position in the employment relationship with businesses, particularly in the food sector, where work may be short-term

[133] See ch 4.V.D.
[134] EHO-A2; EHO-A3.

and on unfavourable terms, such as zero hours contracts. Further, businesses may restrict EHO access to employees if information is to be used in enforcement, damaging prospects for control.

A. Obtaining Information from Businesses

Businesses are generally keen to cooperate in the investigation and control of incidents of food-borne illness. File notes studied in this research demonstrate that businesses freely provide information requested by EHOs.[135] Most incidents arise from mistakes, not deliberate conduct; and most businesses are keen to ensure that an incident is controlled and further risks to consumers reduced. This enthusiasm may be driven both by genuine concern for the affected 'cases' and by self-interest, such as limiting damaging publicity and managing potential financial losses by minimising of the scope of the incident. Businesses therefore voluntarily provide information that assists with the control of the illness. Further, particular businesses may also have a close working relationship with an individual EHO, particularly where the EHO has provided compliance advice in the past, and therefore may wish to assist the EHO and preserve the relationship.

Businesses are naturally more reluctant to cooperate where they perceive that they are primarily subject to an investigation that may lead to enforcement action. Where information is not aimed at control, there is a greater reluctance to provide such information. Environmental Health Officers attempt to make clear, through their words and actions, that information is to be used for the purposes of control. An important means of signalling this is by conducting an interview not under caution, turning an 'interview' into a mutually beneficial 'conversation'. Conducting an interview under caution is thought to demonstrate that criminal proceedings being contemplated by the EHO, inhibiting the information provided for the purpose of control. It may also trigger a business's decision to consult a solicitor, which is perceived by EHOs as likely to mean that the business will be more reluctant to provide information voluntarily, damaging the ability of EHOs to control the spread of food-borne illness. They are therefore loath to use their power to interview under caution, for fear that control objectives will be damaged.

For the same reason, EHOs are reluctant to use formal powers (such as those under Public Health (Control of Disease) Act 1984, section 45I) to obtain information, as this may jeopardise the relationship between business and EHO, preventing cooperation in control. Further, if used in enforcement action, information obtained through the use of formal powers may be subject to challenge as information obtained under compulsion.[136]

[135] Eg, in A/I/5; A/I/16; and A/I/23.

[136] See, eg, *R v Hertfordshire CC, ex p Green Industries* [2000] 2 AC 412.

B. Obtaining Information from Employees

Although information could theoretically be obtained from employees, they are often reluctant to talk to EHOs investigating incidents of food-borne illness. One of the possible explanations for an incident of food-borne illness (particularly viral illness) is contamination of the food by an infected food handler. Therefore EHOs will often wish to ask employees about their health at the time of the incident. However, EHOs have found that food handlers are reluctant to answer questions or provide faecal samples in these circumstances, and in particular will not admit they worked whilst ill. It was suggested by EHO-A3 that this reluctance arises because the sickness policies of most food businesses make working whilst ill a disciplinary offence, and thus could result in the employee's being dismissed. Despite these policies (and the potential consequences of contravention), staff will often work whilst ill. This was explained by EHO-C2: 'People aren't going to admit they puked up that morning or have been up all night, they don't want to lose their money by not turning up.' Most food handlers are in low-paid jobs, and many cannot afford to lose wages. Staff may not receive pay as long as they are unable to work, and this perversely incentivises working whilst symptomatic. Despite their duties to report food-borne illnesses, both in law and in the employment contract, employees typically do not report, and in some cases have an incentive to conceal, illness.

Food handlers may justifiably perceive that if they admit illness to the EHO, they are endangering their job. Cooperation between an EHO and the business poses a perceived risk that information given to the EHO will be passed on to their employers. Information from food handlers about their health is consequently unlikely to be available to EHOs following an investigation. In order to increase cooperation in such circumstances, EHOs must ensure that employees are comfortable about disclosing information, and not afraid that it will be immediately disclosed to employers. They do this by assuring employees of anonymity, which prevents the use of information in enforcement action but ensures that it is available for the purpose of control.

In A/I/14, where infection by a food handler was suspected, all handlers were interviewed but none of them admitted that they had come to work whilst unwell, closing down this potential route to explaining the outbreak. The reluctance of food handlers to inform EHOs about any gastric illness they have suffered also hampers enforcement action alleging that a business did not have in place an adequate sickness policy to ensure that ill food handlers did not work. This is an offence under Food Safety and Hygiene (England) Regulation 2013,[137] but prosecutions are unlikely to be brought

[137] By virtue of reg 19, which makes it an offence if a food business fails to comply with Regulation 852/2004, annex II, ch VIII.

in the absence of evidence from food handlers that the policy did not operate in particular circumstances.

The EHOs interviewed in this study feel that businesses should be responsible for ensuring greater employee cooperation with enforcement actions.[138] It was argued by EHO-A3 that it is necessary for food businesses to ensure that handlers are not incentivised to work whilst ill, and are not penalised financially for complying with sickness policies. If financial incentives to work whilst ill exist, employees are likely to continue to work whilst ill. Encouraging compliance is a matter for food businesses, and EHOs struggle to address the problem through formal action, both due to a lack of information and because suitable powers are not available.

As well as a reluctance to give information about working whilst ill, employees may, in general, be concerned about losing their jobs in the event that they speak to EHOs. If employers are not cooperating with EHOs, the officers perceive that employees take this as a signal that they also are not to cooperate.[139] If asked to cooperate by their employers, employees may provide good quality information. If not so ordered, EHOs find employees routinely uncooperative. Therefore, if they wish to get information from employees for the purposes of control, EHOs must preserve a cooperative relationship with the food business, refraining from using formal investigative powers that may be associated with enforcement action. Food handlers may be casual workers or employed on short-term contracts, and may be reluctant to speak to EHOs for fear of providing their employer with a reason to dispense with their services. Whilst such fears may be overplayed by food handlers,[140] they are perceived by EHOs as having the potential to affect the way that staff members interact with them.[141]

C. The Effect of Inadmissible Interview Information on Enforcement

The decision to question businesses and individuals who may have information about an incident of food-borne illness not under caution is made in order to secure the maximum amount of information. Such information is needed to assist with the control of an incident of food-borne illness, and therefore the investigation is structured in order to secure this information. However, this reluctance to caution may have knock-on effects on the decision whether or not to take enforcement action. Environmental Health Officers treat all information obtained in interviews conducted not under

[138] EHO-A3; EHO-C2.
[139] EHO-A3; EHO-C2.
[140] Dismissal on such grounds would likely amount to unfair dismissal.
[141] EHO-A3.

caution as *de facto* inadmissible. It is therefore not considered when deciding whether the evidence assembled offers a realistic prospect of conviction.

Section 78 of PACE 1984 provides:

> In any proceedings the court may refuse to allow evidence on which the prosecution proposes to rely to be given if it appears to the court that, having regard to all the circumstances, including the circumstances in which the evidence was obtained, the admission of the evidence would have such an adverse effect on the fairness of the proceedings that the court ought not to admit it.

Exclusion under section 78 is 'discretionary', ie a matter for contextual judgement.[142] A judge may exclude information obtained without the administration of a caution as required by PACE Code C on the basis that the admission of the interview would have 'such an adverse effect' on fairness that the court ought not to admit it.[143]

Environmental Health Officers have constructed a bright-line working rule under which they operate: if obtained without a caution, replies to questions will not be admissible (BAR-1; SOL-1; EHO-A3). This means that EHOs will not use information obtained from conversations not conducted under caution when attempting to build a case following an investigation into an incident of food-borne illness. Working to such a rule has the benefit of clarity, and is easier to instruct EHOs about this when they are trained in the rules of evidence.

In contrast, courts have generally refused to construct bright-line rules about the exclusion of evidence under section 78.[144] By presuming a rigid exclusionary rule, and refusing to use evidence obtained not under caution, EHOs go beyond the discretionary approach operated by the court, depriving themselves of some evidence that might otherwise have been admitted. The working rule does not reflect the complexity of the cases decided under PACE 1984, which have not rigidly held that a failure to caution when required should result in the exclusion of evidence derived from an interview conducted without a caution.[145] Generally only 'significant and substantial' breaches of PACE 1984 and its Codes will result in exclusion.[146] Whilst the failure to caution where required will be seen as a significant and substantial breach in most cases,[147] in *Gill* the Court of Appeal held that the decision of a Crown Court judge not to exclude information obtained by questioning not under caution, during an Inland Revenue 'Hansard interview', was

[142] *R v Mason* [1988] 1 WLR 139, 143.

[143] See, eg, *R v Absolam* (1989) 88 Cr App R 332.

[144] See *R v Samuel* [1988] QB 615, 630, per Hodgson J: 'It is undesirable to attempt any general guidance as to the way in which a judge's discretion under section 78 or his inherent powers should be exercised.'

[145] See *R v Delaney* (1988) 88 Cr App R 338; *R v Gill* [2004] 1 WLR 469.

[146] *R v Keenan* [1990] 2 QB 54, 69. See further Michael Zander, *The Police and Criminal Evidence Act 1984* (6th edn, Thomson/Sweet & Maxwell 2013) ch 8.

[147] See, eg, *R v Sparkes* [1991] *Crim LR* 128.

correct, because 'if a caution had been administered, the appellants would [not] have done anything different from what they did'.[148] Utilising a bright-line rule means that the EHOs are not concerned with the complexities of the mass of case law that has grown up around section 78, and the training of EHOs is simpler.[149]

De facto 'inadmissibility,' and the accompanying epistemically deprived enforcement decision making, is the result of two actions of EHOs: first, favouring control over enforcement and therefore choosing not to interview under caution; secondly, creating a clear rule that all information gained from these interviews will be inadmissible. Despite knowing that the absence of a caution will lead to answers to questions being inadmissible in enforcement action, EHOs choose to ask questions without cautioning. As explained above, this deliberate choice is made to improve the chances of obtaining information necessary to control an incident of food-borne illness. By choosing not to caution individuals whom it is reasonable to suspect of committing an offence, EHOs limit the information that can be used in enforcement action, and by extension reduce the chances that enforcement action can ultimately be taken, at an early stage in the investigation. Whilst it may be possible to build a case without this information, the lack of evidence derived from interviews is likely to harm enforcement action brought following an outbreak of food-borne illness.

Any decision to privilege the obtaining of information for the purposes of control over the possibility of subsequent enforcement action influences enforcement decision making, and should be acknowledged as a positive choice by EHOs, rather than as an inevitable consequence of normal practice. In reality this is not a question of inability to present the information, but instead is an example of reluctance to obtain admissible evidence due to the anticipated harmful consequences of doing so. Environmental Health Officers make the decision that information for the purposes of control is more important than obtaining information usable for the purposes of enforcement.

VIII. CONCLUSION

Building a case following an investigation into an incident of food-borne illness is not simple. Challenges, in the form of information that is unavailable

[148] *R v Gill* above n 145, para 48.

[149] The even more complex question of 'curing' a failure to caution by conducting later interviews under caution did not directly arise in the cases considered in the study, although it was adverted to by BAR-1 when considering ways in which admissibility difficulties could be tackled, and implicitly arose in the South Wales case, see above n 17, as the police interviewed William Tudor under caution subsequent to some questioning by EHOs conducted not under caution. However, the questions asked were different. See *R v Ismail* [1990] *Crim LR* 109; *R v Singleton* [2002] EWCA Crim 459, para 10, 'where an early interview is excluded[,] admission of a later interview must be a matter of fact and degree'.

or inadmissible, impede EHOs' ability to do so. Information about food-borne illness is often difficult to obtain, with the difficulties exacerbated by delay and the way in which food is consumed, with destruction a normal part of food business. In many cases, investigations do not produce enough information for the EHO to come to a firm conclusion about the source of the incident (including whether the incident had a food or non-food source), the food vehicle involved, and whether there was a breach of food safety or food hygiene regulations at food businesses implicated in the incident. In such circumstances, formal enforcement action cannot take place.

Given the epistemic challenges of proving offences following incidents of food-borne illness, EHOs do not need to confront the difficult public interest decisions about whether or not to bring enforcement action. Such decisions have been explored in detail in much of the literature surrounding enforcement and the compliance strategies adopted by regulators, but are not directly relevant in these circumstances. Whilst EHOs' investigatory decisions with effects on enforcement actions are sometimes framed in terms of the need to preserve cooperative relationships with business, the transactions described in this chapter are framed in relation to a short-term necessity, enabling control, rather than in relation to the long-term necessity of ensuring and enabling compliance. The public interest calculation is never engaged.

Whilst the decisions highlighted in chapters four and five and in this chapter, which are aimed at preserving the EHO–business relationship, may appear to mirror decisions made by a compliance-focused regulator, control is the motivating factor. Where there is no continuing risk of further infection, the balance moves towards enforcement, and investigatory decisions are made that preserve the evidential value of information collected. For example, EHOs are more willing to conduct interviews under caution (South Wales;[150] *R v Muriel Morris*[151]).

Information necessary to produce a complete picture of an incident of food-borne illness is often difficult to obtain. Enforcement is difficult without such a complete picture. The EHOs are often unable to obtain information from consumers, medical professionals or food businesses. In some cases the lack of information is unavoidable, whereas in other cases it results from a decision by EHOs to forgo information in an admissible form. Information is obtained, but in a form that can be used only for control purposes, not for enforcement.

Delay between the consumption of food and the onset of symptoms creates particular problems for obtaining information, as memory may degrade over (even the short) periods of time between consumption and onset, and may fix on particular foods or businesses as the source of illness; potential food samples may be destroyed in the relevant time period; and faecal

[150] See above n 17.
[151] See above n 35.

samples may no longer contain food-borne illness organisms. Lack of information makes it difficult to show, 'beyond a reasonable doubt', that there has been a breach of food safety and/or food hygiene regulations. When applying the evidential test, EHOs cannot satisfy themselves of a realistic prospect of conviction. In such cases, EHOs will not take enforcement action.

Lack of information will not, however, usually dissuade EHOs from taking control action. Control action is taken on a precautionary basis, as EHOs wish to control the possible risk of secondary spread. They are prepared to use this route when data are missing, whereas enforcement action is seen as requiring information demonstrating breaches to the required standard.

Admissibility is an important part of the decision-making picture when considering whether formal enforcement action should be taken. Inadmissible evidence will be taken into account when EHOs are taking control decisions, as they are not bound by the rules of criminal evidence in this area of their work. Questions of admissibility are familiar to lawyers. This study found that they are also familiar to EHOs. The EHOs interviewed in this research consider the admissibility of information before taking enforcement actions, and used only admissible information in taking enforcement decisions. This is in accordance with the Code for Crown Prosecutors, which binds EHOs through the Food Law Code,[152] which provides that 'when deciding whether there is sufficient evidence to prosecute, prosecutors must consider whether the evidence can be used'.[153] Conceptions of admissibility are in practice based on bright-line working rules that form the basis of the decisions taken by EHOs. Interviews not under caution are regarded as inadmissible; OCT reports *de facto* are inadmissible; information subject to medical confidentiality cannot be used. Some hearsay evidence is treated more selectively, with EHOs seeking creative ways to place it before the court. Once inadmissible evidence is removed, cases built following an incident of food-borne illness frequently do not present a realistic prospect of conviction.

The action that renders the evidence (de facto) inadmissible is often the action of EHOs themselves. Steps taken by EHOs in their response of food-borne illness may render evidence inadmissible according to the working rules adopted. The prime example is a decision to interview without a caution. Where EHOs appreciate the consequence of their decision, they accept this as the price of controlling the spread of food-borne illness and achieving their primary goal. In other cases, however, where inadmissibility is an inadvertent result of EHO actions, they may seek to take enforcement action in

[152] Food Standards Agency, *Food Law Code of Practice for England* (Food Standards Agency 2008) para 3.1.10.

[153] Crown Prosecution Service, *Code for Crown Prosecutors* (CPS 2010) para 4.7.

any event, using a work-around to build a case, such as including hearsay evidence in their witness statement.

The 'working rules of evidence' used by EHOs do not, in some cases, reflect the complexities of the rules operated by a court. Therefore, some information is not considered, despite the possibility that it may be deemed admissible. Some potentially usable information collected during the investigation is therefore not considered in the assessment process that takes place once the investigation is concluded and the food-borne illness controlled. In other cases, EHOs judge that evidence will usually be admissible, despite the possibility that a court will later deem it inadmissible. Where such evidence is challenged in a high-profile and widely reported case, this may contribute to the working rules and inhibit future uses of such information by EHOs (*South-West Water*).

Environmental Health Officers are more aware of some rules of evidence than others. Hearsay evidence is often part of an enforcement case prepared by EHOs. In particular, EHO witness statements often contain hearsay information, and legal professionals may advise EHOs to prepare new statements that are not infected with hearsay. In contrast, having been held to be hearsay in *South-West Water*, EHOs will not rely on OCT reports to build a case.

Where the available and admissible information does not present a realistic prospect of conviction, enforcement action cannot lawfully be pursued. Unavailability of evidence presents the greatest practical difficulty for EHOs seeking to build successful enforcement cases. In addition, inadmissibility of evidence often means that cases cannot be built on the basis of important information known to EHOs (EHO-A3). A combination of these two epistemic challenges means that the evidential test for prosecutions is rarely satisfied, and enforcement action is consequently not taken following the majority of incidents of food-borne illness. For this reason, questions of public interest were never reached in most of the cases examined in this study.

7

Reacting to Incidents of Food-borne Illness: The (Im)Possibility of Investigation, Control and Enforcement

A COMPLEX AND multifaceted regulatory network responds to reports of food-borne illness. As we have seen above, this response involves investigation of the incidents and the gathering of information, taking control action where necessary to prevent further primary or secondary cases, and attempting to take enforcement action where it is both possible (when sufficient evidence is both available and admissible) and proper to do so. In chapters four, five and six we considered these different steps in the response in turn, and illustrated the challenges faced by the regulatory network when taking action. In this chapter it is necessary, first, to extract and examine the themes that appear from the response of network actors to food-borne illness, and to make suggestions for tackling the challenges revealed during the examination of the response by network actors.

It is clear from chapter six that in many cases the admissible information assembled by EHOs is insufficient to demonstrate a realistic prospect of successful enforcement action. It is necessary to consider why this problem arises, and to provide an analysis of the factors that influence (un)successful prosecution case building after an incident of food-borne illness, before turning to possible solutions that may enable the different goals of the investigation to be achieved.

Chapters four and five demonstrated great success by the control network in managing incidents of food-borne illness. It is enforcement, rather than control, that is most inhibited by the evidential challenges identified in chapter six. The willingness to take control action where a risk may be present, without evidence reaching the standard required by the 'realistic prospect' test, means that control action will be taken on the basis of less certain information than is required for enforcement. Indeed, precautionary decisions to take action are common when control is the main objective of the actor. Further, the information may be obtained in a form usable for control decisions, but not usable for enforcement. In particular, information obtained in an interview conducted not under caution, or from an employee who provides it on condition of confidentiality, is used to make control decisions, but it cannot be taken into account when considering potential enforcement action.

I. KEY THEMES IN INVESTIGATION, CONTROL AND ENFORCEMENT

Several thematic strands can be drawn from the foregoing examination of evidence collection and assessment processes, which shed light on responses to incidents of food-borne illness by network actors, and particularly by EHOs. Each theme provides insight into the decision making of the regulatory network, and provides a partial explanation for the steps taken by officers in response to a notification.

A. The Power of the Network

The importance of a networked response to food-borne illness is borne out by the empirical investigations. The presence of a network enables more data to be gathered than could be harvested by a single entity engaged in the response to an incident. A broader range of control powers may be available to a network than to a single entity. A network is essential to the response to food-borne illness, as illustrated by the response to the *South Wales E Coli* outbreak,[1] where coordination between numerous actors was necessary to ensure that both primary and secondary spread was controlled, particularly because of the geographical scope of the incident.

It is essential that participants enrol into the network in order to provide it with information that would not always be available otherwise. Individual consumers, workers employed by food businesses and frontline medical professionals have information about symptoms, food histories and regulatory compliance that would not be available to regulators from other sources. It is therefore necessary to ensure that barriers to actors' enrolling into the network are minimal, enabling those who have information to feed in to the network. It should therefore be easy to identify the way in which an individual can enrol, by providing a clear pathway for him or her to contact network participants. In large incidents it is often the case that a dedicated telephone number and e-mail address will be set up to allow individuals to make contact, whereas in smaller incidents individuals may contact a local authority direct. It is therefore necessary for contact details to be easily accessible. In some cases it may be necessary to allay fears, particularly held by the workers of a food business, of adverse consequences as a result of

[1] Full details available at <http://wales.gov.uk/ecoliinquiry/?lang=en>.

enrolling into the network. Such fears may dissuade individuals from passing on information of which they are aware, reducing the information-gathering capacity of the network.

B. The Centrality of Information

This book provides empirical evidence that collection and assessment of information plays a central role in the response to food-borne illness. The collection of information underpins all the actions of network participants during the response. Information is necessary for control: EHOs need to know the extent of an incident before control measures can be put in place. Information is necessary to identify the products, places or people that need control. Informational challenges are a key driver of decisions not to take enforcement action following an incident of food-borne illness. Difficulties of both availability, where evidence about a particular fact cannot be found or does not exist, and admissibility, where information exists but is not admissible evidence, prevent EHOs taking formal enforcement action. Both considerations impact on the evidence that may be adduced to demonstrate a breach, either during a prosecution or as a prerequisite to taking non-prosecutorial enforcement action.

The impact of lack of information on enforcement reflects research findings in other areas. Of all cases discontinued by the CPS, 43.9 per cent were abandoned due to evidential factors.[2] Only 25.3 per cent of discontinuances were attributable to public interest factors.[3] This distribution reflects this study's finding that a failure to take enforcement action following an incident of food-borne illness is more likely to be due to evidential rather than public interest factors, although this study suggests that evidential issues are likely to constitute the reason for a greater proportion of the cases where enforcement action was not taken than in the CPS study.

More than 20 per cent of CPS discontinuances were due to a lack of available evidence to establish an essential element of the crime charged.[4] Availability factors appear at least this significant in food safety cases. Admissibility factors were less significant. Only 1.1 per cent of the failure of cases in the CPS study was due to admissibility factors. Whilst admissibility factors are less important than availability, we have seen that some information obtained during an investigation into food-borne illness is routinely treated as inadmissible. This implies that inadmissibility plays a greater role in food-borne illness cases than those examined in the CPS study.

[2] Her Majesty's Crown Prosecution Service Inspectorate, *Thematic Review of Attrition in the Prosecution Process (The Justice Gap)* (HMCPSI 2003) (hereinafter 'the CPS study').

[3] Ibid.

[4] Ibid.

Environmental Health Officers often have the will to prosecute (and decide that this would be in the public interest),[5] but do not have the information necessary to take enforcement action. This is so even though, according to EHO-B1, enforcement action is focused on information: '[I]t's evidence, evidence, evidence; you're taking everything you can, photos, photocopies of documents, witness statements, anything you can find.'

Environmental Health Officers see the collection and assessment of information as central to their food safety and food hygiene roles. Routine inspections are information-gathering exercises, with the captured information forming the basis of a judgement about the compliance (or otherwise) of a food business with regulatory requirements. Whilst information gathering is important in all regulatory fields, it is particularly important when regulatory network responds to an incident of food-borne illness. The details of the incident may not be immediately clear to EHOs. The control and enforcement responses are dictated by the information collected. Contaminated products, premises and people have to be identified, with control action to manage the risk of primary and secondary spread taken accordingly. Before enforcement action can be taken, though, the available and admissible evidence must present a realistic prospect of conviction.

The function of information in building a case that a strict liability offence has been committed, has perhaps been overlooked in the past. Consideration of regulatory and prosecutorial behaviour in strict liability cases has focused on discretionary decision making. But a discretionary decision cannot be made unless there is a case with realistic prospects of success. Information collection and utilisation are therefore key drivers in enforcement decision making, even where offences are strict liability.

This study suggests that assembling information is a difficult task. Obtaining information to substantiate a breach of a regulatory requirement causes difficulties for EHOs. The epistemic difficulty of strict liability offences,[6] at least as they relate to food-borne illness, is clear from the empirical findings presented in this book. Environmental Health Officers attempt to collect information that illuminates the incident, and which can identify risks of primary and secondary spread. This process may also expose the violation that led to the incident. Where such evidence is either unavailable or inadmissible, EHOs will not proceed to take enforcement action.

[5] Reversing the order in which the tests should be considered according to the *Code for Crown Prosecutors* (Crown Prosecution Service, *The Code for Crown Prosecutors* (CPS 2010)), as adopted by the Food Law Code (Food Standards Agency, *Food Law Code of Practice for England* (Food Standards Agency 2008)).

[6] See Alvin Goldman, *Knowledge in a social world* (Oxford University Press 1999); and ch 3, text associated with n 150.

C. Evidential Decision Making is not Discretionary

Environmental Health Officers view evidential decision making as measuring information against an external, objective standard, and therefore not as discretionary. If that standard is not reached, enforcement action cannot be taken. This is contrasted with public interest decision making, where the decision whether a case should be pursued is more idiosyncratic, without a external yardstick against which the decision can be measured. The EHOs interviewed for this study commented in some of the cases examined that they wanted to take enforcement action, and felt that such enforcement action would be in the public interest, but were unable to do so because they 'didn't have the evidence'.[7] There is a will to take enforcement action, but EHOs find there is not a way. The question of discretionary, public-interest, decision making does not arise.

However, viewing evidential decision making purely as an objective exercise, lacking in discretion, is too simplistic. Obtaining information and evidential decision making requires discretionary choices by EHOs. Choices about the investigative steps to be taken are discretionary, and influenced by factors other than prosecutorial case-building needs. In particular, there is a conscious decision to favour obtaining information quickly for the purposes of control over preserving evidential value for enforcement.

In enforcement decisions, evidence must be assembled and assessed against food safety and food hygiene standards. This requires considerable choice on the part of EHOs about the availability and admissibility of particular pieces of information (and, in the regulatory standard against which they are judged, particularly whether a food hygiene standard or a food safety standard is chosen). Further, the overall strength of a case must be considered. A judgement about the standard that the evidence must reach, and whether it reaches that standard, is invariably a subjective exercise, although bright-line working rules are adopted that reduce the discretionary space available to enforcement officers. However, it must be appreciated that the decision whether information is probative is a matter for the EHO, exercising his or her professional judgement.

Therefore, rather than case building's being a non-discretionary, 'objective' exercise, EHOs inevitably bring their subjective interpretations of evidence and standards to it.

[7] Whilst the evidential and public interest tests are meant to be considered sequentially, previous research has shown that they are, in fact, considered concurrently. The cases examined in this study reflected these findings. EHOs expressed a concluded view on the public interest in prosecution, despite the failure of a case at the evidential stage.

D. Strict Liability Cases are Epistemically Difficult

Strict liability cases have often been conceptualised as simple to prove.[8] This research paints a different picture, at least following an incident of food-borne illness. Proving a strict liability offence presents difficulties for EHOs in practice, even if such offences are relatively simple to prove in theory. The evidential challenges discussed in chapter six are a stark illustration of the difference between metaphysical difficulty (which is not present in a strict liability offence) and epistemic difficulty.[9]

Building a case demonstrating a strict liability regulatory breach is an exercise similar to building a case demonstrating a breach that requires proof of an advertent mental element. The process involved in proving the *actus reus* element in a strict liability crime is the same as proving the *actus reus* element in a crime that requires proof of *mens rea*. The potential challenges in proving *actus reus* are the same for both crimes, all else being equal.

Whilst *mens rea* offences have an additional element or elements that need to be demonstrated beyond a reasonable doubt, the problems of proof that arise in such offences are not solely associated with the proof of the mental element. It may be simple to prove the mental element or not, as the case may be. This depends on the information that is available and admissible. It is fallacious to suggest that because *mens rea* offences may be difficult to prove in some circumstances, offences of strict liability must be simple.

If the argument is that the *actus reus* of the typical strict liability crime is less burdensome to demonstrate than the *actus reus* of the typical crime that requires proof of *mens rea*, then this book gives equivocal support to this contention. Hygiene offences are seen by some EHOs as epistemically simple to prove, as they have few *actus reus* elements that need to be established, and such elements can be demonstrated with relatively little evidence (perhaps through photographs, environmental samples or witness statements from the EHO). However, the *actus reus* of food safety offences, particularly those alleging breach of the requirement that food placed on the market must be safe, is not epistemically simple to prove.

Strict liability offences should be assessed on their merits. The epistemic challenges of proving a particular offence should be considered by examining the methods that enforcement bodies utilise to prove that offence. This book has attempted to implement this particularistic approach in relation to enforcement following incidents of food-borne illness. Epistemic problems loom large in this area. Food businesses identified as the (or a) source of an incident of food-borne illness are not 'almost certain to be convicted', contrary to the traditional view of strict liability crime.[10]

[8] See above ch 3, text associated with nn 143 et seq.

[9] Goldman, above n 6, 278.

[10] See ch 3, text associated with n 137.

E. Prioritising Control over Enforcement

Perhaps the central trend that can be discerned from this examination of responses to food-borne illness is the balance struck by regulatory network actors, and particularly EHOs, between information needed for control and information needed for enforcement. The balance weighs heavily in favour of control.

In some cases information that is collected is rendered inadmissible by the deliberate or accidental actions of EHOs. These actions consciously or unconsciously trade off enforcement in order to achieve control. Here, lack of admissible information stems from a reluctance to demand information in an admissible form for fear that this would damage the amount and quality of the information supplied, compromising an EHO's ability to control the spread of food-borne illness. The inadmissibility of the information in case building has a negative impact on the ability of EHOs to take enforcement action.

A decision to prioritise gaining information over preserving admissibility for future enforcement action is in accordance with the primary goal of a local authority dealing with an incident of food-borne illness—to prevent further primary and secondary cases.[11] Such a prioritisation of control over enforcement is understandable, with the protective and preventative role of the regulatory network gaining priority over the prosecutorial role of EHOs.

This prioritisation leads to EHOs' focusing on control objectives to the exclusion of enforcement. It was felt by EHO-CON1 that the primary feeling once an incident is under control is, first, relief and then 'exhaustion'. Unless evidence demonstrating a breach can be found within the information collected prior to the control of the illness, in the standard case there is little enthusiasm and energy to undertake further investigations to produce such evidence. Prioritisation of control may therefore mean that a cut-off in information collection is imposed at the point where the primary goal is achieved.

In investigating incidents of food-borne illness, EHOs are prepared to accept 'some information' rather than 'no information', accepting a less than optimal amount in order that effective control action may be taken. Control action is often taken on a precautionary basis, where a object of control is identified with likelihood rather than certainty. By accepting the second-best option, EHOs favour obtaining some information, which can establish this likelihood, over obtaining perfect information, accepting that control requires compromise. Information obtained through such compromise is not well suited to demonstrating regulatory breaches to the criminal standard.

[11] Food Standards Agency, *Management of outbreaks of foodborne illness in England and Wales* (Food Standards Agency 2008) para 2.1.

Enforcement becomes more difficult. As has been observed in a different context, decisions that affect enforcement do not take place at 'a fixed temporal moment, or even [as] a series of discrete decisions at nodal points in the … process'.[12] They take place throughout the period of response to an incident of food-borne illness, whilst gathering information and whilst taking control decisions.

There is only a loose fit between the two goals of EHOs responding to food-borne illness. Priorities for control and enforcement do not match each other exactly. Investigations into incidents and outbreaks are not designed to produce evidence for a criminal prosecution; they are designed to produce information allowing prompt control action to be taken quickly: 'Outbreak control teams are not set up with a remit to collect evidence for a criminal prosecution.'[13] Outbreak Control Teams, and the broader regulatory networks, are created to *control* outbreaks. The terms of reference of an OCT found in the management guidance do not refer to enforcement. The objectives are stated to be

> [t]o agree and coordinate the activities of the agencies involved in the control and investigation of the outbreak in order to understand the aetiology, mechanism and source of the outbreak and to employ control measures to bring the incident to a speedy resolution.[14]

Outbreak Control Teams do not typically include legal professionals to provide advice on the collection of evidence in order to ensure admissibility. They may not even include regulators with enforcement experience, who may be able to offer such advice.[15] An OCT is simply concerned with gaining information to stop the spread of illness as quickly as possible. Whilst the management guidance suggests that the provisions of PACE 1984 requiring the cautioning of individuals suspected of an offence should be complied with,[16] this research indicates that this practice is subsidiary to the overarching goal of obtaining sufficient information to allow control measures to be put in place.

Further, whilst the management guidance states that 'in cases where contraventions of the law are identified, the risk they pose to public health should be considered and enforcement action commensurate with the risk taken',[17] this guidance ignores the difficulties of identifying provable

[12] Paul Roberts and Candida Saunders, 'Piloting PTWI—A Socio-Legal Window on Prosecutors' Assessments of Evidence and Witness Credibility' (2010) 30 *OJLS* 101.

[13] Mick Waite, Principal Inspector, Drinking Water Inspectorate (quoted in Anon, 'Water watchdog rethinks evidence after case fails', *The Lawyer* (10 July 1997)).

[14] Food Standards Agency, above n 10, para 3.9.

[15] See the makeup of the OCT in *R v South-West Water* (Bristol Crown Court, 16 September 1997), which did not include the Drinking Water Inspectorate, which was the authority responsible for enforcement in cases of an unsafe water supply.

[16] Food Standards Agency, above n 10, para 5.14.

[17] Ibid, para 5.14.

regulatory breaches and conceptualises an enforcement decision as something that takes place after information has been collected and assessed, rather than as an iterative process of case building during the investigation. The practical question of how the investigation should generate sufficient available and admissible information to demonstrate a breach is not addressed.

F. Difficulties Taking Enforcement Action—Four Additional Explanatory Factors

Four further factors were observed to create practical obstacles to enforcement action:

(a) delay in the collection of evidence;
(b) the challenges of proving causation;
(c) the limited resources of the regulatory networks, and particularly local authorities; and
(d) the inexperience of EHOs in building cases following incidents of food-borne illness.

A fifth factor, risk aversion, was suggested by some informants, but was contested by network actors, and is examined separately in section I.G.iii. below.

i. Delay in the Collection of Evidence

Delay is a major factor preventing collection of information in response to food-borne illness. In contrast to other types of regulatory breach,[18] investigators will often not be able to collect evidence of food-borne illness immediately after the point of crisis where the regulation is breached and the risk eventuates. Delay impedes the collection of microbiological information, epidemiological information and environmental information. It means that EHOs are deprived of valuable information that might be obtained if the investigation were to begin sooner. This information is unavailable to EHOs taking control and enforcement decisions. This is not such a problem in relation to control action taken on a precautionary basis, but can seriously impede enforcement.

The variable, and often lengthy, incubation periods of food-borne illnesses are structural impediments to information collection. Difficulties caused by delay cannot easily be resolved, as features inherent to food-borne illness are responsible for the problems. A person may not become ill for a period of days following consumption of contaminated food. Further, individuals

[18] In contrast to the investigation of a fire.

often delay reporting their symptoms to a local authority until they are on the road to recovery, as during their illness they simply are too sick to contact an EHO.[19] During this time the situation will have changed: food will have been destroyed; 'cases' may have stopped excreting micro-organisms;[20] the environment in which the food was produced may have been cleaned, or may have deteriorated.

Delay is particularly problematic for the collection of microbiological samples from retailers, especially retailers who prepare food on-site. Food is likely to have been eaten or thrown away by the time food-borne illness manifests. Food was available in the South Wales *E. coli*[21] and Cadbury *Salmonella* cases,[22] as the incidents emanated from food businesses higher in the supply chain than the retail level, and therefore other participants in the supply chain retained food from the same batch and the food was relatively microbiologically stable. However, it was not available in any of the retail-level cases dealt with by Local Authority A, where food was destroyed prior to the time of notification to EHOs.

ii. Causation Matters

Food safety and food hygiene offences do not generally require proof of causation. However, evidence linking the food with symptomatic individuals is a powerful probative tool when enforcement action is contemplated by EHOs, particularly where they seek to argue that unsafe food was placed on the market by the business. Evidence of linkage seeks to pre-empt any argument that may be advanced by the business that other food consumed by the individual is responsible for his or her illness (or that the illness was contracted through person-to-person spread). This argument is likely to be advanced in the absence of analyses of food samples that demonstrate microbial contamination.

Causation arguments become particularly important in food safety prosecutions where a food sample is not available. Evidence capable of linking food to illness allows a decision maker (both those making decisions to take enforcement action and, in the case of prosecutions, magistrates or members of a jury) to infer that the food was microbiologically contaminated, and therefore unfit for human consumption or injurious to health. In this

[19] This is why the enrolment of medical professionals into the regulatory network is important, and is encouraged. They are able to report that a person is suffering from symptoms suggestive of a food-borne illness as soon as the patient presents to them.

[20] Whilst some illnesses remain in the digestive tract once a person is non-symptomatic, others, particularly viral illnesses, do not.

[21] Above n 1.

[22] Outbreak Control Team, 'National increase in *Salmonella* Montevideo infections, England and Wales: March to July 2006' (2006) 16(29) *CDR Weekly*.

way, demonstrating a chain of causation becomes central to the exercise of enforcement powers by EHOs because of the pragmatic realities of proving that the food placed on the market was unsafe. Whilst in law the linkage between food and illness is not a textually apparent element of the offence, in fact, proof of the linkage is often necessary to prove the offence, due to the difficulties of proof through analysis of samples.

Two informational pathways may be used to demonstrate the linkage. First, epidemiological evidence that shows a statistical linkage between the food and the illness may be used to support an inference that the food was unsafe. Secondly, analytical samples may be taken from the environment where the food was produced. If micro-organisms disclosed in the analysis match micro-organisms shown in the analysis of faecal samples taken from the affected individuals, it is possible for the decision maker to conclude either that the food was contaminated by the environment, or that the environment was contaminated by the food. In either case, the food was unsafe.

Therefore, demonstrating linkage between food and an ill person matters. It is a major evidentiary concern, despite the linkage's not being an element of the offence. In some cases, evidence cannot be adduced to show the linkage, as 'it is almost impossible to prove that causal link' (EHO-A2). Similar sentiments appear in files A/I/18 and A/1/21: 'It was not felt that there was a strong case to be able to prove beyond a reasonable doubt that the infection was caused by poor practices at [Food Business H], although this does remain a possibility'; 'Without any samples of the actual food which your party ate we could not analyse this food to identify any causative organism.' This may lead to a decision that the regulatory breach cannot be demonstrated and enforcement action cannot be taken.

iii. Resourcing and Evidence Collection

Resources have a large impact on the investigation into an incident of foodborne illness. Local authorities have limited resources. As one EHO put it,

> there is only so much we can do in the investigation. We could do more, but it would involve putting a lot more resources and time and energy in. From the files you'll notice that it is very rare that we will interview everybody under PACE; you probably wouldn't talk to every member of staff, just because of the time involved in it. You could build a better case, if you had enough time and resources to do it. (EHO-A3)

Large urban authorities have greater resources. These authorities may also have more specialist regulatory lawyers. Local Authority A has these advantages, and there are still not enough resources to 'build a better case'. Suggestions that changes to the practice of EHOs would produce more enforcement action through better case building were dismissed by

EHO-A3,[23] who argued that that this would work only in a 'theoretical world' where EHOs did not have so many responsibilities. Responding to an incident takes significant manpower and time, and it is necessary to use limited resources first to control food-borne illness (EHO-C2).

Greater resources have been expended on investigations of food-borne illness where the police have become involved. In South Wales,[24] PACE interviews were conducted with William Tudor; a large number of witness were tracked down and interviewed; and experts were instructed to give opinions on matters ranging from how the cleaning checklists were completed, to the suitability of the vacuum-packing machine, to the state of the premises and the compliance of Tudor with the requirements of food hygiene law. If the incident had been investigated solely by EHOs, resourced solely by a local authority, it is unlikely that all these steps would have been taken. More extensive investigative steps can be taken where greater resources are available.

There was some dispute amongst interviewees over whether the police investigations were helpful in both that specific case and cases in general. Officer EHO-B1, who stated that police involvement could be useful as '[the police] can sometimes dig things out that we couldn't', can be contrasted with EHO-CON2, who felt that the police have difficulty understanding food law and tend to aim at the more difficult to prove safety offences rather than hygiene offences, the evidence for which can usually be collected without police involvement. Whether the police investigation was necessary in the South Wales case to the successful prosecution of William Tudor for both food safety and food hygiene offences was disputed by EHO-CON2, given that the CPS ultimately rejected the possibility of a manslaughter prosecution.

iv. Inexperience of Environmental Health Officers

Reported incidents of food-borne illness are rare. Within Local Authority A, where a generous definition of 'incident' operated, there are between three and four incidents each year. Other authorities had lower rates of incidents, in line with national statistics. Between 2000 and 2010, a total of 1,458 incidents of microbiological contamination were reported to the Food Standards Agency.[25] Whilst reporting is based on a more restrictive definition of 'incident' compared to Local Authority A's working definition (and excludes cases where a report was made but no microbiological contamination was

[23] EHO-A3 identified Richard North as a particular proponent of this school of thought.
[24] South Wales *E. Coli* above n 1.
[25] Food Standards Agency, *Annual Report of Incidents 2010* (Food Standards Agency 2011) 23.

found), this approximates on average less than one incident per year per local authority.[26]

The rarity of incidents means that EHOs, particularly in authorities with small numbers of food businesses, do not deal with food-borne illness very often. Interviewees BAR-1 and BAR-2 felt that this meant that EHOs, whilst skilled in responding to incidents, did not have the opportunity to hone their practical skills of gathering and assessing information necessary for enforcement in practice. Where enforcement takes place it is generally based on information gathered during inspections, which are simpler environments for gathering information necessary for enforcement. Lawyers interviewed in this study expressed the opinion that the lack of preparation for complex evidence collection and case building in initial training and the continuing professional development of EHOs contributed to evidential problems (BAR-1; BAR-2; SOL-1).[27] A contrast was drawn between the training given to police officers and the training given to EHOs (BAR-1). Due to this inexperience, some investigations may not be performed in accordance with the law that regulates information collection during a criminal investigation (BAR-1). Any training that is given is not reinforced through practice due to the rarity of incidents.

Information collected by EHOs may be excluded from presentation to the court if investigative actions render it inadmissible (or may render it inadmissible at the discretion of the judge). Alternatively, evidence collected during an investigation may be presented in an inadmissible format. In these cases, legal professionals will advise that the case cannot go forward, because the prosecution will be unable to prove the case by admissible evidence (BAR-1).

Environmental Health Officers often have difficulty gathering the necessary evidence, and particularly knowing which witnesses it is necessary to approach (BAR-1; BAR-2). They do not know what is, and who are, needed in order to build a case (BAR-1). Evidence is often not obtained in accordance with legal norms (EHO-A3). This may be deliberate or inadvertent. This potentially compromises later legal action arising out of an incident of food-borne illness. There is often little awareness of the requirements of PACE 1984. Interviews are consequently not conducted in accordance with the applicable Code of Practice (BAR-1; EHO-A3).

The EHOs themselves felt that they were properly aware of evidential requirements (B-EHO1; B-EHO2). However, producing admissible information was not their goal in investigating incidents of food-borne illness. Control has priority. As we have seen, EHOs' ability to produce admissible evidence is constrained by the requirements of dealing with incidents of

[26] There are around 430 local authorities in the UK.

[27] The relative difference in importance of evidence collection in the day-to-day work of police and EHOs can be suggested as a reason for the difference in training.

food-borne illness. According to EHOs, structural challenges that restrict availability cause greater problems than admissibility. Inadmissibility of evidence was not due to lack of training, but instead due to the structure and requirements of the investigation, which is shaped by the need for control.

The training that EHOs receive was described by ACD-1: it involves a practical illustration of building a case, including matters such as drafting a witness statement. A recently qualified EHO, EHO-B2, felt that she had received adequate training in evidence collection, but thought that she would become stronger and more confident as she gained further experience. Both EHO-A3 and EHO-B1 suggested that the specialisation system, where they were tasked with being the primary EHO responding to incidents of food-borne illness, meant that they had a significant amount of experience and training in dealing with such incidents.

However, EHOs felt that when they were faced with difficult decisions about information collection, where it was necessary to ensure admissibility, they would like to be able to consult a specialist legal officer for advice on meeting admissibility requirements. Particularly within small local authorities, this level of legal specialisation may not be available:

> [Internal legal officers are] a waste of time. We have specialist cases dealing with food, and they are not that regular. And what do you get in this smallish local authority? You get turnover of people, and they haven't got a clue. They don't know how to serve summonses under the Act. You end up telling them about the law. What you really need are specialist solicitors. They could probably cut down how much time you spend on a case, because they know exactly, this is what we need for this case, boom, boom, boom, this is what I want from you. They can argue the case, and if there is a smart lawyer on the other side who tries to argue about the evidence, they can deal with it because they are experienced in food safety work. (EHO-CON3)

Local authority solicitors may have little experience of building a case following an outbreak of food-borne illness. They receive no specific training, and may not be experienced in criminal practice, particularly in rural authorities.[28] Even criminal specialists may not come from a prosecution background, or may not have experience of dealing with outbreak cases. Most local authority solicitors may not see cases arising out of an incident for years, and therefore may not appreciate the intricacies of building a successful enforcement case (BAR-1). Building a case takes significant resources, from proofing large numbers of witnesses to researching the law. Local authority legal departments may not have the resource to devote to thorough and effective case building.

[28] These rural authorities may be the home to large food-processing plants, and therefore be in need of specialist legal support. Suggestions for providing such support are explored below ch 7.II.A.vi.

G. Environmental Health Officers as Risk-averse Actors

In addition to their alleged inexperience, interviewees suggested that EHOs exhibited risk-averse behaviour, and were therefore unwilling to bring cases they thought would not be successful. This risk aversion would influence the actions of the network, as the EHOs are the network actors with the power to take enforcement action. It was argued that, before taking enforcement action, EHOs required a higher standard of proof than is required by the evidential test contained in the *Code for Crown Prosecutors*.[29] Therefore, when considering whether to bring enforcement action, the evidential test is applied so that risky cases are not taken forward. If a higher standard is being applied, that would imply that EHOs are acting in an excessively risk-averse manner, rejecting more cases than they need to.

i. Desire for Success and Positive Results

A suggested key aspect of risk-averse behaviour by local authority EHOs, perhaps linked to the inexperience of EHOs in dealing with incidents of food-borne illness, is a fear of bringing unsuccessful enforcement action. This reflects the findings of Cranston's study of the decision making of trading standards officers.[30] Cranston found that officers were unwilling to bring prosecutions in circumstances where the case was unlikely to be successful.[31] The view was expressed by EHO-A3 that cases would be brought in circumstances where the evidence was 'very strong', but would be unlikely to be brought otherwise. Similarly, EHO-B1 adverted to the difficulty that EHOs face when confronted with incidents of food-borne illness, where the lack of 'overwhelming evidence' means that the case may be unsuccessful.

Environmental Health Officers are well aware of the evidential standards that a successful case must reach. It is incumbent upon them to prove their case beyond a reasonable doubt. Most EHOs interviewed explicitly referred to the burden and standard of proof. In particular, EHO-A3 used the standard of proof as a touchstone in his analysis of the difficulties of bringing successful enforcement action: 'in a nutshell it's very difficult to prove beyond a reasonable doubt, which is the burden that we have to discharge in a criminal proceeding'; and '[i]n the majority of cases we can't prove it beyond a reasonable doubt'.

The EHOs are unwilling to risk scarce resources by bringing an unsuccessful prosecution. Cases require a great deal of work, and environmental health departments have only a limited budget from which to bring

[29] Above, ch 3.II.B.i.

[30] Ross Cranston, *Regulating Business: Law and Consumer Agencies* (The Macmillan Press 1979), 616ff.

[31] Ibid.

proceedings (EHO-C2; EHO-CON3). If money expended will not be reflected in results, criminal proceedings will not ensue (BAR-2, EXP-MIC1). Therefore, evidential assessment is linked to an analysis of the costs and benefits of bringing enforcement action, with limited resources offering a possible explanation for EHOs use of a standard beyond 'reasonable prospect of conviction'.

In prosecutions, risk aversion manifests itself with the evidential test becoming 'beyond a reasonable doubt', tending towards 'certainty' of a successful prosecution rather than merely a 'realistic prospect of conviction'. According to BAR-1, this may be operationalized by EHOs using the likelihood of a guilty plea, which is seen as rising as the probability of success rises, as a decision-making factor. Plainly, the 'beyond a reasonable doubt' standard should not be applied to enforcement decisions. It is a standard for judicial fact-finders rather than for prosecuting bodies. By considering whether the evidence assembled can prove a case to this standard, EHOs are going beyond the realistic prospect of conviction standard required by the Food Law Code.

A possible result of risk aversion is to be seen in A/I/9. This investigation produced a large amount of epidemiological information that strongly suggested that the business had placed food unfit for human consumption onto the market. A number of people, who could not be linked in any other way, suffered the same, microbiologically-confirmed illness after eating at the business. However, there was no sample evidence, and environmental investigations (which took place some time after the affected individuals had eaten at the business) did not produce evidence of non-compliance with hygiene requirements. A decision was taken by the EHO, and ratified by an internal solicitor, that the case should not be proceeded with because of insufficient evidence. This seems a conservative decision, especially given the EHO's belief, expressed in file notes, that the business was responsible for the incident.

It was the opinion of BAR-1 that not all cases are prepared with the thought that they may go to a full trial. Some cases are chosen because they are likely to extract a guilty plea through the pressure of a summons. These are the cases that are the easiest to prove with the evidence available, and tend to be cases alleging breach of hygiene requirements. Cases that attract an early plea are less expensive than cases that are contested, as costs of preparation for trial and trial itself will not be incurred.[32] Therefore, there is an economic incentive to prosecute where the case may attract a plea. It was suggested by BAR-1 that decision making that seeks to achieve guilty

[32] Assuming that a basis of plea can be agreed. Where a guilty plea is tendered, but there is dispute about the matters to be taken into account at sentencing, a *Newton* hearing (*R v Newton* (1983) 77 Cr App R 13) will be held, which will still require detailed and expensive preparation, including the examination-in-chief and cross-examination of witnesses.

pleas is an example of 'the cart-before-horse thinking which characterises local authority decision-making in this area'.

In the Bradford *Salmonella* outbreak, the facts of which are summarised in *R v Quadir*,[33] the intention of the EHOs was 'to present so much overwhelming and logical evidence that the defendant would plead guilty'.[34] It was felt by BAR-1 that this focus on guilty pleas could have negative effects, as in some cases, brought because of their high plea probability, the defendant might opt to test the evidence, and might win. This could create negative feedback, with EHOs being more reluctant to bring cases for fear of something similar happening.

Legal professionals interviewed in this study felt that it was necessary to combat plea-driven decision making (BAR-1; BAR-2). They suggested that a virtuous cycle must be created, where there is no consideration of what the defendant will do, or what will happen in court, and where instead the EHO focuses solely on the essential legal question: 'Does this case have a realistic prospect of conviction?' This refocusing should produce more enforcement action, by reinstating a lower decision-making standard. Combined with more focus on evidence collection and greater use of hygiene offences, discussed below, this could contribute to reducing the epistemic obstacles to prosecuting incidents of food-borne illness.

Aversion to the risks of unsuccessful prosecution also manifests itself in EHOs' favouring enforcement in food hygiene offences over food safety offences. Hygiene offences are seen as easier to prove. In A/I/12, EHOs initially favoured prosecution for a serious food safety offence. However, they decided (after consultation with the CCDC) that evidence was inadequate, as the lack of microbiological results meant that it could not be shown beyond a reasonable doubt that the food was 'injurious to health'. Having rejected the possibility of food safety offences, two pieces of enforcement action were contemplated against the nursing home involved. Both were to be based on breaches of the Food Safety (General Food Hygiene) Regulations 1995.[35] It was determined that these breaches could be demonstrated beyond a reasonable doubt. First, EHO-A2 determined that the home had failed to put in place an adequate HACCP plan. This determination was based on an assessment of the existing plan following seizure of the HACCP documentation during a visit to the premises. Secondly, EHO-A2 determined that the home had failed to train staff adequately, based on interviews with the staff (exploring their awareness of food safety risks and the methods for reducing such risks) and copies of the training records held by the food business. Prosecutions were contemplated, and it was determined

[33] *R v Quadir* [2005] EWCA Crim 2800 [3]–[4].

[34] David Clapham, Angela Brindle and Jim Aveyard, 'Food Outbreak Response', *Environmental Health Practitioner* (31 March 2006).

[35] SI 1995/1763.

that the evidential test was satisfied. In the event, however, a prosecution was not brought. Instead, the business took steps to prevent a repeat of the incident by voluntarily agreeing to send all staff on a training course. A formal advisory power was used in relation to the HACCP plan, with an improvement notice being served on the business. Enforcement was seriously contemplated in relation to breaches of hygiene norms, rather than food safety law. The EHOs took the less risky enforcement option, rather than either choosing to take a case based on food safety breaches, or to prosecute both safety and hygiene offences concurrently.

ii. The Unwillingness to Rely upon Epidemiological Evidence

Environmental Health Officers are reluctant to rely upon epidemiological evidence alone as the basis for taking enforcement action in a food safety case. Evidence suggesting that food was unfit for human consumption was not seen as sufficiently 'strong' when it was purely epidemiological. This partly reflected an awareness of the evidential difficulties of epidemiological evidence, which is typically incomplete and open to challenge on a methodological basis. However, epidemiology was also categorised as more risky than sample analysis evidence, which can also be incomplete.

Epidemiological evidence is difficult to fit into a framework that demands proof beyond a reasonable doubt. As Roland Salmon, a consultant epidemiologist, explained,

> the nature of epidemiology is that it's a probabilistic science, so ultimately, whatever you find, there is some fraction associated with this that someone could turn round and say 'This represents the chance that actually whatever we think was responsible for it wasn't responsible for it,' and quite how that sits with processes that demand that things are beyond reasonable doubt is … uneasy…[36]

Whilst it is both difficult and unnecessary to attempt to quantify the standard of proof,[37] it is demanding to fit statistically expressed evidence within the framework of the 'certainty' requirements adopted by EHOs as their modified evidential test. When this evidence is the only substantial evidence that links particular food to the symptomatic individual, and therefore is the basis of an inference that the food was unsafe, statistically expressed conclusions appear to fall short of the standard required by EHOs. Epidemiological evidence is expressed with explicit uncertainty, in terms of significance testing, and this uncertainty may be seen as suggesting reasonable doubt.

Environmental Health Officers are trained in epidemiological methods during both the academic and the practical stages of their professional

[36] PEN/RS/LIVE-10-3-pg39line25 et seq.

[37] See Paul Roberts and Adrian AS Zuckerman, *Criminal evidence* (2nd edn, Oxford University Press 2010), 253ff; See also Alexander Volokh, 'n Guilty Men' (1997) 146 *University of Pennsylvania Law Review* 173.

development.[38] They therefore appreciate the uncertainties of such evidence. This research did not identify any frustration with the lack of a definitive conclusion in epidemiological evidence, or detect any pressure on epidemiologists to make a more authoritative pronouncement on the 'cause' of the food-borne illness.[39]

Appreciation of uncertainty influences decision making by EHOs. From the enforcement perspective, they seek evidence that offers a strong prospect of conviction; however, with scientific training they appreciate that the epidemiological evidence available often cannot reach the standard required. To the trained EHOs, the probabilistic nature of epidemiological evidence often appears to create doubt, which contrasts with the strong evidence needed to satisfy the 'beyond a reasonable doubt' (or beyond) standard. Conversely, EHOs do not believe that as high a standard is required for control, and therefore they are not concerned about taking control action on the basis of less certain epidemiological evidence, being prepared to take action on a precautionary basis.

The problems of relying on epidemiological evidence are also apparent to experts. Roland Salmon, a consultant epidemiologist, commented that even though he was satisfied that the probabilistic results of his epidemiological calculations demonstrated the source of the South Wales Outbreak in school meals, 'experience tells me not everybody finds [those calculations] satisfying in quite the same way'.[40]

Environmental Health Officers do not appear to find epidemiology satisfying to the level required by the *Code for Crown Prosecutors*, or at least appear to anticipate (whether rightly or wrongly) that the court may not find it satisfying. They appear unwilling to utilise epidemiological evidence on its own, requiring it to be supported by microbiological and environmental evidence that increases the strength of the case. This may be justified where epidemiological evidence is the only information available. Simply using statistical evidence to prove a regulatory breach is often seen as unconvincing,[41] as the use of epidemiology alone would be unlikely to be

[38] EHO-A1; EHO-B1.

[39] In contrast to some criminal justice professionals, who put pressure on forensic science experts to come to definitive conclusions about scientific evidence, rather than introducing shades of uncertainty into testimony (Paul Roberts and Chris Willmore, *The role of forensic science evidence in criminal proceedings* (HMSO 1993) ss 2.3, 2.4, 2.6(b), 2.8, 3.5, 3.6 and chs 4–5).

[40] PEN/RS/LIVE-3-10-pg36line17.

[41] See, eg, Robert J Rhee, 'Probability, Policy and the Problem of Reference Class' (2007) 11 *International Journal of Evidence and Proof* 286, 288: 'While the probability between propositions *x* and not-*x* stated as a ratio may lean greatly to one or the other given the available evidence, the possibility of error may nevertheless be great because the amount of evidence creates a sufficient number of possibilities, yet unknown, such that reasonable minds cannot be confident in the truth of this proposition despite its probabilistic superiority over its counterpart given the evidence and the case theory.'

sufficient to satisfy court to a standard 'beyond a reasonable doubt' (and, indeed, on its own could perhaps not satisfy an objective observer to a 'reasonable prospect of conviction' standard). However, EHOs should seek out and consider contextualising evidence, about the foods eaten, about the victims and about the food-borne illness, in order to bolster the 'story' of the incident, and to support their oft-expressed certainty that a particular food was the source of the incident. Constructing and supporting a theory of case should not necessarily require sample evidence, whether from sick individuals or the preparation environment.

Environmental Health Officers are prepared to rely on epidemiological evidence in order to make decisions about withdrawing products or shutting premises, but are unwilling to take enforcement action on this basis. This reflects the different functions of control and enforcement action. As noted above, control is precautionary in nature, and seeks to prevent future harm. The EHOs are more prepared to take the risk of a false positive, taking control action where none is necessary. The potential benefit of, for example, prohibiting a food business outweighs the risk of a false positive. In enforcement decisions EHOs are more prepared to risk a false negative, choosing not to take enforcement action where the action might have been successful. It is notable that when seeking to identify sources of food-borne illness, the Report of the Pennington Inquiry explicitly uses a balance of probabilities standard,[42] rather than the 'beyond a reasonable doubt' standard required in criminal cases.

iii. Rejecting Risk Aversion

Environmental Health Officers do not feel that they act in a risk-averse manner. They characterise their actions as conditioned by the law and the facts. They conceptualise themselves as being unable to act, rather than as failing to act. For example, EHO-B1 stated:

> I'm not averse to bringing prosecutions, I've brought three in the last year, but you have to work with what you have. If you can't prove a case beyond a reasonable doubt, or if another course of action will cause a better result, then you don't prosecute. (EHO-B1)[43]

Instead, EHOs in the sample cases and the expert panel identify in-house legal officers as being risk averse, and as unwilling to countenance enforcement actions following incidents of food-borne illness. In A/I/12, EHO-A2 said, '[w]e went to our legal department, and they said that it would be difficult to conduct a prosecution'. Similarly in A/I/2, the file was referred

[42] Hugh Pennington, *The public inquiry into the September 2005 outbreak of E coli O157 in South Wales* (Welsh Assembly Government 2009), 14, 58 and 316.

[43] The cases mentioned by EHO-B1 arose out of routine inspections that demonstrated serious non-compliance with hygiene requirements, not incidents of food-borne illness.

to the legal department with a recommendation that a prosecution be instituted against the business, either for selling food that was unfit for human consumption under the General Food Regulations 2004[44] or for breach of the hygiene requirements under the Food Safety (General Food Hygiene) Regulations 1995. However, the legal department felt that there was not enough evidence to prove, beyond a reasonable doubt, that the identified food vehicle was responsible for the reported illnesses. This was cited as an example of a case where an EHO was willing, but the lawyers were risk averse.

Environmental Health Officers argue that their job should not be conceptualised simply in terms of their prosecutorial role. Further, the role of the regulatory network should not be seen in such a manner. Disinclination to bring prosecutions should not be equated with risk aversion. As seen throughout this book, EHOs regard control as the more important objective. Prosecution is seen as a useful tool for ensuring 'just deserts' for those who have committed a criminal offence (EHO-B1). However, EHOs were concerned that prosecution-focused regulation could be counter-productive. It might encourage businesses to attempt to 'beat the law', trying to comply with the letter of particular provisions whilst failing to comply with the more socially important values embodied by the 'spirit' of the law. They justified the use of standards such as HACCP, with decisions devolved to business and assessment of the decision making being the focus of regulators' practise, as attempting to prevent this. This mirrors the arguments of Ayres and Braithwaite, who contend that prosecution should be available to prosecutors only as a 'benign big gun': the threat of prosecution increases the ability of regulators to achieve present compliance with regulation and deters future non-compliance.[45] The availability of formal prosecution presents a 'spectre of awesome and authoritative power', which encourages food businesses to act in a socially responsible manner and voluntarily comply with the law.[46] Ayres and Braithwaite argue that the availability of prosecution should not become the primary focus of regulators, as this may lead to lack of cooperation between business and regulators. Whilst Ayres and Braithwaite focus on compliance, similar concerns motivate EHOs' prioritisation of control (and their interest in ensuring future compliance with, in particular, hygiene requirements, as shown in the use of Hygiene Improvement Notices). Enforcement is not, and should not be, the primary concern, and therefore operational decisions will not necessarily support it.

Environmental Health Officers argued that decision making that others might view as risk-averse reflected the control focus of their approach.

[44] SI 2004/3279.

[45] Ian Ayres and John Braithwaite, *Responsive Regulation: Transcending the Deregulation Debate* (Oxford University Press 1992), 47–48.

[46] Ibid.

In the event that the evidential test is satisfied, it may also be seen as an example of a compliance strategy, similar to that identified in much of the existing regulatory literature. In general, EHOs are able but unwilling to take formal enforcement action in respect of a failure to register a food business with a local authority (A/I/26; EHO-B2). This contrasts with most other cases examined, where EHOs are willing but unable to take formal action. It was suggested by EHO-B2 that the ease of remedying the breach in the former circumstances meant that he would not bring enforcement action without something more. The preferred course of action, when faced with an establishment that has not registered, is to 'ask the business to complete a registration form as soon as possible' (EHO-B2). Once a form is completed, the breach is remedied in a practical way that deals with the omission more efficiently than prosecution. However, appropriate formal action will be considered for other breaches observed.

iv. Are Environmental Health Officers Risk-averse Actors?

This book has demonstrated that investigation of food-borne illness is demanding. Where crucial information is either unavailable or inadmissible, EHOs cannot take enforcement action. They tend to see the problems of building a case as immutable, given the legal and institutional structures that currently govern responses to food-borne illness, exemplified by EHO-A3:

> It is difficult. It's just the nature of the situation that makes it difficult to prove, and I'm not sure what could be done that would make it better, because you've got to have the rules of natural justice there as well. I don't think we should move towards a balance of probabilities standard, and the civil courts are there if people do feel that they have got a case that they want to bring because they think that somebody has caused the illness that they have had. (EHO-A3)

Lawyer interviewees, on the other hand, felt that EHOs could be more aggressive, taking action based on the cases currently being built, notwithstanding the perceived evidential problems. In some cases, EHO-A3 suggested, he would be willing to take action despite perceived obstacles. He noted that, in response to a serious outbreak, action may be taken, and 'I suppose it is up to the magistrates (or the jury) to decide whether the evidence proves the case to the required degree'. This perhaps suggests that what is perceived as risk aversion is instead a balancing exercise, with EHOs being prepared to take greater risks of enforcement action (and utilise resources that prosecution requires) where the incident is particularly serious.

Negative judgements about the viability of an enforcement case are influenced by conservative assessments of information on the basis of EHOs' interpretations of the standard of proof and their working rules of evidence. This is not conscious risk aversion, but if EHOs are unwilling to bring a case unless the evidence is 'very strong', this will result in few prosecutions, as such evidence is rarely available given the nature of investigations into food-borne illness. Only the clearest cases will be brought. In order to reduce the difficulties of obtaining admissible evidence, some argue that hygiene offences, seen as less difficult to prove, and which could therefore more regularly reach the standard required by EHOs, should be favoured over food safety offences.[47]

H. Summary

Several trends were identified from the empirical data. Information plays a key role in the decision making of EHOs: information is at the heart of the challenges EHOs face in taking enforcement action. Some of these epistemic problems arise from inherent features of food and food consumption, whilst others arise from, or are compounded by, the decision-making culture of EHOs.

Problems of availability exist because food is destroyed through consumption and degrades with delay. As there is a time lag between infection and an individual's becoming symptomatic, the combined effect is often that suspect food is not available to EHOs who are investigating incidents of food-borne illness. This prevents those EHOs from demonstrating a nexus between particular food and the incident of illness, which is a pivotal factor in enforcement decision making.

The main challenge of initiating prosecutions arises from the difficulty of balancing the need to control the spread of food-borne illness against the desire to bring enforcement actions. The primacy of control means that information is collected in ways that damage its admissibility as evidence. Environmental Health Officers, and the regulatory network more generally, place control at the centre of their role. They are willing to accept the unwanted side-effects of this. These are compounded by the inexperience of some EHOs in bringing enforcement action following incidents of food-borne illness. Steps that could improve both the quality and quantity of evidence collected are examined in the next section.

The skills, attitudes and experiences of EHOs influence the lack of enforcement action following incidents of food-borne illness. By requiring a chance of success beyond that required by the evidential test set out in the Food Law Code, some cases are discontinued despite presenting a realistic prospect of conviction. Whilst EHOs reject an argument that they are risk averse, before deciding to bring enforcement action they do require a case to demonstrate a chance of conviction beyond that required by guidance documentation. They are (perhaps rightly) reluctant to use epidemiological evidence alone to bring enforcement action alleging breach of food safety

[47] See section II.B. below.

requirements, and use bright-line working rules of evidence to remove information from their consideration.

II. MEETING THE EPISTEMIC CHALLENGES OF INCIDENTS OF FOOD-BORNE ILLNESS

The difficulties of obtaining admissible evidence, and therefore the limited possibility of formal enforcement action following incidents of food-borne illness, have been highlighted above. Chapters five and six explored how this lack of evidence is often the result of the primacy accorded to controlling the spread of food-borne illness.

Whilst EHOs accept and support the need for control, and feel satisfied when the further spread of food-borne illness is prevented, they express their frustration with the difficulties of bringing enforcement action. Some EHOs contrasted the lack of food safety enforcement following an incident with the situation after an industrial accident, where enforcement is brought under health and safety regulations (EHO-C2). They see themselves as willing to bring enforcement action, but as prevented by the difficulties of proof (EHO-B1). Whilst this book suggests that epistemic challenges often result from their primary focus on control, EHOs do not accept that an inability to take enforcement action should be an inevitable result of the response to an incident of food-borne illness. They therefore both seek and suggest solutions to these evidential challenges.

This prompts consideration of whether changes could be made to the nature of investigations and enforcement actions that would make enforcement action, and particularly prosecution, easier. Despite the desire of EHOs to bring prosecutions in some cases, the EHOs interviewed preferred an educative and advisory stance, focusing on ensuring business compliance rather than enforcement (EHO-A1; EHO-B1; EHO-C2). They do not favour any changes that would affect their ability to rely on informal compliance strategies or restrict their discretion. Further, of course, EHOs do not favour any changes that would limit their ability to control the spread of food-borne illness, and in particular that would limit their ability to identify products, premises or places that should be made the subject of formal control action.

Environmental Health Officers contend that the inability to prove a breach is not necessarily a failure of the system requiring remedial intervention; it may be an example of the system, and particularly the presumption of innocence, working as intended. Whilst they express their belief that a business is responsible for the incident, this belief must be based upon admissible evidence. Whereas control action, and sometimes less dramatic forms of formal action, such as improvement notices, can be taken at a lower level of proof, and sometimes on a precautionary basis, enforcement (particularly prosecution) must be based on a firmer footing. Weakening evidential requirements might damage the system of checks and balances that underpins regulatory enforcement action.

Therefore, changes proposed by EHOs in this study focus on better case building and adapting to the legal environment. Interviewees did not favour weakening the evidential and/or procedural requirements that must be surmounted by any enforcement action taken.[48]

A. Improving the Collection of Evidence: Seven Suggestions for Increasing Expertise and Experience

The difficulty of transforming information obtained from an investigation into high quality admissible evidence has been identified as a weakness that partly explains the problems encountered in bringing prosecutions following incidents of food-borne illness. Whilst in some cases it will be impossible to obtain information, and a proposed enforcement action will fail the evidential test, in other cases admissibility is identified as the issue preventing enforcement. Inexperience in collecting admissible evidence amongst EHOs was identified by interviewees as a possible reason for this difficulty. The rarity of incidents provides an explanation for inexperience.

Local authorities already seek to counter this difficulty, and to produce higher quality evidence, by adopting measures aimed at increasing specialisation, such as designating a lead EHO for food-borne illness (EHO-A3).[49] Further steps that could be taken were suggested by interviewees or in the literature, and these are examined below.

i. The Need to Build an 'Evidential Culture'

The need for an 'evidential culture' was suggested by both SOL-2 and BAR-1. Such a culture would place the collection of *admissible* information at the heart of the role played by EHOs, whereas information gathering for the purposes of control, without necessarily ensuring that the evidence is admissible, currently appears to be their dominant concern. It was suggested by BAR-1 that an evidential culture would mean that EHOs ask themselves 'How do I ensure that this evidence is admissible?' before collecting information. Environmental Health Officers steeped in this culture would identify potential challenges and seek to minimise them, although it would not prevent the collection of information necessary for control if admissibility could not be ensured, but would instead, in the view of interviewees, ensure that information collection decisions were made with full awareness of their

[48] Through, say, the use of a balance of probabilities standard of proof.

[49] Although, of course, designating a lead EHO is designed to increase expertise in control, and therefore lead to better outcomes in this area.

consequences. This should produce more admissible information when EHOs seek to build cases following control of an incident.

Fostering such an evidential culture involves training, at both the academic and continuing professional development stages. This training must foster a mind-set focusing on evidential matters, and particularly on evidential decision making in real situations (BAR-1). Training should be designed to ensure that preservation of evidential value becomes an automatic consideration when EHOs begin to collect information in response to an incident of food-borne illness.

An evidential culture could not tackle the difficulties that mean information is often unavailable. Such a culture cannot reduce the difficulties of delay; or reduce the fallibilities of human memory; or change the way food is destroyed by consumption, preventing the examination of vital evidence. Further, EHOs made it clear that it is necessary to ensure that fostering such an evidential culture does not lead to lost opportunities to obtain information for control purposes (EHO-A1; EHO-C2). The prevailing culture, which prioritises control, is clearly expressed in documentary guidance, and by EHOs in words and deeds. The ability to control must not be compromised by the need to collect more admissible evidence. Whilst information is to be collected with an eye to preserving evidential value, flexibility must still be built into the culture, enabling EHOs to sacrifice evidential utility for preventative efficacy where the situation warrants it.

ii. Greater Use of Guidelines, Check-lists and Aides-memoires

A further suggestion aimed at bolstering an 'evidential culture' is to standardise the response to food-borne illness, through increased guidance, check-lists and aides-memoires (SOL2). By requiring that investigations are conducted in a standardised way, the same, admissible information should be collected in each case. The information that EHOs are directed to collect would be designed to be sufficient to build a case under the food safety and/or food hygiene regulations.

The use of guidance, check-lists and aides-memoires was supported by EHO-A3. Some guidance is available from the Local Government Association Knowledge Hub,[50] or is adopted at the level of individual authorities. Checklists and aides-memoires appeared in a number of the files examined. However, there was little support for a significant increase in such guidance. The EHOs feared that prescriptive guidance might stifle their discretion in the response to incidents of food-borne illness, restricting their ability to fulfil the network's primary role of control.

[50] The Local Government Association Knowledge Hub has replaced the Local Authority Co-Ordinators of Regulatory Services (LACORS) as the method of sharing information amongst regulatory professionals, available at <https://knowledgehub.local.gov.uk/>.

If a standardised approach were required, EHOs would be limited in their actions. They might be unable to obtain the information necessary for control purposes as quickly and efficiently as they currently do (EXP-MIC1). The more voluminous and complex the policy documentation, the more likely it would not be followed.[51] An example of unwise policy was given by EXP-MIC1—requiring a new pair of sterile gloves to be worn before a sample is taken. Where large numbers of samples are needed, EHOs may not have enough gloves to take samples, and therefore may either take them in contravention of the policy because of the need to obtain information for the purposes of control (with the policy contravention possibly rendering the evidence inadmissible),[52] or not take the samples at all.

Guidance cannot have a positive effect on the availability of unobtainable information. Whilst it may encourage collection of information that is not routinely collected, this is often not the difficulty as regards unavailable information. Such information simply does not exist. Guidance can, however, attempt to ensure that the information that is obtained is gathered the way most likely to ensure its admissibility.

iii. A Two-team Solution—Dividing Control and Enforcement

It has been suggested that in large outbreaks, two teams of EHOs should be set up. One team 'should investigate, identify the cause of the unfit food and gather evidence, trace contacts and stop the spread of the disease', and the other, smaller team 'should concentrate on gathering evidence for a ... prosecution'.[53] The smaller team could collect evidence untroubled by the need to obtain information for the purposes of control, and the team responsible for controlling the incident of food-borne illness would be able to take action to secure information necessary to control the spread of illness.

The evidence collection team could devote its efforts towards obtaining admissible evidence for the purposes of criminal proceedings, and could work in a way (and at a speed) determined by the needs of the enforcement investigation rather than the desire to obtain information to control primary and/or secondary spread of food-borne illness. The smaller team would be experienced in evidence collection. The idea is that better quality evidence could be collected for a potential prosecution.

Separation of the investigation and enforcement teams must be ensured. This is to guarantee that the actions of the investigative team do not compromise the admissibility of information obtained by the enforcement team; and that businesses do not become reluctant to cooperate with the

[51] The more rigid the guidance adopted, the more likely evidence obtained in contravention of the guidance is to be deemed inadmissible under, eg, PACE 1984, s 78.
[52] See ch 6.III, text accompanying n 29.
[53] Clapham, Brindle and Aveyard, above n 34.

investigation team because of a fear that the enforcement team will access the information, if, of course, they are aware of the difference.

It is possible that former police officers who are experienced in evidence collection could (following additional environmental health training) be employed to collect evidence in cases where prosecution appears likely. Alternatively, EHOs could be provided with specialised training to allow them to become enforcement team members.

Despite the apparent elegance of this two-team solution, it is unlikely to produce the desired outcome. First, the separation of control and enforcement functions may lead to duplication of effort, with samples of the same material taken for control and evidential purposes. Given finite local authority and laboratory resources, and the pressures of a large outbreak situation, there would almost certainly have to be some communication and sharing of information between control and enforcement teams, compromising the benefit accruing due to separation, that control and enforcement would not influence each other.

Further, in a large outbreak, obtaining information for the purpose of control will be an exceptionally large task, and depriving the control team of the manpower diverted to the enforcement team may materially impair the regulatory network's ability to carry out the control function, particularly in small local authorities with a limited number of environmental health personnel.[54]

Employing and training specialist enforcement personnel, or training existing EHOs to act as part of the 'enforcement team' during an incident, may not be cost-effective for local authorities. Incidents of food-borne illness are rare. It would be difficult to justify the expense of setting up the two-team response within each local authority for such a small number of cases. For this reason, the enforcement team may be better situated at regional or national level.

iv. A National Body with Responsibility for Incidents of Food-borne Illness

Some interviewees suggested that the control and enforcement components of the response to food-borne illness should be handled by different agencies. This division of institutional labour would attempt to ensure that evidence collection is carried out by officers experienced in collecting evidence suitable for prosecution, and in identifying and responding to evidential challenges. These officers would not be involved in the control of illness, which would remain the responsibility of the current control network, and particularly local authority EHOs. This would therefore be a two-team

[54] See the amount of resources necessary to respond to the South Wales *E. coli* outbreak, detailed in the Pennington documentation, above n 1.

solution, but the enforcement team would come from a national body. The national body would be a key player in surmounting the problem of lack of admissible information, identified as a key roadblock in bringing formal enforcement action following outbreaks.

a. The Health and Safety Executive

The Health and Safety Executive (HSE) is a national body with experience of investigation and enforcement of health and safety law following incidents of work-related illness. It has been responsible for the investigation and prosecution of a number of incidents of legionnaires' disease. Responsibility for the control of the illness, however, remains with the regulatory network, coordinated by the OCT, with much resource provided by the local authority.[55] The HSE prosecuted Barrow Borough Council and Gillian Beckingham following an outbreak of legionnaires' disease that was linked to seven deaths. Neither defendant was found guilty of manslaughter, although the Borough Council pleaded guilty to charges under the Health and Safety at Work, etc Act 1974.[56]

Enforcement by the HSE after an outbreak would not necessarily be more successful than enforcement led by the local authority. Assembling information identifying the party responsible remains problematic. When investigating a 2010 outbreak of legionnaires' disease in South Wales, the HSE had difficulty identifying a single source of the illness.[57] Collection of evidence from the many possible sources of *Legionella* made the investigation time-consuming and resource-intensive. Samples could not be obtained to link sources to individuals, due to the difficulty of growing cultures of legionnaires' disease from either human or environmental samples. A national body cannot solve difficulties of availability. The barriers to obtaining and comparing samples encountered in this incident reflect a problem that is also present in food cases.

Officers of the HSE are experienced in preparing cases for enforcement action, but do not routinely confront the complexities that arise because of the nature of a food-borne illness. Without the benefit of the food science and epidemiological training undertaken by EHOs, significant further training would be required. The additional burden of investigating incidents of food-borne illness would require further resources to be allocated to the HSE.

[55] This is similar to the arrangement that applies when microbial contamination of the drinking water supply is suspected. In such a case, the OCT and the broader regulatory control network are responsible for the control of the incident, and the DWI is responsible for enforcement. As we have seen, this did not result in a successful prosecution in *R v South-West Water* (see ch 6.V.A.ii.).

[56] *R v Barrow BC and Beckingham* (Preston Crown Court, 31 July 2006).

[57] See Outbreak Control Team, *The South Wales 'Heads of the Valleys' Legionnaires Disease Outbreak 2010* (Public Health Wales 2011) and <http://www.wales.nhs.uk/sitesplus/888/news/17248>.

b. The Food Standards Agency

Alternatively, it was suggested by some interviewees (SOL-1) that the Food Standards Agency could engage in enforcement following incidents of food-borne illness. It already brings formal enforcement action when a meat-processing plant is implicated in an incident. Unlike the HSE, the Food Standards Agency (other than former Meat Hygiene Service staff) does not have extensive experience in the investigation and enforcement of regulatory breaches, as much of the enforcement of food law is shared with, or devolved to, local authorities. It would seem that new capacity for the investigation of incidents would have to be built from the ground up, either by recruiting and training staff, or by importing experienced staff from elsewhere. Building capacity requires resources, and may take significant time. However, the Food Standards Agency will be fully apprised of the complexities of food and food-borne illness.

The Agency already plays a key role in the networks *controlling* outbreaks of national or international scope, coordinating control using FAFAs, FAFIs and Recall Notices. This requires information from a food business about the product and its distribution network. Were the Food Standards Agency to be given enforcement responsibility, the ability to coordinate this response might be compromised.

c. A New Body

An entirely new body could be created, specialising in investigation and enforcement following incidents of food-borne illness. However, such a body would initially face capacity-building problems. Whilst a single focus and expertise in food-borne illness might allow the body to build enforcement cases, the availability of epidemiological and microbiological information would remain an issue that is unlikely to be remedied by a specialised agency. Given the epistemic difficulties, and the rarity of incidents of food-borne illness, it seems unlikely to be worthwhile to create a new agency, particularly if routine inspection and advisory roles remain with local authorities.

d. Is a National Body a Plausible and/or Desirable Solution?

Unless one concludes that the availability and admissibility challenges identified above are entirely due to inexperience amongst EHOs, any different body responsible for enforcing following incidents of food-borne illness will face at least some of the epistemic problems identified in this book. Whilst the expertise and experience of the new body, with a greater focus on incidents of food-borne illness, may lead to some epistemic advantages, as may the split of control and enforcement functions, structural difficulties remain, which will prevent evidence being obtained.

v. Increased Investigative Cooperation on a Regional Basis

If nationalisation of food-borne illness investigation is not seen as a viable solution to the challenge of building more viable enforcement cases, then sharing of expertise on a regional basis should be considered. If a regional approach were to be adopted, local authorities could utilise the expertise of neighbouring authorities when responding to incidents of food-borne illness. Environmental Health Officers (perhaps one from each authority) could specialise in investigation and enforcement in situations of food-borne illness, others could specialise in control, and all could gain more exposure to incidents by responding on a regional basis, enrolling into a network when their special skills are needed. When designated EHOs are not engaged directly in responding to incidents, they could remain within the food team of their own authority, carrying out inspection and advisory functions as usual.

Regional enforcement teams are currently being deployed in trading standards enforcement. Recent consultation on modernising local authority enforcement approaches discusses a number of instances where authorities function as regional leads in investigating regulatory breaches that extend beyond their boundaries.[58] The consultation supports this regional approach, and seeks to extend it within the trading standards context. Whilst it is likely that there would be more work for a regional trading standards team than a regional food-borne illness team, a similar approach could be adopted in relation to food. In particular the regional Trading Standards 'Scambuster' Teams,[59] which work through one authority to tackle breaches of trading standards regulation, could provide a model for a regional food enforcement team, which would have responsibility for enforcement following incidents of food-borne illness, as well as wide-ranging food standards, food safety and food hygiene enforcement, particularly where breaches are more than simple breaches detected during inspections.

Regional responses to incidents of food-borne illness currently take place on an *ad hoc* basis. Where an incident extends across local authority boundaries, the affected local authorities will all take part in the regulatory network that aims to control the incident, with information transferred between them to assist control action. For example, in South Wales,[60] information was transferred between the different local authorities covering symptomatic individuals' homes and workplaces. This facilitated, where necessary, the formal exclusion of the individual to reduce the risk

[58] Department of Business Innovation and Skills, *Consultation on Consolidating and Modernising Consumer Law Enforcement Powers* (BIS 2012), ch 3.

[59] See <http://webarchive.nationalarchives.gov.uk/+/http://www.bis.gov.uk/policies/consumer-issues/enforcement-of-consumer-law/trading-standards/scambuster-teams>.

[60] South Wales *E. Coli*, above n 1.

of secondary spread. This was assisted, of course, by the OCT's acting as a formal network mechanism for the exchange of information.

Cooperation and resource sharing may improve responses, as experienced EHOs would form the core team responding to an incident. Expertise would be built within the team of regional EHOs through training and experience. These experienced EHOs could anticipate epistemic challenges and take action to minimise them, with the evidential culture desired by certain interviewees growing through experience and practice. This may lead to higher quality case preparation, with a greater likelihood of successful enforcement action.

However, the advantages of localism may be lost. The relationships built with businesses, which can be advantageous in enrolling business into the network and obtaining information necessary to take control measures, may not be present if regional EHOs are used to respond to food-borne illness. If the regional EHOs are seen as outsiders, they may prove less effective than local EHOs in enrolling a business into the control network, and therefore obtaining information necessary for control.

vi. Involvement of Specialist Lawyers in Case-building

We have seen that local authority solicitors are perceived by some EHOs to be risk-averse.[61] They generally do not have a background in regulatory crime, and therefore do not possess the specialist skill and knowledge that these cases require.[62] Those EHOs complain that local authority solicitors are often unwilling to take a risk by stepping outside of their comfort zone to bring a case. These problems may be greater in rural authorities, which employ generalist legal officers, whereas large urban authorities may employ regulatory crime specialists. A suggested solution is to employ more specialists (EHO-C2).

Environmental Health Officers recognise the need for support from legal experts who can advise on the building of a case and address any evidentiary or procedural issues that may arise. Legal officers should form part of the regulatory network, so that they can advise about information that should be collected to improve the chances of successful enforcement action. Given the perceived complexity of the law of food safety and hygiene, and of the law of evidence, and their interaction, the availability of specialised advice is seen as a necessity.

However, the limited resources of most local authorities mean that the appointment of specialist solicitors might be restricted to large urban authorities with substantial budgets. These authorities have a sufficiently

[61] See section I.G.iii. above.
[62] Ibid.

large case load to justify the employment of a specialist regulatory solicitor on a full-time basis. Regionalisation and the sharing of expertise may be a route by which resource costs could be shared amongst local authorities, all of which would then benefit from the services of a specialised solicitor.

Where there is not a sufficient workload to justify a full-time post, it may be possible to use external solicitors to provide specialist advice. An external solicitor may be supplied by another local authority, or may be in private practice. Outside legal advisers are not as closely integrated into the team as an internal lawyer would be, and may be more expensive, particularly if a lawyer in private practice is instructed. These drawbacks reduce the desirability of this option.

vii. The Possibility of Civil Sanctions

Rather than bringing a prosecution in response to an incident of food-borne illness, the use of civil sanctions should be considered. Two alternative regimes of civil sanctions are available:

(a) those provided for in the Regulatory Enforcement and Sanctions Act 2008; and
(b) those provided for the in Enterprise Act 2002, part 8, as amended and supplemented by the Consumer Rights Act 2015.

The Regulatory Enforcement and Sanctions Act 2008 provides regulators with the ability to make orders imposing fixed or variable monetary penalties, steps that must be taken to ensure that there is no repetition of the breach and steps that must be taken to restore damage caused by the breach, and orders stopping the business from acting in a particular way. The Enterprise Act 2002 allows the enforcement authority to apply to court for an order that businesses stop acting in a way that breaches regulatory requirements and, following the changes made by the Consumer Rights Act 2015, for orders that businesses provide redress, take steps to allow consumers to exercise choice or take steps to ensure compliance in future. Under both regimes, enforcers may accept an undertaking from the business rather than requiring that an order is made.

Neither of these regimes currently applies to regulatory non-compliance of the sort that may be detected during investigation and control of an incident of food-borne illness. The civil sanctions under the Regulatory Enforcement and Sanctions Act 2008 are currently available to the Environment Agency and Natural England, with no political enthusiasm to extend their use to other regulators, and particularly not to local authorities. The powers under the Enterprise Act 2002 extend to domestic infringements and community infringements, as defined by sections 211 and 212. The food safety and hygiene breaches that may be detected during the response to an incident of food-borne illness are neither community[63] nor domestic[64] infringements. The powers under the Enterprise Act 2002 are more limited, as they, in particular, do not allow the imposition of a fixed or variable monetary penalty and, in contrast to the powers contained in the Regulatory Enforcement and Sanctions Act 2008, require a court order.

If available, how might these civil sanctions be of use to regulators and reduce the challenges arising from the epistemic difficulties posed by these offences? The major benefit of civil sanctions under the Enterprise Act 2002 is the burden of proof, with regulators only needing to satisfy the court that there has been a regulatory breach on a balance of probabilities rather than beyond a reasonable doubt.[65] This could enable regulators to bring a case using evidence that they do not feel would discharge the evidential burden in a criminal prosecution. This is not the case under the Regulatory Enforcement and Sanctions Act 2008, where the regulator must be satisfied that there has been a regulatory breach beyond a reasonable doubt before an order can be made.[66] In both cases, the strict rules of criminal evidence are unlikely to apply, so evidence such as an OCT report could be used to demonstrate a regulatory breach.

The advantage of the Regulatory Enforcement and Sanctions Act model is that regulators can impose sanctions without the resource-draining need to take court action. This may encourage regulators to take action more readily, although it is more likely to overcome public interest test objections to regulatory action, rather than the epistemic challenges highlighted by the examination of empirical evidence.

A final advantage is the ability to accept undertakings from businesses, which function as sanctions in the particular case. Rather than imposing sanctions externally, the business can choose to take particular steps, including the payment of a monetary penalty. An enforcement undertaking is unlikely to be as costly to obtain as a final court order. Regulators could explore the possibility of such an undertaking, without committing the level of resources demanded in obtaining court-based formal enforcement action.

However, civil sanctions appear unlikely to be introduced into the food safety and food hygiene spheres. Whilst they have benefit in terms of evidence and proof and resource, it is unlikely that they would lead to a wholesale change in the practice of the regulatory network. Whilst admissibility issues may be ameliorated, case building would remain stunted by availability concerns. If the Regulatory Enforcement and Sanctions Act model were

[63] See Enterprise Act 2002, sch 13.

[64] See Enterprise Act 2002 (Part 8 Domestic Infringements) Regulations 2003, SI 2003/1593, sch 1.

[65] Enterprise Act 2002, s 217.

[66] Regulatory Enforcement and Sanctions Act 2002, ss 39(2) (in relation to fixed monetary penalties) and 42(2) (in relation to variable monetary penalties, compliance notices and restoration notices).

to be adopted, the interpretation of the 'beyond a reasonable doubt' standard would remain a barrier to enforcement in a number of cases. The focus of the regulatory network's response would remain control, and the use of civil sanctions would still have the potential to inhibit this by damaging the relationship between the business and the regulator. Whilst civil sanctions would be useful tools, they are not a silver bullet for resolving the epistemic problems exposed in this book.

B. Easier Prosecution Case-building: Adapting to or Altering the Legal Framework

Food safety and hygiene law presents particular practical obstacles to successful enforcement action. It was suggested by some EHOs and legally qualified interviewees that, in order to bring more successful prosecutions, changes to the strategy for dealing with cases arising out of food-borne illness may be necessary. Rather than seeking to prove that food is unsafe, it was suggested that EHOs should focus on the premises, and seek to prove that food hygiene regulations have been breached.

Amongst EHO interviewees this was generally seen as a second-best response, with food hygiene offences not reflecting the gravamen of the offence, exposing the public to the risk of food-borne illness.[67] The EHOs do not feel that the culpability of the defendant is reflected when hygiene charges are brought. However, hygiene offences are less demanding in terms of proof, as they can be based on environmental evidence alone, collected by an EHO during an inspection.

Hygiene requirements were often found to be breached during inspections. However, these breaches cannot necessarily be linked, beyond a reasonable doubt, to the incident of food-borne illness. In A/I/26, the person who supplied the food was found not to have notified Local Authority A that she was operating a food business. The case showing breach of the notification requirement was built using statements taken from the source of the outbreak identifying the supplier, and a statement from EHO-A3, who detailed the steps he had taken to check the register of food businesses held by the local authority, confirming the supplier was not found on the register. Enforcement action was contemplated, but the supplier gave an undertaking to cease business, and to notify the authority if she decided to restart.

It was felt by EHO-A3 that prosecution for a hygiene offence was a second-best solution, assigning responsibility for this incident of food-borne illness. However, no prosecution was brought, as he felt that it was not in the public interest to use such offences where they could not be linked

[67] BAR-1 advanced a similar criticism, basing his argument on fair labelling, arguing that the offence utilised would not reflecting the reason for taking enforcement action.

to the illness, bringing epistemic considerations into public interest decision making. Similar sentiments were expressed by EHO-B1, who felt that prosecutions for hygiene offences were more likely to be brought where the regulatory breaches could be linked to the incident of food-borne illness. Where the detection of the breaches is incidental to the incident, formal enforcement action is unlikely.

Prosecuting a hygiene offence, with evidence given by EHOs and/or lay witnesses, without microbiological or epidemiological evidence, involves less case building and evidential assembly than in a case brought under food safety regulations. An EHO may therefore be satisfied that there is a reasonable prospect of conviction using less evidence than would be necessary for a safety offence. These provisions could be used to ameliorate epistemic challenges.

A criticism may be advanced. As hygiene problems can often be remedied through the use of lesser actions, such as advice or improvement notices, local authorities may decide that there is no public interest in bringing a prosecution, even if evidence can be assembled to demonstrate a breach. This allows those who cause incidents of food-borne illness to be treated the same as those who are found to have deficiencies in their hygiene compliance during an inspection, whereas there is a distinction between them based on outcomes. Interviewee BAR-1 believes that the move away from enforcement in these circumstances may damage the public protection provided by enforcement following an outbreak.

C. Can the Epistemic Challenges be Met?

None of the suggestions for building better cases canvassed in this chapter should be seen as a silver bullet. The inherent difficulties caused by the characteristics of food and food-borne illness, particularly the challenges of obtaining samples and the delay between consumption and investigation, cannot be addressed by the solutions suggested above. Further, the financial costs of many of the suggestions make them unlikely to be implemented.

Whilst building an evidential culture through better training and greater experience is to be supported, this culture change must not compromise the ability of EHOs to control incidents of food-borne illness. Use of guidance may assist with the development of such a culture, but this guidance should not rigidly restrict EHOs in their evidence collection and assessment. Creation of a specialised national agency is unlikely, but the possibility of regional cooperation amongst experienced EHOs and lawyers should be explored. Further, the use of hygiene offences rather than safety offences following incidents of food-borne illness could be seen as a viable method for taking action in some cases where food safety offences cannot be made out and fair labelling objections are not overwhelming.

8

Conclusions

THIS BOOK HAS explored how EHOs respond to incidents of food-borne illness. It has asked what the key goal of EHOs is in such circumstances, and how they obtain and use information when investigating and managing an incident.

We began by exploring the regulatory network that responds to food-borne illness, and mapped the pitfalls and possibilities of the normative landscape in which the network must operate. A wide range of individuals and institutions may become involved in the network, but EHOs are a constant presence, and it is their practice that has formed a gateway through which the activities of the network have been examined. Chapters four, five and six described and assessed the investigation, control and enforcement aspects of the response. Control was seen to be the primary goal of the regulatory network, and of EHOs in particular; and chapter five explored how this objective is operationalised. Chapter six demonstrated the challenges to enforcement posed by the (un)availability and (in)admissibility of information. Unavailability and inadmissibility often result from the control-orientated nature of the response.

I. SUMMARY OF FINDINGS AND CONCLUSIONS

Incidents of food-borne illness highlight EHOs' multiple professional roles as criminal law, regulatory and public health actors. The book presents original empirical research exploring the relationships between these roles. Interviews were conducted with EHOs, and documents produced during and after responses to incidents were examined. This is the first research project of its kind, investigating EHOs' responses to incidents of food-borne illness, with a particular emphasis, derived from practice, on information gathering.

The regulatory network, when responding to food-borne illness must:

(a) investigate the incident, gathering and assembling information;
(b) control primary and secondary spread of the illness; and
(c) take enforcement action, where possible and appropriate.

The key findings of the research may be summarised as follows:

- Preventing further infection is the primary goal of EHOs confronted with an incident of food-borne illness.
- In conducting investigations, EHOs seek to maximise the information necessary to achieve control of food-borne illness.
- Investigations conducted in this manner often fail to produce adequate admissible information on which to base formal enforcement action.

Investigations of incidents of food-borne illness are of central importance to the role of local authorities as regulators of food and public health. Huge amounts of epidemiological, microbiological and environmental data are collected and analysed. These data enable the authorities to identify products, places or people in need of control. Once something is identified as posing a risk of primary or secondary spread, action will be taken to reduce the risk. Control actions are not sanctions. They are based on status as a risky object, rather than on responsibility for a regulatory infraction. Information that informs control actions therefore need not be as developed, evidentially speaking, as information underpinning enforcement action. Control action may be taken under conditions of uncertainty, with decisions made on a precautionary basis.

Empirical examination of responses to food-borne illness demonstrates the importance placed by EHOs on ensuring that the spread of illness is controlled. They see controlling an incident of food-borne illness as soon as possible, preventing further primary and secondary spread, as their key role in responding to a notification of food-borne illness.

Control actions can be modelled as small-scale biosecurity measures, aimed at preventing the spread of harmful micro-organisms from the sick to the well. The principal regulatory technologies adopted by EHOs, of spatial separation and market control, backed by punishment for those who breach the requirements, are used together to create a secure environment for the uninfected. This is the overarching goal of responses to food-borne illness. Allocation of responsibility is a secondary concern. The role of the regulatory network as a regulator of public health trumps its role as a prosecutor.

Enforcement following incidents of food-borne illness presents EHOs with epistemic challenges. This book has explained why it is difficult to gather information and build cases showing breaches of strict liability offences. Contrary to the prevailing assumptions in much academic literature, such offences are not easy to prove in practice. The book demonstrates that epistemic challenges for enforcement action are often the result of discretionary decisions by EHOs, favouring the collection of information necessary for achieving the primary goal of control over preserving the evidential value of information required for enforcement. The investigations examined in this book do not follow the pattern of traditional criminal law or regulatory investigations. They do not, primarily, have the goal of demonstrating that a crime has been committed.

Epistemic considerations are more influential in EHOs' enforcement decision making than regulatory considerations. In contrast to the findings of previous regulatory scholarship, the decision not to bring enforcement action is not a function of the need to ensure compliance. It arises chiefly from evidential difficulties. In most cases of food-borne illness, EHOs are willing to bring prosecutions but are unable to show a realistic prospect of conviction when they assess the available and admissible evidence.

The demands of case building following an incident of food-borne illness loom large. Whilst in some contexts the existence of a provable regulatory offence can almost be treated as a given, following food-borne outbreaks EHOs have to work hard to make sure that enforcement cases will stand up to judicial scrutiny. They often feel that 'they know what happened' and that enforcement would be in the public interest, but the evidence does not enable a case with a reasonable prospect of conviction to be built. This contradicts the prevailing assumption, which suggests that non-enforcement in strict liability cases is the outcome of discretionary choices by regulatory actors.

Evidential issues cause enforcement action to move from formal to informal, from sanctions to advice. Taking action towards the top of Ayres and Braithwaite's pyramid is difficult to do,[1] with significant procedural checks and balances restraining formal enforcement action, including a requirement of proof beyond a reasonable doubt, as well as the more well-known public interest restraints on high-level action. Evidential difficulties cause proposed formal actions to drop down the regulatory pyramid, until the action reaches a level at which safeguards can be satisfied by the information available and admissible as evidence. In many cases this may mean that only advice action is taken, with businesses offered guidance on avoiding future incidents of food-borne illness.

This book links the fact-finding steps taken by EHOs with the enforcement consequences of these decisions. Investigative actions properly taken in order to obtain information enabling the EHO to control fast-spreading food-borne illness, may entail that the information cannot be used in building a case for enforcement action. By taking these decisions early in the investigation, EHOs limit their discretion to bring enforcement action in future, trading away the possibility of enforcement in order to achieve timely control of incidents. The key example of this behaviour is the decision of EHOs not to interview businesses under caution for fear that this might limit cooperation in control, rendering the information obtained inadmissible, at least in the eyes of the EHOs. The possibility of enforcement action is traded away for information. Although this trade-off is often not explicit, it reflects the high importance of public health and control to EHOs when compared to criminal enforcement.

[1] Ian Ayres and John Braithwaite, *Responsive Regulation: Transcending the Deregulation Debate* (Oxford University Press 1992).

Combined with their reluctance to obtain admissible evidence where this will damage the prospects of control, EHOs tend to be conservative in their assessment of evidence, taking action only where success is likely. This is a more restrictive test than the 'realistic prospect' standard contemplated by the *Code for Crown Prosecutors*.[2] This creates a vicious circle, where cases are not brought due to uncertainty and uncertainty cannot be resolved as no cases are brought. The EHOs in the study vigorously denied this charge, arguing that admissible evidence is simply not available in many cases.

Previous research and commentary have focused on public interest decision making as central to regulatory enforcement. This book argues that information gathering and case building are also central to decision making by EHOs. Whilst previous studies have considered decision making after it has been determined that a breach exists, this study examines a point further from the end of the enforcement process, considering how EHOs gather information to determine whether enforcement action should take place. It also addresses evidence collection, rather than focusing on information that has already been gathered.

II. LIMITATIONS

Two substantive limitations to the findings should be mentioned here. Both mean that the extrapolation of the conclusions of this book to other regulatory contexts ought to be treated with caution.

First, is should be stressed that foods, and food-borne illnesses, have particular characteristics that increase the difficulties of taking enforcement action. Delay is likely to be longer than in other regulatory spheres; the way that food is consumed destroys the product alleged to have breached regulatory requirements.[3] These characteristics have an impact on evidence collection that does not affect other regulatory environments.

In health and safety investigation (apart from those into *Legionella* and other illness) the priority objective for information collection is enforcement. There is not usually a continuing risk to workers or members of the public, as the risky activity (such as work on a building site) often ceases after the incident. With food, the continuing nature of an incident typically means that information is required for control,[4] and its collection takes place under pressure of time.[5] However, similarities between case building

[2] Crown Prosecution Service, *The Code for Crown Prosecutors* (CPS 2010).

[3] Nicole Coutrelis, 'Product Liability in the Food Sector' (2000) 28 *International Business Lawyer* 222, 224; Richard Hyde, 'Why Separate the Regulatory Regimes Applicable to Food Safety and Product Safety?' (2013) 33(4) *Legal Studies* 509.

[4] Eg, interviews will not take place under caution; the fear that a caution will prevent cooperation in control means that a caution will not be administered.

[5] The need for information as soon as possible is in contrast to the longer time frames in which an investigation into other regulatory breaches can be conducted.

in food and other areas do exist. Cases must be proved beyond a reasonable doubt in all regulatory spheres, and this is not easily achieved. The peculiarities of the legal architecture underlying the regulatory area influence the precise nature of informational challenges that arise, but all regulators must grapple with these issues at some level.

Whilst food is special, commonalities between regulatory regimes[6] suggest that at least some epistemic problems are not unique to food. At the very least, the use of availability and admissibility as a vocabulary to describe the evidential difficulties faced by investigators could be applied to other regulatory spheres. The nature of the difficulties faced is dependent on the incidents to which regulators must respond. Further empirical research is necessary to expose these.

Secondly, one local authority lawyer expressed the view that the recently introduced national food hygiene rating scheme meant that enforcement action following incidents of food-borne illness would often be inappropriate (SOL-A2). Control would still be necessary, but formal actions would not be needed. Information about food-borne illness could be integrated into the national food hygiene ratings system; hygiene ratings could be altered to reflect this information; and market forces could determine the sanction appropriate for the wrongdoing. However, this book did not examine the potential role of publicity-based sanctions in enforcement following incidents of food-borne illness.[7] Further work, examining the interrelationships between publicity, information collection, control and enforcement, is therefore necessary to supplement this study.

III. RECOMMENDATIONS

Several concrete policy recommendations to address impediments to case building in the response to food-borne illness arise from the findings of the book. It seems reasonable to suppose that EHOs should remain focused on control in response to such incidents. Control should not be sacrificed in order to achieve enforcement. It must be accepted that structural factors relating to food mean that enforcement is not possible in many circumstances. However, training should be given to EHOs to enable them to make investigative decisions with greater confidence, fully aware of the epistemic consequences of their investigative choices. Sharing of resources across local authorities could be explored more fully, in order to provide necessary support in taking enforcement decisions. Amendment to the regulatory regime is not necessary, but better guidance and training might increase the possibility that enforcement action could be brought successfully.

[6] Adverted to by officers with experience in more than one type of regulation (EHO-C2).

[7] See Peter Cartwright, 'Publicity, punishment and protection: the role(s) of adverse publicity in consumer policy' (2012) 32 *Legal Studies* 179.

In terms of future academic research, this book has indicated that the assembly and handling of information in regulatory enforcement is a subject ripe for further study. More attention should be paid to case building by regulators, and this should be taken into account in studies of regulatory decision making. By taking a step back from the discretionary decision making of regulators, and examining what happens prior to that point in the process, a new perspective may be gained on the working practices of regulators. Insights useful to scholars concerned both with regulatory processes and with evidence law may be discerned. These insights have general application, outside of the food sphere. Whilst some of the obstacles to successful enforcement described in this study are caused by characteristics unique to food, the questions considered are of general applicability, and deserve wider evaluation.

Bibliography

Almond, P, 'An inspector's-eye view—The prospective enforcement of work-related fatality cases' (2006) 46 *British Journal of Criminology* 893

—— 'Investigating health and safety regulation: Finding room for small-scale projects' (2008) 35 *Journal of Law and Society* 108

Andrews, C, *The Enforcement of Regulatory Offences* (Sweet & Maxwell 1998)

Anon, 'E.coli family's manslaughter call' *BBC News Website* (13 September 2007), available at <http://news.bbc.co.uk/1/hi/wales/6993508.stm>

—— 'Legionnaires' Outbreak: "We Are Giving Enough Information'—Health Bosses', *South Wales Argus* (17 September 2010), available at <http://www.southwalesargus.co.uk/news/8397721.LEGIONNAIRES_OUTBREAK_We_are_giving_enough_information_health_bosses/>

—— 'Water watchdog rethinks evidence after case fails' *The Lawyer* (10 July 1997), available at <http://www.thelawyer.com/water-watchdog-rethinks-evidence-after-case-fails/82302.article>

Antle, JM, 'Economic Analysis of Food Safety' in Gardner, B and Rausser, G (eds), *Handbook of Agricultural Economics*, vol 1 (North Holland Publishing Co 1999)

Arden, A, Baker, C and Manning, J (eds), *Local Government Constitutional and Administrative Law* (2nd rev edn, Sweet & Maxwell 2008)

Ashworth, A, 'Should Strict Liability be Removed from all Imprisonable Offences?' (2010) 45 *Irish Jurist* 1

Ashworth, A and Fionda, J, 'The New Code for Crown Prosecutors: Part 1: Prosecution, Accountability and the Public-Interest' [1994] *Crim LR* 894

Ayres, I and Braithwaite, J, *Responsive Regulation: Transcending the Deregulation Debate* (Oxford University Press 1992)

Baker, K *et al*, 'An outbreak of norovirus infection linked to oyster consumption at a UK restaurant, February 2010' (2011) 33 *Journal of Public Health* 205

Barker, K, 'Flexible boundaries in biosecurity: accommodating gorse in Aotearoa New Zealand' (2008) 40 *Environment and Planning A* 1598

Barker, K, Taylor, SL and Dobson, A, 'Introduction: Interrogating bio-insecurities' in Dobson, A, Barker, K and Taylor, SL (eds), *Biosecurity: the socio-politics of invasive species and infectious diseases* (Routledge 2013)

Barrett, SP and Lau, YK, 'Incompleteness of statutory notification of bacterial gastro-intestinal infection' (1997) 111 *Public Health* 183

Bingham, N, Enticott, G and Hinchliffe, S, 'Biosecurity: spaces, practices, and boundaries' 40 *Environment and Planning A* 1528

—— and Hinchliffe, S, 'Mapping the multiplicities of biosecurity' in Lakoff, A and Collier, SJ (eds), *Biosecurity Interventions: Global Health and Security Questions* (Columbia University Press 2008)

—— and Lavau, S, 'The object of regulation: Tending the tensions of food safety' (2012) 44 *Environment and Planning A* 1589

Black, J, 'Enrolling Actors in Regulatory Systems: Examples from UK Financial Services Regulation' [2003] *Public Law* 63

—— 'Tensions in the Regulatory State' [2007] *Public Law* 58.

—— 'The decentred regulatory state?' in Vass, P (ed), *CRI Regulatory Review 2006/2007* (Centre for the Study of Regulated Industries, University of Bath 2007.

—— 'A review of enforcement techniques' in Law Commission (ed), *Criminal Liability in Regulatory Contexts—Consultation Paper 195* (Law Commission 2010)

Bowers, KJ, Johnson, SD and Pease, K, 'Prospective hot-spotting—The future of crime mapping?' (2004) 44 *British Journal of Criminology* 641

Bray, SL, 'Power Rules' (2010) 110 *Columbia Law Review* 1172

Carter, S, 'Disease and Infection in the City' in Bridge, G and Watson, S (eds), *The Blackwell Companion to the City* (Wiley Blackwell 2011)

Cartwright, P, 'Publicity, punishment and protection: the role(s) of adverse publicity in consumer policy' (2012) 32 *Legal Studies* 179

Caywood, C, 'Buffets and Cross-Contamination' *Food Safety News* (20 July 2010), available at <http://www.foodsafetynews.com/2010/07/buffets-and-cross-contamination/>

Choo, ALT, *Abuse of process and judicial stays of criminal proceedings* (2nd edn, Oxford University Press 2008)

Clapham, D, Brindle, A and Aveyard, J, 'Food Outbreak Response' in *Environmental Health Practitioner* (31 March 2006)

Collier, SJ and Lakoff, A, 'The Problem of Securing Health' in Lakoff, A and Collier, SJ (eds), *Biosecurity Interventions: Global Health and Security Questions* (Columbia University Press 2008)

Coultate, TP, *Food: the Chemistry of its Components* (4th edn, The Royal Society of Chemistry 2002)

Coutrelis, N, 'Product Liability in the Food Sector' (2000) 28 *International Business Lawyer* 222

Cowden, JM, 'Investigating outbreaks of infectious intestinal disease: How, why and when do you take action?', speech given to Health Protection Scotland and NHS Scotland, Glasgow (19 November 2007)

Cranston, R, *Regulating Business: Law and Consumer Agencies* (The Macmillan Press 1979)

Crown Prosecution Service, *The Code for Crown Prosecutors* (CPS 2010)

Department of Business Innovation and Skills, *Consultation on Consolidating and Modernising Consumer Law Enforcement Powers* (BIS 2012)

Department of Environment and Department of Health, *Cryptosporidium in Water Supplies* (HMSO 1990)

Department of Health, *Health Protection Legislation (England) Guidance 2010* (Department of Health 2010)

Dinsdale, S, 'Microbiological results from foods—their use and abuse in food safety prosecutions' [2000] *New Law Journal Expert Witness Supplement* 771

Donaldson, A, 'Biosecurity after the event: risk politics and animal disease' (2008) 40 *Environment and Planning A* 1552

Elson, R, 'A National Outbreak of Salmonella Montevideo Infection June 2006' available at <http://www.hpa.org.uk/web/HPAwebFile/HPAweb_C/1207293973143>

Emery, N, 'The Role of the Environmental Health Officer in Fighting Human Infectious Disease' *Memorandum to the House of Lords Select Committee on Science and*

Technology (8 October 2002), available at <http://www.parliament.the-stationery-office.co.uk/pa/ld200203/ldselect/ldsctech/23-vi/2121002.htm>
Ericson, RV and Haggerty, KD, *Policing the risk society* (Clarendon Press 1997)
Evans, R, 'Challenging a Police Caution Using Judicial Review' [1996] *Crim LR* 104
Fairgrieve, D and Howells, G, 'General Product Safety—a revolution through reform' (2006) 69 *MLR* 59
Fisher, E, 'Is the precautionary principle justiciable?' (2001) 13 *Journal of Environmental Law* 315
Food Standards Agency, *Annual Report of Incidents 2010* (Food Standards Agency 2011)
—— *Food Law Code of Practice for England* (Food Standards Agency 2008)
—— *Food Law Practice Guidance (England)* (Food Standards Agency 2006)
—— *Management of outbreaks of foodborne illness in England and Wales* (Food Standards Agency 2008)
—— *The Framework Agreement on Official Feed and Food Controls* (5th amended edn, Food Standards Agency 2010)
—— and Scottish Health Department, *Guidance on the Investigation and Control of Outbreaks of Foodborne Disease in Scotland* (Food Standards Agency 2006)
Foucault, M, *Discipline and punish: the birth of the prison* (Penguin 1979)
Fozzard, J and Murphy, G, 'Public Perception of the Local Authority Pest Control Service in the UK' (2014) 14 *Journal of Environmental Health Research* 17
Garner, BA (ed) *Black's Law Dictionary* (9th edn, West 2009)
General Medical Council, *Confidentiality: Guidance for Doctors* (GMC 2009)
Glaser, BG and Strauss, AL, *The Discovery of Grounded Theory: Strategies for Qualitative Research* (Aldine 1967)
Goldman, AI, *Knowledge in a social world* (Oxford University Press 1999)
Hall, DE, *Criminal Law and Procedure* (5th edn, Cengage 2009)
Hawkins, K, *Law as Last Resort: Prosecution Decision-Making in a Regulatory Agency* (Oxford University Press 2002)
Hawkins, W, *Treatise of the Pleas of the Crown* (7th edn, GG Robinson 1795)
Health Protection Agency, *Foodborne illness at The Fat Duck restaurant: Report of an investigation of a foodborne outbreak of Norovirus among diners at The Fat Duck restaurant, Bray, Berkshire in January and February 2009* (HPA 2009)
Henson, S and Traill, B, 'The Demand for Food Safety: Market Imperfections and the Role of Government' (1993) 18 *Food Policy* 152
Her Majesty's Crown Prosecution Service Inspectorate, *Thematic Review of Attrition in the Prosecution Process (The Justice Gap)* (HMCPSI 2003)
—— and HMIC, *A Report on the Joint Inspection into the Investigation and Prosecution of Cases Involving Allegations of Rape* (HMCPSI 2002)
Herring, J, *Medical law and ethics* (5th edn, Oxford University Press 2014)
Hetherington, D and Dinsdale, S, 'Successfully defending food prosecutions' (2001) 12 *International Food Hygiene* 5
Hinchliffe, S *et al*, 'Biosecurity and the topologies of infected life: From borderlines to borderlands' (2013) 38(4) *Transactions of the Institute of British Geographers* 531
—— and Bingham, N, 'Securing life: the emerging practices of biosecurity' (2008) 40 *Environment and Planning A* 1534

Hirst, M, 'Guilty; but of what?' (2000) 4 *International Journal of Evidence and Proof* 31

House of Lords Science and Technology Committee, *Fourth Report—Fighting Infection* (House of Lords 2003)

Hoyano, A *et al*, 'A Study of the Impact of the Revised Code for Crown Prosecutors' [1997] *Crim LR* 556

Hutter, BM, *Managing food safety and hygiene: governance and regulation as risk management* (Edward Elgar 2011)

—— *The reasonable arm of the law?: the law enforcement procedures of environmental health officers* (Clarendon 1988)

—— and Amodu, T, *Risk Regulation and Compliance: Food Safety in the UK* (LSE Enterprise 2009)

Hyde, R, *Responding to Incidents of Food-borne Illness: An Empirical Study* (PhD Thesis, University of Nottingham 2013)

—— 'Why Separate the Regulatory Regimes Applicable to Food Safety and Product Safety?' (2013) 33(4) *Legal Studies* 509

——, Hoflund, AB and Pautz, MC, 'One HACCP, Two Approaches: Experiences with and Perceptions of the Hazard Analysis and Critical Control Points (HACCP) Food Safety Management Systems in the US and the EU' (2015) *Administration and Society* (forthcoming), available at <http://www.dx.doi.org/10.1177/0095399714548266>

Incident Management Team, *An Outbreak of Food-borne Botulism in Scotland, November 2011* (IMT 2012)

Independent Investigation Committee, *Review of the major outbreak of E. coli O157 in Surrey, 2009* (IIC 2010)

Jiggins, P and Waite, WM, 'Cryptosporidium in England and Wales' in Hunter, PR, Waite, WM and Ronchi, E (eds), *Drinking Water and Infectious Disease: Establishing the Links* (CRC Press 2002)

LACORS, *Guidance on Food Sampling for Microbiological Purposes* (LACORS 2006)

Lauterberg, D, *Food Law: Policy and Ethics* (Cavendish 2001)

Levi, M, *The phantom capitalists: the organization and control of long-firm fraud* (rev edn, Aldershot 2008)

Llewellyn, L, Burtonwood, M and Mukerjee, A, 'Non-notification of Food Poisoning—Whose Fault' (1995) 16 *Journal of Public Health Medicine* 368

London Economics, *Consumer Detriment under Conditions of Imperfect Information (OFT Research Paper 11)* (Office of Fair Trading 1997)

Lowe, N, 'Learning From Major Incidents: Cadbury Salmonella Outbreak' available at <http://www.ips.uk.net/Admin/uploads/ResourceInfo/presentations/confectionaryoutbreak.pdf>

Macrory, RB, 'Reforming regulatory sanctions—a personal perspective' (2009) 11 *Environmental Law Review* 69

—— *Regulatory Justice: Making Sanctions Effective* (Better Regulation Executive 2006)

Mather, C and Marshall, A, 'Biosecurity's unruly spaces' (2011) 177 *Geographical Journal* 300

—— 'Living with disease? Biosecurity and avian influenza in ostriches' (2011) 25 *Agriculture and Human Values* 153

McHale, J, *Medical Confidentiality and Legal Privilege* (Routledge 1993)
Ministry of Justice, *Simple Cautions for Adult Offenders* (MOJ 2014)
Morrison, C, 'Traceability in Food Processing: An Introduction' in Lees, M (ed), *Food Authenticity and Traceability* (Woodhead Publishing 2003)
North, RAE, Duguid, JPI and Sheard, MA, 'The quality of public sector food-poisoning surveillance in England and Wales, with specific reference to salmonella food poisoning' (1996) 98 *British Food Journal* 1
O'Neil, EA and Naumova, EN, 'Defining outbreak: Breaking out of confusion' (2007) 28 *Journal of Public Health Policy* 442
Ockleton, M, 'Documentary Hearsay in Criminal Cases' [1992] *Crim LR* 15
Ogus, AI, *Regulation: Legal Form and Economic Theory* (Hart Publishing 2004)
Ormerod, DC, Smith, JC and Hogan, B, *Smith and Hogan Criminal Law* (13th edn, Oxford University Press 2011)
Outbreak Control Team, *The investigation of an outbreak of diarrhoeal illness in participants of the Builth Wells Mountain Bike Marathon July 2008* (OCT 2008)
—— 'National increase in *Salmonella* Montevideo infections, England and Wales: March to July 2006' (2006) 16(29) *CDR Weekly*
—— *Outbreak of cryptosporidiosis in North West Wales, 2005* (OCT 2006)
—— *Outbreak of Cryptosporidium Infection in a swimming pool complex in Merthyr Tydfil South Wales Summer 2009* (OCT 2010)
—— *The Outbreak of E. Coli O157 at New Deer Millennium Scout Camp May/June 2000* (OCT 2000)
—— *Outbreak of E. coli O157 infection Auchinclech, Aberdeenshire August 2008* (OCT 2009)
—— *Outbreak of Norovirus Infection amongst Guests attending a Concert at the Music Hall Aberdeen May 2004* (OCT 2004)
—— *Outbreak of Norovirus Infection at Marathon Oil UK, Aberdeen March 2008* (OCT 2008)
—— *The report of the Outbreak Control Team of the investigation of an outbreak of listeriosis in the Belfast Health and Social Care Trust during May to November 2008* (OCT 2009)
—— *The South Wales 'Heads of the Valleys' Legionnaires Disease Outbreak 2010* (Public Health Wales 2011)
Overview and Scrutiny Committee, *Report of the Scrutiny Review of the E. Coli O157 Outbreak at Feltham Hill Infant and Nursery School* (London Borough of Hounslow 2010)
Paulus, I, *The search for pure food: a sociology of legislation in Britain* (Martin Robertson 1974)
Pennington Group, *Report on the circumstances leading to the 1996 outbreak of infection with E. coli O157 in Central Scotland, the implications for food safety and the lessons to be learned* (Scottish Office 1997)
Pennington, H, *The public inquiry into the September 2005 outbreak of E. coli O157 in South Wales* (Welsh Assembly Government 2009)
Porter, G, 'A new theoretical framework regarding the application and reliability of photographic evidence' (2011) 15 *Evidence and Proof* 26
Prosser, T, *The regulatory enterprise: Government, regulation, and legitimacy* (Oxford University Press 2010)

Rabinow, P, 'Episodes or incidents: Seeking significance' in Lakoff, A and Collier, SJ (eds), *Biosecurity Interventions: Global Health and Security Questions* (Columbia University Press 2008)
Ramsay, I, *Rationales for Intervention in the Consumer Market Place* (Office of Fair Trading 1984)
Rawcliffe, C, *Leprosy in Medieval England* (Boydell & Brewer 2006)
Reid, K, 'Strict Liability: Some Principles for Parliament' (2008) 29 *Statute Law Review* 173
Rhee, RJ, 'Probability, Policy and the Problem of Reference Class' (2007) 11 *International Journal of Evidence and Proof* 286
Ritvo, H, 'Mad Cow Mysteries' in Watson, JL and Caldwell, ML (eds), *The cultural politics of food and eating: a reader* (Blackwell 2005)
Roberts, MT, 'Mandatory recall authority: A sensible and minimalist approach to improving food safety' (2004) 59 *Food and Drug Law Journal* 563
Roberts, P, 'Law and Criminal Investigation' in Newburn, T, Williamson, T and Wright, A (eds), *Handbook of Criminal Investigation* (Willan 2007)
—— and Saunders, C, 'Piloting PTWI—A Socio-Legal Window on Prosecutors' Assessments of Evidence and Witness Credibility' (2010) 30 *OJLS* 101
—— and Willmore, C, *The role of forensic science evidence in criminal proceedings* (HMSO 1993)
—— and Zuckerman, AAS, *Criminal Evidence* (2nd edn, Oxford University Press 2010)
Sandin, P, 'The Precautionary Principle and the Concept of Precaution' (2004) 13 *Environmental Values* 461
Savage, A and Hyde, R, 'The Response to Whistleblowing by Regulators: A Practical Perspective' (2014) *Legal Studies* (forthcoming) available at <http://www.dx.doi.org/10.1111/lest.12066>
Simester, AP, 'Is Strict Liability Always Wrong?' in Simester, AP (ed), *Appraising Strict Liability* (Oxford University Press 2005)
—— 'Preface' in Simester, AP (ed), *Appraising Strict Liability* (Oxford University Press 2005)
—— (ed), *Appraising Strict Liability* (Oxford University Press 2005)
—— *et al*, *Simester and Sullivan's Criminal Law: Theory and Doctrine* (5th edn, Hart Publishing 2013)
Simon, J, *Governing through crime: how the war on crime transformed American democracy and created a culture of fear* (Oxford University Press 2007)
Stafford, SL, 'Should you turn yourself in? The consequence of environmental self-policing' (2007) 26 *The Journal of Policy Management and Analysis* 305
Steinzor, RI, 'High Crimes, Not Misdemeanors: Deterring the Production of Unsafe Food' (2010) 19 *Health Matrix: Journal of Law-Medicine* 175
Syed, Q, *Outbreak Report: National Outbreak of Vero cytotoxin-producing Escherichia coli O157 infection associated with lemon and coriander chicken wraps in England & Wales June–July 2007* (Health Protection Agency 2007)
Tversky, A and Kahneman, D, 'Judgment under Uncertainty—Heuristics and Biases' (1974) 185 *Science* 1124
Unnevehr, LJ and Jensen, HH, 'The economic implications of using HACCP as a food safety regulatory standard' (1999) 24 *Food Policy* 625

Van Wagner, E, 'The practice of biosecurity in Canada: public health legal preparedness and Toronto's SARS crisis' (2008) 40(7) *Environment and Planning A* 1647

Vogel, KM, 'Biodefence: Considering the Sociotechnological Dimension' in Lakoff, A and Collier, SJ (eds), *Biosecurity Interventions: Global Health and Security in Question* (Columbia University Press 2008)

Volokh, A, 'n Guilty Men' (1997) 146 *University of Pennsylvania Law Review* 173

Waite, WM, *Assessment of Water Supply and Associated Matters in relation to the Incidence of Cryptosporidiosis in Torbay in August and September 1995* (DWI 1997)

Wallace, P, 'A Dreadful Heritage: Interpreting Epidemic Disease at Eyam, 1666–2000' (2005) 61 *History Workshop Journal* 31

Wechsler, H, 'The Modern Penal Code' in Edwards, JLJ (ed), *Modern Advances in Criminology* (Centre of Criminology, University of Toronto 1965)

Wilson, JM, 'Infectious Disease Events, Crises, and Disasters: An Operational Definition' (*Biosurveillance Blog*, 2010)

Yeung, K, 'The Regulatory State' in Baldwin, R, Cave, M and Lodge, M, *The Oxford Handbook of Regulation* (Oxford University Press 2010)

Zander, M, *The Police and Criminal Evidence Act 1984* (6th edn, Thomson/Sweet & Maxwell 2013)

Index

A
Absence and sickness records, 110
Admissibility *see* **Inadmissible evidence**
Advisory powers
  following incidents, 60–1
  improvement notices, 61–2
  local authorities, 25, 43
Aides-memoires, 220–1
Analysis of information
  epidemiological investigations
    building a hypothesis, 87–8
    cohort studies, 90–1
    mapping, 89–90
    overview, 86–7
    paired-sampling, 91
    testing a hypothesis, 88–9
  testing and analysis of samples, 98–100
Animals
  effect of illness, 8
  epidemiological investigation of special factors, 84–5
Avian illness, 8

B
Biosecurity
  control techniques
    market management, 136–9
    spatial separation, 133–6
  enforcement, 139–41
  examination of preventative measures, 8–9
  focus on illness prevention, 8
  no consideration of enforcement, 9
  practice and procedure in action
    precautionary approach, 127–8
  relevance to food-borne illness, 145
  theoretical framework, 126–7
Buffets, 153–4
Businesses *see* **Food businesses**

C
Campylobacter, 159
Causes *see* **Epidemiological investigations**
Cautions
  enforcement powers used following incidents, 59–60
  informal approach to enforcement, 11–12
Checklists, 220–1
Civil sanctions, 227–9
Cohort studies, 90–1
Confidentiality *see* **Medical confidentiality**
Consultants in Communicable Disease Control (CCDCs)
  analysis of epidemiology, 86
  delegated authority, 25
  local authority affiliation, 26
  network role, 6
  powers and duties, 26–7
  specialist epidemiologists, 86
Consumers
  identifying 'cases' and 'controls', 73–4
  key network actors, 29–30
  market management, 136–9
  notification of illness, 66, 67
  provision of samples for microbiological investigation, 93–4
  unavailability of epidemiological evidence
    memory failures, 151–3
    'source fixation', 148–50
  underlying rationale for food regulation
    food preparation out of public view, 4
    information deficit, 4
    prevention of market failure, 3–4
Control
  see also **Enforcement**
  alternative techniques
    market management, 136–9
    overview, 132–3
    spatial separation, 133–6
  biosecurity
    theoretical framework, 126–7
  biosecurity enforcement, 139–41
  collection and sorting of information, 131–2, 145
  dividing control and enforcement, 220–1
  incidents, 125
  key objective, 124
  limitations on findings, 234–5
  local authority powers, 43
  powers used during incidents
    environmental control, 52
    people control, 50–2
    premises, 48–50
    product control, 45–8
  practice and procedure in action, 127–32
  prioritisation over enforcement, 201–3
  process of risk management, 124–5
  realised risks, 11
  recommendations, 235–6
  regulatory context, 141–5

regulatory imperative, 125–6
relationship with investigation and enforcement, 130
small-scale approach, 126
summary of findings and conclusions, 231–4
unique characteristics of food-borne illness, 126

Criminal offences
see also **Enforcement; Prosecution**
apportionment of responsibilities, 9
biosecurity enforcement, 139–41
breaches of food production regulations, 31–2
premises, 37–8
product control, 47–8
Regulation 178/2002, 32–3
strict liability offences
breaches of food production regulations, 31–2
decisions to prosecute, 56–7
epistemic difficulties, 200
premises, 37–8

Cross-contamination
buffets, 153–4
employees, 95
evidence bags, 97
preventative measures not open to scrutiny, 4
proper food flows and storage, 105
secondary transmission, 51
taking of environmental samples, 98
value of absence and sickness records, 110

Cryptosporidium
control in action, 129
identifying 'cases' and 'controls', 72
inadmissible evidence
medical confidentiality, 165–6
Outbreak Control Team Reports, 174–83
mapping, 89–90
role of information, 132
symptoms, 80

D

Data protection, 167–8

Descriptive epidemiology
analysis of epidemiology, 87
mapping, 89
testing a hypothesis, 88

Documentation
examination of retained documentation at premises
absence and sickness records, 110
food safety management systems, 108
importance, 107
other documents, 110
preparation instructions, 109–10
procedure, 107–8
temperature records, 109

E

E. coli
adverse publicity if no enforcement, 144
economic, social and political effects, 1
food history, 81
human samples, 94
role of information, 131–2
role of police, 28
'source fixation', 150
testing and analysis of samples, 99–100
unavailability of faecal samples, 161

Emergency Control Orders, 20

Employees
environmental investigations, 117
inadmissible evidence, 188–9
key network actors, 29
participants in regulatory network, 18
provision of samples for microbiological investigation, 94–5

Enforcement
see also **Control; Criminal offences; Prosecution**
additional difficulties
delay in collection of evidence, 203–4
inexperience of EHOs, 206–8
proof of causation, 204–5
resources for evidence collection, 205–6
assessment of information, 146
biosecurity, 139–41
dividing control and enforcement, 220–1
epistemic challenges, 230
evidential difficulties, 147, 191–4
formal and informal approaches, 11–12
inadmissible evidence
conversations with business owners, 186–7
effect on enforcement, 189–91
information from employees, 188–9
medical confidentiality, 164–72
Outbreak Control Team Reports, 172–86
key themes
control prioritisation, 201–3
decision making based on objective standards, 199
epistemic difficulties with strict liability, 200
limitations on findings, 234–5
local authority powers, 23–4, 43
no part of biosecurity consideration, 9
possible use of civil sanctions, 227–9
powers used following incidents
cautions, 59–60
prosecution, 53–9

primary obstacles, 146–7
recommendations, 235–6
relationship with investigation and enforcement, 130
risk-averse behaviour of EHOs, 209–12
role of information, 11
summary of findings and conclusions, 231–4
unavailability of epidemiological evidence
buffets, 153–4
consumer memory failures, 151–3
consumer 'source fixation', 148–50
lack of information, 148
limitations on enforcement decisions, 154–6
unavailability of evidence
food samples, 156–9
human samples, 159–64

Environmental control, 52

Environmental health officers (EHOs)
see also **Investigation; Local authorities**
advisory powers
following incidents, 60–1
improvement notices, 61–2
powers used during incidents, 43
centrality of control, 127–8, 145
difficulties created by inexperience, 206–8
'knowledge workers', 11
limited regulatory capacity, 25–6
methodology of research, 12–13
methods for improving collection of evidence
dividing control and enforcement, 220–1
greater use of guidelines, check-lists and aides-memoires, 220–1
increased regional cooperation, 225–6
involvement of specialist lawyers, 226–7
need to build 'evidential culture', 219–20
two-team solution involving national agency, 222–4
participants in regulatory network, 18
powers of entry, 102
powers used during incidents
premises, 48–50
product control, 45–8
primary professionals, 25
risk-averse behaviour, 209–12
assessment based on research, 216–17
conclusions, 217–18
desire for success and positive results, 209–12
rejection of characterisation by EHOs, 214–16
unwillingness to rely on epidemiological evidence, 212–14

Environmental investigations
assessment of problems, 101
attendance at premises, 101–2
examination of documentation, 107–11
initial contact with food business, 103
observation of working practices, 118
physical inspection of premises, 103–7
purpose, 100–1
questioning of employees, 117
questioning of business owners
under caution, 111–14
importance, 111
not under caution, 114–17
questioning of employees, 111

Environmental samples, 97–8

Epidemiological investigations
analysis of information
building a hypothesis, 87–8
cohort studies, 90–1
mapping, 89–90
overview, 86–7
paired-sampling, 91
testing a hypothesis, 88–9
evidential difficulties facing enforcement, 147
identifying 'cases' and 'controls'
case definition, 70–3
consumer snowballing, 73–4
information from event organisers, 75–6
information from food business, 74–5
information from medical professionals, 76–7
key focuses, 69–70
lack of evidence for enforcement
buffets, 153–4
consumer memory failures, 151–3
consumer 'source fixation', 148–50
lack of information, 148
limitations on enforcement decisions, 154–6
questioning affected persons
information about 'cases' and 'controls', 78–9
information about other risk factors, 84–6
information about symptoms, 79–80
obtaining food histories, 81–4
overview, 77–8
risk-averse responses of EHOs, 212–14

European Union (EU)
participant in regulatory network, 18
standard-setting for regulatory framework, 19–20

Event organisers, 75

Evidence
see also **Information**
additional difficulties
problems with delayed collection, 203–4
proof of causation, 204–5
resources for evidence collection, 205–6

decision making based on objective standards, 199
decisions to prosecute, 54–6
difficulties facing enforcement, 147, 191–4
inadmissible evidence
conversations with business owners, 186–7
effect on enforcement, 189–91
information from employees, 188–9
medical confidentiality, 164–72
Outbreak Control Team Reports, 172–86
inspection of premises
photographs of premises, 106–7
sketch plans, 107
methods for improving collection
dividing control and enforcement, 221–2
greater use of guidelines, check-lists and aides-memoires, 220–1
increased regional cooperation, 225–6
involvement of specialist lawyers, 226–7
need to build 'evidential culture', 219–20
two-team solution involving national agency, 222–4
unavailability of epidemiological evidence
buffets, 153–4
consumer memory failures, 151–3
consumer 'source fixation', 148–50
lack of information, 148
limitations on enforcement decisions, 154–6
unavailability of food samples, 156–9
unavailability of human samples, 159–64

F

Faecal samples *see* **Human samples**
'Food Alerts for Action' (FAFA), 21
'Food Alerts for Information' (FAFI), 21
Food-borne illness
economic, social and political effects, 1
fluid nature of risk, 7–8
limitations on findings, 234–5
need for networked response, 2–3
recommendations, 235–6
sui generis interactions between regulators and businesses, 2
summary of findings and conclusions, 231–4
unique characteristics, 5
Food businesses
see also **Employees**
environmental investigations
assessment of problems, 101
attendance at premises, 101–2
examination of documentation, 107–11
initial contact with food business, 103
observation of working practices, 118
physical inspection of premises, 103–7
purpose, 100–1
questioning of business owners, 111–17
questioning of employees, 117
food histories, 83–4
identifying 'cases' and 'controls', 74–5
inadmissible evidence, 186–7
key network actors, 28–9
notification of illness, 66
participants in regulatory network, 18
prosecution following incidents, 54
questioning of owners
under caution, 111–14
importance, 111
sui generis interaction with regulators, 2
Food history
consumer memory failures, 151–3
cross-tabulation, 89
example, 82
importance, 81
information from implicated businesses, 83–4
limitations on enforcement decisions, 154–6
methodology of compiling, 81–3
underlying rationale, 81
Food Law Code, 56–9
Food premises *see* **Premises**
Food production
criminal offences, 31–2
Regulation 178/2002
criminal offences, 32–3
injurious to health, 34–5
unfit for human consumption, 35–7
unsafe *per se*, 33–4
Food safety management systems, 108
Food samples
evidential difficulties facing enforcement, 147
lack of evidence for enforcement, 156–9
microbiological investigations, 95–7
Food Standards Agency
key role, 21
'main objective', 20–1
participant in regulatory network, 18
two-team solution for collection of evidence, 224
Foot and mouth, 8

G

Government
long-standing preoccupation with regulation, 1–2
networks as necessary state response, 5–6
participant in regulatory network, 18
standard-setting for regulatory framework, 19–20
sui generis interaction with business, 2
Guidelines, 220–1

H
Hazard analysis critical control point (HACCP), 40–2
Health and Safety Executive (HSE), 223
Hearsay evidence
difficulties facing enforcement, 147
Outbreak Control Team Reports, 178–82
History *see* **Food history**
Human rights
effect of biosecurity, 141
entitlement to information, 180
justified interferences with rights, 143
people control, 51
Human samples
from consumers, 93–4
from employees, 94–5
evidential difficulties facing enforcement, 147
lack of evidence for enforcement, 159–64
Hygiene Emergency Prohibition Notices (HEPNs), 48
Hygiene improvement notices (HINs), 61–2
Hygiene requirements
condition, 42
general obligations, 38
hazard analysis critical control point (HACCP), 40–2
microbiological safety, 39–40
notification of operations, 42
temperature control, 39

I
Illness *see* **Food-borne illness**
Improvement notices, 61–2
Inadmissible evidence
conversations with business owners, 186–7
decisions to prosecute, 55–6
difficulties facing enforcement, 147
effect on enforcement, 189–91
information from employees, 188–9
medical confidentiality
case studies, 165–6
ethical reasoning, 166–9
overview, 164–5
policy reasoning, 169–72
need for change, 218–19
Outbreak Control Team Reports
case study *R v South-West Water*, 174–83
effect on enforcement, 183–6
overview, 172–4
Incidents
control imperative, 125
control powers used during incidents
environmental control, 52
people control, 50–2
premises, 48–50
product control, 45–8
defined, 10
enforcement powers used following incidents
cautions, 59–60
prosecution, 53–9
two-team solution involving national agency
advantages, 224
creation of new body, 224
Food Standards Agency, 224
Health and Safety Executive (HSE), 223
Information
see also **Evidence**; **Investigation**
assessment for enforcement, 146
basis of all decisions, 64
centrality, 10–11, 197–8, 217
challenge of controlling torrent of information, 3
consumer information deficit, 4
'Food Alerts for Information' (FAFI), 21
network benefits, 6–7
relationship to control, 131–2, 145
sources, 64
use in enforcement, 11
Injurious to health, 34–5
see also **Unfit for human consumption**; **Unsafe *per se***
Interviews
environmental investigations
business owners not under caution, 114–17
business owners under caution, 111–14
importance, 111
questioning of employees, 117
epidemiological investigations
information about 'cases' and 'controls', 78–9
information about other risk factors, 84–6
information about symptoms, 79–80
obtaining food histories, 81–4
overview, 77–8
methodology of research, 13–14
Investigation
commencement, 68–9
environmental investigations
assessment of problems, 101
attendance at premises, 101–2
examination of documentation, 107–17
initial contact with food business, 103
observation of working practices, 118
physical inspection of premises, 103–7
purpose, 100–1
questioning of employees, 117
epidemiological investigations
analysis of information, 86–91
identifying 'cases' and 'controls', 70–7

key focuses, 69–70
questioning affected persons, 77–86
importance of information, 123
limitations on findings, 234–5
local authority role, 24
microbiological investigations
environmental samples, 97–8
food samples, 95–7
human samples, 92–5
overview, 92
testing and analysis of samples, 98–100
overview, 69
range of techniques, 123
recommendations, 235–6
relationship with control and enforcement, 130
summary of findings and conclusions, 231–4
supply chain investigations
examples, 120–2
importance, 118–19
necessity of tracing, 119
regulatory requirements, 119–21
torrent of information, 3

L

Lawyers
involvement of specialist lawyers in case-building, 226–7
methodology of research, 13–14
participants in regulatory network, 18

Listeria
economic, social and political effects, 1
food history, 84
notification by medical practitioners, 65
unavailability of epidemiological evidence, 148

Local authorities
see also **Environmental health officers (EHOs)**
advisory powers, 25, 43
control powers, 43
control powers used during incidents
environmental control, 52
people control, 50–2
coordination of network, 19
county and district division of responsibilities, 22–3
enforcement powers, 23–4, 43
enforcement powers used following incidents
cautions, 59–60
prosecution, 53–9
formal enrolment in network, 24–5
investigation, 24
key actors, 22
notification of illness, 66
participants in regulatory network, 18

M

Mapping, 89–90
Market management, 136–9
Medical confidentiality
case studies
Cadbury case, 165
R v South-West Water, 165–6
ethical reasoning
confidentiality, 168–9
data protection, 167–8
privilege, 166–7
evidential difficulties facing enforcement, 147
overview, 164–5
policy reasoning, 169–72

Medical practitioners
Consultants in Communicable Disease Control (CCDCs)
analysis of epidemiology, 86
delegated authority, 25
local authority affiliation, 26
network role, 6
powers and duties, 26–7
specialist epidemiologists, 86
identifying 'cases' and 'controls', 76–7
key network actors, 26–7
notification of illness, 64–6

Methodology of research, 12–14

Microbiological investigations
environmental samples, 97–8
food samples, 95–7
human samples
from consumers, 93–4
from employees, 94–5
hygiene requirements for food premises, 39–40
overview, 92
testing and analysis of samples, 98–100

N

Networks
see also **Regulation**
formal mechanisms for coordination, 18–19
importance, 2–3, 17, 196–7
key actors
consumers, 29–30
employees, 29
European Union (EU), 19–20
food businesses, 28–9
Food Standards Agency, 20–1
government, 19–20
local authorities, 22–6
medical practitioners, 26–7
police, 28
methodology of research, 12–13
necessary state response, 5–6
need for information, 6–7

need for polycentric network of different actors, 18
numerous roles played by various actors, 6
particular responsibilities, 6, 18
powers, 62–3
risk management, 7, 30
role, 17
Norovirus
closure of mollusc harvesting grounds, 50
economic, social and political effects, 1
identifying 'cases' and 'controls', 75
notification by medical practitioners, 65
supply chain investigations, 120–2
unavailability of faecal samples, 161–2
Notification
pathways to local authorities, 68
premises involved in food production or preparation, 42
sources
consumers, 67
food businesses, 66
medical practitioners, 64–6
overview, 66

O
Organisers *see* **Event organisers**
Outbreak Control Teams
coordination of network, 18–19
inadmissibility of reports
case study *R v South-West Water*, 174–83
effect on enforcement, 183–6
overview, 172–4
prioritisation of control over enforcement, 202
role, 10
Outbreaks defined, 10

P
PACE Code C, 111–13
Paired-sampling, 91
Photographic evidence, 106–7
Police
key network actors, 28
participants in regulatory network, 18
Policy
decisions to prosecute, 59
medical confidentiality, 169–72
Premises
control powers used during incidents, 48–50
criminal offences, 37–8
examination of retained documentation
absence and sickness records, 110
food safety management systems, 108
importance, 107
other documents, 110
preparation instructions, 109–10
procedure, 107–8
temperature records, 109
hygiene requirements
condition, 42
general obligations, 38
hazard analysis critical control point (HACCP), 40–2
microbiological safety, 39–40
notification of operations, 42
temperature control, 39
physical inspection, 103–7
Preparation of food
examination of instructions at premises, 109–10
underlying rationale for food regulation, 4
Privilege, 166–7
Product control, 45–8
Prosecution
see also **Enforcement**
adapting legal framework to simplify task, 229–30
following incidents
decisions to prosecute, 54–6
procedure, 53
relevant conduct, 54
statutory powers, 53–4
formal approach to enforcement, 11–12
main challenges, 217
risk-averse behaviour of EHOs, 210
Public Health England
functions, 27
notification by, 65
participant in regulatory network, 18
relationship with medical professionals, 171
specialist epidemiologists, 65
Public interest
cautions, 59
decisions to prosecute, 55, 58–9
disclosure of patient information, 169–70
discontinuance, 197–9
key findings of the research, 229–34
whistle-blowers, 29
Punishment *see* **Criminal offences**

Q
Quarantines, 50–2
Questioning *see* **Interviews**

R
Recall of products, 47
Regulation
see also **Networks**
control imperative, 125–6
control objectives, 141–5
food production
Regulation 178/2002, 32–7
strict liability offence, 31–2

key concepts, 10
local authority enforcement, 23–4
long-standing preoccupation of state, 1–2
premises
control powers used during incidents, 48–9
hygiene requirements, 37–42
strict liability offences, 37–8
Regulation 178/2002
criminal offences, 32–3
injurious to health, 34–5
unfit for human consumption, 35–7
unsafe *per se*, 33–4
seizure powers, 45–7
standard-setting by EU and government, 19–20
traceability requirements, 119–21
underlying rationales
consumer information deficit, 4
food preparation out of public view, 4
prevention of market failure, 3–4
unique characteristics of food, 4–5
Risk
averse behaviour of EHOs
assessment based on research, 216–17
conclusions, 217–18
desire for success and positive results, 209–12
rejection of characterisation by EHOs, 214–16
unwillingness to rely on epidemiological evidence, 212–14
control of realised risks, 11
epidemiological investigation of special factors
animals, 84–5
swimming pools, 85
travel, 86
untreated water, 85–6
fluid nature of risk in food-borne illness, 7–8
management through control, 124–5
role of regulatory network, 7, 30

S
Salmonella
control in action, 128
economic, social and political effects, 1
mapping, 90
medical confidentiality, 165
notification by medical practitioners, 65
questioning of business owners under caution, 114
'source fixation', 150
surveillance study, 9–10
unavailability of faecal samples, 161
Samples
environmental samples, 97–8
evidential difficulties facing enforcement, 147
food samples, 95–7
human samples
from consumers, 93–4
from employees, 94–5
lack of evidence for enforcement
food samples, 156–9
human samples, 159–64
testing and analysis of samples, 98–100
Seizure powers, 45–7
Severe acute respiratory syndrome (SARS), 8, 9
Sketch plans, 107
Snowballing, 73–4
'Source fixation', 148–50
Sources *see* **Epidemiological investigations**
Spatial separation
biosecurity requirement, 9
control technique, 133–6
Strict liability offences
breaches of food production regulations, 31–2
decisions to prosecute, 56–7
epistemic difficulties, 200
premises, 37–8
Supply chain investigations
examples, 120–2
importance, 118–19
necessity of tracing, 119
regulatory requirements, 119–20
Swimming pools
building a hypothesis, 87–8
special risk factor, 85
Symptoms
epidemiological investigations, 79–80
people control, 52

T
Temperature
examination of records at premises, 109
hygiene requirements for food premises, 39
Traceability *see* **Supply chain investigations**
Travel, 86

U
Unfit for human consumption, 35–7
see also **Injurious to health; Unsafe *per se***
Unsafe *per se*, 33–4
Untreated water, 85–6

W
Whistleblowers, 18, 29
Withdrawal of products, 47
Working practices, 118